THE CULTURE OF

AUTOBIOGRAPHY

✛

Irvine Studies in the Humanities

Robert Folkenflik, General Editor

CONTRIBUTORS

Lindon Barrett

Jerome Bruner

Robert Folkenflik

Barbara D. Metcalf

Genaro M. Padilla

Ronald Paulson

Linda H. Peterson

Roger J. Porter

John Sturrock

Julia Watson

THE CULTURE OF

Autobiography

Constructions of Self-Representation

Edited by Robert Folkenflik

STANFORD UNIVERSITY PRESS, STANFORD, CALIFORNIA 1993

Stanford University Press
Stanford, California
© 1993 by the Board of Trustees of the
Leland Stanford Junior University
Printed in the United States of America

CIP data appear at the end of the book

A Note on This Series

This is the sixth in a series of volumes on topics in the humanities and the first in the new series published by Stanford University Press. This volume originated in a conference on autobiography and self-representation held at the University of California Humanities Research Institute.

For help with a broad range of problems, I am indebted to the Editorial Board of Irvine Studies in the Humanities: Ellen Burt, Lucia Guerra-Cunningham, Anne Friedberg, J. Hillis Miller, Jane Newman, Spencer Olin, John Carlos Rowe, Aliko Songolo (now of the University of Wisconsin), Linda Williams, and especially Murray Krieger, who chaired the board while this volume was under consideration. I am grateful to former Dean Terence D. Parsons of the School of Humanities for his support. Joann McLean and Lisa Ness provided secretarial help for Irvine Studies. Philip Baruth, our Research Assistant, proofread the text and compiled the index, among other contributions. His own interest in and knowledge of autobiography proved valuable. My undergraduate mentees Georgina Dodge, now a Mellon Fellow at UCLA, and Maria Iannetta, now a President's Fellow at the University of California, Santa Cruz, were also helpful. Helen Tartar, Humanities Editor at Stanford University Press, is responsible for the new series and I am particularly indebted to her for this volume.

Robert Folkenflik, General Editor

Acknowledgments

The conference that provided the basis for this volume was held at the University of California Humanities Research Institute on March 3–4, 1990. Many people made that conference possible. The participants, apart from those represented in this volume, were James Breslin, who helped me organize it; Marc Blanchard, who originally took part in a workshop that led to the conference; Paul John Eakin, who moderated our round table discussion; and Rafia Zafar. Jerome Bruner, Roger Porter, and Julia Watson delivered different papers at the conference. The essays of Genaro M. Padilla (who moderated a section), Lindon Barrett, and Linda H. Peterson also appear originally here, as does mine. I am grateful to the former Dean of the School of Humanities, Terence D. Parsons, and the former Chair of the English Department, Edgar Schell, who shared the sponsorship with the Institute. In my department I have been helped in innumerable ways by Janet Stevens, Rachel Pardee, and especially Sharon Doyel. In the Humanities Research Institute we are grateful to the former Director, Murray Krieger, who has dwindled again to a University Professor, the current Director, Mark Rose, and members of his staff: Julie Van Camp, Debbie Massie, and Molly McGuire. We are also indebted to Vivian Folkenflik.

As editor I would like to thank for help with my own contributions Ruth Angress, Philip Baruth, Wolfgang Iser, Margot Norris, and Jane Newman. The Wessenberg Library of the city of Konstanz made available to me a number of useful eighteenth-century German books, and the University of Konstanz Library extended its privileges while I was Visiting Professor. As usual I am indebted to the library of the University of California at Irvine, especially its Special Collections and interlibrary loan facilities. A few names here stand for many: Roger Berry, Cathy Palmer, Pamela LaZarr. The contributors join me in thanking our copy editor, Bud Bynack, and our editor, Helen Tartar. We are also grateful to Karen Brown Davison and Julia Johnson Zafferano at Stanford University Press.

A few paragraphs of Linda H. Peterson's discussion of Mary Robinson's *Memoirs* were originally published, in different form, in *Studies in the Literary Imagination* 23 (1990): 165–76. Parts of Ronald Paulson's essay, which was written especially for the conference and is essentially as delivered, have appeared in expanded form, with full annotation, throughout the following books: *Hogarth, I: The Modern Moral Subject, Hogarth, II: High Art and Low,* and *Hogarth, III: Art and Politics* (New Brunswick, N.J.: Rutgers University Press, 1991, 1992, and 1993).

R.F.

Contents

Contributors   xi

Introduction: The Institution of Autobiography   1
     Robert Folkenflik

Theory Versus Autobiography   21
     John Sturrock

The Autobiographical Process   38
     Jerome Bruner

Toward an Anti-Metaphysics of Autobiography   57
     Julia Watson

Institutionalizing Women's Autobiography:
Nineteenth-Century Editors and the Shaping of an
Autobiographical Tradition   80
     Linda H. Peterson

Self-Knowledge, Law, and African American Autobiography:
Lucy A. Delaney's *From the Darkness Cometh the Light*   104
     Lindon Barrett

The Mexican Immigrant as *: The (de)Formation of Mexican
Immigrant Life Story   125
     Genaro M. Padilla

What Happened in Mecca: Mumtaz Mufti's *Labbaik*   149
     Barbara D. Metcalf

Contents

"In *me* the solitary sublimity": Posturing and the Collapse of
Romantic Will in Benjamin Robert Haydon   168
    Roger J. Porter

Hogarth's Self-Representations   188
    Ronald Paulson

The Self as Other   215
    Robert Folkenflik

Notes   237

Index   267

Contributors

LINDON BARRETT, Assistant Professor of English and Comparative Literature at the University of California, Irvine, is the author of essays published or forthcoming in *Callaloo, Cultural Critique, SubStance,* and in the anthology *Teaching Theory to Undergraduates.* He is currently writing a book on value, representation, and authority in relation to African American literature and culture.

JEROME BRUNER, Research Professor of Psychology at New York University and most recently Senior Research Fellow in Law there, has published numerous books, among them *Acts of Meaning; In Search of Mind: Essays in Autobiography;* and *Actual Minds, Possible Worlds.* He is currently working on *Autobiography and the Construction of Self.*

ROBERT FOLKENFLIK, Professor of English and Comparative Literature at the University of California, Irvine, is the author of *Samuel Johnson, Biographer* and other books. He has published numerous essays on autobiography, the eighteenth-century novel, and the artist as hero. He has held fellowships from the Guggenheim Foundation, the National Endowment for the Humanities, and other sources.

BARBARA D. METCALF, Professor of History at the University of California, Davis, was recently a fellow at the National Humanities Center. Her publications include *Islamic Revival in British India; Moral Conduct and Authority: The Place of Adab in South Asian Islam;* and *Perfecting Women: Maulana Ashraf ʿAli Thanawi's Bihishti Zewar.*

GENARO M. PADILLA, Associate Professor of English at the University of California, Berkeley, has published numerous essays on Chicano literature and autobiography. His book *History, Memory and the Struggles of Self-Representation: The Formation of Mexican American Autobiog-*

raphy will appear in the American Autobiography series of the University of Wisconsin Press in 1993.

RONALD PAULSON, Mayer Professor of the Humanities at The Johns Hopkins University, is the author of numerous books, including *Hogarth: His Life, Art and Times*; *Representations of Revolution*; and, most recently, *Breaking and Remaking: Aesthetic Practice in England, 1700–1820*. A three-volume revision of *Hogarth* is being published by Rutgers University Press. He is Senior Editor of *English Literary History*.

LINDA H. PETERSON, Professor of English at Yale University, has published *Victorian Autobiography: The Tradition of Self-Interpretation* and a number of essays on women's autobiography that will appear in a forthcoming book.

ROGER J. PORTER, Professor of English at Reed College, is co-editor of *The Voice Within* and the author of numerous articles on autobiography. He is currently completing a book on that topic.

JOHN STURROCK, Consulting Editor with the *London Review of Books* and sometime Regents' Lecturer at the University of California, Los Angeles, has published a variety of books, including *Structuralism*; *Paper Tigers: The Ideal Fictions of Borges*; and *The French Pyrenees*. His *Language of Autobiography* will be published in 1993 by Cambridge University Press.

JULIA WATSON, Associate Professor of Humanities at the University of Montana, writes on gender and the theory and practice of autobiography. She is co-editor with Sidonie Smith of *De/Colonizing the Subject: The Politics of Gender in Women's Autobiography*. Her essays include "Shadowed Presence: Women's Autobiography and the Other" (in *Studies in Autobiography*), and pieces on Montaigne, Rilke, and new German film.

THE CULTURE OF
AUTOBIOGRAPHY

Introduction:
The Institution of Autobiography

Robert Folkenflik

The culture of autobiography is discovered in part in its institutions, and this collective work is an appropriate place to consider in a limited way the institution of autobiography as well as the state of its study. I would like first to examine the word *autobiography* itself. This brief history of the term and its synonyms is significantly different from what has appeared in print even as recently as Felicity Nussbaum's *The Autobiographical Subject* (1989). In fact, as far as I know this is the first attempt to put all the pieces together, add new ones, and interpret them.[1] Until 1961, thanks to those Baker Street Irregulars of lexicography, the compilers of the *OED*, it was thought that the first use of the term in English was that of Robert Southey in 1809, whose usage is matter-of-fact and unapologetic: "This very amusing and unique specimen of autobiography."[2] But James Ogden, working on a biography of Isaac D'Israeli, noticed its use in an anonymous review of D'Israeli's *Miscellanies or Literary Recreations* (1796), which appeared in the *Monthly Review* in 1797.[3] (His observation was institutionalized in the *Supplement* to the *OED*, 1976.) Commenting on D'Israeli's "Some Observations on Diaries, Self-biography, and Self-characters," the author, who has been identified as William Taylor of Norwich, says, "We are doubtful whether the latter word ["self-biography"] be legitimate. It is not very usual in English to employ hybrid words partly Saxon and partly Greek: yet autobiography would have seemed pedantic."[4] Here the author is conscious of his term as a neologism.

The first published use of the term *autobiography* in any language, however, occurred in the adjectival form in the preface to the 1786 edition of Ann Yearsley's *Poems* as an "Autobiographical Narrative" of her strained relations with her patron, Hannah More.[5] Hence, the first use of any form of the term appeared in the apologia of a lower-class woman poet generally condescended to in literary histories under the name Lactilla, the Milkmaid Poet. To continue with this little band of early users, Robert Southey, who later wrote of Yearsley in an essay on the "Lives and Works of our Uneducated Poets" (1831), was a friend of both D'Israeli and Taylor by the time he came to use the term in 1809. And D'Israeli was a close reader of the reviews of his work in the *Monthly*, which were frequently by Taylor.[6] It is a pity that the *OED* chose to institutionalize Southey's usage. In addition to being the cause of the first use of the term *autobiography* in print, and the contributor of his own neologism, *self-biography*, D'Israeli used *auto-biography* a number of times in the first decades of the nineteenth century, including once in the same issue of *The Quarterly Review* in which Southey's "first" appeared.[7] He was also the first to apply the term to a series of paintings. In "Of a Biography Painted," published in the second series of his *Curiosities of Literature* (1823), he comments, "The idea is new of this production, an auto-biography in a series of remarkable scenes painted under the eye of the describer of them." Most would quarrel with this notion of the autobiographer as setting the program rather than as self-portraitist. Another essay in the book, "Sentimental Biography," distinguishes that subject from "auto-biography." And in the sixth edition (1817) he referred to Baxter's "voluminous auto-biography."[8] Taylor's etymological point may have convinced the punctilious D'Israeli, and his works would have done much to popularize the term.

German usage of both substantives in print came earlier. Christian Friederich Daniel Schubart's *Leben und Gesinnungen* (1791)—like Tristram Shandy's, his "life and opinions"—shifts from "biography" to a new term: "Therefore biographers [*die Biografen*], especially autobiographers [*die Autobiografen*], become so intimidated that they often suppress the very circumstances that would highlight their hero and would give him, so to speak, his selfhood."[9] The evidence is good that he actually wrote the book in prison in 1779. There are some other contenders for the earliest uses in German. Gunter Niggl claims that Theodor Gottlieb von Hippel's "Hr. Bahrdt . . . um seine Selbstbiographie auszumeubliren," published in 1801, was written in 1789. An article in the *Deutsche Monatsschrift* for February 1795 entitled "Ueber Selbstbiographien" makes the distinction for German that William Taylor was to make for English in his review two years later: "selfbiographies [*Selbstbiographien*], or if one prefers to avoid the hybrid word, autobiographies [*Autobiographien*]."[10]

Despite the precedence of *autobiografen* and the objection voiced in both Germany and England to the etymological contradictions of its synonym, *self-biography* dominated in Germany until quite recently in this century. In a title it first appeared in a collection of "Selfbiographies of Famous Men" (*Selbstbiographien berühmter Männer*) edited and introduced by David Cristoph Seybold, a classicist, in 1796. In the introduction, which also uses the term, Seybold credits Johann Gottfried Herder's *Briefe über die Humanität* with giving him the idea for his collection, though Herder does not use the term himself there or earlier. Niggl claims that after the turn of the century occasional comments betray the unfamiliarity of the new words.[11] By 1802 Daniel Jenisch had published the first book on the theory of Life-writing, *Theorie der Lebens-Beschreibung*.[12]

Autobiographie does not appear in the Grimms' *Wörterbuch* of 1853. But then, neither does *Biographie*, despite the fact that it appeared in Karl Philipp Moritz's *Grammatisches Wörterbuch der deutschen Sprache* (1793), where it is characterized as preferable to the polysyllabic *Lebens-beschreibung*. The superiority on the same grounds of either *Autobiographie* or *Selbstbiographie* to a term such as *selbstverfasste Lebensbeschreibung*, which Seybold also uses, is immediately apparent.[13] The fact that Taylor later wrote *A Historic Survey of German Poetry* (1828–30) suggests the possibility that he was influenced by a German predecessor, though I doubt it. In that history he uses the word with no self-consciousness, and no consciousness of having been the first to use it in print in England.

The most revealing eighteenth-century usage appears in one of the *Athenaeum* fragments of Friedrich Schlegel (1798):

Pure autobiographies [*Autobiographien*] are written either by neurotics who are fascinated by their own ego [I], as in Rousseau's case; or by authors of a robust artistic or adventuresome self-love, such as Benvenuto Cellini; or by born historians who regard themselves only as material for historic art; or by women who also coquette with posterity; or by pedantic minds who want to bring even the most minute things in order before they die and cannot let themselves leave the world without commentaries. [They] can also be regarded as mere *plaidoyers* [legal pleadings] before the public. Another great group among the autobiographers [*Autobiographen*] is formed by the autopseusts [self-deceivers].[14]

The two uses in this paragraph are remarkable because they are part of a thumbnail account of autobiography touching on some late-eighteenth-century publications that we continue to think among the most important for the modern tradition of the form. Schlegel may well have provided the context for a leap into the consideration of autobiography that did not actually obtain until well into this century. The comment on Gibbon as not only a born writer of history but himself the stuff of historical art presents an insight that has not been put to use until quite recently. The notion of "pure autobiography" (*reine Autobiographien*) with which the fragment begins is again a strikingly advanced construct, though it probably means here a work that is intentionally written as autobiography.

Georges Gusdorf, who refers to this passage, claims that the use of *autobiography* does not suggest a neologism.[15] But it is worth noting that the passage is part of a series of fragments that consider such topics as *Individualität* and *Originalitätssucht*. The paragraph contains another term with "auto" that is almost certainly a neologism. One of Schlegel's other aphorisms in this highly metaphoric collection suggests what he was doing in coining *autopseusts*, which even Schlegel's translators do not gloss: "The surest method of being incomprehensible or, moreover, to be misunderstood is to use words in their original sense, especially words from the ancient languages."[16] I take the term to mean "self-deceivers" because the Greek *pseustos* originally means a liar or cheat. I think that he employed this method in coining the terms *Autobiographien* and *Autobiographen*, as well as *Autopseusten*. His brother August Wilhelm's testimony may help to support my sense of this usage: "He succeeds with aphorisms better than with articles and with self-coined words better than with aphorisms. In the final analysis, his entire genius might be reduced to mystical terminology."[17]

Even though *autobiography* has now been pushed back behind the literary curtain generally dropped between the eighteenth and nineteenth centuries, most of the early uses, those of Taylor, D'Israeli, Schlegel, and Southey, came from members of the younger generation (born 1765, 1766, 1772, 1774, respectively), the Romantics, and not those, even though autobiographers, associated with Enlightenment or neo-classical thought. Although it is a Greek term, it did not exist in Classical Greece. The late Hellenistic period yields *Idion Bion*,[18] a usage that would lead to *idiobiography*. If we return to D'Israeli, however, we ought to note that he published an essay called "The History of New Words" and was born in the same year as Taylor. His use of *self-biography*, used (among others) by Coleridge in 1804 and James Field Stanfield in 1813, never caught hold, but he went on to convert to *auto-biography*—which he spelled, like Southey, with a hyphen. (The *OED* does not even recognize *self-biography* as a word.) It is an accident that in England, unlike Germany until this century, *autobiography* won out. If we think of D'Israeli, an early belle-lettrist with a distinctly expressive poetics, and Schlegel, we may note the Romantic fondness for neologisms, whereas eighteenth-century writers in general preferred a common vocabulary and shied from the singular or idiosyncratic. Interestingly, the English neologists included two radicals and an outsider as well as a woman laborer, a suggestion that *autobiography* in its inception came from the margin.

To sum up, the term *autobiography* and its synonym *self-biography*, having never been used in earlier periods, appeared in the late eighteenth century in several forms, in isolated instances in the seventies, eighties, and nineties in both England and Germany with no sign that one use influenced another. The two terms not only were invented but reinvented during this period. In France, a more linguistically conservative country, the term first appears in the *Dictionnaire de l'Académie française* (1836), defined there as "biography made by hand, or manuscript," and it did not appear in its accepted modern form until 1838, with the *Dictionnaire* putting it into its supplement in 1842. It is confessedly of English origin. Larousse's *Grand Dictionnaire universel* (1866) goes even further and claims that "very few French memoirs merit the name of *autobiographie*"; it is more an "English and American genre." Georges May remarks that the word seems to have been taken as what we now call Franglais.[19] It was not fully naturalized until this century. The French got along happily with *les mémoires*.

In a discussion of subjectivity in the early nineteenth century, Jerome Hamilton Buckley claims *autobiography* was "a comparatively new word in the 1830s."[20] But it might be worth noticing that in 1824 T. F. Dibdin in *The Library Companion*, under the heading of "Memoirs and Anecdotes," uses the term *autobiography* five times to refer to the memoirs of Gilbert Wakefield, Richard Cumberland, and Gibbon, the life of Herbert of Cherbury, and Cellini's *Vita*. The text itself uses the hyphenated form of the word a few times in the course of a discussion of Gibbon's *Memoirs*, which Dibdin calls "the most popular production, of its kind, of modern times."[21] This includes a use of *auto-biographical* that also antedates that of Carlyle, the first cited by the *OED*. Around this time a writer of an earlier generation, Henry Mackenzie, in the context of a comment on Rousseau includes the following ironic definition among his *Anecdotes and Egotisms*: "Autobiography, the confession of a person to himself instead of the priest,—generally gets absolution too easily." This was probably written in 1825; Mackenzie died in 1831, and his manuscript was only published in this century.[22]

But such usage was established even earlier. Just three years after Southey, Leigh Hunt claims, in a *Reflector* essay "Letters on Biography" (1812), "the first place is due to those who are their own historians—or, if the word be sufficiently naturalized, the class of autobiographers." Early in *An Essay on the Study and Composition of Biography* (1813), the first book on biography in English, James Field Stanfield says, "It may be here

suitable to introduce a few observations on the subject of auto-biography."
He also speaks of the "self-biographer," and "self-biography."[23] In 1826 a
series began with the title *Autobiography: A Collection of the Most Instructive and Amusing Lives Ever Published, Written by the Parties Themselves*. So by the middle of the 1820's there was an institutional recognition
of the term and a budding canon. (Linda Peterson discusses below the implications for women's autobiography.) Jacques Voisine called the first use
in a book title W. P. Scargill's *The Autobiography of a Dissenting Minister*
(1834), which is probably fiction, but John Galt preceded Scargill in publishing both autobiographical fact and fiction with *The Member: An Autobiography* and *The Radical: An Autobiography* (both 1832, the former
in January), and *The Autobiography of John Galt* (1833).[24] The reviews
of the novels employed the word in a familiar way. A number of books
appeared with "autobiography" in the title in England and America in
the late twenties and early thirties: William Brown, *The Autobiography,
or Narrative of a Soldier* (1829); Matthew Carey, *Auto biographical
Sketches. In a Series of Letters Addressed to a Friend* (1829); Asa Greene,
A Yankee Among the Nullifiers: An Auto-biography (1833), published
pseudonymously by Elnathan Elmwood, Esq. (the book is fiction). James
Browne published *The 'Life' of the Ettrick Shepherd Anatomized in a Series of Strictures on the Autobiography of James Hogg* (1832), under the
pseudonym "an old dissector." The ubiquitous Sir Egerton Brydges published *The Autobiography, Times, Opinions, and Contemporaries of Sir
Egerton Brydges* in 1834. Women's autobiography was a little slower to
use the term. While Elizabeth Wright Macauley's very short, privately
printed *Autobiographical Memoirs* appeared in 1834 and Caroline Fry's
Christ Our Example: To Which Is Prefixed an Autobiography in 1839, the
frequency of the term in titles did not pick up until the mid-forties.[25] Charlotte Brontë's *Jane Eyre: An Autobiography*, perhaps the first novel by a
woman with *autobiography* in the title, appeared in 1847.

The first personal document by a woman to be explicitly called an autobiography was probably *A True Relation of the Birth, Breeding, and Life*
(1814), by Margaret Cavendish, Duchess of Newcastle. Her editor, Sir
Egerton Brydges, says in the opening sentence of his preface: "AUTO-
BIOGRAPHY is so attractive, that in whatever manner it is executed, it
seldom fails both to entertain and instruct." This may well have been the
first application of the term to any English text of an earlier century. In
1819 Samuel Weller Singer claims in the preface to his edition of Joseph
Spence's *Anecdotes . . . of Mr. Pope* (published in 1820) that "a complete
though brief Auto-Biography of Pope may be gathered from it. . . ." The
first use in English of any form of the term applied in a title to poetry was

Charles Armitage Brown's *Shakespeare's Autobiographical Poems: Being his Sonnets Clearly Developed with his Character Drawn Chiefly from his Works* (1838).[26]

In our own day there has been both an occasional return to the use of "self-biography" (e.g. Felicity Nussbaum), and an attempt to develop an entirely new terminology in order to address problems within the field: "Autography" (H. Porter Abbott), "Autogynography" (Domna C. Stanton), "Otobiographie" (Jacques Derrida).[27]

Of course, autobiography existed before the term came into being, just as one could catch a disease before it was diagnosed or named. There was, as May puts it, "autobiographie avant la lettre." At the same time it is easy to think that one of the scholarly pioneers, Georg Misch, wrote a number of large volumes about autobiography in periods that had, properly speaking, little or none.

Yet there is something appropriate about the focus of the present volume largely on works from the late eighteenth century forward because this has been the high tide of autobiography and of a growing awareness of the genre's importance. The late eighteenth century, according to a number of writers, witnessed the beginning of a tradition of autobiography, and some of the most characteristic achievements of the Romantic period were original uses of autobiographic form, such as Wordsworth's *The Prelude* and Coleridge's *Biographia Literaria*. Of course, if autobiography claims to be the unique record of an individual, the notion of a tradition of autobiography is paradoxical at the least.

Let me begin with the late-eighteenth-century interest in the subject. Samuel Johnson is best known as a biographer and lover of biography. His *Rambler* no. 60 is one of the great statements on behalf of biography, yet his preference of autobiography to biography in the later *Idler* no. 84 is far less well known. That he himself is not known as a great autobiographer may be due to his having destroyed all but a small portion of the autobiography he had written. Johnson prefers autobiography to biography for its antiheroic and domestic qualities:

Those relations are therefore commonly of most value in which the writer tells his own story. He that recounts the life of another, commonly dwells most upon conspicuous events, lessens the familiarity of his tale to increase its dignity, shews his favourite at a distance decorated and magnified like the ancient actors in their tragick dress, and endeavours to hide the man that he may produce a hero.[28]

For Johnson, autobiography is preferable because the autobiographer is closer to useful truth, and because he knows it, he will be less likely to distort that truth than a partisan. (Johnson also makes the qualification that such works may be best trusted when published posthumously.) What is clear, however, is that Johnson does not need a special word for autobiography because he thinks of it as a form of biography. Typically, he once tried to cajole Oglethorpe, the founder of Georgia, into writing his own life, but said he would do it himself if Oglethorpe supplied the materials. Johnson's dominant intention was the didactic value of the life for the reader. Yet the fact that he was willing to destroy his own autobiography (though that is not a habit limited to eighteenth-century authors) suggests it played a role for him that took precedence over any role it could have as part of a publicly accessible genre.

At the beginning of the nineteenth century, so shrewd an observer as Mme de Staël claimed "there is nothing at all in England of memoirs, of confessions, of narratives of self made by oneself; the pride of English character refuses to this genre details and opinions: but the eloquence of writers in prose often loses through too severe an abnegation all that seems to come from personal affections."[29] When she wrote this in 1800, she could hardly have known that the great age of English autobiography, which even the Larousse would acknowledge, was beginning.

The emphasis on autobiographies from the late eighteenth century to the twentieth, then, marks a coming of age of autobiographical literature, but the new importance must be taken together with the fact that the study of autobiography is only now coming into its own. It is worth corroborating these claims with testimonies, more or less conscious, of some recent critics. Karl Weintraub, a practicing historian, says, "What I consider genuine autobiography turns out to be very much rarer prior to 1800 than might be expected."[30] Our inquiry into the earliest uses of the term suggests several reasons why the major tradition of autobiography began with (or slightly before) the advent of Romanticism in the eighteenth century. First, such writings, building upon eighteenth-century empiricism and individualism, were encouraged by Romantic subjectivity and its expressive poetics. Second, the Romantic search for origins and its child cult led writers to narrate their own lives from the beginning, and to find more significance in their early years. Third, the breakdown of the prestige of genres encouraged the multiplicity of forms of writing.

In the introduction to L'autobiographie, Georges May says, "If one can imagine a chronological list, nearly complete, of all the known autobiographies and a parallel list of all the critical and historical studies consecrated to autobiography, the first would only need several pages in order to lead up to the middle of the eighteenth century, then the second would only contain very few titles before the second half, if not the last third of the twentieth century."[31] Although this is not perhaps scrupulously accurate—the sectarian autobiographies now in print from seventeenth-century England alone could fill a few of those pages—the timing and the proportions are correct. May quickly draws one important conclusion from these observations: the criticism and theory of autobiography have lagged several centuries behind the practice.[32]

Recent changes in this literature have led William C. Spengemann, perhaps the most acute of those examining the criticism and theory of autobiography, to comment with ironic self-consciousness in his introduction to *The Forms of Autobiography* (1980):

The years that have slipped by since I began to work on this little book have seen autobiography move from the borderlands of literary study to a place much nearer the privileged center traditionally occupied by fiction, poetry, and the drama. Had I written this introduction even five years ago, I could have begun, as was then the custom among critics of autobiography, by lamenting the scholarly neglect of this worthy literature. Now that the genre has become critically respectable, not to say fashionable, however, prefaces like this one are obliged to open on a softer note, with some acknowledgment of the great deal that has already been said on the subject, as well as some justification for adding yet another handful of pages to the steadily mounting pile.[33]

Such observations also appear in *Women's Autobiography: Essays in Criticism* (1980), the first collection of essays devoted to its subject and the harbinger of an important development in the decade. In her preface, Estelle C. Jelinek says, "The idea for this collection came to me in 1976 when I was writing my dissertation on the tradition of women's autobiography. I found practically no criticism on women's autobiographies, except for that on Gertrude Stein." And in her introduction she says that "it has only been since World War II, when the formal analysis of all branches of literature flourished, that autobiography began receiving consideration as a literary genre worthy of serious critical study."[34] The timing is justified, but the heritage of formalism (especially in its embodiment in this country as New Criticism) is certainly ambiguous for autobiography.

New Criticism emphasized the work of art as object, but it took the poem as the highest form of literary art and privileged the imaginative over "non-fiction." In such an atmosphere autobiography did not get much of a hearing, although so important a formalist as R. P. Blackmur devoted a major work (only published in its entirety posthumously) to Henry Adams, and Kenneth Burke would as willingly consider autobiography as anything else. But these were the mavericks of the period, and such critics as Ransom, Tate, and Brooks in America, and Richards and Empson in England, had little or nothing to say about the subject. If we think of the importance of Eliot to the movement, and of his dictum that poetry is "an escape from personality," we may see one of the ways in which the New Critics were inimical to autobiography (as well as biography). It is one of the ironies of literary history that we can now see how implicated Eliot was in hiding autobiography between the lines in so "impersonal" a poem as *The Waste Land*. At any rate, none of the New Critics shows up as a writer of critically or theoretically important essays on autobiography. On the other hand, philosophers and philosophically inclined critics, such as Georges Gusdorf, Paul de Man, and Jacques Derrida, have been part of the more recent interest in autobiography.[35]

Although Spengemann is undoubtedly right to say that "the New Critical animus against historical, biographical, and psychological interpretation . . . severed the already attenuated connections between autobiography and historiography and left the genre a freestanding literary form, to be read like any other narrative," by and large the New Critics were leaving it free for others to read in this way. I think that Northrop Frye's explicit willingness to read autobiography ("confession") as one of the four major forms of prose narrative was a more decisive if later (1957) contribution.[36] Certainly, the return of Freud to high standing in literary theory has had a large role in the increasing respect given to autobiography.

Charles Ryecroft claims that

In the early, heroic days of psychoanalysis, it would not, I imagine, have been difficult to find an analyst prepared to propound with confidence *the* psychoanalytic theory of autobiography. In a paper entitled, perhaps, "The Psychopathology of Autobiography" or "The Autobiographer as Narcissist and Exhibitionist," the infantile fixation points and the unconscious perverse phantasies of the autobiographer would have been located and defined, and autobiographers added to the list of those who, like children, savages, neurotics, lunatics and artists were impelled by the primitive, primary processes of their Id.[37]

Ryecroft says this "reductionist approach would be inconceivable today." But the essay that it is so easy to imagine any of a number of early psychoanalysts writing was never written. A number of recent students of autobiography have made use of Freudian insights. Jeffrey Mehlman has even drawn extensively on Freud, in this case a Lacanian version, and James Olney has relied extensively on Jung, but no book on autobiography with a primary allegiance to Freudian psychoanalysis has appeared as yet with the exception of Paul Jay's *Being in the Text* (1984). This is a surprising fact, because Freud's "talking cure" would seem to provide an obvious model for the writing cure that autobiography offers.[38]

A quick glance at some of the books of the last decade suggests the critical change that has come about. Paul John Eakin (1985): "Formerly neglected by critics, autobiography is now receiving the lively attention it deserves, and it becomes increasingly difficult for me to identify all those whose work on this subject has contributed to the development of my own ideas." Sidonie Smith (1987): "Suddenly everyone in the universe of literary critics and theorists seems to be talking about autobiography, a genre critics described until recently as a kind of flawed biography at worst, and at best a historiographical document capable of capturing the essence of a nation or the spirit of an age." Herbert Leibowitz (1989): "Anybody who embarks on a study of autobiography quickly learns that he or she cannot go far without frequently consulting the vast number of scholarly and critical works on the subject that serve as navigational charts."[39]

A number of recent critical tendencies in different fields have combined to give autobiography its new importance. First, the use of linguistic or rhetorical models for literature displaces poetry from its privileged position and makes "nonfiction" as viable a form of literature (or discourse) as poetry, drama, or the novel. Second, and opposed to this development, the emphasis on "reality," especially reality presented in a seemingly direct form, has led to a strong interest in the reading of autobiography. As one of my undergraduates once put it, "When I read a bad novel, I wind up with nothing; but when I read a bad autobiography I still have something." An age that has become distrustful of history is still willing to read avidly the first-person account, one by the eyewitness or the participant true to his or her subjective response. (At least it is willing to weigh them against other such documents.) "Witness literature" has become especially important in third world countries. Such a position is hardly uncontested. Paradoxically, the interest in autobiography has been furthered by some critics and theorists who, following linguistic or poststructuralist models, are skeptical of the possibility of writing autobiography at all.[40]

Autobiography, I would argue, now occupies the position held during the time of high New Criticism by the poem, a time when such titles as "*Macbeth* as Poem" and "*Wuthering Heights*: The Novel as Poem" were common. The difference in our more self-conscious age, however, is that whereas the poem was the exemplary form for the New Critics, autobiography is a battlefield on which competing ideas about literature (and for that matter history) are fought out. It is a highly problematic form (some would say genre) that encourages the asking of questions about fact and fiction, about the relations of reality and the text, about origins. Is autobiography to be found in referentiality, textuality, or social construction? Is there a self in this text? The subject is radically in question.

At the same time, despite its new importance, autobiography is marginal in all the disciplines in which it has significance in the university. This volume addresses from different vantage points the larger problems posed by the form and the question of its institutional and cultural marginality. These last two concerns are not unrelated. Part of the current appeal of autobiography has to do with its democratic potential, with its suggestion that each person has a possible autobiography allotted him or her, and with its connections to a "bottom up" historiography that would enfranchise anyone ready to tell his or her tale (including orally). From this perspective the weak canonical status of autobiography is an advantage, and its importance especially in recent years as a vehicle for members of minorities and inhabitants of third world countries is obvious.

Autobiographies take the form of both written and oral narratives. Oral autobiographies, recorded and transcribed, have been one characteristic part of the attempt to enfranchise peoples such as the African Americans who have been denied a personal history through laws prohibiting them from learning to read or write. Literacy has been an important theme in the autobiographies of Olaudah Equiano, Frederick Douglass, Harriet Jacobs, and others. The ex-slave narrative in this volume is the written discourse of Lucy A. Delaney, but Genaro M. Padilla interrogates the oral autobiography of a pseudonymous Mexican immigrant produced by an American sociologist, and Jerome Bruner, who has studied the "autobiographical" narratives produced by a two-year-old on the verge of sleep, shows what the social sciences can do when their work is informed by the self-awareness of literary theory in eliciting familial autobiographies that it then subjects to analysis.

Self-representation of a different unwritten sort is found in self-portraiture. Below, Ronald Paulson considers William Hogarth's autobiography in relation to his art, but some artists have clearly thought of their self-portraits as a kind of autobiography. Courbet is explicit about this in writing to his patron concerning his *L'homme à la pipe* (1854):

I was struck on seeing it. It's a terrific element in our solution. It's the portrait of a fanatic, an aesthetic, a man disillusioned with the rubbish that made up his education, and now trying to live in harmony with his principles. I have painted many self-portraits in my life, corresponding to the changes in my state of mind. In a word, I have written my autobiography [j'ai écrit ma vie].[41]

This may to some extent have been telling Bruyas things he wanted to hear, but certainly the autobiographical impulse was strongest in his great self-portrait, *The Studio of the Painter, Real Allegory Determining a Phase of Seven Years of My Artistic Life*. In such a conception he tried to overcome the inherent limitations of painting as an autobiographical medium and give duration to what otherwise would seem to be only a particular moment in his life, however much it may have summed up the character and experience of a lifetime. The oxymoronic phrase "real allegory" (*allégorie réelle*) was interestingly anticipated by Daniel Defoe in his *Serious Reflections of Robinson Crusoe* with strong hints that he was himself the subject of *Robinson Crusoe*—a line that leads to the relationship between auto-biography and the novel. Other painters of numerous self-portraits early and late, particularly Rembrandt and Reynolds, may give us a special kind of serial autobiography, as Courbet suggests. Edvard Munch claimed, "My paintings are my diaries." Even the composer (as expected, in the Romantic tradition) can experiment with autobiography. Richard Strauss's *Ein Helden-Leben*, with its self-quotations of his work, was meant to be a kind of musical autobiography, but it can only chronicle his career and in doing so make a case for its heroic significance.

Samuel Johnson warns that "definitions are hazardous," and the definition of autobiography has proved elusive. Philippe Lejeune's attempt (1971) has been eroded by his own work as well as by that of other theorists: "We call autobiography the retrospective narrative in prose that someone makes of his own existence when he puts the principal accent upon his life, especially upon the story of his own personality."[42] More recently so sophisticated a critic as William Spengemann admits not just fiction (a frequent decision in recent books on the subject) but such a seemingly unautobiographical work as Hawthorne's *Scarlet Letter* (Hester Prynne, c'est moi?). Indeed, it would seem that Spengemann's whole teleological book exists to make that argument. The strong argument here is Paul de Man's contention that autobiography is a "figure of reading," specifically, prosopopoeia.[43]

Autobiography, as I understand it, has norms but not rules. It is usually but not exclusively in the first person. Some of the greatest, such as Henry Adams's *The Education of Henry Adams* (an autobiography despite his contention that it is not one), are in the third person, and bring up problems considered below in "The Self as Other." Autobiographies may be in prose or verse, though a verse autobiography such as Wordsworth's *Prelude* presents special problems, and the conventions of poetry are often at variance with those of autobiography. Autobiography may be truthful or mendacious, for factuality is not crucial to its autobiographical interest, despite some critics' neo-Romantic insistence on sincerity. The autobiography of Edmund Backhouse, known at this time only from Hugh Trevor-Roper's account of it in his fascinating biography, *The Hermit of Peking*, is evidently highly revealing of its subject, whose sexual and other fantasies or lies are given as authentic experiences. Autobiographies may also be ostensibly fiction, though the subject of autobiography presented as fiction needs more theoretical examination. Some works are autobiographical despite being principally or officially something else—Boswell's *Life of Johnson* and Mark Harris's *Saul Bellow, Drumlin Woodchuck* (influenced by Boswell and ostensibly a biography of Bellow) come to mind. But the autobiographical and autobiography are not the same thing, though the question of the significance of autobiography in any writing has a long, complex history of its own. The autobiographer, as John Sturrock puts it, cannot help writing autobiography. But I would add as a corollary that others can.[44]

Autobiography is usually written in old age, or at least in mid-life (the Dantean *Nel mezzo del cammin di nostra vita*), but it may be written by the young. Frank Conroy's *Stop-Time* and Beverly Nichols's *Twenty-Five* are cases in point. The latter insists that that age is the oldest one should be when writing autobiography. It is usually one book, though possibly of many volumes, since lives come one to a customer. Beverly Nichols is again a useful exception, since he wrote three separate autobiographies. Autobiography is usually an avocation rather than a vocation, though the autobiographer is often a writer. But some autobiographies have been the first or only productions of their authors. Like the fictional Tristram Shandy, these writers seem to exist only to tell the story of their lives. Richard Rodriguez's *Hunger of Memory: The Education of Richard Rodriguez* (with its echo of Henry Adams) is in many ways the story of what he has become: a man who writes in English of Hispanic parents who could not speak English. He is a writer, but the writing of this book was the central fact of his early life. Such an instance should remind us of the situation of the modernist novel. A first novel was often autobiographical and told us, as in the paradigm case of *A Portrait of the Artist as a Young Man*, how the writer became the man who wrote the book we are reading. As Paul Fussell shrewdly observed in 1970, "Twenty years ago Frank Conroy's *Stop-Time* would have been costumed as a 'first novel.' Today it appears openly as a memoir."[45] One may make the same claim of Maxine Hong Kingston's more recent *The Woman Warrior*.

The case of fiction may seem to offer a crude dividing line: autobiographies are generally written by those who bear the same name as the protagonists of their narratives. But of course some have been written in collaboration with others or entirely ghostwritten. Alex Haley billed himself as the "author" of *The Autobiography of Malcolm X*. Conversely, we have cases like that of Gertrude Stein, who wrote her own autobiography, but wrote it as though it were that of her friend, Alice B. Toklas.

Autobiographies are generally narratives about the past of the writer. We reserve the terms "diary" and "journal" for accounts of present activities. Augustine certainly makes a number of his modern readers uneasy when he shifts in his *Confessions* to the present and turns more directly to prayer and hermeneutics. This is not to say, however, that the past takes precedence over the present moment or moments, which often provide the point of departure that organizes the autobiography. In *Roland Barthes by Roland Barthes*, at once the paradigmatic title for an autobiography and a parody of it, the author organizes his book by alphabetical subjects and moves freely from first to third person and back.

The difference between autobiography and biography would seem to be grounded upon consciousness. Louis Marin is fond of reminding us that there are two things that an autobiographer cannot say of himself from knowledge: "I was born," and "I died." The biographer can say, "he was born," "he died." Biography is about a completed life, a telos; autobiography, about a life in process. But there are a number of things that an autobiographer can say and a biographer cannot. A recent letter to the *Los Angeles Times Book Review* (July 20, 1990) by one Daniel A. Jenkins helps to clarify the point: "I am writing my autobiography and would appreciate hearing from anyone who can remember anything interesting or exciting about my life." This request amuses as a parody of the biographer's usual letter to such publications. In autobiography the narrator has, to some extent at least, a privileged knowledge of the consciousness of the protagonist of his narrative. If autobiography were merely a variety of first-person narration, it neither would receive the popular attention it does, nor would it be as interesting a form for critics. Henry James, after all, considered first-person narration as an artistically inferior form for the novelist. Northrop Frye would circumvent such problems by seeing all autobiography as "confession," one of his four forms of fiction, but surely the fictional encoding of the factual is one of the great problematics of autobiography.

Many theorists would deny that autobiography is a genre, and yet since the eighteenth century it certainly has been recognized as such by its writers and readers. If in closing we look at what is perhaps the strongest of all autobiographical generic conventions, the telling of one's first memories, we should see the centrality of consciousness to some of the philosophical and psychological thinking of the last three hundred years that shapes it. I start with a few examples of its force. Robert Graves begins *Goodbye to All That* by saying, "As proof of my readiness to accept autobiographical convention, let me at once record my two earliest memories."[46] And E. L. Woodward, who quarrels with the notion of significance attached to earliest memories, nonetheless starts his autobiography, *Short Journey*, the same way: "I have not seen many elephants in my life. Therefore, my first memories, which are of elephants, are not very relevant to my future career." (It is revealing that he sees life in terms of its *res gestae*, career rather than consciousness.) The description is followed by a summary dismissal: "I mention the elephants because they serve to show that my recollections of childhood may be entertaining to myself, but are not likely to interest anyone else. Therefore, I pass over them quickly in a general survey of the world in which I have lived."[47] And yet the last sentence of the book returns to them: "Wise or unwise, content or still questioning, the little creature who laughed at elephants half a century ago in a suburban field, must come, soon, to the end of his distractions." This, for all the denials of the opening paragraphs, is more than slick autobiographical closure. The note of absurdity that accompanies the self-deprecation and the skeptical poise is just right. The heavy breathing of the punctuation works up to an unmentioned but strongly suggested death, yet the term "distractions" covers such entertainments as circuses as well as the darker thought that "all is vanity" (an echo of Ecclesiastes appearing a page before). Perhaps the dynamics of this unremarked (and largely unremarkable) autobiography of an English academic have much to do with the seeming irrelevance of elephants and the seeming relevance of career in his "short journey."

Locke's definition of personal identity goes a long way towards explaining the convention of first memories in autobiography:

For, since consciousness always accompanies thinking, and it is that which makes every one to be what he calls self, and thereby distinguishes himself from all other thinking things, in this alone consists personal identity, i.e. in the sameness of a rational being: and as far as this consciousness can be extended backwards to any past action or thought, so far reaches the identity of that person.[48]

This is the point of departure for all conceptions of self that find their way into the modern conception of autobiography, and for the critique of personal identity that starts with Hume.

If Locke gives us the philosophical basis for the convention of first memories in autobiography, Freud gives us the psychoanalytic reasons for their necessity. Locke tells us that personal identity coexists with these memories; Freud tells us that what we remember as our first memory will be significant because we have remembered it, that we will remember it because, even if distorted, it has a special significance. (It would not be too hard to give a Freudian reading of Woodward's elephants, which come with the telltale accompaniment of a denial of their importance on the part of the subject—just the sort of resistance that Freud found highly suggestive of repression on the subject's part.) Freud's own showpiece for this claim comes from Goethe's *Dichtung und Wahrheit*. Freud notes that Goethe's first memory, one of breaking the family crockery in the street, egged on by three odd orphan brothers who lived opposite his house, seems at first glance a silly and essentially meaningless incident, and in "preanalytic days one could read this without finding occasion to stop and without surprise."[49] Yet he conjectures "that what had remained in memory was the most significant element in that whole period of life, equally so whether it had gained subsequent importance from the influence of later events." (Freud's alertness to crucial moments of autobiographical time should be noted.) Here his reading does not depend on the direct interpretation of symbols, but on the analogy of symbolic action on the part of patients encountered in practice. Freud reveals the meaning of this memory as a "magical action, by which a child . . . violently expresses his wish to get rid of a disturbing intruder," in Goethe's case a new-born brother, who is not so much as mentioned in the autobiography, though he lived to be six.

The essays brought together here are intended to provide contemporary perspectives for the reading and understanding of autobiography through a recognition of its social construction and cultural conditioning. Devoted to the history, theory, and practice of autobiography, they consider either in themselves or by implication the relations of mainstream and marginal, of the canon and its other. While the focus is on written autobiography, the oral also is given attention, especially by Genaro Padilla.

John Sturrock's inquiry into the relationship between autobiography and theory turns on the observation that autobiography, with its insistence on presence and sympathy, would seem to be at a remove from theory. Sturrock, whose "new model autobiographer" was a pivotal conception in recent studies of autobiography, goes on to contrast the theorist of autobiography to the "lay reader" who is seeking to further his or her knowledge about a known figure. This leads him from questions about the theorist's proper agenda to an examination of a series of those whose thought rather than their activities has led to their "singularization" as autobiographical figures.

Jerome Bruner's wide-ranging consideration of the conditions of autobiography explores through anthropology, psychology, philosophy, sociology, law, portraiture, and speech acts, the process by which autobiographical utterance, both oral and written, comes into being. It provides a critique of the "fact," insists upon the social construction of autobiography, and points to a number of studies in different fields that need doing.

Like Bruner, Watson provides a critique of common notions of autobiography through an investigation of theory and autobiographies, but her very different rejection of essentialism and totalization rests on opposition to what she calls the "*bios*-bias." Through a consideration of autobiographies that test canonical notions and a survey of some important recent theories of autobiography, especially by a variety of feminists, she attempts to resituate our notion of what autobiography is and to exemplify it in the work of Christa Wolf. Implicit here is a different idea of the reader of autobiography as well as its theorists.

Linda Peterson's essay may be taken as a complement to Watson's in its examination of the canon of women's autobiography as it was constructed in the nineteenth century. Her close historical account focuses on the publication or republication of seventeenth-century texts (mainly religious) and the publication of the scandalous autobiographies of Mary Robinson and Charlotte Charke in the Hunt and Clarke collection, the canonizing moments that she calls the institutionalizing of women's autobiography.

The next three papers, which focus on specific autobiographers, extend the consideration of questions of canon and the social or cultural construction of autobiography, and they do so by focusing on relations between the autobiographer and some "other."

The institutional other considered by Lindon Barrett is the court of law, which defines identity in the autobiography of the ex-slave Lucy Delaney in a way on which her freedom depends. By focusing on the problematics of self-definition for African Americans, Barrett deals with the construction of selves as a means of highlighting the relation between the individual and the communal that is explicitly or implicitly a central concern of African American autobiography.

Genaro Padilla interrogates the way in which sociologists have constructed the narratives of anonymous American Mexicans and Mexican Americans through the publication of oral autobiographies by "editors."

He provides a close examination of the case of Ramon Gonzales*, whose asterisk points to the eliding of his identity by the very process that is presumably bringing him to light.

Barbara Metcalf examines the pilgrimage narrative of the highly westernized Mumtaz Mufti as a way of showing the conventions of Islamic self-representation and their difference from Western expectations. However, within the narrative itself, Mufti, as a skeptical intellectual, represents himself as one of the least likely pilgrims to Mecca.

Like these three essays, Roger Porter's contribution considers an autobiographer who in some sense is relatively "unknown." (These four essays in different ways deal with the ironies of such a situation.) Porter reads the diaries and autobiography of the artist and suicide Benjamin Robert Haydon in terms of Romantic concepts of the artist and Rousseau's autobiographical tradition.

Porter is concerned with the artist-failure as writer, but the next contributor, Ronald Paulson, the biographer of Hogarth, considers both Hogarth's autobiography and his self-representations in his art as ways of arriving at Hogarth's psychological projection of self, carefully establishing what it tells us of his biography.

Ranging from Augustine to Roland Barthes, the editor focuses on the moment in autobiography when the autobiographer sees himself or herself as other. This begins with a focus on the mirror image, but it takes in autobiography as a whole, with its implied Lacanian late mirror stage, and addresses some of the issues of the split subject.

If this collection includes such canonical autobiographers as Augustine and Rousseau, Henry Adams and John Henry Newman, it also includes the women of various sects who wrote religious autobiographies in the seventeenth and eighteenth centuries; Charlotte Charke, the cross-dressing daughter of Colley Cibber, and Mary Robinson, two scandalous actresses of the eighteenth century; Lucy Delaney, an ex-slave; the lesbian women of color who collectively wrote *This Bridge Called My Back*; and Christa Wolf. It also considers, among numerous others, an obscure professor (along with those less obscure professors Vico and Primo Levi); the two-year-old Emmy; an anonymous American Mexican; Mumtaz Mufti, virtually unknown in the Western world, though the foremost modern Urdu author; a great English artist, Hogarth; and a major artistic failure, Benjamin Robert Haydon. The autobiographers represented here are African, American, English, French, German, Italian, Mexican, Pakistani, and Roman Moroccan. By including both canonical and noncanonical authors, "mainstream" and marginal, and interrogating the ideas of canon, main-stream, and margin, the volume collectively attempts without totalizing to come to grips with questions of what autobiography has been and is, and what it can become. It interrogates the cultural status of autobiography now.

Theory Versus Autobiography

John Sturrock

A leading question, appropriate to this liminal moment of my own removal from a social to a textual setting: Should we feel bad when we theorize about autobiography? Or, supposing all literary theory to have something unsociable about it, should we feel particularly bad when theorizing about autobiography? My answer, briefly, is that we should sense in ourselves a discomfort that is specific to theorizing about autobiography, a discomfort brought on by responding with the hardheadedness of the analyst to a kind of writing that, more than any other, is intended to work on our sympathies. But this sense of discomfort is not a reason for giving up the theoretical study of autobiography; quite the reverse, it is a feeling around which we might one day make a successful theory of autobiography to turn. For if autobiography does not lend itself altogether comfortably to theorization—or, better, if it seems to resist theorization—that makes it a most promising case, both in itself and because it may have something to tell us about the wider question of whether literary theory in general derives its energy from the theorist's sense of himself as a defaulter from certain ideals of sociability. An autobiography is a text that would draw us into itself without reservations, one that we are more strongly than ever inclined to read as dignified by a "metaphysics of presence," when not to do so is to refuse the peculiar appeal of the autobiographer. That text is the certificate of a unique existence, and the theorist who comes to it full of questions, and with a will to formalize its uniqueness away, knows himself to be playing a reprehensible part; he is not as other, innocent readers of autobiography.

Autobiography precedes theory, and it will do so here. Let me take advantage of the license allowed to its theorists of referring to episodes from their own lives in support of their theoretical case. Some years ago I was

asked by a publisher in London to report on a manuscript whose subject
was modern literary autobiographies, exclusively British ones as I recall.
It covered a good many examples, summarizing what was in them, and
adding some paragraphs of analysis or judgment before it passed on. It was
essentially a list of autobiographies categorized more by the circumstances
of their authorship than by similarities of structure. The manuscript struck
me as falling heavily but interestingly between two stools. It was neither
sufficiently empirical, by which I mean adequately descriptive of the contents of the books it discussed, nor sufficiently theoretical, since it skimped
or else avoided any true classification of them. It never inquired into what
the possible generic determinants of autobiography might be and what
these particular examples had to tell us about them.

But here comes the theoretical point of this pre-theoretical anecdote.
Who was going to respond to such a book, supposing it were published?
What kind of reader collects autobiographies? Only those of us, presumably, with some theoretical interest in them as together making up a recognizable literary genre. The theorist will willingly pass from reading one
autobiography to another, will read, it may be, nothing but autobiographies for months on end, in the furtherance of his strange professional interests. In the preface to his attractive study of autobiography, for example,
Richard N. Coe records having read "some six hundred" texts during the
eight years he worked on it.[1] Such are the demands, or the anxieties, of
comprehensiveness for the literary theorist, who can but proceed towards
his general conclusions by induction from individual cases. The lay reader,
whose interests are the opposite of generic, does no such thing. For the lay
reader, an autobiography is not one more contribution to a genre or ty-
pology, but the unique self-presentation of author X or author Y, some
public figure this reader already knows, and about whom he or she wants
to know more. The lay reader does not normally read the autobiographies
of previously unknown authors, or of authors without a name; the theorist
on the other hand reads them indiscriminately, in search of formal or textual variety, the better to accumulate examples of the genre that preoccu-
pies him. The theorist's concern is with the genre, not the autobiographer.

The author of the manuscript I have been citing had done something
more revealing than merely fall between two stools; he had fallen victim
to the strong tension or opposition between the writing of autobiography
and its subsequent ordering into a theory. His program was a theoretical
one, he had planned a generic study, but what he had then written was a
catalogue, dimly raisonné, of individual titles or autobiographers. It could
be argued that even to give a précis of an autobiography, to retell it as a
story of one's own, is tacitly to theorize it, since however we choose to re-

duce a text we do so according to some set of rules or choices, so that a collection of potted autobiographies produced by a single author is sure to reveal a consistency of method amounting to a potential theory of the genre. But what the précis does very much more obviously is to pay its respects to the integrity of the text it is summarizing. It sets difference above sameness. This half-hearted and ultimately failed theorist had stumbled in practice over what the profoundly theoretical Paul de Man wrote of as the "disreputability" of autobiography, and "its incompatibility with the monumental dignity of aesthetic values."[2] De Man, in common with others who have turned their thoughts to the specific nature of autobiography, asked whether we can define it as a literary genre at all, given not so much the apparent miscellany of the forms in which the autobiographical project may be realized, as the essentially contra-generic intentions that are its very source.

The autobiographer of course is on the side of the lay reader of autobiography, not of the theorist. It is the lay reader with whom he means to associate. He becomes an autobiographer because his name is already in the public domain: he has done or written something that ensures him a readership. Although he is in part known already, he may feel he is misleadingly or inadequately known, and write in order to correct that, to impose an image of himself whose authenticity no reader is in a position to question. An autobiography is offered as a textual accessory, either to its author's extra-textual life, which is the text's seductive but otherwise inaccessible ground, or else to his published oeuvre. Its relation to that oeuvre may vary according to the extent the autobiography acts as an explication of that oeuvre's hitherto unsuspected unity or serves merely as a chronological account in which its serial publication constitutes a succession of episodes. In either case, what the autobiographer has taken in hand is his own public integration, whose logic may be that of narrative or of orderly self-portraiture.

But for the theorist, the autobiographical text has to be brought out from under this too close tutelage of the life it represents; it has to be isolated even from the oeuvre of which it may purport to be the final rationalization. The theorist's loyalty is to the genre, and he reads autobiographies not as gratifying evidence of how it is possible textually to establish one's coherence as a living entity but in order to integrate these texts successively in whatever theoretical model of the genre he has thus far been able to build, either as confirmation of its soundness and capacity to incorporate new evidence, or else of the need to overhaul and enrich it. If we accept that the property rights of all autobiography lie inalienably with the author, then what the theorist is set upon is an act of expropriation, or of dismemberment. He assumes that we can, with profit, distinguish the dance from the dancer, or the self as impersonal performance from the self as unique and transcendent originator of the text. The theoretical task is to relate one autobiographical performance to others, and so to reclassify particular examples of autobiography in generic terms. Autobiographers themselves have done something of the same sort. They have learned how to write autobiographically from their own writing and reading of history, or fiction, or (auto)biography; they have acquired the rules by which alone any narrative or essay in self-presentation can proceed. But if they are themselves already generically adept when they set out to write autobiographically, they do not write in order to be read generically, as faceless new recruits to some ancient and familiar standing army. Rather, they naturalize the conventional methods of narrative or self-analysis so that it strikes us as a failure of our own goodwill if we pause to draw attention to them. There has never yet been an autobiography written for a readership of theorists, although, as we shall shortly see, there is a strand of extreme self-consciousness among some contemporary autobiographers that ought in the future to make any naive practice of the genre impossible.

The theorist of autobiography faces a serious dilemma in fixing the direction and bounds of his research: How far ought he to pursue the vital or intellectual context of the autobiographies he reads? If the autobiographer is or was a literary figure, how much of the rest of his or her oeuvre does the theorist read in order to give an informed reading of the autobiography? And should the theorist read it before or after reading the autobiography? Again, how much external historical evidence needs to be brought in, in order to relate a particular autobiography to circumstances of its author's life and times that have gone unrecorded, or that are perhaps taken for granted in the text itself? These, after all, are the directions in which the lay reader of autobiography will be led, or indeed the directions from which he or she may have come to the autobiography in the first place. Take the case of an autobiographer wholly remote from us, in time, in condition, and very likely in his creed: Augustine, whose *Confessions* no theorist of autobiography could conceivably ignore. When, as theorists, we read that extraordinary text and draw our formal conclusions from it, can we be quite easy in our minds doing so without having read anything else of Augustine's huge oeuvre, or any other account of his life apart from his own? Can we justify to ourselves knowing little or nothing of the intellectual or ecclesiastical traditions within which he worked?

Of course not. But if we want to get on with formulating theorems of autobiography, we must not allow ourselves to be led astray by the feeling of unease that goes with this singling out of examples. The autobiographical theorist cannot afford to yield to the historical appeal of a text such as the *Confessions*, or be so drawn into it as to want to study patristic theology, it might be, or the psychology of religious conversion, or those others of Augustine's writings that it would always be possible to relate to the *Confessions* for their similarities of theme or form. The temptation always will be there, to know more of Augustine the better to interpret this one text in the documentary sense in which it was intended. It is a temptation to which most theorists of autobiography I am sure give in. It would be good one day to have their own autobiographical confessions, to discover how strictly they have been able to defend their virtue as theorists, to what extent they compromise it by reading around the text they are concerned with, and how far they are prepared to go in this contextualizing endeavor before feeling free to pass on to the next autobiography. Autobiography is unquestionably an appeal to us as its readers to progress in intimacy with the autobiographer, and there could be no more callous response to it than to register that appeal as characteristic of the genre without ever acting on it.

The theorist of autobiography is, in short, a singular reader of autobiography, someone whose motive for reading accounts of human lives written by those who have lived them is not to satisfy a humane curiosity about the privacy of others, or to encompass other lives as gratifying wholes in recompense for the perceived incoherence of his or her own life, but to know more about a certain kind of writing. The theorist is committed to a study that runs very suggestively counter to the task to which the autobiographer is committed. This I make, necessarily, as a theoretical point: the opposition intended is between the activity of the theorist and the activity of the autobiographer as understood in the perspective of the theorist, and not that of the individual autobiographer.

The autobiographer's wish is to single himself out by the writing of a book, to construct in prose an attractive identity for himself. We need perhaps the traditional notion of the book here, rather than that of the text, as standing more positively for the entity that the autobiographer aspires to create as a worldly representative among those for whom he can never be a bodily presence. The autobiographer, in quest of a shelf life, memorializes himself in the form of a book; the theorist takes down that book from the shelf, suspicious of its claims to integrity, and anaesthetizes it, in the hopes of conducting on this temporarily lifeless specimen a biopsy full of advantage to the literary specialist. The theorist knows, but is not deterred by the knowledge, that the autobiographer is already the interpreter of his life, already a textualist, and not some godlike chronicler mysteriously exempted from the equivocations of language. To an extent the theorizing of autobiography begins in the writing of autobiography.

The writer's urge to establish his singularity is an inaugural topos of the genre. It may be expressed very robustly, as it is by Nietzsche at the start of the preface to *Ecce Homo*: "*Listen! for I am such and such a person. For Heaven's sake do not confound me with anyone else.*"[3] Thus speaks Zarathustra: the mood is the imperative, the typeface italic. It is this recognition of the autobiographer's predicament that has called for words of such vehemence to be spoken. Nietzsche is not unknown to the world because he has addressed it a good many times before, in the books he has published, but he has not been heard, he is not, he concludes, "alive." Hence the demand for attention, urgently required because of the disparity he observes between the "greatness" of his task as the transvaluer of all our values and the "smallness" of his contemporaries, that is, ourselves as his timid or benighted readers. It is his unacknowledged singularity that entitles him to address us now in this bullying form and that we are to be brought to recognize by attending to his declaration of "who and what I am." Nietzsche may count as an extraordinarily brash autobiographer, but he is not behaving any differently from his kind in proclaiming as he does his fated "genius." Such singularity of destiny is the promise held out to us by all autobiographical retrospection; it is simply held out with what one can but call a unique immodesty by Nietzsche, not least in the title he took over for his work of self-presentation, *Ecce Homo*.

The most celebrated statement of this generic promise is to be read at the opening of Rousseau's *Confessions*: "I have formed an undertaking for which there has never been a model, and whose execution will have no imitator. I wish to show my fellow-creatures a man in all the truth of nature; and that man will be me. Me alone. I feel my heart and I know men. I am not made like any of those I have seen; I dare to think I am not made like any of those who exist. If I am not better, at least I am other."[4] The emphasis here is different from that found in *Ecce Homo*: where Nietzsche cherishes the uniqueness of his destiny, Rousseau cherishes that of his nature, which is a more extravagant assertion for him to make. Without laying claim thereby to the status of Ubermensch, we can all be certain that the life we have lived is ours alone; few of us would go on, however, to presume the uniqueness of our nature. On the strength of Rousseau's proclamation of his own singularity of essence, as opposed to that of his past existence, one might decide that among autobiographers he is remarkable for the intensity with which he holds to that belief. It is an intensity made painfully sharp, as in Nietzsche's case, by his knowing, or imagining, that the image of himself already circulating as a consequence of his earlier public appearances as author or human agent is in desperate need of correction. It is not necessary to be paranoiac in order to write one's autobiography, but it surely helps to have a weakened sense of contingency, to be able to believe that one has been the victim either of ill-informed attention in the past or else of an unmerited neglect. The autobiographer is seeking to plot the course of his remembered life after the event(s); he is, by virtue of his calling, a conspiracy theorist, and it matters not whether the machinations of which he sees himself as the center be those of fate and favorable to him, as with Nietzsche, or those of society and unfavorable, as with Rousseau, whose conviction of his own uniqueness is underwritten by his anxiety to rescue his self-image from the custody of others.

The writer's singularity is at once a premise and an end of autobiography. The autobiographer already has a proper name that is known to others as a result of the public achievements that entitle him to come forward as an autobiographer; he is singular to start with. The function of the account he will give is to reaffirm his singularity from within, by justifying it not as an original given but as a lived process. Autobiography is the record of a singularization. In reflecting on his life, the autobiographer traces the purposeful, seemingly anticipated course of his own separation out from others, his escape from among the great mass of the anonymous. Anonymity means the death of autobiography. If we ever get to read a book called "The Autobiography of an Anonymous Man," it will be a cheat, since we shall be reading the work of someone determined to abolish his anonymity by the presumed singularity of authorship. Just as the Grossmiths' original Nobody became a distinguished Somebody long ago, with the publication of his *Diary*, so the anonymous autobiographer can but give us the story of how he has lost his anonymity.

The process of singularization is one peculiarly easy to find recorded in autobiographies written by philosophers or other thinkers who have become singular in the world for their ideas rather than for their actions. It is to them I shall turn for examples, in the belief that the theory of autobiography has much to learn from the autobiographies of theorists. Thinkers habitually wish us to know that the ideas associated with their names are, genetically speaking, theirs, that they were, when first thought of, new, original ideas, not ones recovered from the oblivion of the past or found in intimate collaboration with other thinkers. This possessiveness is a strong theme of the accounts they have left of their lives.

I go straight to an extreme and therefore instructive case: that of Descartes. Descartes was a mighty innovator in the philosophy of mind, but was he as mightily innovative as he asks us to believe in the account he published of the genesis of his thought in the *Discourse on Method*? This is a text written in the vernacular, it is worth noting, in French, and only subsequently translated into the Latin in which, had Descartes been following the scholarly conventions of the time, he would have published it from the start. The reason he gives for this unorthodox procedure is his hope "that those who rely entirely on their unspoiled natural reason will be better judges of my opinions than those who give credence only to the writing of the ancients."[5] Latin was the language used by those who had taught Descartes, the Jesuits of the college of La Flèche, and of received, authoritative opinion in general. The philosopher's decision to write and publish the *Discourse* in French is thus all of a piece with his wish to tell there the story of his radical and complete break with intellectual authority, of his utterly distinctive desire to think afresh, from the beginning, for himself, trusting only in the "unspoiled natural reason" inscribed in each one of us from birth. The choice of the vernacular is a first, important step in the philosopher's singularization.

Read today, the *Discourse* seems remarkable for achieving its philosophical ends by way of a narrative tracing the philosopher's formation. The element of story is crucial to Descartes, even if it contradicts his desire to establish his own autonomy. Towards the end of the first part of the *Discourse* he tells us that "as soon as my age allowed of my passing from under the control of my teachers, I entirely abandoned the study of letters; and resolving to seek no other science than that which can be found in myself and in the great book of the world, I spent the remainder of my youth in travel . . . amassing varied experiences . . . and at all times making reflections on the things that came my way, and by which I could in any wise profit."[6] Descartes needs this polarity between letters and life, whereby the immediacy of life, and the autonomy of one's own reactions to it as a man of the world, are opposed to the cloistered, unreliable mediacy of books or teachers. And yet, in order to persuade us that the lessons of immediacy were the more profitable to him in the furtherance of his philosophical purpose, Descartes has to resort to certain lessons in mediacy acquired during his education; he has to show that he has learned well enough the power of letters and how to bend it to his own rhetorical ends. Among the discoveries of his schooling that he would have us believe he has now transcended was the effect on our minds of narrative: in the Schools he had once learned that "fables charm and awaken the mind" and that "the histories of memorable deeds exalt it." This is a teaching of which he can now make use as a writer in advancing the case of his own preeminence as a thinker who has dared to reoriginate philosophy from a new, apodeictic datumline. Descartes makes beautifully devious use of the power of narrative in the *Discourse*:

Thus my present design is not to teach a method which everyone ought to follow for the right conduct of his reason, but only to show in what manner I have endeavoured to conduct my own. Those who undertake to give precepts ought to regard themselves as wiser than those for whom they prescribe; and if they prove to be in the least degree lacking, they have to bear the blame. But in putting forward this piece of writing merely as a history, or, if you prefer so to regard it, as a fable, in which, among some examples worthy of imitation, there will also, perhaps, be found others we should be well advised not to follow, I hope that it will be of use to some without being harmful to anyone, and that all will welcome my plain-speaking.[7]

He is in seeming retreat here, willing to exchange authority, the taking possession of which he is in fact recounting, for the modest conviviality of narrative, or that power of stories to charm and perhaps, charmingly, to point a moral. Here is a giver of precepts willing to steal the clothes of a humble *littérateur*, the better to compel acceptance of his precepts.

Descartes was equivocal towards his singularity, able apparently both to assert it as his philosophical aim and to abdicate from it, as from an unwanted isolation within society. (This equivocation recurs, interestingly, in the first biography written of him, that by Adrien Baillet, who more than once equates singularity with "affectation" and stresses the philosopher's wish accordingly to avoid it.) But then it was important for him to remind us that his intellectual distinction had not been bought at the cost of his humanity; there is a cleverly managed egalitarianism in the *Discourse*. The text opens, famously, with the proposition that "Good sense is of all things in the world the most equitably distributed," good sense being here defined as "the power of judging well and of distinguishing between the true and the false." Descartes accepts that this power is "by nature equal in all men" on the curious ground that all men believe themselves "amply provided with it" and all men cannot be wrong. But whatever its persuasiveness as an axiom of his philosophy, Descartes requires the premise of an innate "good sense" for his purposes as an autobiographer. It is the most promising point of departure for the story of his singularization. If we are all equally in possession of this fundamental faculty of accurate judgment, how does it happen that so few of us distinguish ourselves by its application? We start equal and end unequal. The opportunity is there, then, to tell us by what singular path or process René Descartes has elevated himself above the crowd of those identically endowed. The moral of his fable is that we are not born singular but that we can rise to singularity, and do so by being singularly unencumbered by intellectual debts to those who have been our teachers.

One might ask, taking a cue from the distinction observed by Descartes himself, whether in the *Discourse* he is writing as the historian of his own intellectual formation, or else as a fabulist, as the kind of serious storyteller for whom what matters is not exactitude but the moral to be drawn. Bluntly put: do we believe the story Descartes tells us, or discount its truth claims by seeing it as having been shaped by the requirements of the literary form he is practicing? It is not being unduly skeptical to come to the conclusion after reading the *Discourse* that his desire to affirm his singularity has got the better of him, and that he has gone egregiously far in protesting his own independence of mind by eliminating the influence of other minds on his own and reducing the essentials needed by the successful philosopher to the barest minimum, the congenital "good sense" common to us all. Can this be the credible history of how his thought came to be what it is? By thus clearing away from his path all evidence of an outside contribution to his philosophy, the self-sufficient Descartes has given us not the truthful record but what might better be called the *fabula rasa* of his past.

Two of his close successors in philosophy did not trust what they read in the *Discourse*. Leibniz thought it an excellent idea that original thinkers should leave behind a record for others of the successive steps by which they had arrived at their intellectual discoveries, so that as their readers we might take those same steps for ourselves and understand more clearly that knowledge and understanding are gradual attainments. Descartes's was an initiative of the right kind, but, declared Leibniz, he had exaggerated his own originality: "Descartes would have had us believe that he had read scarcely anything. That was a bit too much."[8]

Leibniz was forbearing towards his distinguished predecessor in comparison with another thinker from whom an account of his intellectual evolution along Leibnizian lines was commissioned in Venice in the 1720's: Giambattista Vico. Vico's was to have been one of many such accounts in which distinguished Italian scholars were to trace the process by which their own ideas had emerged and establish pedagogical models the young could follow for the future advancement of learning in Italy; his *Life* is the only one of these exemplars to have survived. The model he had in mind when writing is very clearly Descartes. Like Descartes, Vico wrote not in Latin but in the vernacular, having by this point in his academic career in Naples given up all hope of an advancement in keeping with his remarkable but unrecognized abilities. The break in language is, as with Descartes, if for a less highminded reason, a break with the intellectual establishment. Unlike Descartes, however, who had, ironically, used the first person in order to tell the story of how he came to identify himself with the etiolated or universal first person of epistemology, Vico writes of himself in the third person; the title of his work is *The Life of Giambattista Vico Written by Himself.*

Vico intends that we should read him as the historian of himself, not as a fabulist. By this stage of his intellectual development, he is opposed to Cartesianism, or to rationalism, which by its a priori claims concerning the presence of "good sense" in all of us from birth presupposes the very faculty whose genesis it is the historian's task to narrate. Vico believes rationality to be the laborious product of thought, not its prerequisite. The individual is no different in this from whole societies, progressing through time and circumstances towards the rational state rather than being born into it. So the rational man looking back over the growth of his mind is not entitled to interpret that uncertain growth in the light of his subsequent rationality, or to ascribe to himself all the credit for having procured it. The Vichian autobiographer has to see himself as product, not as progenitor of his past. Descartes's rationalism precludes his ever giving us a true account of his slow coming to maturity or of the real plasticity of his thought as it developed, and Vico wastes no time in telling him off for misleading his readers:

We shall not here feign what René Descartes craftily feigned as to the method of his studies simply in order to exalt his own philosophy and mathematics and degrade all the other studies included in divine and human erudition. Rather, with the candor proper to a historian, we shall narrate plainly and step by step the entire series of Vico's studies, in order that the proper and natural causes of his particular development as a man of letters may be known.[9]

One might think, then, that the true historian Vico would be very careful to abjure all suggestion of the fabulous in chronicling for us the stages of his development, if only to show himself the superior as an autobiographer of the presumptuous Descartes. Yet the *Life* starts with an episode that it is extremely hard for us to take simply as history. At the age of seven, Vico tells us in the first few lines, "he fell head first from the top of a ladder to the floor below, and remained a good five hours without motion or consciousness."[10] A story that opens with a fall, however banal, is likely to remind us of a far from banal story that also begins with a Fall, the story of humankind in its disobedience towards God as told in the book of Genesis. Vico attributes his "melancholy and irritable" temperament to his own fall, but at once indicates that this temperament has stood him in good stead, since it goes with the possession of "ingenuity and depth" of mind. Indeed, his fall has been the making of him. By keeping him at home, convalescent, for three whole years, it delayed his formal education and so made the boy's great precocity the more visible. Having gone back to school, the young Vico is in no time at all far in advance of his coevals and offering us the admirable spectacle of "a pupil acting as his own teacher." Remembering that, as Nelson Goodman once put it, the Garden of Eden was lost "not for sex but for science,"[11] one may decide that Vico's fall too has exchanged the paradise of nescience for the arena of a highly advantageous knowledge, leading in his case to the elaboration of the great work on which he was already embarked when he wrote his *Life, The New Science*. Interestingly, a little later in the *Life* he records rather obscurely how in his search for the principles of an ideal justice he first tried reading Aristotle and found him wanting, and then passed on to Plato, where he discovered what he now recognizes that he then needed, the idea of "the eternal idea," an immanent, creative principle that Plato imagined at work in the formation of "an ideal commonwealth, to which he gave, in his laws, an equally ideal justice." Since that discovery, whose importance for him he did not at the time fully appreciate, Vico has gone beyond Plato in "meditating an ideal eternal law that should be observed in a universal city after the idea or design of providence." This was "the ideal republic" that Plato, given his metaphysical premises, should have devised for himself, but he was alas prevented from doing so by the accident of birth, having been "shut off from it by ignorance of the fall of the first man."[12] From this we must gather that it was a considerable advantage to Vico over Plato to have entered history when he did, so that he could take into account the story of the biblical Fall, and that the episode of his childhood fall is, at the very least, a happy accident by which to originate the story of his own acquisition of knowledge.

Vico's *Life* is not the corrective of Descartes that its author claims it to be; it does not escape the influence of the *Discourse*, which is its chosen intertext. Vico remains throughout the brilliant pupil who instantly becomes, by virtue of what is apparently a destructive mischance but in truth a providential blessing, "his own master." He is the devious chronicler of an education conducted or influenced over the years by numerous others but perfected in isolation, an education that serves ultimately to equip him with the nickname by which he tells us he was eventually known, the "Autodidact." Providence, for Vico, is able to play the same narrative role as an arrogant hindsight plays for Descartes, by appearing to absolve the autobiographer himself from any responsibility for presenting his earlier life entirely as a preparation for what was to come later.

But if the *Discourse* of Descartes was his textual model, we can agree that Vico departed from it to remarkable effect; as an autobiographer he singled himself out formally just as he singled himself out in his life, by coming to be the man capable of writing *The New Science*. The *Life* displays symptoms of that condition we now know as the anxiety of influence; it purports to show, contra Descartes, that Vico is a humble enough person to admit to having been influenced by the thought of others in the elaboration of his own, but succeeds in showing, to the contrary, that Vico is, intellectually speaking, his own man. Such are the compulsions of autobiography.

Let me exemplify them further from another source, this time from the twentieth century: the short *Autobiographical Study* written by Freud, a prime record if ever there was one of the means by which a preeminent theorist has established his intellectual authority over others. Freud, like Vico, was sufficiently the historian of his developing thought to acknowledge at least some of the outside contributions to it, because he has to show where he parted company with other thinkers or went beyond them. The story of psychoanalysis, as told by its creator, is one of a highly unpopular independence of mind encouraged over many years by the resistance that Freud experienced from others, beginning with the anti-Semites of Vienna who made him aware even as a student of belonging to the "Opposition" and not to what the English text calls the "compact majority." (Are all majorities "compact"? In autobiography, where the author is committed to singularizing himself, they surely have to be.) At the narrative crux of the *Autobiographical Study*, where he turns from tracing the inner, intellectual process by which his analytical method took shape to tracing the more public process of its institutionalization, Freud declares himself to have then stood formidably alone: "For more than ten years after my separation from Breuer I had no followers. I was completely isolated. In Vienna I was shunned; abroad no notice was taken of me."[13] When followers came to him, as we know well from the historians of the movement, the regular pattern was one of a professional association with Freud leading sooner or later to an often ill-tempered split.

Freud the autobiographer shows a marked fear of revealing his intellectual indebtedness. This comes out most strikingly in his defensive remarks concerning what he calls, late in the *Autobiographical Study*, "philosophy proper." His avoidance of this "has been greatly facilitated by constitutional incapacity." He does not, however, spell out the nature of this incapacity. One can but assume he means an incapacity for abstract thought. But can Freud, the solitary creator of the remarkable theory of psychoanalysis, seriously claim to have no capacity for that? He can, but only if he is set on defending himself against being seen as a theorist rather than as a practical healer of the mentally disturbed. The charge against which he is implicitly defending himself by suggesting that his mind is so constituted as to make of "philosophy proper" literally a closed book to him—it is a charge that has of course been made against him repeatedly— is that he became a theorist, a man of abstractions, when he should have remained a physician; that he chose to generalize and to advance his own name as a thinker at the expense of his unhappy and anonymous or pseud-onymous patients. (In this he is at one with the guilty theorist of auto-biography, ambitious to formulate a generic model from the unique evi-dence of the cases presented to him.) Freud goes to the strange lengths of naming two very powerful non-influences on him: Schopenhauer and Nietzsche, both of whom he recognizes as having achieved certain of his own insights into the human unconscious before he did. But his theory was already in place, he assures us, before, "very late in my life," he read Scho-penhauer. And Nietzsche, "another philosopher whose guesses and intu-itions often agree in the most astonishing way with the laborious findings of psychoanalysis, was for a long time avoided by me on that very account; I was less concerned with the question of priority than with keeping my mind unembarrassed."[14] Here the opposition between philosopher and psychoanalyst is stark: the "guesses" and "intuitions" of the one are set against the "laborious findings" of the other. Freud is inviting us to sym-pathize as ordinary mortals like him, with the hardworking scientist of the mind who has to proceed carefully from experience, instead of leaping po-etically to the grand conclusions of a Nietzsche. The empiricist is covering himself. But then why should Freud find the agreement between Nietz-sche's guesswork and his own empirical research to be so "astonishing"? If he himself is right in the conclusions he has come to about human nature, he should surely expect to find others in agreement with him, since it would seem difficult, even for a Freud, to suppose that he was uniquely right on such a matter. The *Autobiographical Study*, however, gives just such an impression, that Freud is set on outfacing all possible rivals, even those who preceded him historically. His ill-found astonishment at the concord-ance of his own views with the insights of Nietzsche leads us to suspect that, contrary to what he writes, Freud was very uneasily concerned with the question of priority, and that his well-known authoritarianism as a the-orist finds its reflection in his anxiety to singularize himself as an author.

The three autobiographies of theorizers from which I have been quoting concur in showing that the desired process of singularization is carried through at a price of isolation from the community, from the uncomprehending, ignorant, or resistant "other." Descartes, it is recorded, once condemned the English philosopher Thomas Hobbes for having been "dangerous even in his singularity." As it happens, Hobbes wrote a very cursory chronological account of his life in Latin verses; perhaps he should have done as Descartes did and explained himself to society at large in the vernacular, because the writing of an autobiography removes the curse from the very singularity whose achievement it celebrates: it is a strong token of the writer's wish to be reunited with those from whom he has singled himself out. In his life, according to the *Discourse*, Descartes's great quest was for assurance, not simply for those first principles in epistemology that he believed would immunize his philosophy against contradiction by others, but also for security in daily life, by the avoidance of such "singularity" as he thought had placed Hobbes in peril. It is a chief moral maxim of the *Discourse* that it is wise to live according to the prevailing laws and customs of your country. Descartes's autonomy is limited to the sphere of epistemology, of mathematics and of "pure" thought; as a citizen he yields prudently to the order of the world. His prudence in respect of society indeed is what guarantees him the peace of mind in which to think and spares him from the unpleasantness that might result were he to live his life with the same freedom from precedent as he sought in constructing his philosophy.

In this sense, the writing of an apologia, be it the *Discourse* of Descartes, Vico's *Life*, or the *Autobiographical Study* of Freud, is equally prudential. The autobiographer is making his peace with society, and counteracting that very drive towards singularity of which his text is the record. It is true that the actual writing of the text must still take place in isolation, in the security of a place apart, the model for which might well be the famous *poêle* or hot room into which Descartes one day retreated, in an interval of his exposed and extrovert life as a soldier, there to have the first revelation of his "method." The autobiographer finds a deep and productive use for such moments of asylum, first to integrate himself textually in his perceived separateness as an individual, and then to reemerge from his guilty solipsism in the form of a document whose publication asks that we readmit him to the community, as author and as human being. He is playing a double game.

Let me illustrate finally just how double that game can be from an autobiographer who is so much the theorist, even when writing about himself, as rather to spoil things for those of us who hope to press autobiographies into theoretical service against the grain of the text: Jean-Paul Sartre. Sartre's *The Words* is anti-autobiography; it is a very clever attempt to unmask from within the bad faith of what Sartre takes to be a reprehensible, because essentially bourgeois, literary genre. He knows however that such an exercise as he is himself engaged in is ambiguous: how can he avoid being taken for an autobiographer, even as he demonstrates the bad faith on which autobiography rests? Is it possible to kill off the genre by practicing it in a peculiarly self-aware manner, simultaneously acknowledging that whoever writes autobiographically declares himself to be a singular being but that he, Jean-Paul Sartre, is different, inasmuch as he has now come to the realization that he is not singular at all and has written an autobiography to prove it?

Among the books that Sartre tells us in *The Words* he knew as a small boy was one called *L'Enfance des hommes illustres*. This was a school prize, won by his uncle Georges, and a very bourgeois volume indeed, a collection of exemplary accounts of childhood, as virtuously lived by boys predestined to greatness. The boy Sartre had an odd, double relationship with the book. On his first discovery of it he rejected it, finding the child subjects insipid, like himself, in their virtuousness, with none of the qualities of the *enfant prodige*, which is what he then believed himself to be. The book vanished for a year—he had "decided to punish it by hiding it." A year later he went looking for it again, for now he needed it; in his own words, "The child prodigy had become a great man who was having trouble with his childhood." Reread, it spoke to him of himself, and Sartre says that he became afraid of it, as being his own particular kind of "poison" as a young reader. The poison he had found in it was that of predestination; the childhoods narrated were not those of just any young boys, but of boys destined to become celebrated and whose stories were told accordingly: "These children lived in a state of error. They thought they were acting and talking at random, whereas the real purpose of their slightest remarks was to announce their Destiny."[15] This is the pernicious effect of narrative, to represent a life as if it were lived backwards, with its end determining its beginning and so robbing it of its true contingency. In *The Words*, Sartre would have us believe that he had already as a small child grasped the falsity of such a representation: to protect himself against the "poison" of this profoundly deceptive volume he sat by the window to read it: "in case of danger, I would let the true light of day come into my eyes."

This episode alone would be enough to qualify *The Words* as a fabulous text and as a story of childhood fit to be included in any collection of the *enfance des hommes illustres*. Sartre's story too is told backwards because it has to be, there is no other way to tell it. But we do not read it in the same superior way as he once read the stories of the young Molière, or Johann Sebastian Bach, as another story of "fake mediocrities" unaware of their glorious future, because Sartre is on hand in the text to tell us how to read this story, as an exorcising of that same sense of "God-like" superiority with which he had long been possessed but which he is now finally overcoming. His story too is an improving one; it is exemplary. The example it would teach us is: do not be led astray as I, Jean-Paul Sartre was, into thinking yourself an *enfant prodige*, an elite being, a potential autobiographer. *The Words* is presented as Sartre's belated farewell to that enduring error, because from this time forward he means to live out his proclaimed solidarity with the proletariat, to be a practicing egalitarian. The lesson of the episode I have quoted is that we should all of us get to the window and read our own lives by the "true light of day," as Sartre is finally reading in *The Words* the text of his own very corrupt early life; that way we will not be deluded into taking the fable of singularity for our own truth, but assume our full Sartrian freedom of action in restoring ourselves to the community—or to an ideologically favored part of it, in his case.

As an anti-autobiographer, narrating the temptations and delusions of narrative, Sartre prepares us throughout for the much quoted last words of *The Words*, for his eventual abdication from the false role he has been playing. His illusions having now been erased in this public process of recollection, what, he asks, is left? "A whole man, composed of all men and as good as all of them and no better than any."[16] Just as Descartes began in the *Discourse* by separating himself out from the crowd, so Sartre, able by the time he writes this final sentence of his text to assume the part of the repentant autobiographer, will now fall anonymously back into it. Of the two gestures, Descartes's is the more persuasive, because the more sincere. We don't believe Sartre's own good faith when, at the end of a volume that has demonstrated what a remarkably clever and singular person he has been, he protests his ordinariness. Even in Sartre's hugely self-aware case, the theorist of autobiography is thus required to argue against the autobiographer's artful and seductive claim that he is nothing of the kind, or is an autobiographer only *malgré lui*. The theorist's position is that the autobiographer can never quite be one of us, but can never not be one of them: never not be an autobiographer, that is.

The Autobiographical Process

Jerome Bruner

 utobiography is altogether too familiar a form to be taken at
 face value. Its very familiarity risks obscuring its secretive metaphysics and its tacit presuppositions, both of which would be the better for
some airing. Autobiographical "theory," such as it is, too often loses its
way amidst these same obscurities. So I would like at the start of this essay,
which is unabashedly given over to autobiographical theory, to get some
of my own metaphysical-presuppositional skeletons out into the open so
that you can get to know them a bit before we get down to particulars.
Since skeletons, like stick figures, are more easily defined in motion than
at rest, I shall try to make my skeletons dance for you a little so that you
can sense in what manner they are strung together and what roles they may
play in later discussion. You will recognize the dancing as sometimes philosophical, sometimes psychological, and all too often polemical.

To begin in just that last mode, I want to assert that an autobiography
is not and cannot be a way of simply signifying or referring to a "life as
lived." I take the view that there is no such thing as a "life as lived" to be
referred to. On this view, a life is created or constructed by the act of autobiography. It is a way of construing experience—and of reconstruing and
reconstruing it until our breath or our pen fails us. Construal and recon-
strual are interpretive. Like all forms of interpretation, how we construe
our lives is subject to our intentions, to the interpretive conventions available to us, and to the meanings imposed upon us by the usages of our culture and language.

Some lives actually get written down, though a very small number.
Most are accounted for "locally" and patchily in the form of excuses for
this particular act, or justifications for having that particular belief or desire. The local patches provide glimpses of a more general narrative about

a life that is largely implicit—a narrative that almost "goes without say-ing," what lawyers call *res ipse loquitur*. The very malleability of this im-plicit autobiography probably serves to keep possibilities of interpretation from being frozen or shut down. But for all that, autobiography, however implicit or explicit, always risks becoming self-sealing in the sense that it may tempt the teller into a "life" that suits circumstances so comfortably that it even conceals the possibilities of choice. It is usually the case that the conversions and turning points in literary autobiography are dramat-ically about such "awakenings" from self-sealing autobiographical pe-riods. It is no less true of the "spontaneous" autobiographies I have been studying.[1] At least two psychoanalysts have proposed that the object of therapy might be better conceived as an effort to help "awaken" patients from frozen narratives about their lives so that they can risk forging new ones.[2]

But we do not fall into self-sealing autobiographical traps just for ego-defense and dissonance-reduction. They are just as much an instrument of cultural stability. Those in the micro-culture around us would usually just as soon we stayed self-sealed, because autobiography also functions as an instrument for cultural constraint—sometimes explicitly, as in traditional Indian culture, often implicitly in extremely egalitarian cultures, where high autobiographical aspirations provoke the "cutting down of tall pop-pies," to use an Australian expression. It is not surprising that political and cultural revolutions often create demands for brusque changes in self-accounting, as we've seen during China's cultural revolution, or when Ital-ian students paint the walls of their universities with autobiographical slo-gans like "I am an orphan." An autobiography can be read not only as a personal expression, as a narrative expressing "inner dynamics," but as a cultural product as well.

Obviously, then, there is no such thing as a "uniquely" true, correct, or even faithful autobiography. This should warn us away from the heavy-handed judgment that autobiography is particularly subject to "self-deception." Such a judgment is surely based on some curious presupposi-tions about self-knowledge—that somehow "we" know all (or, rather, the Id knows all) and that "we" are hiding something from "ourselves." This, of course, is high Freudian "received wisdom," and it is a view that has become so uncritically accepted that it deserves a moment of deconstruc-tion. The notion of self-deception rests on a faith that our minds are equipped with an all-seeing panopticon scanner that has access to every-thing we have experienced, which in some mysterious way is stored in memory in a form transparent to that scanner. On this view, it is self-

interest, "defenses," or whatever, that get in the way of this all-seeing scanner. But everything we know about the structure of direct experience and
of memory storage and retrieval tells us this is a deeply misleading view.
Perceiving and remembering are themselves constructions and reconstructions. What is "laid down" in memory is not some aboriginal encounter
with a "real world," but is already highly schematized. There is no mental
reference shelf of our aboriginal "real world" encounters, any more than
there is an aboriginal real world "out there" made available to us by means
of them. Any autobiographical reconfiguring of a life, then, is not so much
a matter of making new discoveries in the archeological record of our experiences, or of revealing the contents of previously hidden "memories,"
but of rewriting a narrative along different interpretive lines. In the process,
to use Sir Frederic Bartlett's celebrated phrase, we "turn round upon" the
older "schemata" of memory and what before may have seemed irrelevant
may now become newly so.[3] In rewriting our autobiographies, we often
"rewrite culture" as much as we rewrite our lives, privileging different conventional turning points such as adolescence or retirement. I suspect that
the epithet "self-deception" (which, as far as I can tell, Freud never used)
is more of a political instrument than a useful tool in dissecting the ex-
quisite acts of sham ontology and sedulous epistemology involved in putting together the account of one's own life. This leads directly to the next
point.

The "rightness" of any autobiographical version is relative to the intentions and conventions that govern its construction or its interpretation.
But that is a statement that obviously needs further explanation. By the
"intentions and conventions" of an autobiography I mean something
roughly corresponding to a genre in fiction because it is authorial intentions embodied in a conventional form and style that constitute a genre.
In autobiography these provide more or less canonical ways of organizing
the account of a life. The conventional autobiographical genres, of course,
reflect idealized cultural patterns. Many are familiar: the selfless seeker after the public interest, the sacrificing family man, the *Bildungsroman* with
its assurance of learning from experience, the ironic and detached observer
of the absurdities of the contemporary human condition (in any age), the
guardian mother shielding the young, the seeker after spontaneous self-
expression, the forgiving victim of society's outrages, the apologia of the
misunderstood public man, and so on. Each contains a conception of human agency, a view of the vicissitudes that beset it, an account of the protagonist's location in a "virtual" culture, and a theory or a story of how
the narrator's protagonist managed to get from there and then to here and

now. Though it may seem a strange way to put it, we may properly suspect that the shape of a life as experienced is as much dependent upon the narrative skills of the autobiographer as is the story he or she tells about it. It is probably in this sense that Henry James intended his famous remark that adventures happen only to people who know how to tell them.

Autobiography can be written in one genre and interpreted by its readers in another. From this banal point there follows another less obvious one. First, let me illustrate. The contemporary feminist critic who is trying to understand, say, how male-defined autobiographical genres marginalized women, reads and writes about earlier women's autobiography from within the concerns and public goals of contemporary criticism, which has its own generic intentions, forms, and styles. It may be precisely the unconsciousness and generic "non-intentionality" of these works that interests such critics, and that enables them to place earlier autobiographies within current discussions about gender.[4] So while autobiography exists, as it were, in the private intentions of the autobiographer, it also exists for its public interpretive uses, as part of a general and perpetual conversation about life possibilities. Eulogies, "minutes" on the lives of parliamentary members, and obituaries all can be considered as canonical commentaries on autobiography. Perhaps this is one of the reasons why the autobiographies of the rogues, swashbucklers, and instant tycoons have always been so popular, providing as they do an opportunity to explore canonical limits. In any case, the "publicness" of autobiography constitutes something like an opportunity for an ever-renewable "conversation" about conceivable lives.

What is it that makes all autobiography alike? Is there some fundamental set of requirements that all autobiography must meet to earn the name, the kind of contract that the French critic Philippe Lejeune calls the "autobiographical pact"?[5] "DEFINITION: Retrospective prose narrative written by a real person concerning his own existence, where the focus is his individual life, in particular the story of his own personality."[6] But as Lejeune willingly admits, this is a hybrid lot of criteria—some about language, some about subject matter, some about the situation of the author (that he be the same person as the protagonist), and some about the narrator (that he take a retrospective point of view). He thinks of them as defining properties of an autobiographical genre. But might they not better be considered as conventional "felicity conditions" imposed on acts of self-revelation generally? In this sense, self-revelation might be conceived of as a conventional speech act with its own felicity conditions, much as promising, warning, and declaring are speech acts with theirs.[7] My own view is that definitions of a genre (particularly autobiography) serve principally as challenges to literary invention. Does Lejeune really want to do battle with Santayana's *The Last Puritan* (in the form of a novel), Mary McCarthy's *Memories of a Catholic Girlhood* (first published as short stories and then regrouped with interstitial comments as an autobiography), or Michel Leiris's *Manhood* (which strives to break the rules of narrative and retrospection)? And what of Wordsworth and the prose criterion? Finally, what about those of us, somewhat perverted though we may be, who find autobiography in everything we read, and who find Henry Adams's *Mont-Saint-Michel and Chartres* quite as revealing a self-account as the *Education*? This is not to make the absurd claim that autobiography has nothing to do with authorial intent, but only that there is a readerly side to the matter that can be summed up in the evident truism that any text can be read as revelatory of the author, so long as it can be interpreted as fulfilling intentionally or inadvertently the conditions imposed on speech acts of self-revelation. As for the author, all we need say is that sometimes he or she cooperates openly, often not. When he or she does, we are somehow bound by a pact of communicative courtesy to judge the autobiography that results in terms of the genre that he or she intended, but we would be poor critics indeed if we stopped at that.

If the "rightness" of an autobiography is relative to genre conventions in the mind of its writer or its readers, the same surely cannot be said about its "depth" or "power." There is some sense in which, whatever the genre, there is an element of "radical reflection" that assures depth or power—a term I borrow from Charles Taylor.[8] Radical reflection involves exploring not only the nature of one's commitments but the value presuppositions on which they are based.

Obviously, St. Augustine's radical reflections in the *Confessions*—his struggle to reconcile faith and reason, God and self—are not the same as the equally radical brooding of an honest Ilongot in the Philippines over the fit between his passions and his reason before undertaking a headhunt, or Bertrand Russell's equally honest autobiographical conflict between personal compassion and impersonal abstraction.[9] That is not the point. The issue, rather, resides in both the general form of the reflection and in its honesty.

James Boyd White, in his remarkable book, *Heracles' Bow*, attempts to clarify this cloudy domain in a most interesting way. His interest is not so much in autobiography as in the conditions of existence in a society that can assure a requisite degree of congruence between a citizen's sense of himself and his sense of his rights and obligations under law in a broader community.[10] Can one conceive of oneself and of one's community in a fashion to permit one to live without alienation? He sees the challenge not as simply "establishing," say, a just order. The task of living with oneself and within a society, he argues, is an exercise in "constitutive rhetoric." That is to say, the discourse of social life (and, in his central argument, the discourse of the law) is designed not just to settle differences and resolve conflicts, but to constitute or construct realities that each individual can live with in a fashion that does not produce alienation. There can be no effective self, he argues, unless a person can construct a sense of the world that is congruent with it. He uses as an illustrative text for his discussion Sophocles' *Philoctetes*. Philoctetes is the injured self, abandoned to his bad luck on the island of Melos by the Achaeans on their way to the Trojan War. Heracles had bequeathed him his unerring bow. Odysseus has been sent back to get the bow, which prophecy reveals is essential for victory against Troy, and he offers Philoctetes restored health from the sons of Aesculapius if he will return the bow. Odysseus is accompanied by young Neoptolemus, the son of Achilles. To Odysseus, Philoctetes is a mere instrument in the war against Troy to be convinced at any cost. To the suffering Philoctetes himself, the Achaeans who abandoned him on Melos are anathema. Young Neoptolemus is caught between the two of them. The play is about three men coming to terms with self-respect in an imperfect world through their efforts to construct versions of the world that each can accept individually but that will convince the others. For White, it is the type-case of constitutive rhetoric.

What Sophocles (or White) is arguing is that one cannot reflect upon self (radically or otherwise) without an accompanying reflection on the nature of the world in which one exists. And one's reflections on both one's self and one's world cannot be one's own alone: you and your version of your world must be public, recognizable enough to be negotiable in the "conversation of lives." So emerges the classic criterion of what constitutes "good" autobiography—that it be communicable through its representativeness. Late nineteenth-century scholars made much of "representativeness." An autobiography must be "representative" of its times, however unusual or special it might be. On this view, autobiography is as much historical as personal. Dilthey, in his formulation of the "human sciences," for example, saw autobiography as the human side of history, as somehow exemplary of it.[11] And when Ranke proposed that history itself is nothing other than a distillation of participant subjectivities, his was yet another voice in the chorus of perspectivalism that included Nietzsche and many others.[12] History and autobiography were taken to be two sides of a common coin. A *geschichtsblind* autobiography consequently was as poor as one lacking human insight; indeed, insight was impossible without a sense of history. The Great Man was supposed to be the one who could bring the two together.

Students of narrative have, of course, been much concerned with just this issue—the question, as Greimas puts it, of relating the "landscape of action" to the protagonist's "landscape of consciousness."[13] Greimas elaborates his point in a most original way by positing an "axis" extending from inwardness to outwardness, from the subjective to the objective. This axis is linguistically memorialized in the primitive system of modal verbs— I *want* to eat, I *can* eat, and so on. In French, an axis of modals extends from *vouloir*, through *savior* and *pouvoir*, to *faire*. To *desire* is to implicate little in the world; to *know* what one desires moves one outward toward the world; to feel one is *able* to achieve *what* one desires is yet another step outward. *To be able*, of course, implicates both senses of the term: epistemic and deontic, what one is able or not able to do by virtue of skill and knowledge, and what one is permitted or not permitted to do by virtue of the social world. Finally one acts or *does*, and impinges directly upon the world.[14] For Greimas, self-accounting has to exploit the full axis from desire to action if it is to bridge the gap between the subjective and the objective, between inner and outer.

Yet this is too abstract, too Cartesian, to be altogether convincing. It requires what linguists refer to as "realization rules" that describe how one gets from the deep order of language to its local expression in a particular language. As already noted, autobiography can only enter the "conversation of lives" when it achieves localness.[15] Localness is, in practice, something like a speech register or idiolect that one's effective community shares. Our Western version, for example, emphasizes individuality, power, and autonomy in explicating lives. The rural Malaysian version, on the other hand, is incomplete without the shamanistic notion of "inner wind" based on ancient humoral medicine uniquely mixed with cosmological and aesthetic beliefs about what controls life.[16] Autobiography in each case is a constitutive act, one designed to construct a reality about a life in a place and time, one that can be negotiated with somebody. It can no more be placeless and timeless than it can be "self-less." Nor can its composition be disembodied from the interlocutors who constitute the dialogic imagination of the teller.

Let me elaborate a little more on what is involved in writing or telling "your life story." It is a unique process. It involves, as already noted, a narrator here and now telling about a protagonist of the same name, there and then. The narrator, obviously, must have recourse to memory, must retrieve information about the past. But given the von Neumann architecture of all known systems of memory, retrieval must be steered to the appropriate storage "addresses" by some sort of program. The program of retrieval must be guided by some criteria of relevance, by something like a "theory" about how the isolated "facts" of a life cohere. That theory (or narrative plot) not so much "selects" the so-called facts, but rather creates them and then organizes them. The "facts," we might say, are partly made, partly found. We must examine this process now.

Autobiographical discourse involves, at the outset, a discourse of witness: accounts of happenings in which one participated if only as an observer. These accounts are most often marked by the past tense, by verbs of direct experience such as *see* and *hear*, and by declarative speech acts. Witness creates existential immediacy for both the writer and the reader. Its object is to make "the facts" seem like just that. It is mimesis, and its cunning is to make the facts seem in the world, ontologically given.

Then there is a discourse of interpretation, which is diegesis in the classical sense. The cunning of diegesis, as we already know, is that it creates "facts" to fit its needs, much as the law creates facts to fit its requirements: guardianship, breach of contract, statutory rape. Since well-framed "facts" seem able to speak for themselves, it remains for diegesis to give them wider significance. It organizes the detailed constituents of witness into larger-scale sequences (holidays, careers, "declining years," and the like) and it places them into evaluational frames (instances of "struggle," of "devotion," or whatever). Diegesis has a way of being more subjunctive than mimesis: it considers paths not taken; it is couched retrospectively and counterfactually; it is more apt to ride on epistemic verbs like *know* and *believe* rather than *see* and *hear*; and it is usually couched in the present or timeless tense. In a corpus of spontaneously spoken autobiographies that my colleagues and I have gathered, as many as forty percent of the propositions in some narratives are framed in these tenses—"As I look back, I realize that I should never have quit that job."[17]

Autobiographies are also marked by another feature. I shall call it "stance," though it has also been called "diatactics."[18] It is the autobiographer's posture toward the world, toward self, toward fate and the possible, and also toward interpretation itself. Unlike ordinary discourse, which presupposes intention, stance seems innocent of it. Linguistically, it is marked by such seemingly uninformative markers as *just*, *even*, and *only*—as in "I'm just a housewife" or "I'm only an associate in the firm."

It is Patrick White's painful reticence in *Flaws in the Glass*, Tennessee Williams's "caught-on-the-fly-paper" urgency in his *Memoirs*, or Richard Feynman's buoyant and boyish braggadocio.[19] It succeeds (or fails) in giving human substance to the mimetic and diegetic play of autobiography.

The task of autobiographical composition consists, of course, in combining witness, interpretation, and stance to create an account that has both verisimilitude and negotiability. Let me consider verisimilitude first.[20] It is perhaps best likened to the believability of a legal brief as pled in court, but without explicit benefit of the rules of legal evidence. The autobiographer does not have to confront the accused, or submit to cross examination by the reader, or even take an oath to perform according to Professor Lejeune's pact. Yet in some implicit way the "truth" of autobiography plainly rests upon some signs of evidentiary probity—something like "fairmindedness" toward others' views, an absence of reticence about one's mistakes, and so on. Fair-mindedness, of course, is no easier to define than most other evaluative concepts. In this respect, again, an autobiographer's task is not unlike that of legal pleading. Both depend on the achievement of a convincing reality.

Verisimilitude also depends on the fitness of the genre to the "facts." The "victim of circumstances" genre rarely fits the Mafia chief well, even when he soft-pedals his "deals." Autobiographical genres can be likened to what the French "annales" historians refer to as *histoire* in the scale that descends from *histoire* to *chroniques* to *annales*. *Annales* are the bare bones (crop failures, assassinations, kings coming to the throne or being deposed, and so on). These in turn are then "bound" into *chroniques*, like "the prosperous reign of Charlemagne," which can then be put into the yet broader context of, say, "the emergence of Europe from Charlemagne's coronation at the Vatican in the year 800 to the realization of the European Community in 1992."

As any historiographer will remind us, not every *histoire* fits the available *annales* equally convincingly, selective though we may be in choosing the latter to fit the former. There are matters of consensual public record to be taken into account. A history of Europe whose theme is the implacability of ethnic minorities will mine a quite different vein of *annales* from one that trumpets the emergence of the idea of Europa. But however tendentious it may be, it is constrained by "the facts," that corpus of recorded events that comprise cultural memory. The ethnicist must cope with the "fact" of the Swiss Federation, the Europeanist with the persistence of "Little Englanders" in Britain, or with French farmers dumping Italian wine tankers at the frontier. Ignoring "matters of record" makes bad history, elaborate "explainings away" even worse. Some histories just fit "the facts" better, unfashionable though such a remark will seem to some revisionist historians.

So it is with genre choice in autobiography. A "wrong" choice, an inappropriate "model" for a life, ends up lending an aura of unbelievability or "forcedness" to the episodes and the detailed enterprises of that life. Tellers and hearers are both sensitive to it. "It just doesn't make sense," we say. Often the autobiographer is alienated from his own "forced" account. He feels he has been "pompous" or "frivolous" or "too linear by twice." More often than not, he has simply chosen the wrong genre. There is a well-known Martin Buber tale about a certain Rev Moshe who, upon arrival in Heaven for the entry interview, begins by excusing himself to St. Peter for not having been as deeply dedicated, perhaps, as Albert Schweitzer, or as intellectually penetrating as Einstein. St. Peter listens for a while and then, consulting the Great Book, replies: "But the problem I'm supposed to ask you, it says here, is not whether you've been like Schweitzer or Einstein, but whether you have been enough like Rev Moshe." Autobiography is perpetually caught between the mimetic rendering of its unique detail and the requirement of finding a negotiable genre in terms of which to render those details into a life.

I come now to what I earlier called the "negotiability" of an autobiography. It is whatever makes it possible for an autobiography to enter into the "conversation of lives." I used to refer to this quality as its "forgivability," but that does not make a definition any easier. Negotiability, I suspect, inheres far more in an autobiographer's stance toward his own life than in mimesis, diegesis, or the fit between them. Is the autobiographer *sympathique* and worth caring about as a human being? Is the Great Man bearably modest or decently self-mocking? Is the trickster forgivably free of contempt for his victims? Are we prepared to accept this life as part of the community of lives that makes up our world?

I must make one comment about both "negotiability" and the autobiographical stance upon which it is usually based, for I shall want to come back to the subject later in a more concrete way. Ours is a generation that gave birth to the craft of "impression management," and we have had a president whose "handlers" were obsessed with making him *sympathique* even when he was either unbelievable or vacuous. We have also had a feast of scholarship, principally inspired by Erving Goffman, on the "presentation of face in public places"—though, to the best of my knowledge, there has been no systematic study of "face presentation" in autobiography.[21] We know some obvious things: there is a profession of "hired pens" who do others' autobiographies, and their conventions would be worth studying. There are even literary stories about writing "formula" autobiographies like the one that ended up entitled, "I Shot a Bear for the FBI and Found God." Indeed, we know a very great deal about "impression formation," much of it quite illuminating, virtually all of it based upon exposing undergraduates to lists of trait names.[22] But we know virtually nothing that goes by way of being, say, a "reader response" analysis of autobiography.

How is it that artless autobiography comes so easily to us? Some colleagues and I had the good fortune of analyzing the bedtime soliloquies of a child between her second and third birthdays—lengthy monologues after lights were out and parents had withdrawn.[23] Many of her monologues were autobiographical, *pace* Professor Lejeune's definition. It was a year in which a baby brother was born and in which Emmy, our child, entered the noisy, brawling world of nursery school. In her soliloquies she goes over her daily life, seeking to establish what is reliable and canonical, what is steady enough to "should be." She "tries on" stances toward the people and events recounted, expressing them by such locutions as "I wish that . . . " or "I don't really know whether. . . ." It became plain to us in the course of this lengthy study that the act of self-accounting is acquired almost with the acquisition of language itself—even the dual landscape, the narrator-protagonist relation (at first, the narrator is "I," the protagonist "Emmy"), and other features of more adult artless self-accounting. The answer to the question of why autobiography is so much easier than it ought to be according to "technical" philosophical standards is that there must be some push even in the earliest normal development toward the elaboration of a reflective self, and this push must be aided by the models of self portrayed in the words, acts, and expressions of those around the child. But like many human achievements, it is probably a fragile gift. It is generally coming to be believed now, for example, that the autistic child has a marked defect both in such self-reflection and in being able to "read" the minds (or subjective selves) of others.[24]

Is there something like a "natural genre" of artless autobiography that precedes more "artificial" literary forms of autobiography? I strongly doubt that there is such a thing, though I suspect that it is virtually always the case that the stories of our lives take some sort of narrative form—which hardly makes a genre. More likely, each particular culture favors a canonical form of autobiographical telling that is its own mark. In ours, for example, it is chronological, oriented around emblematic events and

"stages" of life, focused on the voyage from the private to the public domain (home to school to work), voluntaristic, and marked by the "life
crises" made so familiar by Erik Erikson.[25] Vincent Crapanzano reports,
on the other hand, that his Moroccan informant offered a life story that,
by our standards, was "scrambled" chronologically and seemed to leave
the protagonist more a sport of outer forces than an active agent with recognizable crises.[26] It must surely be the case that these canonical forms,
located as they are within local cultural convention, provide an enormous
assist in the "conversation of lives" that is so prominent a part of cultural
exchange. And insofar as there are subcultural forms—women's autobiography being the most striking example—they must also serve to impose
and maintain a culture's internal hegemonies, as Sidonie Smith observes.[27]

Why does autobiography ever become "literary," innovative and in-
ventive? Probably for the same reason writers break away from other forms
of received wisdom. But there is a particular poignancy in autobiographical innovation because it represents a radical effort to redefine the nature
and possibilities of the self. As such, radical autobiography has important
political reverberations. Current attacks on the unreflective folk belief that
"life" is simply "there to be led," a belief ingrained in our canonical forms
of autobiography, are also attacks on the "arbitrariness" of hegemonic
power as embodied in prevailing life styles. But alas, resistance to enslavement by conventional life styles by no means guarantees inventiveness in
autobiographical form. The rebellious obsession of the 1960's with life
styles and their recreation has produced little invention in the way of memoirs or autobiography.[28] Perhaps (as I shall argue later) a generation needs
first to formulate new forms of fiction. Perhaps, too, one needs the curious
chemistry of a "literary culture" even for life-shaping fiction—whether
Bloomsbury in London, the Mauve Decade in Paris, Greenwich Village
and the WPA Writers Project in New York, or even the short-lived bur-
geoning of consciousness in Moscow and Leningrad in the decade immediately after the Russian Revolution. If this is the case, then it is surely the
most concrete instantiation yet of the Wildean adage about life imitating
art.

James Young reports that more than a few concentration camp inmates
during the Holocaust were obsessed with making a record of the horrors
that they were living through and often risked their lives to do so secretly.[29]
These memoirs almost always have the harrowing immediacy of witness,
but few attempted to go beyond that and one could not imagine that
Auschwitz or Ravensbrück would have provided the distancing needed for

invention in the art of self-representation. Prisons and torture chambers defeat radical reflection about the shapes that life can take. Suffering finally silences autobiography.

The richness of Black and feminist life writing inheres, I suspect, not so much in the intensity of protest that they represent as in the inventiveness of the literary traditions they call upon for their inspiration. Contemporary African American autobiography nourishes itself on a literary tradition that goes back to fugitive slave memoirs (many of them composed to Abolitionist formulae), to the covert apologetics of a Booker T. Washington, to the ironies of writers like Richard Wright, and to the disciplined self-consciousness of a Frederick Douglass. Its literary power is in its tracing out these lines of descent through the perspectivalism of postmodern fictional sensibility. It is curious to quote William Butler Yeats in this context, but his lines catch the sense of unfinishedness and tension that characterizes so much of the best of African American autobiographical writing. In his "Dialogue of Self and Soul," he writes of "That defiling and disfiguring shape / That mirror of malicious eyes" "until at last / He thinks that shape must be his shape." And he ends,

> And what's the good of an escape
> If honor finds him in the wintry blast?

First in fiction and drama (which, of course, can also be taken in its autobiographical sense), but then followed by "direct" autobiography, African American writing has created a new poetics of alienation and redemption, new images of identity and visibility, of irony and detachment. But it is a literary achievement, not simply a political one. So too with women's autobiography: it also lives in a literary tradition as well as in "political life," a literary tradition that includes not only the protestations of a Margaret Fuller, an Emma Goldman, and the suffragettes, but even the male-created images of Emma in *Madame Bovary* and Nora in *A Doll's House*. It is the convergence of the politics and the poetics that marks the best of the present writing. In that writing, the politics gains a new freshness by finding expression in a literary poetics, Maxine Hong Kingston's *Woman Warrior* being as good an example as one needs.

I want to explore now one fragment of autobiographical text to examine some of the abstractions I have set out. I choose a brilliantly crafted passage from the work of Primo Levi. It is his account of life at the chemical factory close by Auschwitz where he was sent to work as a slave chemist. He recounts it in preparation for telling us about stealing cerium rods from the factory, returning each night with them to the Auschwitz camp. It is from the chapter in his *The Periodic Table* given over to cerium, the book as a whole being a human metaphor of Mendeleev's profoundly fundamental table of the elements.

I was a chemist in a chemical plant, in a chemical laboratory (this too has been narrated), and I stole in order to eat. If you do not begin as a child, learning how to steal is not easy; it had taken me several months before I could repress the moral commandments and acquired the necessary techniques, and at a certain point I realized (with a flash of laughter and a pinch of satisfied ambition) that I was re-living—*me*, a little university graduate—the involution-evolution of a famous respectable dog, a Victorian, Darwinian dog who is deported and becomes a thief in his Klondike *Lager*—the great Buck of *The Call of the Wild*. I stole like him and like the foxes: at every favorable opportunity but with sly cunning and without exposing myself. I stole everything except the bread of my companions.[30]

It is a curiously moving passage. There is first the matter-of-fact witness of almost unbelievable, yet compelling facts: Auschwitz, the chemical plant, working as a chemist in the midst of his own inhuman degradation. Then the touchingly incongruous stance of repugnance toward stealing, even if in hell. But once this is overcome, the little victory against conventional morality produces impromptu laughter and satisfied ambition, bespeaking a kind of human constancy under the most bizarre adversity. He confesses to the irony of his position as a "little university graduate" rising to thievery, and sees the parallel in Buck, a dog debased by circumstances, who though surviving in a Darwinian sense, yet maintains a certain Victorian decorum, never stealing from friends. The mix of the comic and the tragic, the moral and the biological, the bizarre and the banal, all evoke a hard-edged reality that is too unreal to tell. And all this dehumanizing transiency is placed in the metaphoric setting of Mendeleev's periodic table of the elements, of which there could be no stabler image of reality.

Then Levi elaborates on the stolen iron-cerium rods, "an alloy from which the common flints of cigarette lighters are made." He and his friend Alberto trade them with the guards at the *Lager*, once they are properly thinned down to fit a lighter, in exchange for food. Thinning the rods is night work, to be done under your meager blanket if you are not to be caught. Being caught is the beginning of death: the threshold act. Not being caught leaves chances for exchange with the very guards who are the agents of death if you fail. Those who enforce death are the very ones who enable life by trading food for cerium lighter flints you've risked your life to make. So long as you win the deadly and banal game of not getting caught, you can go on living a life that seems less and less worth living, yet all the more precious. The effect is a surrealist nightmare. It is a surrealism played out between the stability of the elements and the equally certain dehumanization of Auschwitz. The stable element cerium, the furtiveness of stealing, the metaphor of the camp guard as complicit torturer-trickster rendered approachable by a weakness for lighter flints that only the "little chemist" could provide: the mimetic, diegetic, and diatactic become one. Levi must have felt in the end that the story could not survive human desire for the comforts of reality. We know from his last work his doubts about making believable this dark episode in the history of human inhumanity.[31] If the life there could not be made negotiable in the minds of others, then humanity would never learn the lesson. He took his own life in despair. Perhaps that was the final autobiographical stance that might communicate if all else failed.

Kirk Varnedoe, in a most perceptive essay on portraits and self-portraiture, remarks that the modern self-portraitist, forswearing almost altogether the earlier ideal of *resemblance*, reveals (and conceals) himself by recourse to "equivalents."[32] In our times, he remarks, "the Self, paradoxically, has become so important that it cannot be dealt with directly, but demands instead a complex mixture of disclosure and disguise." Whereas a Dürer or others could mask themselves in such public disguises as the Harlequin, the Knight, or the Martyr, this does not fulfill the more self-conscious modern's need for disguise. The modern artist draws his disguises not from the public stock of images, but from personal mythologies and fantasies. So, for example, Claes Oldenburg's "Symbolic Self-Portrait with Equivalents" presents as his persona a mask that is part clown, part shaman, with neat geometrical designs surrounding it. Surmounting it is an ice bag that serves as artist's beret and a symbol of "cool." The tongue that lolls from the mouth is a Good Humor Bar upside down, a comment on commercial culture. The portrait is an impersonation of a set of private beliefs, attitudes, and identities. "Impersonation," Varnedoe proposes, becomes "the fundamental modern means of self-expression." He reminds us that impersonation is yet another version of the artist's "inversion and perversion of all conceptions and realities" in the search for "truth."

We have come increasingly to recognize that what the artist "inverts and perverts" is not an enduring hard-rock reality beyond human consciousness, but, as philosophers like Nelson Goodman make so clear, a set of conventions (often exploitative) about what constitutes "reality."[33] "We" includes the physicist and his paradigms, the poet and his visions, and perhaps it will next include the autobiographer and his "life." Increasingly, in our age, we abandon the comfortable hope of achieving "a view from nowhere." Even in the austere domain of the law, a new nominalism intrudes, whether in the "critical legal studies" of a Roberto Unger, the "constitutive rhetoric" of a James Boyd White, or the "narrativism" of a Robert Cover.[34]

It is as if contemporary conceptions of "reality," and even of "life," have caught up with yesterday's imagination. Freud's daring becomes today's received wisdom: life catches up with art. It is like Pablo Picasso's portrait of Gertrude Stein. Picasso had fashioned the face after an ancient Iberian mask. Her friends complained to him that it did not look like her. Picasso is reported to have urged them to be patient: "Everybody thinks she is not at all like her portrait but never mind, in the end she will manage to look just like it."[35] What then of Varnedoe's "impersonation" formula for self-portraiture in autobiography? Is autobiography the artist's finding a model to impersonate or recognizing the model that he has already impersonated—all disguised in a personal idiom? Is it that the literary autobiographer (or any autobiographer) is in the act of modeling himself or herself on "art," whether newly invented or taken whole from the world of convention?

At the Queens entrance to the Midtown Tunnel in New York City there is a large billboard that for several years has been dedicated to displaying anti-drug messages. During the Christmas season of 1990 there appeared on it the message, "Do clothes, not drugs." It contained three panels, each portraying attractive young people dressed in highly stylized "New Age" sweaters and jackets. As with the emblems in Oldenburg's self-portrait, the clothes in the billboard were impersonations—in this case, impersonations of anti-conventionalist solidarity, of middle-class bohemianism, of "clean" drug-freeness: self-portraits of the redeemed. The day I first saw the billboard, I read in the *National Law Journal* a front-page feature about the increase in drug problems in large law firms all over the country. The long feature story was supplemented by a shorter "case report" under the headline, "There *Is* Hope for Addicted Lawyers." Atop this headline was a picture of a 36-year-old Fort Lauderdale lawyer, Howard Finkelstein, who had, it was reported, won out against cocaine addiction. Not only had he kicked the habit, but he had kicked the lifestyle that went with it. Throwing over his lucrative practice, he had rejoined the Broward County Public Defender's Office, where he had started his career. "With renewed idealism," the story states, "he's teaching younger lawyers the art of making the legal system work for the poor and the oppressed."[36] In the picture, Mr. Finkelstein is neatly dressed in canonical lawyerly garb. We see a mature man

whose face shows intelligence and concern earnestly counseling an obviously indigent client, around whose chair his arm is draped. The shot is
taken from behind. The lawyer's hair descends to the middle of his back,
but it is decorously gathered at the nape of his neck. He is a study in impersonations, but it remains appropriately obscure what he is impersonating. Who is revealed, who concealed? Is it the hippy hairdo or the im-
peccable three-piece suit that carries the message? This is the Varnadoe
formula mimicked to perfection in photojournalism.

As might be expected, writers of modern fiction are "into" this intrigu-
ing phenomenon. In Don DeLillo's two most successful (and widely read)
novels, the major characters are caught in the act of impersonation.[37] In
White Noise, a professor is impersonating a "professor." He has neither
the languages nor the knowledge needed to pursue his trade. Eventually he
and his family flee a toxic cloud that is traveling cross-country, a cloud
whose very existence is being vehemently denied by the authorities, much
as the professor is engaged in denying his own reality. In *Libra*, a motley
crew of impostors, nearly all of them pseudonymous impersonators, are
engaged in hatching what will turn out to be (unbeknownst to them,
though not to the reader) the assassination of President Kennedy. It is a
novel of meticulously researched detail whose vividness of witness contrasts with the wild inadvertence of the "plot" itself. Is it the "plot" of history or of the novel? Which is intended as the "truth"?

Eventually the trope of impersonation finds its way into literary autobiography. In Philip Roth's *The Facts*, the autobiographer enters into debate with Zuckerman, a major character out of Roth's fiction. In a final
"essay," Zuckerman accuses Roth of dissimulation, of trying to placate his
critics by a display of his virtues as a good son or a good Jew. He, Zuckerman, with no axe to grind, can tell it better. Who really can tell it better,
the fictional Zuckerman or the real Roth? Is Zuckerman like the shaman's
mask in Claes Oldenburg's self-portrait? I find myself somewhat beguiled
by the irresistible spillover of this "interior" autobiographical debate into
the novel that followed shortly after *The Facts*, appropriately entitled
Deception.[38]

Commenting on the phenomenology of self, Hazel Markus and Paula
Nurius propose that we have "Possible" selves along with a "Now" self.
The Now self is rather a routine, workaday figure. "Possible selves represent individuals' ideas of what they *might* become, what they would *like*
to become, and what they are *afraid* of becoming."[39] They tempt us to action occasionally, and more often they challenge the mundane acts of the
Now self. Markus and Nurius, of course, could have gone beyond their

"roster" of Possible selves to speculate about how these selves finally become a cast of characters in an internal drama of their own. Had the two investigators let their subjects go on talking about it—unfortunately, their study is based principally on check lists and rating scales—they might have encountered the condition to which the Varnedoe formula, the DeLillo novels, and the Roth autobiography are addressed.

I suspect that the "condition" in question is the compartmentalization of life in postmodern bureaucratic life, and the requirement of impersonation it imposes on those who live it. At the office, all "lawyer"; at home, all "husband." The Fort Lauderdale lawyer is quoted as saying about his cure, "I am so grateful that I really don't have the words for it, because [doing drugs] could just as easily [have] resulted in my being dead, being disbarred, losing my wife and losing my children."[40] It is as if, before, being an addict, being a lawyer, and being a family man had each been an impersonation, with none of the characters impersonated able to communicate with the others—a mild version of Multiple Personality Disorder, a rapidly growing illness that, interestingly, seems to have its locus classicus in North America.[41]

I have no grand conclusion to offer, save that autobiography is life construction through "text" construction. To look at a life as if it were independent of the autobiographical text that constructs it is as futile a quest for reality as the physicist's search for a Nature that is independent of the theories that lead him to measure one rather than another phenomenon. But while the culture of science creates the paradigms that guide our construction of some version of nature (with a lowercase n), it is the culture in a more loosely defined sense that provides the formulae for the construction of lives. The principal instruments by which the culture does so are its narrative forms, its genres, its modes of "packaging" forms of life. We can get away from the culture of science somewhat, but there is no escaping the broader culture: it is us.

I persist in thinking that autobiography is an extension of fiction, rather than the reverse, that the shape of life comes first from imagination rather than from experience. Plato was not faced with having to keep autobiographers out of the Republic; there were none—only poets, purveyors of story, drama, and metaphor. Autobiographers would have been as dangerous as poets, however, for they practice essentially the same art. As for contemporary autobiography, I have tried to suggest that contemporary literature has it firmly by the hand. As postmodern bureaucratic life becomes more unbearably compartmentalized, we are compelled increasingly to "play a role" in each of the compartments we may occupy—to impersonate what we are supposed to be. Just as "postmodern" social science—I single out Erving Goffman—explores the presentation of face, so the novel becomes preoccupied with the drama and the ironies of impersonation. Soon autobiography follows. Can life be far behind?

Toward an Anti-Metaphysics
of Autobiography

Julia Watson

*I*t has become a critical topos to begin discussions of the theory of
autobiography by rehearsing the changing positions assumed by
critics throughout the last three decades. I too will begin with this over-
view, but only to foreground the persistence of certain concepts about life
writing in many "new model" theorists. Despite the post-structuralist dis-
mantling of the metaphysics of subjectivity, the metaphysical self is alive
and well in much "new model" theory of autobiography. "Mainstream"
or dominant critical theorizing of autobiography, however, is destabilized
by critiques of the subject and, from another vantage point, by alternative
autobiographical practices such as those exemplified in feminist and multicultural non-canonical life writings, with their narratives of multiple,
non-hierarchical difference. These critical positions contest not just the legitimacy of the canon but the definition of what constitutes a "life" in autobiography. This latter question of *bios*, the accumulated historical events
that comprise the "biography" of the writer, is problematic from the perspectives of both women's autobiography and the critique of a metaphysics
of the subject. I want to invoke both critical discourses here in examining
the multiple sites at which the metaphysical self of canonical autobiography is being interrogated and redefined.

Practitioners of mainstream theorizing of autobiography have maintained a canon of autobiographical texts that clearly is narrow and insufficiently representative, but theorists who challenge metaphysical readings
of autobiographical texts, whether from the point of view of feminism or
of post-structuralism, need to grapple more intensively with how the historical practices and traditions constituting Western subjectivity have
shaped a metaphysics of selfhood that informs the texts even of those who
attempt to write against it. I want to examine practices and traditions in

the work of autobiographers who engage the Western metaphysical tradition's representation of subjectivity, both to write against it and to rewrite it. Montaigne is one of a few canonical but anti-metaphysical life-writers located at an uneasy margin of the autobiographical genre; De Quincey and Rilke occupy similar positions. By exploring the challenges to metaphysical concepts of the autobiographical subject posed in the "anti-autobiographical" texts of Montaigne, De Quincey, and Rilke, and, more extensively in the work of Christa Wolf, I will argue that these are sites from which we can decenter *bios* in rethinking the genre along lines already proposed by the autobiographical theory and practice of women and people of color. But first I wish to explore the privileging of *bios* as the persistence of a metaphysical view of the self.

Autobiography is often understood as literalizing its own definition by the translation of the three Greek words that comprise it, *autos, bios, graphē*, as "the story of one's life written by himself."[1] William Spengemann points out that "self-written biography" or the factual account of one's life has traditionally been a synonym for autobiography.[2] In many standard critical works before 1970, autobiography was treated as a variant of biography that must largely renounce fictional invention in its fidelity to historically based "fact." The *bios* component of autobiography signals an expectation that the significant, usually public, events of the life of a "great" person will be recounted. Autobiography becomes a retrospective reflection on how this greatness was achieved, on actions and ideas that characterize a life as in some sense exemplary. The life thus represented is by definition one that has entered into history, so that it is "worth" reading about and imitating. By the same definition, those denied the subject status achieved by white European-oriented males—women, people of color, or those of low social status—lack the public dimensions of the life "worth" living and recounting. To privilege *bios* is to accept that one's cultural status as a subject is externally authorized in this way. *Bios*, then, is not synonymous with identity, but signals the significance of a life within authorized traditions of representing lives in Western culture. The delineation of actions signifying greatness in Plutarch's *Lives*, for example, indicates the monumental public stature of "the great." European philological traditions look to such a concept of classical greatness in reading *bios* as the indicator of the exemplary life, the life demonstrably worth imitating.

Georges Gusdorf epitomizes this position, privileging autobiography as a uniquely Western form and one of the highest achievements of the

Western civilizing mission precisely for its fidelity to, and celebration of, *bios*. Gusdorf praises autobiography as the "conscious awareness of the singularity of each individual life," an awareness that he sees as marking the epitome of Western civilization, the "precious capital" of the biographical self that achieves meaning by its separation and singularity. Autobiography is therefore a genre for memorializing those who are self-evidently wise and "great," as their autobiographies show us: "the great artist, the great writer lives, in a sense, for his autobiography."[3] Gusdorf authorizes his reading of autobiography as timeless, transcendent memorializing by appealing to the principles of nineteenth-century *Geistesgeschichte*. Like Georg Misch and other European critics in the *Geistesgeschichte* tradition who read autobiographical writing as consciously glossing the literary production of great men on the model of the Ancients, Gusdorf regards autobiography as a cultural monument to the individualized subject of Western culture—inevitably white, male, and highly literate—and to the metaphysical aspiration of that culture itself, whose achievement was to produce a universalizing, transcendent subject memorialized by life writing in metaphors of stasis and permanence.

Because the transcendent metaphysical subject has become suspect in recent critical theorizing, autobiography takes on new importance as a site for exploring the rhetoric of metaphysical selfhood and posing alternative readings of self-representation. But as the more recent history of theorizing autobiography suggests, its dominant tradition of criticism has paid only lip service to deconstructionist gestures, while stubbornly retaining the adherence to *bios* that I call the "*bios*-bias." Those who view the recording of the individual's life events as the center of autobiography generally have not been sympathetic to critiques of the Cartesian subject. Much theorizing of autobiography has seemed to make a double gesture of acknowledgment and recuperation, as a focus on biographical materials as the reliable "documents" of autobiography suggests.

Roy Pascal's *Design and Truth in Autobiography* was a kind of initiatory book for theorizing autobiography as something other than a subset of biography because he announced a shift in emphasis to narrative shaping and distinguished the order of fact from that of "truth."[4] This revision was expanded and developed by the "new model" theorists gathered in an important 1977 issue of *New Literary History.*[5] The most illuminating and enduring of these theorists—Philippe Lejeune, Louis Renza, John Sturrock—situated autobiography at an intersection of history and fiction, temporally complex in both its readership and its multiple "I's." Such a location argued for importing autobiography into the literary canon as a prime site for probing the constitution of the subject. But while the new model theorists claimed that autobiography was a worthy textual focus, they tended to restrict that discussion to canonical writers whose autobiographies had been underread, such as Goethe and Sartre, or to argue for autobiographical readings of texts such as Descartes's *Discourse on Method*. The limitations of this approach are clear. The hermeneutic circle involved in revising a theoretical model while adhering to its canonical texts is evident if we recall Lejeune's identification of autobiography with "a passion for the proper name," a transformation of the person analogous to the signature in writing.[6] For those who are not authorized by patronymic privilege, autobiography is by this definition an inaccessible means of self-inscription. In the new model theorists, the implicit assumption remained that autobiography is a First World genre of the dominant culture written by persons whose lives are culturally endorsed, that is, "worth" writing.

Only a few theorists, such as Louis Renza, with Teresa of Avila, and Mary G. Mason, with British women autobiographers, introduced writers outside the literary canon into the discussion, and their examples were canonical within the larger framework of prose genres such as the familiar letter and the journal.[7] Indeed, many discussions of autobiography, while explicitly insisting on its apparently non-biographical character by stressing its fictional invention, either remain located in texts that are canonical or consider as exemplary selected examples that mimic the dominant tradition's categories. But too often these exemplary representatives of other traditions used in formulating autobiographical theories have modeled their lives on literary paradigms informed by canonical models. Thus, Mary McCarthy is discussed by some autobiographical theorists as an exemplary figure for "woman," although her proximity to the world of New York publishing, the Great Tradition, and the *New York Review of Books* hardly makes her typical of the great majority of women, particularly those writing autobiography outside the United States; to an extent the same might be said of Lillian Hellman, and of "sanitized" treatments of Gertrude Stein and Maxine Hong Kingston that efface the lesbianism of the first and the multicultural dissonance of the second.[8] Similarly, one might consider *Black Elk Speaks*, as told to Charles Neihardt, as a problematic representative of Native American life writing in the same way that the work of James Baldwin, Richard Wright, or *The Autobiography of Malcolm X* as told to Alex Haley can be seen as misleadingly exemplary—as texts. Some texts introduced to rewrite canonical parochialism may serve to preserve it.

In these cases, although the *bios*-bias has been revised to undermine the "truth" and stability of the life being represented, the focus on auto-biographies of writers who are canonical or whose life writings have canonical status points to the stubborn persistence of *bios* as giving cultural status to particular lives. In that sense autobiography has remained, in mainstream theorizing, the genre of exemplary lives. All too frequently discussion and theorizing of multicultural and women's autobiographies are absent from critiques that, while claiming to resituate dominant theories, adhere to canonical texts.[9] The canonical texts of autobiography may be read as stories of self-reflection and discovery that produce the writer's insertion into an empowered discourse of cultural validation. But that discourse, and the *bios*-bias on which it rests, is by no means as stable as it seems.

The critical tradition of reading autobiography as the locus of monumental Western selfhood may be destabilized if we read the alter egos of its canonical texts, those equally canonical autobiographies that are too problematic to be inserted easily into the genre as models but that enjoy the status of "great books" despite their resistance to generic norms. As troublingly self-reflexive narratives, the autobiographical writings of Montaigne, De Quincey, and Rilke can be read as transgressive boundary texts that disrupt the genre's *bios*-biased self-definition and reveal the shifting instability inscribed within the representation of any Western self, including their own. The disruption of that self-definition will afford us the opportunity to look at one "other" of the autobiographical tradition, namely women's autobiographies, and to examine current claims that they offer an alternative mode in which *bios* is reinterpreted and the monument to stable selfhood is seen in the light of alterity and dialogue.

I have argued that autobiography as "self-written biography" is a *geistesgeschichtliche* importation that restricts and biases the genre toward *bios*. Recent critics of genre such as Lentricchia and Hernadi in the wake of post-structuralist "de-facement" of autobiography have acknowledged that genres are defined by their boundaries, which historically have been "policed" to exclude non-normative works. Even within the canonical texts of autobiography, extensive readings have demonstrated just how contradictory the claims to a universalized subject and solid presence are in such autobiographical memorializers as Wordsworth, Rousseau, and Augustine. Metaphysical concepts of self that emphasize the "content" of self in, for example, metaphors of place—an enduring edifice, a repository of recollections, a theater for dramatizing the masks of a central self—have been unmasked as "always already" impossible by the critiques of Derrida, de Man, and a host of deconstructionist critics. To de Man, autobiography is to be unmasked or "defaced" as the most suspect of genres because of its claim to write the essence of a self.[10] Here, instead of continuing this deconstruction of canonical writers, I want to explore the problematic of metaphysical selfhood in writers who have usually been read as violating the generic norms of autobiography, despite their concern with self-representation. In different ways, Montaigne, De Quincey, and Rilke articulate structures of self-reflection that place the metaphysical self in a *mise-en-abîme* that represents its undoing. In a chain of substitutions and using different narrative strategies, each confronts the speaking self with its irreducible other. Meta-phor replaces metaphysics with a gap that resists the closure and ordering of detail into a *bios*-oriented structure of linear "truth." But each of these writers "graphs" the other, and its critique of stable metaphysical subjectivity, into his autobiography by contesting a concept of referential selfhood as a requirement of autobiography.

Montaigne's *Essais* may be read not just as posing a Renaissance critique of the sign, but as comprehensively subverting the imagined solidity and permanence of the subject who says "I." In a brief, central essay, "Of Giving the Lie," Montaigne poses a set of oppositional self-representations that contrast public and private modes of self-representation. Montaigne's incessant self-reflexivity, the project of "registering" his thoughts, is not biographical in character, and in this essay the autobiographical signature is identified only under erasure.[11] Montaigne's insistence on the non-monumental, fluid, and antimetaphysical character of his book both makes and unmakes it as a personal form of dialogical subjectivity.

Montaigne begins by observing that his is a wholly private project because his life and opinions lack the exemplary qualities to serve as a model for others to imitate, as Antiquity required. He presents his plan of writing about himself thus:

I am not building here a statue to erect at the town crossroads, or in a church or a public square. . . . This is for a nook in a library, and to amuse a neighbor, a relative, a friend, who may take pleasure in associating and conversing with me again in this image. Others have taken courage to speak of themselves because they found the subject worthy and rich; I, on the contrary, because I have found mine so barren and so meager that no suspicion of ostentation can fall upon my plan. (p. 503)

Here Montaigne challenges a central expectation of the *bios*-bias, that one must present a legitimately public face. He celebrates his own private musings as an autobiographical fullness that refuses to be regulated by the norms of either tradition or decorum. Montaigne also refers to a dictum of the Ancients, that one should not praise oneself lest he be thought a vain fool by others. Plutarch, one of Montaigne's most-used and best-beloved sources, considers the problem of how to speak of oneself in the essay, "On Inoffensive Self-Praise."[12] Clearly Montaigne negotiates this dilemma of the autobiographer by representing himself as lacking the statesman's claims to greatness. In the *Essais*, resistance to *bios* generates the self-portrait.

Montaigne goes on to argue that any trace of himself, be it in writing, gestures, clothing, or implements, would serve as a full sign to invoke his "presence" for his loved ones after his death, an intimate presence unavailable in monumental public presentations. Writing, then, has the power not just to record the words but to evoke the fullness of the subject. A subsequent passage, one of the most famous in the *Essais*, develops the "consubstantiality" that is, in a sense, a foundational claim for all autobiography, the presence of the writer in and as the text. Consubstantiality, sacramental coexistence of writer and text, is established, claims Montaigne, between the subject matter presented in his writing and its author: "Painting myself for others, I have painted my inward self with colors clearer than my original ones. I have no more made my book than my book has made me—a book consubstantial with its author, concerned with my own self, an integral part of my life; not concerned with some third-hand, extraneous purpose, like all other books" (p. 504). This passage is often read as one that authorizes autobiography as a complete and faithful self-portrait, an image of the exchange between "self" and text, as well as a moral corrective to the vanity implicit in self-reference.[13] The assertion of mutual interchange and recognition between the writing subject and the represented textual "object" is presented as a moment of transcendent, universalizing subjectivity, the birth of autobiography as the genre of individuation and ego-genesis. Generations of scholars have located Montaigne's "humanism" in this impulse, while critics of autobiography have been both fascinated by Montaigne and reluctant to claim him for autobiography because of his extravagant assertions about self-representation.

In fact the metaphorics of Montaigne's text in several ways deconstruct the metaphysical illusion of "presence" that it here seems to enshrine. In distinguishing his writing from all "third-hand" books, it insists on writing *as* the self, not an imitation of its biographical character. Furthermore, Montaigne follows the moment of self-communion here with a self-conscious flaunting of his embodied textual self and pointedly argues the impossibility of representing or enshrining self-communion in writing. Consubstantiality is both asserted and subverted. The self is constructed over its own impossibility—its impossibility, that is, except as a strategy of writing, a condition of reading. Two sentences after the preceding citation Montaigne continues: "Indeed, the most delightful pleasures are digested inwardly, avoid leaving any traces, and avoid the sight not only of the public but of any other person" (p. 504). Here "consubstantiality" is glossed differently, as a purely private communion—and de-sacralized as digestion—in a process that is by definition unsharable. The intensity of self-communion that the book both brings into being and represents is purely private, like the body's digestion of the food that will become it. Self-experience exceeds and eludes any other's knowledge, and one can write only of its unsharability. Not to challenge his own prior assertion of consubstantiality would indicate insufficient self-understanding, as well as a false modesty about the book and the significance of writing as self-communication. It would reduce the process to a biographical monument observable by others, rather than authorize the intimacy and pleasure that Montaigne attests to and urges his reader to engage. Thus Montaigne's text deconstructs its own autobiographical claims and argues for undoing the norm of representative selfhood at the heart of *bios* that persists in much theorizing of autobiography. Montaigne's *Essais* argue for diversity at the core of claims to unified, coherent selfhood.

In a more extended reading of this essay I would trace the implications of Montaigne's relocation of the writing self outside the sphere of *bios* in several ways: by further exploring the essay's shift of metaphorical categories of communion and embodiment; by noting how its assertions of the equilibrium of textual self-portrait and writing persona continue to be subverted and revised; and by contrasting his speaking positions as subject and as commentator on the history of other subject inscriptions. All of these would help to locate this essay in the virtual space of a metaphysics of presence inscribed upon its own impossibility. Perhaps the clearest evidence of Montaigne's conscious writing against the truth of the self, however, is his inscription of his consubstantial text/self within the essay entitled "Of Giving the Lie." By executing a "lie," a rhetorical test of itself, at its end, that essay goes on to explore and explode the discourse of referential truth that underlies the notion of *bios*. As a further subversion of autobiographical claims, Montaigne's "lying" self-portrait deserves examining.

Montaigne introduces the problem of "lying" or false self-representations by asking, "But whom shall we believe when he talks about himself?", alluding again to Plutarch's critique of self-reference as presumptive (p. 505). He goes on to consider customs of lying as misrepresenting both oneself and the communicative process. He then denounces lying by taking on the voice and argument of a righteous medieval preacher: "Lying is an ugly vice, which . . . is giving evidence of contempt for God, and at the same time of fear of men. . . . He who breaks his word betrays human society" (p. 505). Having made truthful speech the foundation of communication, morality, and civilization, he goes on to execute an elaborate lie designed to test the reader's awareness of self-truth as a non-referential discourse different in kind from objective or "third-hand" truth claims. Montaigne describes "certain nations of the new Indies" who sacrifice human blood from tongues and ears as expiation for lying (p. 505). But the conquest of these nations was so complete that it "has extended even to the entire abolition of the names and former knowledge of the places" (p. 506). In a variation on the Cretan liar paradox, Montaigne unmasks the fictiveness of his own assertion about truthtellers. His "true" narrative of truth-loving tribes that left no record and cannot be recalled by any trace is paradoxically true because he attests to its impossibility. In authoring this example, Montaigne both authorizes and undermines his own reliability.[14] The knowing reader becomes educated neither to believe nor to disbelieve Montaigne's claims to self-presence in the text. Rather, we are invited to reread his assertion of autobiographical consubstantiality through the problematics of self-reference that his own metaphors have pursued.

As Michel Beaujour has persuasively argued, Montaigne's *Essais* cannot be read as an example of *bios*, despite his incessant self-reference; rather, the *Essais* must be read as an "autoportrait," which for Beaujour is distinct from autobiography. They render the mirror of the self-portrait an opaque image in a virtual yet exemplary space.[15] In Montaigne, "self" is a process of investigation into a set of hypothetical textual "I's." These "I's" are interrogated as a particular case of Montaigne's motto and his rationale for writing: "*Que sçay-je?*" (What do I know?). The *Essais* continually subvert the claims of the subject to record the contents of a life and relocate selfhood to the realm of discursive voices that play against one another in multilayered intertextuality. The autobiographical signature that would name Montaigne is suspended in a forever-incomplete dialogue with the reader, who can complete Montaigne's self-representation only by initiating a private self-reflection. In every sense the *Essais*, by resisting *bios*, inscribe the complexity of self-experience.[16]

Montaigne employs the structure of the Cretan liar paradox to create a *mise-en-abîme* of self-reflection as an illusory self-portrait subverting the *bios*-graphical edifice of metaphysical selfhood in autobiography. De Quincey adopts a different strategy for undermining metaphysical selfhood, extending and diffusing his self, in space and time, through the agency of opium. *Confessions of an English Opium Eater* is an autobiographical narrative that is usually ignored because of its apparent celebration of opium as an agent of self-fragmentation and vision.[17] But *Confessions* is both a gripping tale of self-study and a significant rewriting of autobiographical norms. In relocating his biographical self, De Quincey pronounces opium "the true hero of the tale" and becomes an observer of visions that act upon his sense of fixed, bounded identity.[18] His "self" is destabilized through the consciousness-altering effects of massive, regular doses of the drug, and his visions become an occasion for rewriting history from the points of view of non-Western cultural others. De Quincey's autobiography confesses its anxious discovery of its "Oriental" other and unmasks an imperialist bias in Western cultural narratives that privileges the white, male, upper-class, educated author. The encounters and visions of his life are structured in the autobiography so as to locate him in cultural contexts whose authority is unmasked by the agency of opium: the educated young man whose privilege is not shared by his female companion; the outcast among the ravaged poor of London who can retreat to his father's house; the Western subject haunted by dreams of a Malay who accuses and threatens him; the witness to a procession of histories in which the Greco-Roman is but one of several scenarios of grandeur and domination. These multiple phantasmagoric others rewrite his story and challenge the claim to individual autonomy implicit in autobiography.

While a reading of the *Confessions* would be too extended for this discussion, it may be useful to focus on a figure—of both speech and thought—that is central to it. The involute, a form that both turns upon itself and spirals progressively, is found in nature in conch shells and suggested by the human ear, the agent of memory.[19] De Quincey makes the involute a metaphor for human memory and characterizes memory as combining two antithetical senses of time, linear progress and cyclical return. The involute both figures and is figured by the peculiar dialogic structure of his text, in which the "story" interweaves past and future British and Western history with a multiple retrospective view of his own history, moving as it does between vision and memory. For De Quincey, an autobiographical narrative is a historical fiction that imitates, in its privileging of *bios*, the events of a life and, ultimately, the cultural fictions of Western history. His self-study with opium displaces the subject from official history into a critique of its foundations and a rewriting of history as a panoramic procession spiraling into multiple pasts and an unmapped future. There the self becomes neither actor nor author, but is revealed as a destabilized sign and site of collective processes whose human experience is to participate in, and not forget, suffering. In De Quincey, "self" is replaced by hieroglyphs yet to be unriddled.[20] In confessing his inability to sustain a metaphysical self and recording his erasures of ego by the agency of vision, De Quincey offers an alternative view of the autobiographical subject as the ground on which the theater of human history plays out a drama of relationships.

In *The Notebooks of Malte Laurids Brigge*, Rilke initiates a third means of destabilizing metaphysical selfhood.[21] *The Notebooks* is a text of interstices that seems to defy generic limits: Its many brief entries read as poetic prose, neither fully prose nor poetry, though many are the basis for the poems of *New Poems*.[22] Malte's life has striking biographical parallels to Rilke's, but the author explicitly disavowed the biographical similarity.[23] The persona that speaks and attempts to subjectify himself in *The Notebooks* keeps collapsing in on himself; his status is defined by acts of seeing rather than by conditions of existing. Most critics have remarked on *The Notebooks* as a hall of mirrors that constructs a labyrinth of self-reflection in some oblique yet highly self-referential relationship to its other.[24]

The Notebooks clearly is about processes of self-making and unmaking, and the conditions within which an artistic subjectivity may be posed in writing. These processes are metaphorized, rather than monumentalized, in figures of tentative subjectification: in sketches (*Aufzeichnungen*); in the medieval tapestries, such as "La dame au licorne" in Cluny, where Malte reads life histories as cultural stories that allude to artistic mysteries; in the many hallucinatory mirrors, specters, spectacles, and acts of self-reflexivity chronicled; and in *The Notebooks'* compilation as a textual mosaic or collage of fragments only peripherally connected by Malte, the unstable subject that says "I."

As readers of *The Notebooks* know, that peculiar and evocative first-person text is characterized by both the absence of a central metaphysical self and the interplay of a panoply of echoes from the poetic and artistic texts of the Western tradition. Like De Quincey's narrator, Malte is a site at which the collected voices of cultural memory create a meta-commentary about the conditions of subjectification. In its particular attention to the invisible subjects of writing, above all to women and the poor of Paris, *The Notebooks* displaces attention to the historical others of the Western tradition. But Rilke's means of displacing the metaphysical subject differ from De Quincey's. Rather than losing himself through agents of vision, Malte continually escapes from a firm self to elude the oppressive impingement of others' consciousness. A manqué who can make no supra-personal identification, he nevertheless interrogates the conditions of autobiographical "presence." Without an *autos*-nomous center of reference and a *bios*-graphy of coherent events, what is left of Malte/Rilke's autobiographical habit is *graphe*, writing, as the sketching of momentary images.

In *The Notebooks'* central metaphor of learning to see, perception becomes insistently subjective.[25] Seeing is embodied; it rebounds upon the senses by which Malte takes the measure of a tentative "I". The conditions of seeing are unreliable, and change with his vantage point and the temporal moment. No stable self can be affirmed in this fragmentary experience of seeing. But the process of writing, as a recording of discontinuous points of perception, traces a temporal continuum.

In *The Notebooks*, the utterances of an "I" are doubly hypothetical, displaced from Rilke to Malte and directed at faceless and hallucinatory others. The text reverberates with cultural voices, the Biblical narrative of the prodigal son and the medieval allegory of the unicorn, family ghost stories and mystical raptures, fragments of Verlaine and Baudelaire or of regional Danish poets. These dispossessed and fragmentary voices do not so much create a narrative as thwart the reader's expectations that an orderly narrative will underlie and organize efforts at self-making. In repeatedly refusing the terms of coherent selfhood in *Notebooks*, Rilke offers a new challenge to the norms of autobiography. Despite his aristocratic and reactionary pretensions to inhabit the old world of culture, Rilke's unmaking of *autos* and *bios*, as the conditions of writing one's experience of historical time, is a modern and multivocal revision of those norms.

The metaphysics of self-making and authenticating the biographical life is explicitly turned inside out in these examples. As critiques of the edifice of Western selfhood, the "boundary" texts of self-reference that I have discussed call the concept into question. They suggest a method of unmasking the metaphysical selves attributed to texts of the autobiographical canon. Because the texts of Montaigne, DeQuincey, and Rilke create structures of self-interrogation rather than asserting *bios*, are they anti-autobiographical? Or is it autobiography itself that has become identical with the fiction of a stably constructed and continuous self that is at odds with current "alter-ego" concepts of identity? Examining the kinds of autobiography being written and discussed in the last decade mandates that we redefine the genre to fit the complexity and diversity of its practices.

In the process of recovering and reading non-canonical autobiographies of women, African American slave narratives, *testimonios*, and other modes of previously invisible autobiography, critics have posed alternative canons-in-the-making that have begun to alter the autobiographical canon. But has their impact on its theorizing been profound or merely superficial; has the *bios*-bias reinstated itself in more covert ways? The theoretical discussion of women's autobiography is a case in point. (I cannot speak to the many alternative canons of autobiography here, and the terms of the argument would differ with each canon, though all to some extent remain marginalized within dominant autobiography.)

In their collection of essays on women's autobiography, *Life/Lines*, Bella Brodzki and Celeste Schenck have pointed to the notable absence of discussion of radically experimental women or non-white autobiographers in recent mainstream studies of new model autobiography. They have also emphasized the need for "resisting reification and essentialism" by feminist theorists who would relocate experimental selfhood from the singularity of the individual self to a relational model of alterity.[26] Just as mainstream theorizing of autobiography has implicitly continued to assume the legitimacy of *bios* as the criterion for inclusion in the canon, theorizing of women's autobiography has noted the absence of *bios* in women's texts. Brodzki and Schenck argue that exclusionary literary and cultural practices continue to hypostasize the subject as white and male because they cannot value this difference of women's self-presentation and, ultimately, self-experience.

That difference is crystallized in the concept of alterity introduced into the discussion of autobiography by Mary G. Mason and elaborated by Susan Stanford Friedman. Mason argues that women writers delineate identity relationally, through connection to significant others, that "the self-discovery of female identity seems to acknowledge the real presence and recognition of another consciousness, and the disclosure of female self is linked to the identification of some 'other.' This recognition . . . [seems] to enable women to write openly about themselves."[27] Mason positions this alterity in contrast to the self-dramatizing ego of the white male autobiographer à la Rousseau, who, Mason argues, sees others as a kind of backdrop or screen for his solitary performances, and not as relational possibilities in a dialogue.[28] By positing other voices as aspects of the relational autobiographical "I," Mason destabilizes claims for the separateness of lives implied by the concept of individuality, and therefore questions the authority of *bios* itself.

This argument was developed into a theoretical position by Susan Stanford Friedman. Invoking the research of Nancy Chodorow in *The Reproduction of Mothering*, Friedman argues that in women's texts we can find "a consciousness of self in which 'the individual [feels] . . . very much with

others in an interdependent existence.'" Friedman also turns to Sheila
Rowbotham to incorporate concepts of "collective alienation, consciousness, and formation of new identities through reclamation of language and
image."[29] Friedman explores a notion of fluid or permeable ego boundaries
to describe the sense of collective identification and yearning for maternal
nurturance and community that she reads as characteristic of many wom-
en's autobiographies, particularly contemporary ones. The texts she discusses suggest an alternative canon for women's autobiography in the diverse works of Charlotte Perkins Gilman, Anaïs Nin, Isabella Leitner,
Paule Marshall, Ntozake Shange, Maxine Hong Kingston, H.D., and
Audre Lorde. Friedman thus radically rewrites notions of self and authorship to displace *bios* as the determining and validating category of autobiography. In speaking of a model of selfhood applicable to all women,
however, Friedman seems to essentialize "woman" and to privilege the maternal bond. Although interpersonal relationships and a sense of community are assuredly important in many women's self-definition, their modification by social circumstances, and sometimes their complete absence,
are also marked in the above autobiographers. To rewrite Gusdorf's claims
about autobiography by redefining life as "an interdependent existence
that asserts its rhythms everywhere in the community," as Friedman explicitly does, seems more a denial of autobiography's hegemonic claims
than an acknowledgment of their formative yet repressive power.

Domna Stanton strongly makes the case against *bios* as the foundational category of women's autobiography in an influential essay entitled
"Autogynography: Is the Subject Different?" Echoing Virginia Woolf in
her bewilderment at the lack of women's texts, Stanton observes that "in
a phallocentric system . . . the *graphing* of the *auto* was an act of self-
assertion that denied and reversed woman's status." She proposes a different category, autogynography, to designate the fundamentally different nature of the project, as well as to theorize its critical history: "Autogynography, I concluded, dramatized the fundamental alterity and non-presence of
the subject, even as it asserts itself discursively and strives toward an always
impossible self-possession. This gendered narrative involved a different
plotting and configuration of the split subject." For Stanton, then, *bios* signals an entire symbolic order of discourse that enables the subjectification
of the male autobiographer at the expense of silencing his others. While
acknowledging that her renunciation of *bios* denies the possibility of signature to women, Stanton states her preference for the contradictory implications of gynocriticism that opens up a discursive space.[30]

But the problem of representing the diversity of women under a unified gynocentric sign, when their positions with respect to ethnicity and class and their modes of self-identification are not only divergent but organized within a structure of power relations, has made the argument to privilege alterity and to replace *bios*-bias with *gyno*-bias both inadequate and politically suspect. That critique is implied in the work of some theorists of women's autobiography; it is most fully articulated in autobiographical writings by women of color and in theorizing positioned at explicit "margins."

Sidonie Smith has expanded on the implications for literary and cultural tradition of the lack of *bios*-authority in women's autobiography by locating women's textuality in relation to life scripts available at specific historical periods in the West.[31] Smith argues that, historically, Western women's four life scripts—wife, nun, queen, and witch—undermined the possibility of subjectification, of claiming *bios* for their lives, except within prescribed and highly encoded male scripts such as queen or "rationalist." What women could inscribe was their textual invisibility, their absence from history, narrating brief forays into public life recollected after renouncing the public world and acknowledging their ancillary status.

Similarly, Carolyn Heilbrun has noted that until the twentieth century the cultural injunctions against writing one's life as a woman were so powerful that they produced at best self-presentations under erasure. Arguing that women's sense of life was controlled by male narratives, Heilbrun claims that "there will be narratives of female lives only when women no longer live their lives isolated in the houses and the stories of men." For Heilbrun, earlier women's autobiographies were inevitably tales of no life, of silencing. At this time autobiography represents, for women, the possibility of breaking into speech about that silence: "Only in the last third of the twentieth century have women broken through to a realization of the narratives that have been controlling their lives."[32] In that process *bios* will inevitably be remade, though for Heilbrun the project of biographical recounting is as much a narrative as a linguistic issue. For both Smith and Heilbrun, the terms of women's autobiography depend on its opposition to a privileged phallocentric discourse in dominant autobiography. In this opposition women's difference tends to become essentialized as a "lack"— of scripts, of boundaries—that is potentially productive but that has been historically inhibiting. For women, then, autobiography is the site of an alien form of prohibited selfhood, and the acknowledgment of that prohibition is an initial gesture in entering into writing as the other of discourse in search of a voice and a transformative script.

Perhaps no work of women's autobiography has had more important implications for theorizing *bios* outside a metaphysical tradition than *This Bridge Called My Back*, a collection of brief autobiographical writings in many genres by radical women of color in the United States.[33] In a sense, *Bridge* enunciates all that dominant autobiography is not: creative and polemical, it redefines autobiography as the first-person utterances of women whose identities had been construed as contradictory and invisible within both mainstream theory and academic white women's writing. In *Bridge*, autobiography takes on a new meaning as the coming-to-voice of women who had been multiply marginalized and historically silenced for their color and its gradations, for their lack of class and educational privilege, for their predominantly lesbian sexual orientations. The personal histories of ethnic prejudice narrated in *Bridge* collectivize and historicize first-person statements in ways that *bios*, understood as individualized assertion of a life's significance, cannot admit. The self-presentations of many women who speak of the cultural invisibility of their unauthorized lives are inseparable from identity politics in *Bridge*, and argue for resituating autobiography as an inescapably collective and oppositional form.[34] The autobiographical writings of *Bridge* are foregrounded as a site for rethinking identity in Biddy Martin's important essay, "Lesbian Identity and Autobiographical Difference." She emphasizes that its "autobiographical essays, poems, and letters relate psychic and political struggles in ways that make 'identity' irreducible to consciousness. . . . [It is a] discussion, between and among 'women of color,' of the contradictions, conflicts, and possibilities in that constructed but 'potent fusion of outsider identities.' "[35]

In a different voice, Trinh Minh-ha has critiqued the historical and writerly orientation of Western narrative as a silencing of women's speech, the sensory and material stuff of stories. In "Grandma's Story" particularly, Trinh redefines every term of autobiography from the vantage point of women of color.[36] In women's narratives, she claims, story is a living, woven thread, moving generationally through many lives. *Autos* becomes collective; *bios* is fragmentary rather than totalizing, oriented toward the body and the future; and *graphe* becomes a living process of giving voice. For Trinh, life narratives are neither fiction nor nonfiction, but a transformative process of naming what is happening.[37] Her critique, then, is also an autobiographical speaking of her own cultural location, authorized through her maternal ancestry. In valorizing speech over word, voice over mind, story over history, collectivity over the individual, and "Third World" narratives (Silko, Hong Kingston, African folk tales, her own films) over First World autobiographies, Trinh argues for "unwriting" life stories as a rewriting that challenges the norms of autobiography at every point.[38]

Françoise Lionnet, too, privileges voice over word and calls for revising the emphasis in autobiography from *bios* to multiple, irreducible differences.[39] Lionnet addresses herself to women and women's texts across the differences of women living between cultures. She encodes a concept of difference in the untranslatable word *métissage* (roughly, the braiding of different cultures as one identity), arguing that women's differences cannot be essentialized as gynocriticism, but are inflected by cultural specificities of ethnicity, class, time, and location. Lionnet's book is at once a kind of culmination of feminist positions on theorizing autobiography and a beginning gesture toward theorizing multiple, non-symmetrical differences that are inflected by both the texts under study and the critic's own cultural location. Her insistence on rereading autobiographical texts such as Augustine's *Confessions* and Nietzsche's *Ecce Homo* against the histories of their metaphysical readings suggests a practice that I would like to apply here, in conclusion, to an autobiographical writer in whose works the politics of difference and the critique of metaphysical constructions of the self interpenetrate as in perhaps no other writer today. I am referring to the German socialist writer Christa Wolf.

A writer of novels, essays, film scripts, and other literary forms in the former German socialist state since the beginning of the sixties, Christa Wolf has been celebrated throughout Germany as an important "Marxist Humanist." While her political reputation is currently a subject of debate, her extraordinary literary accomplishment seems beyond question.[40] Wolf's reflection on the historical and transpersonal character of subjectivity revises the metaphysical self of autobiography, questions the authenticity of *bios*, and proposes a dialectical inquiry between culture and self. Wolf situates her narratives uneasily at a boundary of history and fiction. She has pursued this project throughout many autobiographical novels, but most notably in two books: *Patterns of Childhood*, in which acts of memory become gestures against collective cultural amnesia about the fascist past of Germany; and the four essays in *Cassandra*, where Wolf both describes the writing of the novel and interweaves reflections on herself as a writer and an unheeded prophetess.[41] While neither of these books is autobiography in a simple sense, their complex explorations of subjectivity rewrite the terms of autobiography in ways that are illuminating for my discussion of the "non-*biosed*" female subject.

Wolf is critical of the aesthetic norms by which subjectivity is objecti-

fied in the "alienated" forms of art. She begins the series of lectures on poetics later published with *Cassandra* by distinguishing the experiences of
subjects from the realm and rules of art: "I feel keenly the tension between
the artistic forms within which we have agreed to abide and the living material, borne to me by my senses, my psychic apparatus, and my thought,
which has resisted these forms. . . . There are no poetics, and there can be
none, that prevent the living experience of numberless subjects from being
deprived of life and buried in art-objects."[42] Thus Wolf separates the lived
experience of subjects from the system of literature and attempts to mobilize her personal, subjective connection to the world as both resistance
and writing. She goes on to ask why and how "art-objects" such as texts
in our culture have come to mirror its alienation, just as other human products reflect a Western desire for self-annihilation. Wolf locates a point of
origin in the fall of Troy and the corresponding patriarchalization of Western culture that, she argues, seems bent on destruction, though no return
to matriarchal culture is possible (p. 142).

In these lectures Wolf insists on the personal character of her response
to literary material, specifically the story of the doomed prophetess Cassandra as developed in the *Iliad* and Aeschylus's *Agamemnon*. Employing
a variety of subjective modes of expression—essay, diary, travel journal,
letter—she insists on the irreducibly autobiographical character of her
(re)writing of literature and refashions autobiography as a cultural inquiry
into the historically conditioned construction of the self. That is, in Christa
Wolf's writing "individuality" is seen as a kind of personal myth that needs
to be subjected to interrogation by the collective and transpersonal events
and configurations of history.

In *Patterns of Childhood* the narrating "I" journeys literally and in the
movement of memory toward an encounter with her past selves. Wolf employs both second and third persons in addressing versions of herself, and
thereby locates herself as both the observed subject, enmeshed in the particulars of circumstance and ideological complexity, and the observing "I."
Wolf specifically rejects the designation of "autobiography" for this text,
although the narrator's life closely parallels her own experience of growing
up in the thirties in Nazi Germany in Landsberg, a small city near Dres-
den.[43] Her disclaimer at the beginning of the book indicates the vehemence
of her rejection of autobiography. In full it reads:

All characters in this book are the invention of the narrator. None is identical with
any person living or dead. Neither do any of the described episodes coincide with
actual events.

Anyone believing that he detects a similarity between a character in the narrative and either himself or anyone else should consider the strange lack of indi-

viduality [*den merkwürdigen Mangel an Eigentümlichkeit*] in the behavior of many contemporaries. Generally recognizable behavior patterns [*Verhaltensweisen*] should be blamed on circumstances [*die Verhältnisse*].

Wolf's double emphasis on fictional invention and the fictionality of individuality suggests one of her purposes in chronicling this voyage of memory: to trace how historical and sociopolitical forces, including the ideology of individuality, shape larger configurations of social action. Self-examination is for her inextricable from the process of history; to reflect on her experience she must necessarily interrogate the "official" histories of fascism and socialism and seek the suppressed, forgotten unofficial histories. To see the self as an "individual," that is, outside of and "transcending" the circumstantial context—the emphasis of traditional autobiography that the *bios*-bias insists on—is for Wolf a willed delusion that, on a national level, may create culture but also permits atrocities against those whose subject status has been denied or revoked. In *Patterns of Childhood* the fictional frame becomes a guarantor of the book's personal engagement, whereas a claim to the factual authenticity of *bios* would discredit it as an act of historical witnessing. Insisting on locating subjectivity at a nexus of historical coordinates, Wolf signals a resistance to autobiography's authorization of private, *bios*-oriented subjectivity and reinscribes it as a collective genre. Mistrusting autobiography as a form of false consciousness, Wolf rewrites the autobiographical paradigm itself as a multiply reflexive, irreducibly plural dialogue with memory about the construction of subjectivity.

   Patterns of Childhood begins with a compelling sentence that both indicts the biographical character of much personal history and insists on the importance of autobiographical reflection: "What is past is not dead; it is not even past. We cut ourselves off from it; we pretend to be strangers" (p. 3). Wolf ruminates on the difficulty and the necessity of memory by describing her dilemma: "to remain speechless, or else to live in the third person" (p. 3). In this gap created from a historical silence about the intolerable past, memory and voice are what constitute the illusion of a chronological life:

The present intrudes upon remembrance, today becomes the last day of the past. Yet we would suffer continuous estrangement from ourselves if it weren't for our memory of the things we have done, of the things that have happened to us. If it weren't for the memory of ourselves.
   And for the voice that assumes the task of telling it. (p. 4)

Memory both creates and structures a sense of cohesive selfhood that "present-ifies" the past.[44] Attempting to mediate between the impossibility of a first-person narrator of her childhood, when the conditions of that childhood (belonging to the Hitler Youth) made speech impossible, and the objective third person, Wolf narrates much of the book in the second person, a telling from the inside, as the self regards and engages itself. The self-reflection woven throughout the text suggests why. Recalling herself as the child Nelly, the narrator remarks:

The child Nelly strikes you as being helpless, and it is you who put her in that position: intentionally, one might say. . . . The closer she gets to you in time, the less familiar she becomes. And you call that strange? . . . Nelly is nothing but the product of your hypocrisy. It stands to reason that anyone who attempts to change a person into an object in order to use that person for a confrontation with the self has to be hypocritical if he later complains that he can no longer expose himself to this object; that it's becoming more and more incomprehensible to him.

Or do you imagine that you can understand someone of whom you're ashamed? (p. 211)

In remembering, the narrator discovers herself objectifying her younger self and adopting a variety of defensive postures toward this other. This emphasis on the otherness of the other, particularly when it is her recent self, suggests Wolf's resistance to the fiction of coherent selfhood and biographical continuity that has long been considered central to Western autobiography.

Furthermore, memory seems mixed with acts of invention; it is inevitably the memory of memories. Particularly in the twentieth century, retrieval of history, available only through personal engagement with the past, is made difficult by both personal and collective amnesia. Characterizing Nazi Germany as "the age of the universal loss of memory," Wolf notes: "You realized you had to fear memory, this system of treachery; that by seemingly exposing it you'd actually have to fight it. . . . We must realize that complete presence of mind can be achieved only when based on a clear past. . . . (Only it's so much easier . . . to invent the past than to remember it)" (pp. 152–53). What passes for remembered history—official accounts, stories, photographs—has been "censored" and objectified into a "fossil," by being distanced from the remembering "I" (p. 153). To remember the time of Auschwitz, to remember the first time she heard the words "the final solution," is to evoke the imagined horror of what she did not observe as part of the German denial of its own death camps (p. 233). As a child she stands uneasily between the roles of perpetrator and victim, yet knows she cannot imaginatively project herself into the victim's horror, because to do so would appropriate it. Her daughter Lenka's demands to know how the Holocaust could have been permitted bring her face-to-face with her own amnesia as a former child and her desire to "eliminate inventions, to use the memory of memories, the memory of fantasies, only as second-hand information, as reflections, not as reality" (p. 217).

The problematic of memory, so central to *Patterns of Childhood*, is intricately traced in the varieties of unraveling Wolf follows throughout this long novel that refuses to be normative autobiography. Charting her voyage into childhood and motherhood in the doubled times—contemporary and pre–World War II—of narration, Wolf imagines arriving, if interrogatively, at the convergence of the three pronouns into whom she has had to divide herself in order to remember and to narrate:

The final point would be reached when the second and the third person were to meet again in the first or, better still, were to meet with the first person. When it would no longer have to be "you" and "she" but a candid, unreserved "I." It seemed very doubtful to you whether you could reach this point at all, whether the road you've taken would ever lead to it. (p. 349)

Writing and remembering, constructing a self as both personal and collective history against the amnesia mandated by her past, is a process that engenders not the construction of a biography but a questioning engagement with the fictions that seem to promise factual closure about self-knowledge. Wolf concludes this searching book in two voices, that of the questioner of the past's power to objectify self-experience, and that of the future-oriented narrating "I":

And the past, which can still split the first person into the second and the third—has its hegemony been broken? Will the voices be still?
   I don't know. . . .
   Sure of finding myself once again in the world of solid bodies upon awakening, I shall abandon myself to the experience of dreaming. I shall not revolt against the limits of the expressible. (pp. 406–7)

In hovering between a desire to remain open to her past selves as an act of resistance to "the mortal sin of our times: the desire not to come to grips with oneself," and a desire to reintegrate and open herself to the unspecified future, Wolf closes her narrative with a refusal of closure, in a sense beyond the imperatives of both narrative and witnessing (p. 406). Resisting throughout the acts of separation and objectification that autobiography would seem to require, refusing to name her to herself as a recognizable "life," she opts instead for an uneasy boundary of history and fiction as a means of examining the German past, her accumulated experience, and "pastness" itself through her personal connection to them.

In *Cassandra* Wolf expands this inquiry into the cultural past of the

West to the borderlines of cultural memory in order to locate herself within
the cultural silencing of both women and poets in the contemporary world,
and to probe the conditions of change. I will be concerned here only with
the four essays that accompany the novel.[45] Wolf's essays intend to explore
"the sinister effects of alienation, in aesthetics, in art, as well as elsewhere"
(p. 142). As a woman writer marginalized, like Cassandra, by her eccentric place in Western history, Wolf poses provocative questions with autobiographical resonance: "The literature of the West [I read] is the white
man's reflection on himself. So should it be supplemented by the white
woman's reflection on herself? And nothing more?" (p. 225). Wolf delineates the difficulty of claiming subjectivity either through, or despite, gender. To be historically invisible and voiceless is to lack identity except as
the unspecified other of a male subject: "The fact that I lack words here:
doesn't this mean that I am losing myself? How quickly does lack of speech
turn into lack of identity?" (p. 161). To come to voice is above all to pose
questions that are inscribed within a double circle of women's historical
voicelessness and contemporary indifference to the personal and experiential: "Shall I try to name the 'meaning' they [the *korai*, or Greek maid-
ens] stand for, which is really a non-meaning? The barbarism of the modern age. The question that disturbs me: Was there, is there, an alternative
to this barbarism?" (p. 159). In political provocations that probe the Western humanistic tradition and its contemporary practice by nation-states,
Wolf entwines the forms of alienation and speaks from the position of a
historically silenced other analogous to Cassandra's: "Who was Cassandra
before anyone wrote about her?" (p. 273). The pre-biographical self, which
is also pre-patriarchal, leaves no trace.

    At the same time that Wolf indicts the Western obsession with the bio-
graphical self as a self-justifying blind spot for its murderous practices, she
self-consciously reveals herself, suggesting the complexity of her relationship to autobiographical discourse. In discussing a contemporary poem by
Ingeborg Bachmann, Wolf alludes to "the grammar of manifold simulta-
neous relations" in which things cannot be thought to be exclusively one
way or the other, an opposition that she reads through gender, class, and
historical conditions (p. 276). The phrase is instructive, as are her interrogation of the conditions and blind spots of subjectivity and her rewriting
of autobiographical discourse as a form of cultural critique in which the
subject understands herself as a nexus of multiple circumstances, a willed
"depersonalization" (p. 284).

    For Wolf, the project of contemporary culture must be to reconstruct
the conditions of subjectivity before the consolidation of the subject of

Western humanism. This would mean discovering "the feeling that everything is fundamentally related," a feeling that was renounced and suppressed throughout Western culture's pursuit of objectivity (p. 287). To re-situate autobiographical discourse at this relational site without reading it as "alterity," one would have to renegotiate *bios* and locate the "I" in the common cultural life as an appropriate historical witness. This understanding of subjectivity would radically reform both our reading and our theorizing of autobiography by returning subjectivity to historically depersonalized subjects. They must now will that depersonalization, Wolf argues, in order not to be seduced by *bios* into a collusion with Western humanism that would subvert their resistance. By interrogating the female autobiographical subject autobiographically, as both a cultural subject and an invisible person, Wolf resituates autobiography at the intersection of personal and political critiques of Western culture. "But how can we write under the glowing sun of reason; in this rigorously cultivated, arrogant, and deciphered landscape, robbed of our possessions, including our words, which could have the power to cast spells? This, too, is a question which can only be approached by asking further questions" (p. 305). In the autobiographical landscape, Wolf's sketching of a virtual space offers the possibility of writing the auto- as "non-*biosed*" and relational, a historical signature and an act of witnessing.

Institutionalizing Women's Autobiography: Nineteenth-Century Editors and the Shaping of an Autobiographical Tradition

Linda H. Peterson

*W*hat is women's autobiography, and when was it first written? Answers are difficult to give. We do not know what Englishwoman produced the first piece of self-writing; what women's texts we have lost from the mid-seventeenth century, the moment that seems to mark the beginning of an unbroken English autobiographical tradition; or what texts we have lost—or lost sight of—from centuries before and after the seventeenth. Despite such lacunae, feminist scholarship of the last decade has attempted to delineate a tradition of women's autobiography. Beginning with Mary G. Mason's "The Other Voice" (1980) and continuing with Estelle C. Jelinek's *The Tradition of Women's Autobiography* (1986), Sidonie Smith's *A Poetics of Women's Autobiography* (1987), and Carolyn G. Heilbrun's *Writing a Woman's Life* (1988), the agenda has been to (re)discover a tradition of women's own.[1]

That agenda has included more specific goals: the (re)discovery of lost or forgotten women's texts, the posing of literary questions about gender and genre, the posing of more general questions about women's self-representation, whether it has always been different from men's or whether women's writings show certain fundamental "human" patterns of development. Whatever the specific goals, as versions of literary history, critical studies of the 1980's have assumed a common argument: that women's autobiography represents a separate and distinct tradition, a genre or subgenre different from autobiographical writing produced by men. In Jelinek's words, "contemporary women are writing out of and continuing to create a wholly different autobiographical tradition from that delineated in studies of male autobiography."[2]

That women's autobiography represents "a wholly different autobiographical tradition" has been a practical, even necessary critical assumption. Prior to 1980 major critical studies of autobiography excluded serious consideration of women's texts. The fact of exclusion seemed to call for new approaches to, and new theories about, women's forms of self-representation.[3] Nonetheless, the argument about a separate women's tradition is worth reexamining—not simply because, as I believe, it misrepresents a significant number of women's texts, but because it involves a blindness about the writing of literary history. To oversimplify, recent studies of women's autobiography have tended to read women's texts as if gender were the hermeneutic key to authorial intention and textual production; they have assumed that gender determines the form of women's autobiography or, at least, that it motivates women writers to seek a separate autobiographical tradition. Other possibilities—that gender may not be a crucial factor in some autobiographical writing, that some women autobiographers may deliberately avoid a female literary tradition, or that a woman's autobiography may self-consciously invoke multiple literary traditions—have been overlooked or avoided. So, too, have possibilities that implicate editors and critics in the process of defining what constitutes "women's autobiography." The desire to define a women's tradition has, in other words, shaped the writing of literary history and practical criticism. I want, therefore, to reconsider the question of women's autobiography not by presupposing the existence of a tradition but instead by asking about possible traditions available to, acknowledged, or created by women writers. And I want to begin not by posing an alternate version of literary history, but by looking at early attempts to define "women's autobiography"—because as it turns out, modern literary critics are not the first to construct a tradition of women's autobiographical writing.

The effort to construct a literary past, a tradition of English autobiography that accounts for women's texts as well as men's, originated in the nineteenth century. By 1797 English literary critics had coined the term *autobiography* for a "new" genre.[4] Within three decades Victorian antiquarians, scholars, and critics had begun to resurrect and publish the texts we cite today when we write about the "emergence" or "origins" of women's autobiography: the *Memoirs of Ann Lady Fanshawe* (1829); *A Legacy, or Widow's Mite, Left by Alice Hayes* (1836); the *Autobiography of Mary Countess of Warwick* (1848); *The Autobiography of Mrs. Alice Thornton* (1875); *The Autobiography of Anne Lady Halkett* (1875); and numerous spiritual accounts written by Nonconformist women. Indeed, except for the autobiography of Margaret Cavendish, Duchess of Newcastle, which first appeared as part of her *Natures Pictures Drawn by Fancies Pencil to the Life* (1656), these seminal women's autobiographies would be lost to literary history were it not for the editorial efforts of the Victorians.

The Victorians rescued and wrote about these texts for reasons similar to our own: for their historical interest, for the social and familial information they contained, for their contribution to literary discussions of the "new" genre, for their relevance to their own lives. Thus nineteenth-century efforts at reconstructing literary history can illuminate our own contemporary efforts at delineating traditions of autobiography, whether men's, women's, or both. They can be used to challenge or affirm critical claims that the "male" tradition of autobiography excludes or misrepresents women's lives; that women's self-representation assumes a form different from men's, one that is "relational" or "contextual" rather than "positional" or "linear"; or that the traditions of male and female autobiography have developed separately—and, by implication, that critics do best to treat them separately.

The important nineteenth-century reconstructions of autobiographical traditions that I shall consider are these: (1) a tradition of spiritual autobiography, embodied in the documents of *The Friends' Library* (1837–1850), a collection that includes more than twenty accounts by Quaker women; (2) a tradition of domestic memoirs, represented not by a single collection but by the publications of various antiquarian societies (1829–1875); and (3) the women's texts chosen for Hunt and Clarke's groundbreaking *Autobiography* series (1826–1833), the first known attempt to create a literary collection of autobiographical writing. As we shall see, the question of "women's autobiography" has been vexed from its origins, with neither writers nor editors agreeing on the relevance of gender to genre.

Has women's autobiography been, from its origins, fundamentally different from men's? A great deal hangs on what one means by "origins." In her survey of "archetypal" women's autobiographies, Mary Mason argues this position categorically: "Nowhere in women's autobiographies do we find the patterns established by the two prototypical male autobiographers, Augustine and Rousseau." Augustine's use of a dramatic structure of conversion, where the "self is presented as the stage for a battle of opposing forces" and where "a climactic victory of one force—spirit defeating flesh—completes the drama of the self," is, according to Mason, essentially alien to women's self-conception; so, too, is Rousseau's "unfolding self-discovery where the characters and events are little more than aspects of the author's evolving consciousness."[5] Such an argument assumes that gender determines generic production—and not, as the late Paul de Man proposed, that what the autobiographer does is "governed by the technical demands of self-portraiture and thus determined, in all its aspects, by the resources of [the] medium."[6] In fact, one early nineteenth-century reconstruction of an autobiographical tradition suggests a view of self-construction quite different from Mason's and more compatible with de Man's; it used women's autobiographies to suggest that gender was an almost negligible concern of (or influence on) life writing.

Between 1837 and 1850 the Quaker historians William and Thomas Evans published a series of spiritual memoirs and journals that included both men's and women's texts, English and American. Their series, called *The Friends' Library*, had a non-literary agenda: it was meant to preserve the seminal texts of Quakerism and, through its representative auto/biographies,[7] set the standard for Quaker self-presentation in life and in print. As the prospectus explained, "It is both our duty and our interest to be intimately conversant with [the early Friends'] writings; to imitate their piety and devotedness, and to strive to be imbued with that fervour and heavenly mindedness which so conspicuously marked their example." The editors assumed, as was generally true for spiritual autobiography, that subsequent writers would imitate these autobiographical models, exemplary as they were in their "heavenly mindedness." They seem also to have assumed that women's and men's texts were equally suitable for institutionalizing as autobiography, equally based on seminal forms (like George Fox's *Journal*) and thus equally imitable by subsequent writers.[8]

Quite apart from stated intentions, what the women's autobiographies in *The Friends' Library* demonstrate is that seventeenth-century women writers readily engaged the traditional model of spiritual autobiography. They treated their lives as a struggle between opposing forces; they delineated a pattern of spiritual progress from bondage in sin to enlightenment and victory over the world, flesh, and devil; most importantly, they composed their lives without a sense that they were appropriating a "male" tradition or that their experiences were radically different from men's. These women's accounts belie the label of the Augustinian or Bunyanesque form as prototypically "male."[9] When, for example, Elizabeth Stirredge wrote *Strength in Weakness Manifest* (1711), included in the Evans collection as her *Life and Christian Testimony* (1838), she followed the general formula for Quaker autobiography, beginning with her earliest recollections of religious seriousness and her "dread and terror" in the contemplation of death. Her autobiography describes at great length her temptations to sin (the most serious being a hankering after "fine clothes"), her wanderings without spiritual guidance (like the children of Israel in the wilderness), her conviction of sin and conversion under Quaker preaching, and finally her persecutions for religious conscience.[10] Formally, Stirredge's account differs little from the male autobiographies included in the same volume. *A Brief Account of the Life and Travels of Thomas Wilson* contains the same testimony to youthful "hungerings and thirstings," the same prolonged conviction under Quaker preaching, the same detailing of religious persecution and perseverance.[11] Equally for the male Wilson and the female Stirredge, the structure of autobiography follows from the Quaker belief that spiritual reality is all-encompassing. Both their accounts rely heavily on the literary models provided by other Quaker accounts and, as Richard T. Vann has shown, on the Puritan literary heritage that many Quakers drew upon as they remembered and inscribed their religious pasts.[12]

Within the autobiographical tradition constructed by *The Friends' Library*, variations in form reveal little correlation with gender. Both men and women may report rebellious episodes (Elizabeth Ashbridge disobediently elopes at age fourteen, Joseph Pike confesses his delight in the company of "wild boys" so that he may digress on the importance of parental supervision). Either gender may incorporate dialogues that record serious clashes with worldly authority (Alice Hayes and Benjamin Bangs recapitulate doctrinal disputes with Anglican priests, Thomas Wilson harangues the Baptists). Both men and women recount their journeys as Quaker ministers (Jane Hoskens subtitles her life, *A Minister of the Gospel*, a claim possible for most of the autobiographers in the collection because Quakers expected the public testimony of both men and women).[13] Such formal homogeneity was encouraged within Quakerism, where a similarity in the representation of experience gave assurance of genuine conversion.

A stylistic homogeneity also marks *The Friends' Library*—in part because of the practice of the writers themselves, in part because of the editorial policies of William and Thomas Evans. Quaker autobiographers, like other Protestant writers, relied heavily on the language of scripture to recount their lives, the ideal being to merge the words of their texts with the divinely inspired words of the Bible. Thus Alice Hayes's multimetaphoric sentence: "Now was the refiner's fire very hot, in order to burn up the dross and the tin," which echoes the words of Malachi and Ezekiel to describe her trials under conviction of sin.[14] This stylistic practice was exacerbated (or improved, it depends on one's perspective) by an editorial decision to modernize and regularize the original documents. Because the Evanses felt that early Quaker texts were often "prolix and redundant," they made "a judicious selection and abridgment," thereby presenting the series "in a more attractive form, [its] intrinsic value enhanced."[15] Or so they claimed. While abridging, they also moderated extremes of style, thus eradicating many telling, individualistic features of style we today associate with autobiographical writing.

The point here is not to lament Quaker stylistics or editorial practice, but rather to stress the virtually genderless form of many early English autobiographies. In its first five volumes alone, *The Friends' Library* reproduces eight examples of women's autobiography, all of them showing women writers who worked comfortably within what today is identified as a masculine form. If these women perceived the world differently from men, they did not register their perceptions in the shape or style of their spiritual accounts.

Nor was their gender registered in special thematic concerns. Modern literary criticism assumes that women autobiographers will show a special facility or predilection for domestic themes, for the exploration of matters relating to marriage, children, or housewifery.[16] This assumption, complemented by modern psychological theories of women's "relational" approach to self-definition,[17] often predisposes critics to foreground those autobiographical episodes in which women writers touch on familial matters or domestic details. Of course such details appear, but no more frequently in women's spiritual accounts than in men's.

If we compare men's and women's autobiographies in *The Friends' Library* on the themes of marriage and the family, we discover that neither develops such themes, although occasionally they appear in the accounts of both. We know that Elizabeth Stirredge was married, for instance, only because the editors preface her account with "testimonies" from acquaintances who refer to her husband James. Stirredge herself gives no account of courtship or marriage; her husband appears incidentally (if effectually) in an episode about persecution, where the king's officers attempt to confiscate their personal goods and James protests with her against the action.[18] Jane Hoskens refers to her marriage in a subordinate clause, written to explain why she left the care of Quaker mentors in 1738; after the reference, she continues her narrative as if nothing special has occurred.[19] Another autobiographer, Mary Pennington, discusses her first and second marriages at some length, but primarily to explain her long search for religious truth.[20] So, too, for male autobiographers. Like Pennington, Joseph Pike gives some account of his marriage, though his interest lies in the "in-

struction and information" he can pass on: after naming his wife and listing their fourteen children, he goes on to cite several paragraphs of scrip-
tural texts that stress the importance of seeking God's light in marriage.
And it may be only coincidental that we read details of courtship in a male
autobiography, Benjamin Bangs's *Life and Convincement*. Bangs's encounters with Mary Lowe, his future wife, occur as interstices between records of his journeys as a Quaker minister. "Although we had often met
together before in our Journeys," he comments, "I never so much as mention'd, one Word of Courtship to her; though my Spirit was closely united
in a divine Fellowship with her."[21] One does not question his silence, given
the tendency of Quaker accounts to efface such moments. The repression
of romance becomes even more complete in *The Friends' Library* version,
where the editors eliminate Bangs's reference to courtship and summarize
his word to Mary Lowe as an "impart[ation]" of his mind.[22] Perhaps the
editors wished to lift Bangs's account to the same level of heavenly-
mindedness that George Fox demanded in his teaching on marriage: "as it
was in the beginning, before sin and defilement was."[23]

Whatever the editorial motive, the tendency to efface details of romance and domesticity demonstrates the powerful operation of generic
conventions and editorial practice on the autobiographer's self-construction—whether the writer is male or female, whether we understand that
operation to occur as the writer lives her life or as she later converts it into
textual form. The spiritual autobiography, unlike the domestic memoir,
does not concern itself with marriage and the family.

Such generic power asserts itself most peculiarly in the spiritual autobiographer's treatment of children, ultimately to the point of obscuring
meaning. One might think that women autobiographers would devote
more space to children and childrearing than men, that they would stress
their maternal concerns even as they detail their inner struggles or report
their travels in the ministry. Indeed, the best female autobiographer in the
Quaker tradition titled her autobiography *A Legacy, or Widow's Mite,
Left by Alice Hayes to Her Children and Others*, and she rationalizes her
authorship by explaining that it is "for the encouragement of the young to
faithfulness and continual trust and confidence in the Lord." But this rationalization was equally common among male writers: Joseph Pike similarly writes "for the benefit and instruction of my children" and "for others
also," while Joseph Oxley prefaces his journal with an address to his children, admonishing them "to follow me, in like manner, only in greater degrees of purity."[24] If we label Hayes's autobiographical stance "maternal,"
then Pike's and Oxley's must be also.

More perplexing is the indeterminacy of the word *children* in the titles of many such autobiographies. Does Hayes refer to her own children or to spiritual offspring, including the reader, left to her care? Perhaps both, for Hayes mentions that her first husband, Daniel Smith, was "an indulgent father to our children," but she also frames her text with prayers for "all the babes and lambs of God."[25] Yet in Elizabeth Stirredge's autobiography the reader can never determine if the "children" are anything other than Quakers under spiritual guidance. When she warns "my dear children" of the "subtle devices" of "the enemy of your immortal soul," she may refer to either natural or spiritual offspring. When she later recounts her testimony before King Charles II, including a plea for the end "of persecuting and shedding the blood of my dear children," she refers to all Quakers. Within the text the referent is never fixed. Stirredge's "maternal" stance becomes a function of her writerly role. This stance demands—for male and female autobiographer alike—the nurturing of a spiritual community.[26]

The minimizing of romantic and domestic concerns in the spiritual autobiography—or, more specifically, in the autobiographical tradition that *The Friends' Library* reconstructs—should challenge the modern critical assumption that gender is always the operative force in self-writing. It should lead us to ask whether theory and criticism of women's autobiography proceeds most perceptively when it emphasizes sexual difference. One might, of course, interpret the documents in the Evans collection and the construction of literary history they represent in different ways. One might argue that the women who wrote such accounts were exceptional or anomalous, or that gender was necessarily a secondary issue among radical English sects under persecution, or that spiritual accounts allow only limited views of human experience. These interpretations—psychological, sociological, literary—have a certain validity, but the existence of such a large body of women's documents contradicts categorical assertions about a distinctively gender-linked origin and history of women's autobiography. More likely, as Nancy Armstrong has argued in *Desire and Domestic Fiction*, "gender" is a category of modern invention, subsuming and even denying the relevance of older categories such as class, status, or religion.[27] In *The Friends' Library* the Evans brothers meant to reassert the importance of one of those older categories by preserving autobiographical texts in which the religious was all-important and by editing out details that might hint of other means by which to interpret life experiences.

If *The Friends' Library* institutionalized a form of women's autobiography that avoided or minimized issues of gender, a different editorial trend helped to authorize a form that was explicitly feminine. This trend was the publication of archival materials that came with no generic label but that increasingly came to be called "autobiography" by their editors. The form they reproduced was, in today's terms, the domestic (or family) memoir, a *res gestae* account rooted not in a conception of an individual self or a religious soul but in the autobiographer as recorder of communal history.

As a form of women's writing, the domestic memoir dates back to the seventeenth century, the earliest examples emerging contemporaneously with the earliest spiritual autobiographies (1654 for Anna Trapnel's *Legacy for Saints*, 1656 for Margaret Cavendish's *True Relation of My Birth, Breeding, and Life*). The domestic memoir placed great emphasis on social continuity and family service in public causes, thus revealing its essentially upper-class origins and modes of self-definition. Indeed, the use of the word *legacy* in the title of many spiritual autobiographies suggests that some lower- and middle-class writers were consciously echoing their secular, aristocratic counterparts but offering a spiritual inheritance instead of a corruptible earthly one of status and wealth. While the forms of the spiritual autobiography and domestic memoir may be historically linked, however, they represent radically different ways of representing subjectivity. The spiritual autobiography focuses on the individual writer's progress or regress, whereas the memoir tends to stress the writer's place in an extended family unit and to make her (since most such writers were female) the repository of its significant accomplishments, more likely those of a husband or a father than her own.

Ann Lady Fanshawe's *Memoirs* (1829) delineates the typical pattern and its conventional features.[28] Lady Fanshawe's account originates in a desire to pass on both her personal and the familial history to children. She addresses her words to her "most dear and only son," beginning not with memories from her own childhood but instead with several paragraphs of Polonius-like advice (pp. 2–4) and a hagiographic character sketch of her late husband, the boy's father (pp. 5–9). She includes two long segments of genealogy, one tracing the paternal line (pp. 9–25), the other the maternal (pp. 25–32), both giving details of the family estates, finances, and public honors. When the narrative proper gets underway, the *Memoirs* follows the career of Lady Fanshawe's husband, who served as Secretary of War to Charles II (then Prince of Wales), later as ambassador to Portugal and Spain.

Because Ann Fanshawe witnessed foreign court life in its official pomp and its unofficial details, her account records many political events from a "feminine" perspective. She takes particular note, for instance, of the perquisites she receives as ambassador's wife, right down to the large silver chocolate pot, twelve fine filigree cups, two large silver salvers, and twelve fine saceret napkins that the English merchants of Seville presented to her and her husband on their arrival from England (p. 204). Because the account is also a domestic memorial, she includes many intimate stories about her marriage, including her husband's tears on their first separation (p. 45), her secret visits while he was imprisoned in Whitehall (pp. 116–17), and even her assumption of cabin boy's garb so that she could fight by his side when pirates attacked their ship (pp. 91–93). In its structure, Fanshawe's is a typically seventeenth-century account: it ends when Sir Richard's life ends. Fanshawe finds it within her power (or desire) only to describe his funeral and then her father's death before she breaks off the narrative.

Despite the autobiographical elements of this and other such documents, and despite their early emergence in the history of self-writing, the domestic memoir was not recognized as an autobiographical form until the nineteenth century. Certainly it was not considered a public or publishable form until then. With the exception of Margaret Cavendish's *True Relation* (1656), all the now-famous memoirs of seventeenth-century women, including Fanshawe's, were kept privately within family archives and published only two centuries later by descendants or antiquarians. When published, the accounts increasingly came to include "autobiography" in the title or editorial preface, as the following chronological listing suggests: the *Life of Mrs. Lucy Hutchinson* (1806), *A Pairt of the Life of Lady Margaret Cunninghame* (1827), the *Memoirs of Lady Fanshawe* (1829), the *Autobiography of Mary Countess of Warwick* (1848), the *Autobiography of Mrs. Alice Thornton* (1875), the *Autobiography of Anne Lady Halkett* (1875). Even Cavendish's account, published during her lifetime in *Natures Pictures Drawn by Fancies Pencil to the Life*, was issued separately only in 1814 by Sir Egerton Brydges, who attached the label "auto-biography" that has stayed with it ever since.

It is worth asking why these texts were published first and in such numbers in the nineteenth century and why they were then given the literary designation of *autobiography* (rather than, say, *history*).[29] A simple answer would note, of course, that the term *autobiography* did not become established until the nineteenth century, along with rising interest in the genre; thus, not until the nineteenth century were these older texts likely to attract literary attention or fashionable terminology. A more complicated answer would point to the cultural conditions—and contradictions—that authorized these forms as "women's autobiography"; it would include consideration of what critics and editors said about such women's texts, what they praised and blamed, what they sanctioned and omitted.

Nineteenth-century editors seem to have been uncommonly nervous

about publishing women's private documents, but they nevertheless articulated the case for doing so and, in the process, authorized certain kinds
of life writing as legitimately feminine. Charles Jackson, editor of Alice
Thornton's autobiography, expresses a common rationale for going public
when he states that such specimens, "hid among the archives of many of
our ancient houses," deserve to be shared with the English nation; "from
their intrinsic merit, [they] have a right to be considered *publici* as well as
privati juris."[30] What does he mean by "intrinsic merit"? One criterion for
merit was historical. Like Charles Jackson, Lady Halkett's editor stresses
"the value of the historical information which she actually imparts"; Lady
Warwick's, the "great historical value" of such records of "the domestic
occurrences of the period, soon after the restoration of Charles II"; the
preface to Lady Fanshawe's *Memoirs* claims that, whether the work "be
read for the historical information which it contains, or with no higher
motive than for amusement," it will "more than amply gratify either object"; Lucy Hutchinson's editor praises the ability of the work to make the
reader feel "a party in the transactions which are recounted."[31]

Amplifying the claims of these last two editors, both nineteenth- and
twentieth-century scholars have added appeals to literary merit to assertions of historical value, praising the works as lively, imaginative examples
of an evolving genre or arguing for them as "contributions to the early development of the English secular autobiography."[32] Despite the defensibil-
ity of the historical and aesthetic claims, the evidence for literary influence
is dubious—at least as formulated by twentieth-century critics. Few (virtually none) of these domestic memoirs were published until the Victorian
period, at which point the secular tradition of autobiography had already
been shaped by male writers. We need another explanation for the Victorian publication of these seventeenth-century accounts and the promotion of their nineteenth-century equivalents, a promotion that did, subsequently, influence a tradition of autobiography.

These documents represent, I think, a literary manifestation of the doc-
trine of separate spheres—at best a form of commitment to the private and
domestic, at worst a form of compensation for loss of the public and
professional. The seventeenth-century women who wrote family memoirs
stayed, as writers, safely within the domestic realm. Their texts were thus
exemplary for would-be Victorian women writers. The memoir—domestic in its focus, relational in its mode of self-construction—allowed women
to write as mothers, daughters, and wives. It allowed them to represent
their lives in terms of "good" feminine plots. It did not, however, allow
women writers to develop—or disturb—the primary male traditions of

autobiography: the public, *res gestae* account of professional life or the more introspective form of spiritual confession.

That there is a cultural link between the publication of seventeenth-century memoirs and the remarkable increase of nineteenth-century domestic memoirs is suggested by the bibliographical records. Whereas women wrote and published significant numbers of spiritual autobiographies from the mid-seventeenth century to the early eighteenth, by the nineteenth century such women autobiographers had virtually disappeared.[33] Instead, women with religious inclinations turned inward to spiritual diaries or outward to what William Matthews categorizes as autobiographies of "clergymen's wives"—actually domestic memoirs of life in a vicarage or on the mission field.[34] At the same time, in the secular arena, editors resurrected memoirs by diplomats' and soldiers' wives like Ann Fanshawe and Lucy Hutchinson and encouraged nineteenth-century equivalents written by women who traveled with their husbands to India, Egypt, the West Indies, and the Far East, published under such titles as *Foreign Courts and Foreign Homes*, *Our Home in Cyprus*, *At Home in India*, or *Garden of Fidelity*.[35] So, too, in the memoirs of Anne Halkett and Alice Thornton, the Victorians edited women's perspectives on the disruptions of the Interregnum, just as they published books by their own politicians' and diplomats' wives on domestic conditions during colonial and internal crises. And they published numerous examples of what William Matthews calls simply "domestic and family life," accounts in which women recorded their memories and the social mores of Victorian Britain.[36] Thus was the domestic memoir institutionalized as an appropriately feminine form of autobiography, as a model for female subjectivity and self-representation.

We should not lose sight of the fact, however, that it was Victorian editors and critics who authorized these works as "women's" autobiography. Had the texts come to light at a different cultural moment, they might not have been labeled "autobiography" at all. But because a feminine sensibility and certain nascent structures seemed evident in seventeenth-century women's self-writing, literary history—in the form of ancient manuscripts and modern critical commentary—seemed to validate the notion of a separate autobiographical sphere and the development of a female autobiographical tradition. After all, didn't the memoirs of these female predecessors represent the origins of women's autobiography? Didn't these original and originating texts add historical weight to the enterprise of writing domestic memoirs and give a sense of a female tradition that women needed?[37]

As I have been arguing, origins are created, not found; traditions constructed, not discovered. The fact that the Victorians created—or, rather, believed they had discovered—a generic link between seventeenth-century women's texts and those of their own era is the significant point. In fact, the texts they resuscitated did not represent a unified feminine tradition or a coherent genre. If we relinquish the nineteenth-century perspective, we can see that Lady Halkett's account reads like a historical romance; Lady Cunninghame's, a legal deposition; Lady Warwick's, a spiritual confession but without the religious ecstasies or hermeneutic vagaries of sectarian practitioners. Alice Thornton's autobiography was compiled from four discrete books of record, its basic structure (so far as we can tell) suggesting a spiritual diary with meditations following each entry.[38] Even within a single autobiography, we can find different modes of self-expression—as in Lady Cunninghame's, which uses a plain, factual style in the primary text but shifts to highly abstract, typological discourse in an extended address to her husband.[39] Despite such diversity, Victorians treated these accounts as a generic unit, as part of a continuous literary tradition. And they gave the texts and the tradition coherence by stressing a fundamental quality: a feminine mode of self-conception.

This mode I shall designate, following modern psychological terminology, as relational. According to theorists like Nancy Chodorow and Carol Gilligan, women's ways of conceiving the self focus on relationships with another person or group. In Chodorow's terms, "the basic feminine sense of self is connected to the world; the basic masculine sense of self is separate." Girls emerge from childhood "with a basis for 'empathy' built into their primary definition of self in a way that boys do not"; they "come to define and experience themselves as continuous with others; their experience of self contains more flexible and permeable ego boundaries." In contrast, boys have "engaged, or been required to engage, in a more emphatic individuation and a more defensive firming of experienced ego boundaries"; hence, their self-conceptions tend to be "positional" rather than "relational."[40] Nineteenth-century editors did not, of course, refer to modern psychology when they characterized seventeenth-century women's texts. But judging from editorial prefaces and critical reviews, we can recognize a comparable language for interpreting women's experience. For virtually every text, the critical commentary and rhetorical weight fall on the woman writer's achievements as daughter, wife, and mother.

Editors viewed these early women autobiographers—and believed these women viewed themselves—in relational terms, in their connections with fathers and mothers, husbands and children. For example, Ann Lady Fanshawe's editor characterizes his authoress as "a beautiful example of female devotion" (p. xxxiv). Although he notes her "literary merits" (p. ix) and frequently remarks on the fascinating historical information she conveys, the self he conceives for his subject is that of wife and mother—as in his descriptive sequence, "an accomplished and clever woman, the wife of one of the most faithful servants of Charles the First and Charles the Second" (p. vi). His emphasis in analyzing her autobiography lies on Lady Fanshawe's feminine virtues, those "instances of conjugal devotion, of maternal excellence, and of enduring fortitude under calamities, which render her a bright example to posterity" (p. ix).

Certainly these seventeenth-century women understood their lives in relation to others. Lucy Hutchinson composed her autobiography (a fragment, never finished) to accompany her massive biographical memorial, the *Memoirs of the Life of Colonel Hutchinson*. Margaret Cavendish, after multiple and contradictory attempts at self-definition, finally concluded her autobiography with an unadorned, relational formula: "I was daughter to one Master Lucas of St. Johns, near Colchester, in Essex, second wife to the Lord Marquis of Newcastle; for my Lord having had two Wives, I might easily have been mistaken, especially if I should dye and my Lord Marry again" (p. 310). And Lady Halkett seems to have found the conclusion to her narrative only when she accepted Sir James and agreed to define herself as his wife; her account may be a quest for a relational (rather than individual) self-definition.

But what signifies more—at least for the institutionalizing of women's autobiography—are the rhetorical maneuvers by which nineteenth-century editors made relational self-definitions not only superior to, but identical with, literary merit. When Sir Egerton Brydges, the editor of Margaret Cavendish's account, states that "her Grace wanted taste," that she "had not the talent of seizing that *selection* of circumstances," that she "knew not what to obtrude, and what to leave out" (pp. 262–63), he refers to her literary productions generally. From this judgment, however, he excludes her biography, the *Life of William Cavendish, Duke of Newcastle*, and presumably her own pendant autobiography. These productions reveal her "great fault" less, Brydges claims, because they are "domestic." Brydges thus implies that the domestic memoirist cannot praise her husband too excessively, that the reader does not expect aesthetic balance anyway, that the evidence of feminine virtue is what really matters in a woman's autobiography.

More subtly, Ann Fanshawe's editor attributes a woman's literary fame to domestic merit. Unlike Cavendish's editor, Fanshawe's praises the style, thought, and reliable historical sense of his authoress: "Celebrated as this country is for female talent and virtue, there is no one with whom Lady Fanshawe may not be compared and gain by the comparison" (pp. viii–ix). But as his link of "talent" and "virtue" hints, the former depends on the latter. The subsequent comments make explicit the point that, in order to achieve a lasting place in the literary canon, a woman writer must be "a bright example to posterity" (p. ix).

The critical responses and rhetorical choices of Victorian editors allow us to sense the immense pressure on contemporary women to make their autobiographies domestic, their self-conceptions relational. These editors express (and helped shape) Victorian assumptions about the proper modes of women's self-writing. One consequence of such assumptions was the rise of the Victorian domestic memoir. Another was the inclusion of domestic patterns—plots of sisterhood, motherhood, conjugal life—in the autobiography of virtually every major Victorian woman writer, even when such patterns caused disjunctions in narrative structure.[41] A third was a fundamental confusion in literary history. Victorian women who wrote autobiography came to believe that they had inherited a domestic tradition from their female predecessors. In reality, they inherited it not so much from female predecessors as from male editors who transmitted to them their literary heritage.

If we compare the editorial work of *The Friends' Library* with the archival (re)productions of seventeenth-century women's memoirs, we can sense the contradictions that Victorian women faced when they conceived of writing autobiography. The two traditions implied different ways of constructing the self: one essentially genderless, the other highly gendered; one inner and psychological, the other social and domestic; one religious, the other secular. Women autobiographers might, of course, have aligned themselves with a tradition simply on the basis of this last difference: religious versus secular. But for writers interested in autobiography as literary production, the choice was not so clear-cut, not simply a matter of religious affiliation or secular interest. As a literary form, women's autobiography was institutionalized with the contradictions embedded in it.

These contradictions appear in the first collection of autobiography as a literary genre. Beginning in 1826, the publishers John Hunt and Cowden Clarke issued a series titled *Autobiography: A Collection of the Most Instructive and Amusing Lives Ever Published, Written by the Parties Themselves*. To my knowledge, the series is the first of its kind, the first to capitalize on the newly named genre and to attempt the construction of an autobiographical canon. Hunt and Clarke explained their project simply as "a diversified study of the human character." But their advertisement in the inaugural volume featured a list of forthcoming works classified by the autobiographers' public roles: statesmen (Sully, Bubb Doddington), men of genius and literature (Gibbon, Hume, Marmontel), religious enthusiasts (John Wesley, George Whitfield), artists (Benvenuto Cellini), dramatists and players (Colley Cibber, Goldini), mystics and imposters (William Lilly, James Hardy Vaux).[42]

Despite the wide range of lives projected, no woman's name appeared in the original list, an omission that suggests either the limited roles available to women or their exclusion from autobiography as a genre—or both.[43] Nonetheless, by the end of 1826 Hunt and Clarke must have decided to add samples of women's autobiographical writing, for volume 7 reproduces the *Memoirs of Mrs. Robinson*, a well-known actress better known as mistress of the Prince of Wales, and *A Narrative of the Life of Mrs. Charlotte Charke*, the daughter of Colley Cibber better known as a transvestite actress.

The first autobiography in volume 7, the *Memoirs of Mrs. Robinson*, seems to adopt feminine roles so readily that it is almost parodic. Its two plot lines juxtapose the autobiographer's progress in one set of roles (daughter, mother) against her regress in the other (wife, mistress). The main plot traces the fall of a beautiful young woman from chastity to infidelity. As Mary Robinson looks back on her history, she sees a sensitive, talented girl—too soon left unprotected by her father (who heads for America with his paramour), too soon married to a dissembling London rake (who neglects her for his many mistresses), too readily exposed to the temptations of the stage (where male viewers accost her virtue), and too fondly charmed by the amorous supplications of a prince (who falls in love with "Perdita" and loses interest after she becomes his lover). This plot repeats the pattern of the *chroniques scandaleuses*, one that depends upon its writer's sex to titillate the reader and then evoke pity. Mary Robinson refuses to complete this plot, however, and breaks off just before she consummates her affair with the prince, leaving it to her daughter to complete the account posthumously.

The intervention of Mrs. Robinson's daughter as editor—indeed, as coauthor and corroborator of her mother's account—represents a characteristically nineteenth-century modification of the memoir form. The daughter's appearance in the text also validates a second plot: that of Robinson as a loving mother and faithful daughter. As autobiographer, Robinson superimposes this plot on the less commendable course of her actions as a wife, explaining her marriage to Thomas Robinson as an act of filial obedience and her fidelity to him, even during the worst of his profligacies, as a commitment to children and, more broadly, the family.[44] Throughout her autobiography Robinson repeatedly juxtaposes these two feminine plots, disturbing the smooth narrative of the scandalous plot with suggestions for an alternative reading. With the maternal plot that punctuates the *Memoirs* she hopes to counter—and thus redeem—her tale of a woman's fall.

Robinson draws attention to the maternal plot in various ways: through rhetorical excess, through abrupt interruptions of the narrative with baby stories, through episodes of maternal solicitude and filial piety.[45] Her nineteenth-century publishers seem to have approved such rhetorical tactics, for while they admit "some little negative disingenuousness," they also suggest that the account "show[s] the exposed situation of an unprotected beauty" and, unlike other "autobiography of this class," it is not "dangerous" (p. v). That they judge the *Memoirs* to be without danger suggests a need to rationalize its risqué elements. But it also suggests a shrewd patriarchal sense that, whether scandalous or maternal, Robinson's autobiographical modes are safe because they stay carefully within the prescribed limits of the "feminine." The shape of the *Memoirs* is determined by gender, by the social roles allotted to women and by literary traditions identified as feminine. These roles stay under the protection of men, at least officially. Even when a female is left socially "unprotected," as Mary Robinson was, she remains literarily enclosed within a safe autobiographical form by her male editors.

Or almost safe. For within Robinson's *Memoirs*, conventional as the account may seem, is a third plot not subject to restrictions of gender. This plot, the account of an artist's career, also punctuates the main narrative, although not as deliberately or coherently as the maternal. During her lifetime Mary Robinson succeeded, as she reminds us, in the roles of actress, novelist, and poet; indeed, her autobiography commemorates this artistic achievement. She demonstrates her verbal ability in the gothic word-painting that opens the *Memoirs* and in scenes of her dramatic recitations of poetry as a child. While she narrates the course of her marriage, she inserts details of her artistic interests—of female friends who write novels (pp. 48–49), of an actress she admires (p. 54), of her first attempt at publication to avoid imprisonment for debt (p. 71), of the patronage of the duchess of Devonshire (pp. 75–77), of her various dramatic roles (pp. 89–90).

Such artistic experiences resist subordination to domestic concerns. Robinson may claim that she turned to poetry and then the theatre to support herself and her daughter, but she never fully convinces us that maternal motives dominated her actions. We sense a real pleasure when circumstances make it possible for her to venture into print, just as we recognize her delight in the fame that her theatrical career accrued. But Robinson's accounts of her artistic experiences, though they disrupt the more conventional feminine modes of self-construction, show her straining between contradictory autobiographical impulses.

For example, when the playwright Richard Sheridan visits Robinson at home to persuade her to appear at the Drury Lane Theatre, she gives this record of their encounter:

> I was then some months advanced in a state of domestic solicitude, and my health seemed in a precarious state, owing to my having too long devoted myself to the duties of a mother in nursing my eldest daughter Maria. It was in this lodging that, one morning, wholly unexpectedly, Mr Brereton made us a second visit, bringing with him a friend, whom he introduced on entering the drawing-room. This stranger was Mr Sheridan.
>
> I was overwhelmed with confusion: I know not why; but I felt a sense of mortification when I observed that my appearance was carelessly *dishabillé*, and my mind as little prepared for what I guessed to be the motive of his visit. I however soon recovered my recollection, and the theatre was consequently the topic of discourse. (p. 82)

Why was Robinson overwhelmed with confusion? We might dismiss her claim, "I know not why," as duplicity, in that Robinson knows retrospectively that her *dishabillé* aroused Sheridan's desire and encouraged his quest as a lover. But the confusion is more complex. Then and years later, when Robinson wrote the autobiography, it was unclear what role she should assume, what self she should construct: the devoted mother greeting a friendly visitor? the erotic object confronting a male viewer? the aspiring actress negotiating with a theatre-owner? Such confusion plagues the entire account, with Robinson alternating details of her dramatic career with comments about her infants' illnesses or her husband's infidelities or her filial relationships. As autobiographer, she seems caught between a (masculine) tradition of public self-presentation and a (feminine) tradition of private self-revelation, between the forms of the "autobiography" or *res gestae* "memoir," on the one hand, and the "diary" or "domestic memoir," on the other.

On the whole, Robinson shows little desire to escape feminine modes. Her tale of Meribah Lorrington, the governess who received a "masculine education" (p. 20) and taught young Mary all she knew, haunts the *Memoirs* as a negative example of the woman who dares to pursue male models. Meribah takes to drink and ends up in the Chelsea workhouse—in Robinson's words, "almost naked" and "completely disfigured." Disfiguration, represented by a marring of facial features and an absence of clothing, is the punishment for "masculine" achievement. The nakedness, the stripping away of sartorial protection, recalls Robinson's obsession with feminine costume and her terror of its absence. We can read her numerous descriptions of dress, ridiculously frequent and detailed in the *Memoirs*, as defensive strategies to ward off the fate of Meribah. She fears that to be without appropriate feminine dress is to be without identity. Perhaps she also fears what we suspect—that feminine identity is only a matter of dress. In any case, she fears patriarchal retribution for seeking to find out.

Robinson's counterpart in volume 7, however, records a different story about a woman's assumption of male models. In a sense, we can read the *Narrative of the Life of Mrs. Charlotte Charke*, an actress famous for cross-dressing, as a version of Meribah Lorrington's tale writ large. Officially— that is, in the view of her eighteenth-century contemporaries, her nineteenth-century editors, and most of her modern readers—Charke's life traces a course of failure in virtually every feminine role: wife, daughter, sister, even actress. Charke confesses that she married too young and foolishly, only to discover within "the first twelvemonth of her connubial estate" that her husband had an "insatiate fondness for the plurality of common wretches, that were to be had for half-a-crown."[46] She also admits that she damaged her career as a London actress by quarreling with Fleetwood, manager of the Haymarket, and then behaving capriciously after he agreed to take her back. That Charke failed in the role of daughter is demonstrated by the entire *Life*, which she published in an attempt to regain the affection of her father, Colley Cibber. In these repeated examples of failure, Charke reenacts what Patricia Meyer Spacks identifies as the most pervasive of eighteenth-century feminine plots: that of woman as victim, as sufferer of marital, filial, or social wrong.[47]

The editorial apparatus that surrounds Charke's text urges us to read this plot as the dominant pattern of its author's life. Hunt and Clarke introduce Charlotte as a creature more "whimsical, wild, heartless, and unprincipled" than her brother; they characterize her tale as one of those "weeds" that "may spring up . . . in the hot-bed of corrupt civilization" (pp. v–vi). Lest this seem too gentle a warning for the errant (female) reader, they conclude Charke's life with a "sequel" giving the known facts of her history from 1755, when she published her account, to 1759, the year of her death. The sequel reports the visit of a bookseller to "a wretched thatched hovel" near the New River Head, "where it was usual for the scavengers to deposit the sweepings of the streets" (p. 165). Surrounded by refuse and attended only by a "squalid handmaid," we get our final glimpse of Charlotte

on a broken chair under the mantle-piece, by a fire merely sufficient to put us in mind of starving. At our author's feet, on the flounce of her dirty petticoat, reclined a dog, almost a skeleton, who saluted us with a snarl. . . . A magpie was perched on the top rail of her chair, and on her lap was placed a pair of mutilated bellows— the pipe was gone. These were used as a succedaneum for a writing-desk, on which lay her hopes and treasure, the manuscript of her novel. (p. 166)

Whether we feel sympathy or only (as the editor recommends) "surprise," the sequel suggests that we interpret Charke's fate as self-victimization; her misfortunes as "altogether of her own creating" (p. 167). In this addendum she is duly punished for her masculine aspirations. Her writerly instruments have been taken away; her treasured manuscript is sold for ten guineas. Whether she has been physically punished for assuming male costume we cannot tell—except that the "squalid handmaid" who lives with her is sexually ambiguous, identified as a woman only by "a blue apron, indicating, what was otherwise doubtful, that it was a female." The sequel remains silent about Charke's appearance.

Despite this effort to make Charke's autobiography conform to a recognizable feminine plot, we can see, if we will, that our responses are manipulated by editorial practice. Hunt and Clarke added sequels to all the lives that lacked them.[48] But if we compare the 1755 edition with their version of 1827, we find no final episode of degradation in the former. Rather, in the original conclusion Charke reaffirms her confidence in the eventual restoration of fatherly affection and declares her "design to pass in the Catalogue of Authors," promising her readers that she "will endeavour to produce something now and then to make them laugh."[49] This note of good humor carries over to the dedication—written at the completion of the autobiography but printed at its beginning—which Charke addresses to herself, "your real friend." We can treat this self-dedication as evidence of the author's pathetic isolation, of her lack of other friends. But we might better read it as a brilliant commentary on the autobiographical act. Autobiography demands, Charke implies, an act of self-performance. If the autobiographer writes to herself as well as to others, she may or may not persuade the others, but she will through "prudence" and "reflection" come finally to know herself—and "for once to call you, FRIEND," says Charke affirmatively, "a name I never as yet have known you by."[50] This is self-acceptance, not self-victimization.

What I am suggesting is that we—like Victorian readers—have learned

to read Charlotte Charke's *Life* through the eyes of its editors, who incorporated her text into a tradition of feminine autobiography only by misrepresenting its form.[51] These editors imposed a conventional shape on it
by emphasizing latent features, adding others, and repressing idiosyncratic
elements. They made her autobiography conformable to their sense of feminine self-writing, even though the work resists, formally and thematically,
such conformity. Why should they have done so?

The motives lie in the danger of Charke's autobiographical approach.
Charke claims a universal application for her narrative: "I have, I think,
taken care . . . that every person who reads my volume may bear a part in
some circumstance or other in the perusal, as there is nothing inserted but
what may daily happen to every mortal breathing" (p. 10). This claim to
represent universal human experience is conventional in early autobiography, its corollary being the readerly habit of searching an auto/biographical
text for personal applications of its episodes or morals. Universal applica-
bility, however, is precisely what Hunt and Clarke wish to deny Charke's
Life. To them the text is "curious," marked by the "extreme singularity" of
its author; it traces the career of a "reckless and anomalous individual";
Charke is a *"lusus naturae* of the moral world" (pp. v–vi). The question
seems to be whether or not Charke, a female writer, may legitimately claim
to represent human experience. Given the deliberate contrast with Robinson's autobiography (the two texts comprise the same volume), we might
surmise that the editors refuse to allow this possibility; instead they present
Charke as a wayward female who is thus anomalous of acceptable feminine
experience. Despite their attempt in the sequel to normalize her account,
the editors seem to recognize a fundamental and irremediable deviation
from feminine patterns. And thus they deny Charke access to—perhaps
deny the existence of—universal patterns of autobiography.

Read apart from its editorial apparatus, Charke's *Life* challenges the
notion of gender-specific patterns of autobiography. The content of the text
focuses on acts of cross-dressing, both social and dramatic, thus arguing
by example that autobiographical writing can be androgynous, if not genderless. During her lifetime Charke made her reputation as a transvestite
actress, beginning her career with successes in feminine roles (Lucy in
George Barnwell, Arabella in *The Fair Quaker*, Thalia in *Triumph of Love
and Honor*), but soon shifting to male parts (Lord Place in *Pasquin*, Rod-
erigo in *Othello*, George in *George Barnwell*, and, her most famous,
MacHeath in *The Beggar's Opera*). About the same time she assumed masculine roles in the theatre, she took to men's clothing in real life. She claims
she did so "for some substantial reasons" (p. 56), the telling of which she

"beg[s] to be excused, as it concerns no mortal now living but myself" (p. 161). All we can deduce from the *Life* is that her "substantial" reasons are partly erotic, partly financial: they are intimately connected with a man she privately "marries" and whose death deprives her "of every hope and means of support" (p. 55).

We should not exaggerate the financial motives, however, for several episodes in the *Life* make it clear that money is not the fundamental issue. Charke begins her autobiography with an episode of cross-dressing meant to reveal the natural bent of her personality: as a child of four, she dresses up in periwig and hat, waistcoat and sword, hoping to be taken for "the perfect representative of my sire" (p. 13). As an adolescent, she takes up riding and shooting, "coming home laden with feathered spoil" and imagining herself "equal to the best fowler or marksman in the universe" (pp. 19–20); she also sets herself up as a physician (pp. 23–26), works as the family gardener (pp. 26–28), defends the house against robbery (pp. 29–30), even takes to horse-trading (pp. 31–32). As an adult, now in male costume, she courts a wealthy young orphan (pp. 64–69), becomes valet to Lord Anglesea (pp. 82–83), takes up as a higgler "in breeches" (p. 84), serves as a waiter in a public house (pp. 95–100), and travels as a strolling actor for nine years under the assumed name of "Mr. Brown," all the while keeping company with a "Mrs. Brown." As this enumeration of episodes suggests, Charke emphasizes her "masculine" preferences through the narrative structure of the autobiography.

Hunt and Clarke never name Charke's transvestism; instead, they refer to her besetting sin as "vagabondism" (p. v).[52] This inability to name Charke's sexual activities may represent the same sort of prudery that moved Hunt and Clarke's contemporary, Thomas Bowdler, to publish an expurgated Shakespeare. But "vagabondism," euphemistic as it sounds, nonetheless describes Charke's social and literary predicament: by acting and writing as a man, she is deemed guilty of its root meaning (Latin *vagari*), of wandering, erring, straying from the prescribed feminine path. This (mis)naming allows the editor to categorize Charke's social crime and justifiably attach the sequel of her shame.

More important, it helps to obscure what was of greater danger than Charke's deviance: her literary cross-dressing. In many features the *Narrative of the Life of Mrs. Charlotte Charke* is a work of what the nineteenth century came to consider "masculine" autobiography. Charke assumes the stance of a male autobiographer, explicitly rejecting conventional female roles and trying out various male substitutes. The danger is not simply that she scorns feminine pursuits—as when she reports that she had little acquaintance "with that necessary utensil . . . of a young lady's education, called a needle" but adds that she understood French well before young ladies were traditionally employed in "ornamenting a piece of canvas with beasts, birds, and the alphabet" (p. 12). Nor is there real danger in the masculine content of the *Life*, in Charke's recital of the male roles she assumed; after all, she admits failure (or frustration) in many of these guises. The danger of Charke's writing lies in its autobiographical mode. This is the mode that Mary G. Mason terms "Rousseauian" and claims that no woman autobiographer has ever adopted. Rousseau's mode in the *Confessions*—"an unfolding self-discovery where characters and events are little more than aspects of the author's evolving consciousness"—stands, according to Mason, in marked contrast to the relational mode of women's self-writing, which recognizes the "real presence" of other consciousnesses and grounds identity "through relation to the chosen other."[53] Whether we name the mode after Rousseau, or call it pre-Romantic, or late picaresque, or simply "masculine," the point seems to be that male autobiographers move through experience, taking from it and others what they choose, whereas women autobiographers live within contexts, being shaped by others who share the space.

If we place Charlotte Charke anywhere in these dichotomies, it must be with Rousseau and men and taking on all kinds of experiences. Despite her references to husband, child, lovers, sisters, brother, mother, and even father, she does not finally define her identity through such relationships. Even her appeals for fatherly affection, which motivate the publication of her *Life*, do not dominate its formal or thematic organization. Rather, she arranges the account as a movement through various (male) roles in a search for her (true) self.

But this right to adopt various roles freely is what nineteenth-century editors refused to credit and what twentieth-century critics resist. Hunt and Clarke read Charke's account as a product of "corrupt civilization," Patricia Spacks as an example of female victimization, Sidonie Smith as the story of a "sentimental heroine, a woman who accepts and reflects the values of the community, including its expectations of appropriate female behavior."[54] None of these readings acknowledges Charke's desire to escape dichotomies of gender.

Charke must have understood the difficulty her autobiography would pose. Although she admits it to be "the product of a female pen," she does not plead feminine inadequacy or excuse its faults on that account. She asks that her narrative be given "the common chance of a criminal, at least to be properly examined, before it is condemned" (p. 9). Her choice of criminality as a trope for self-writing marks her fine sensitivity to the literary code she transgresses. She uses a female pen, but she writes in a male mode, in a forbidden masculine discourse. That we should, in the twentieth century, continue to read the *Narrative of the Life of Mrs. Charlotte Charke* as a criminal act, however, is to mistake it, to accept the restrictive views of gender and autobiography that limited her nineteenth-century editors. It is also to miss the subtler implications of her own use of criminality as a trope for autobiographical writing.

If Charke asks that her autobiography be treated as a criminal, it is with a sense that, before the law, gender does not figure. Justice should be done to a writer's performance whatever the gender, whatever the literary mode: "should it be found guilty of nonsense and inconsistencies, I must consequently resign it to its deserved punishment" (p. 9). What Charke suggests is that critical reading proceed not from considerations of gender, but from concerns with genre. She pleads for a critical stance that nineteenth-century editors and readers were to ignore—indeed, that we in the twentieth century, with our interest in feminine, relational modes of self-conception, have tended to minimize. But there is good argument that we ought now to move beyond the critical practice of identifying only feminine, relational modes with "women's autobiography" and adopt a less restrictive approach to understanding what women have written—and will in the future write—as autobiography. At the very least, we ought to recognize the tensions that critical practice has brought to discussions of the traditions of women's autobiography.

Self-Knowledge, Law, and African American Autobiography: Lucy A. Delaney's 'From the Darkness Cometh the Light'

Lindon Barrett

*T*he autobiographical text this discussion considers is a recollection of antebellum slave life and of release from chattel slavery. Published some 25 years after the Civil War, Lucy A. Delaney's *From the Darkness Cometh the Light*, subtitled *Struggles for Freedom*, recalls as its climax events from 1844, the year in which Delaney's mother, Polly Berry, sued successfully for Delaney's freedom in a Missouri courtroom.[1] The legal case and judgment for Delaney's freedom turned upon the status of Delaney's mother, who was born free in Illinois, kidnapped as a child, and taken to slaveholding territory. Legally a free woman, Berry could not bear enslaved children in the eyes of the law. Thus, successfully establishing the biological mother-daughter relationship between Berry and Delaney amounted to a demonstration of Delaney's legally free status. Despite the singularity of this movement from slavery to freedom in terms of classic slave narratives, Delaney's recollections bear central characteristics of the classic antebellum text in which, during the years from 1836 to the end of the Civil War, "the stigma traditionally associated with slavery [was transferred] from the slave to the slaveholder."[2] What is significant about Delaney's text is that the working out of these traditional concerns and themes occurs at a very novel site: the American courtroom.

The climax of Delaney's narrative in the setting of an American courtroom tellingly resituates the "scene of writing" so peculiar to African American autobiography. The "scene of writing" in these narratives is the scene in which the autobiographer learns to read, write, or respect fully the power of literacy and discursive conventions. The scene provides a sometimes veiled but always undeniable commentary on the construction of the autobiographical self presented by the narrative. The revision suggested by Delaney's narrative tellingly documents the manner in which each African American autobiographer must in some measure recast the hostile construction of African American identity already undertaken by dominant American society. The courtroom setting in Delaney's narrative dramatizes the convergence of the scriptive and the prescriptive, the private and the public, the individual and the social. Put another way, it dramatizes "a complex political technology" by which the self is represented.³ This "complex political technology," as *From the Darkness Cometh the Light* reveals, is ultimately implicated in the terms of American law. The critical reader sees in the courtroom scene of writing the African American self as a manifest fiction—a provisional composite of self-declaration and judicial arbitration.

In addition to prompting the critical reader to consider the American courtroom as a primary site for "political and conceptual" determinations (as well as disclosures) of African American identity, Delaney's text prompts recognition of the technological and epistemological fiction of the genre of autobiography.⁴ This essay examines these intersecting exposures. It begins by analyzing Delaney's portrayal of the nuclear family and her presentation of her own representativeness vis-à-vis all other African Americans; these subordinate elements of the narrative underscore the exposures of the climactic scenes in the courtroom. The essay concludes by claiming a central place for the American courtroom as a site for the writing of African American identity and autobiography.

The convergence at this site is important for investigations of the situation of the self of African American autobiography, because the foremost concern of African American autobiographies has been the relation between the individual and the communal. Accordingly, the academic study of African American autobiography is perennially concerned with this relation. In 1974, in the introduction to his *Black Autobiography in America*, Stephen Butterfield writes: "The 'self' of black autobiography . . . is not an individual with a private career. . . . The self is conceived as a member of an oppressed social group with ties and responsibilities to the other members."⁵ Almost twenty years later it is now routinely acknowledged that there are important distinctions to be made along these lines between autobiographies written by African American women and African American men. These distinctions concern the relation that the narrated subjects of the autobiographies bear to the community of African Americans with whom they share their oppression, or in other words the extent to which the narratives are or are not individualistic, celebrating individual struggles and individual triumphs. The now-classic pairing of Frederick Douglass's *Narrative of the Life of Frederick Douglass* and Harriet Jacobs's *Incidents in the Life of a Slave Girl* is taken to exemplify such distinctions. Douglass more fully fashions a mythic tale of individual perseverance and ingenuity, while Jacobs more fully records her indebtedness to and enduring concerns for the familial community in relation to which she defines herself. The pairing brings together strikingly different models of the way in which African American autobiographies present the dramatic actualization or realization of the self, given a set of intellectual, civic, and legal circumstances operating to prevent precisely that.

Needless to say, one recognizes equally important similarities. One critic describes the shared complexities of African American autobiographical projects as follows: "Autobiography as a genre should be the history of individual craziness, but in black autobiography the outer reality in which heroes move is so massive and absolute in its craziness that any one person's individual idiosyncrasies seem almost dull in their normality."[6] African American autobiographies present readers with narratives that are, in terms of the dominant society, unimaginable. In these texts, what is normally taken for granted becomes, as a matter of course, eccentric. These eccentricities involve defying socially assigned identities and undertaking their revision in light of personally proclaimed identities. The autobiographies of Douglass and Jacobs share, in addition to these traits, more widespread characteristics of autobiography. Both suggest, for instance, that the genre offers "not a simple recapitulation of the past; it is also the attempt and the drama of [persons] struggling to reassemble [themselves] in [their] own likeness at a certain moment of [their] history."[7]

Differences and similarities notwithstanding, these estimations of African American autobiography depend upon notions that Candace Lang, in her reprimand of traditional scholars of autobiography, terms a relatively "unskeptical acceptance of the unified, autonomous self." Writing of Georges Gusdorf and James Olney, among others, Lang invites one to see that "few of the critics in question here manifest an entirely unskeptical acceptance of the unified, autonomous self, but virtually none goes so far as to ponder the consequences of a total rejection of that notion of the subject. To do so would constitute . . . a serious and sustained critique of the 'genre' and its ideological foundations."[8] My contention is that the circumstances of African American autobiography prompt such a sustained critique. That critique operates at the level of the ideological foundations of the genre, but it also operates beyond them, putting into question the ideological foundations of American social custom and law. It thus identifies discursive practices from which African American autobiography must extract itself, practices that it must revise. This critique is suggested, but only suggested, by the pairing of Douglass and Jacobs. The issues setting the two narratives in opposition imply the problematics troubling any definitive declaration of the limits and boundaries of the self. The self, as it turns out, is always a questionable fiction, whether that fiction is exposed in terms of relations to a community, or in terms of narrative complexities that betray a self performing the narration over and against a self being narrated.

African American autobiography stands as a peculiar site at which a critical reader can witness, in diverse realms, the dynamics animating fictions of the self. In addition to observing narrative disturbances fretting a discourse generically premised on the viability of a discrete identity, the reader is privy to disturbances of the enduring national fictions in the United States that propose it is impossible and undesirable, in the words of Abraham Lincoln, to "introduce political and social equality between the white and black races . . . [as a result of] a physical difference between the two, which . . . will probably forever forbid their living together upon the footing of perfect equality."[9] Lucy Delaney's *From the Darkness Cometh the Light* articulates this coincidence of generic and social fictions, providing a fiction of personal identity that also rehearses a systemic fiction of national identity, a coincidence that one might attribute to the terms of all African American autobiography. One is openly prompted by Delaney's narrative to see the autobiographical heroine as multiple and as defined in deeply conflicting ways. Additionally, the climax of the narrative—the courtroom scene that eventually secures Delaney her freedom—graphically conjoins the fictitious self-evidence of autobiography with the imperatives of social and legal systems in the United States that remain hostile to African Americans. The "ideological foundations" of the generic, unitary self and of a racial, gendered, and classed national configuration appear there in powerful complementarity. The equivocal fiction of the self is set in relief against the assumed univocality of an overwhelming system. Accordingly, the official site of the courtroom takes its place as the paramount scene for multiple fictive selves, or what amounts to the same, multiple fictions of the self. The tenuous fiction of the self is inevitable, but is taken as less tenuous at some sites than at others.

Not so oddly, then, the autobiographical self-knowledge to be accrued from reading Delaney's narrative—and by extension all African American autobiography—proves to be the ironic knowledge of another / an Other. For Delaney this odd self-knowledge is a foreign and contrary knowledge

imposed by a hostile and dominant other party and is, furthermore, knowledge of an estranged and, at best, marginalized Other that/who must be
understood as one's self. African American autobiographical acts recapitulate the hostile "knowledge" that discounts them in the first place, as well
as the marginalized personal and community "knowledge" that, oppos-
ingly, promotes them in the first place. For an African American "simply
to write the story of his or her own life represent[s] an assault" on the line
of reasoning that assumes and perpetuates the construct that African
Americans do not live—at the very least—as fully imaginative, significant,
intellectual, and complex lives as the dominant American community,
"since to make oneself the subject of a narrative presumes both the worth
of that self and its interest for a reader."[10] Given this set of circumstances,
From the Darkness Cometh the Light underscores correspondences between the generic dimensions of a social configuration and the social dimensions of a generic configuration; *From the Darkness Cometh the Light*
challenges "ideological foundations" that obscure these conjunctions.

There are two principal ways in which the text imputes the fictive status
to the self. The first returns us to the exemplary concerns of *Incidents in
the Life of a Slave Girl*, since the construct of the family holds priority in
both narratives. Delaney's narrative begins with the abduction of her
mother at the age of five from the state of Illinois "across the Mississippi
River to the city of St. Louis" and shortly "up the Missouri River [where
she is] sold into slavery."[11] Sold and resold as a slave, Polly meets "a mulatto
servant, who was as handsome as Apollo" (p. 11) and eventually the two
are married and begin to raise two daughters. With foreshadowing irony,
Delaney characterizes her early childhood: "With mother, father, and sister, a pleasant home and surroundings, what happier child than I!" (p. 13).
A state of domestic unity and happiness is recuperated from the opening
misdeeds of the narrative; however, as one suspects, the archetypal unity
and happiness prove ephemeral. The ensuing episodes of Delaney's narrative seem to chronicle a quest to reconvene the blissful family unit.

Delaney recalls that "Though in direct opposition to the will of Major
Berry, my father's quondam master and friend Judge Wash tore my father
from his wife and children and sold him 'way down South'!" (p. 14). This
disbanding of the family marks the beginning of the misfortunes from
which Delaney must continually extricate herself. Although the evil of slavery underlies the whole narrative, the disbanding of the family also marks
the first of only two occasions when the text calls the evil by its name. Delaney decries "Slavery! cursed slavery . . . [which means] bondage as parts
husband from wife, the mother from her children, aye, even the babe from

her breast" (pp. 14–15). The terms of this initial and most enduring distress are those of the separation of family member from family member. Conversely, the terms of greatest consolation are implied to be the return of family members into each other's presence. The narrative is structured so that its penultimate moment appears to effect such success, but the equivocal nature of this success suggests the fictiveness that the notion of family bears in Delaney's autobiography—despite the fact that it determines both the autobiographical narrator's dilemma and her delivery from that dilemma. Years after the initial catastrophe, and years after her own emancipation as well as the emancipation and death of her mother, years after the abolition of "slavery [and] involuntary servitude, except as a punishment for crime whereof the party shall have been duly convicted,"[12] Delaney is haunted by the impulse to redress the longstanding disintegration of her family. She locates her father, and calls her sister Nancy down from Canada, then she writes of her triumph of sorts:

Forty-five years of separation, hard work, rough times and heart longings, had perseveringly performed its work, and instead of a man bearing his years with upright vigor, he was made prematurely old by the accumulation of troubles. My sister Nancy came from Canada, and we had a most joyful reunion, and only the absence of our mother left a vacuum, which we deeply and sorrowfully felt. Father could not be persuaded to stay with us, when he found his wife dead; he longed to get back to his old associations of forty-five years standing, he felt like a stranger in a strange land, and taking pity on him, I urged him no more, but let him go though with great reluctance. (p. 61)

Delaney's triumph in effect recapitulates the initial loss. The passage begins with "separation" and ends with references to leavetaking, "a strange land," and "reluctance"—the very markers of the distress wrought 45 years earlier. Indeed, the brief mention of "a most joyful reunion" is encircled by references to "the accumulation of troubles" and "a vacuum . . . deeply and sorrowfully felt." It would appear that the configuration of "family," so heavily privileged in depictions of the African American experience by nineteenth-century white writers like Harriet Beecher Stowe, is one that is strangely never sustained or realized at this or any other point in the narrative. The configuration of "family" is an absent term that nonetheless maintains a brooding, fantastic, and highly rhetorical presence. One must remember that the reunion inevitably falls short of the original union it seeks, since the death of Delaney's mother starkly precludes the possibility. Polly never again faces her husband "who was as handsome as Apollo"; the benevolent romance that introduces and privileges the term "family" within the text survives only as a lost, unattainable fiction.

The teasing impossibility of this presiding fiction is underscored by the scenes immediately preceding the narrative's penultimate episode: after the accidental death of her first husband, Frederick Turner, Delaney is importuned by her mother to remember that death proves a better fate than enslavement. The unexpected separation Delaney must endure is not ordained by American law and privilege, as is the arbitrary legal separation of her father from her mother. In her grief Delaney submits to the judgment that the burden of slavery outweighs the burden of death: "I had been taught that there was hope beyond the grave, but hope was left behind when sold 'down souf'" (p. 57). Even in light of further misfortunes, the fiction of the original family unit and the trauma of its fracture presides. Equally, when the four children she bears in her second marriage (to Zachariah Delaney) all die either in childhood or by the age of 24, Delaney reflects that "one consolation was always mine! Our children were born free and died free! Their childhood and my maternity were never shadowed with a thought of separation" (p. 58). No doubt this claim is an odd one to be made by a mother who endures the deaths of two of her children in childhood and two in young adulthood, for the reader is asked to understand that, as she witnessed the death of each child, she is never troubled with "thought[s] of separation," even though that separation might be effected by physical death as opposed to enslavement. The ultimate outrage of American chattel slavery is portrayed in the narrative in terms of the customary priority accorded to the family in nineteenth-century American life. The principal evil of slavery is the arbitrary severing of African American families. So too the narrative represents this arbitrary severing of families as the preeminent despair of Delaney's life. The fiction of the family represents or pursues the fact of Delaney's despair.

The third in the series of deaths enumerated immediately prior to the scene of the curious family reunion is the death of Delaney's mother, her most cherished and longstanding companion. The focus and tone of this passage is substantially different from that registering her distress at her father's forced removal. Delaney remarks that she is pleased her mother "had lived to see the joyful time when her race was made free, their chains struck off, and their right to their own flesh and blood lawfully acknowledged" (p. 59). The death of her mother represents in the narrative not a traumatic separation but an occasion for satisfying and almost calming reflection. As in describing the death of her children, Delaney moves, if not to hyperbole, to measured lyricism:

Her life, so full of sorrow was ended, full of years and surrounded by many friends, both black and white, who recognized and appreciated her sufferings and sacrifices and rejoiced that her old age was spent in freedom and plenty. The azure vault of heaven bends over us all, and the gleaming moonlight brightens the marble tablet which marks her last resting place, "to fame and fortune unknown," but in the eyes of Him who judgeth us, hers was a heroism which outvied the most famous. (p. 59)

Once again, the reader is asked to overlook the trauma of this separation, while the narrative itself is structured so as never to overlook the imposed separation outlined early in the events of Delaney's life. Strikingly, the episode that immediately follows, Delaney's attempt at a family reunion, returns to the consequences of that early separation.

It is clear that the privileged form of self-definition in Delaney's narrative is the family, yet it is equally clear that within the circumstances of her life and narrative this privileged form operates foremost as a tantalizing fiction. In her life and narrative, Delaney's family disintegrates even as it is invoked. The term enters the narrative to recapitulate its rupture and absence. As Frances Smith Foster comments, "the problem of distinguishing between the individual self and the community self and the desire to present the symbolic nature of one's personal experiences while maintaining one's own inimitability is traditional for autobiographical writers"; nonetheless, for the African American autobiographer "the question is complicated by his [or her] status . . . in the United States." That status is an alien and inferior one that in large part abrogates the prerogatives of self-definition. "The slave narrator," and subsequent writers are aliens "whose assertions of common humanity and civil rights conflict with some basic beliefs" of the society they address.[13] African American autobiographers define themselves in relation to at least two communities, a dominating American community that brooks no identification with African Americans and a community of African Americans with whom they share an imposed singularity. Delaney's narrative outlines ways in which defining oneself beyond these options amounts to pursuing a tantalizing and forever absent fiction. Thus, the privileged term of her narrative, the primary register of her self-evidence proves unprocurable. The central family in her narrative, which the prerogatives of American chattel slavery violate, remains above all in the text what the *OED* calls "a supposition known to be at variance with fact." Delaney recounts her life and defines her self in terms of a fiction, unfortunately a hostile fiction authored by American law and custom. What is more, the fictive status of her family in both the autobiographical narrative and the "reality" of American life implies an equal fictiveness for the self that reference to this family records. Defining the self in terms of what is ultimately fantastic calls into question its "uni-

fied and autonomous" nature, because this fantastic self remains, by definition, "at variance with fact." Presented without fact, the unity and autonomy of the self are not those of a first order reality faithfully recorded
by the autobiographical act, but of a fiction manifestly invented by others.
The principal sign of Delaney's autobiographical self-presence rests outside her self in what is "known to be at variance with fact," so that the text
gives the lie to "the assumption that the . . . [autobiographical] work is the
expression (however inadequate) of an anterior idea originating in the
writing subject and for which that subject was the sole authority."[14] One
must remember that in large part Delaney's persevering fictions represent
a struggle with American law and custom for authorship of and authority
over the terms of her life. Given the plainness of these circumstances and
their attendant fictions, *From the Darkness Cometh the Light* advertises
its fictiveness as opposed to its facticity. The autobiography restates the
conditions of invention determining autobiographical representation as
much as it appears to redact a fixed presence, a unified and autonomous
self.

The even larger irony to be noted here is that every African American
autobiographer wishes to pursue options of self-definition beyond the two
imperatives that allow her or him either no room for resemblance or no
room for difference. In the negative relation African Americans are assumed to bear to the dominating American community we are granted
conversely an inexorable representativeness in relation to all other African
Americans, and the second of the two principal ways in which Delaney's
text imputes the fictive status of the self concerns this assumption of representativeness. Following her rehearsal of the partial, belated reunion of
her family, Delaney concludes her text with an enumeration of her personal
accomplishments, an enumeration immediately recuperated as racial exemplum. Both the brief listing that includes such items as her election as
"President of the first colored society, called the 'Female Union,' which was
the first ever organized exclusively for women" (p. 62), as well as the narrative in its entirety, are offered in the hopes that either "may settle the
problem in your mind, if not in others, 'Can the negro race succeed, proportionately, as well as the whites, if given the same and an equal start?'"
(pp. 63–64). Delaney briefly fashions herself as representative of all African Americans and of their potential. Nevertheless, only three paragraphs
earlier, she writes:

There are abounding in public and private libraries of all sorts, lives of people which
fill our minds with amazement, admiration, sympathy, and indeed with as many
feelings as there are people, so I can scarcely expect that the reader of these episodes

of my life will meet with more than a passing interest, but as such I will commend it to your thought for a brief hour. (pp. 61–62)

Delaney acknowledges a vast multiplicity of individuals who are not easily reducible to one another, and acknowledges as well a multiplicity of feelings that may animate any of those individuals. She characterizes herself as acutely aware that for one to read her text is to make a single choice among many and, accordingly, she asks only "for a brief hour" devoted to her own. In effect, at the moment in the text when she sets her own life as a standard or gauge for millions of other lives she also considers her life in terms of the infinite differences that implicitly make such a substitution impossible. Furthermore, she suggests that not only is it troublesome to imagine one life standing in the place of another or many others, it is equally troublesome to imagine any of the many "feelings" that play their part in any one life somehow standing as indicative of that individual life. Oddly, then, at the same time the impossibilities of representation are briefly considered, the narrative nonetheless claims a representative posture for Delaney. One sees that this representative understanding is openly provisional at best and, therefore, in one further and pronounced way, Delaney's reader witnesses (and witnesses Delaney witnessing) her self as "a supposition known to be at variance with fact."

As with the persistent attention to family, the form of the self being invoked responds to the invocation with rupture and withdrawal. The presented self-evidence underscores its own contrivance. The notion that African Americans are invariably more similar than different, and that one African American may always stand in the place of another, is sometimes a profitable fiction and sometimes is not. The notion remains, in any case, always a fiction, as made clear emphatically and irrevocably by the urbanization of large populations of African Americans early in the twentieth century: "After the war, black intellectuals had to confront the black masses on the streets of their cities. . . . After World War I, the large-scale movement of black people into the cities of the North meant that intellectual leadership and its constituencies fragmented. No longer was it possible to mobilize an undifferentiated address to 'the black people' once an urban black working class was established."[15] The closing paragraphs of Delaney's autobiography comprehend and imply deep conflicts that disturb assumptions of a unitary identity attributed by law or custom to African Americans. Indeed, this is an outcome her narrative shares generally with African American autobiographies. (Of course, this description is necessarily ironic, insofar as it advances a unitary identity.) The conflicts of racial representation are registered in Delaney's text in the terms of her autobiographical self, inasmuch as Delaney equivocally proposes a role for her self in that representative fiction.

In effect, as does the genre in general, Delaney's autobiography leads the critical reader to a meditation on fiction. Importantly, however, suggesting perennial concerns of African American autobiography, the fictions to be imagined and re-imagined in this instance are not simply personal or generic, but also and necessarily social and legal. As much as the scene of writing here is generic, it also is "constitutional" in the social and legal senses of that word—a scene of writing from which one necessarily infers the civic and judicial. Hence, if African American autobiography, this overdetermined scene of writing, always undertakes "a total rejection of the notion of the subject,"[16] then it troubles, by definition—even beyond the ideological foundations of autobiography—the foundations of powerful social and legal practices.

The climactic scenes of Delaney's text powerfully illuminate this imperative and intricate cathexis. Her text lays bare the deeply composite nature and unquestioned priority of these scenes. Although the importance of scenes of writing is well acknowledged within African American autobiographies and the commentaries on them, Delaney's text manifestly draws out and elaborates the non-subjective and systemic nature of this peculiar scene of writing in which she, as African American "subject," discovers her self. The novelty of Delaney's rendition becomes clear if one considers briefly well-known scenes of writing in *Narrative of the Life of Frederick Douglass* and *Incidents in the Life of a Slave Girl*.

In Douglass's text, in keeping with the more individualistic focus attributed to his narrative, the scene is in large part self-centered. Douglass's lessons in literacy provided by Mrs. Auld are stopped by Mr. Auld, since attaining literacy invariably spoils slaves by making them "unmanageable." At this juncture Douglass understands the white man's power to enslave as well as "the pathway from slavery to freedom."[17] He undertakes learning to read and write by tricking and bribing white boys in his neighborhood and by using for practice such communal markers as fences and such markers of his alienation from that community as the discarded schoolbooks of his master's son. The scene of writing outlined here underscores individual acumen, ingenuity, and the remove imposed by hostile, dominating agents. In Jacobs's text, by contrast, the more miscible, promiscuous, or indiscreet nature of the scene of writing is suggested. Initially, Linda Brent's literacy seems a liability, since it means she must endure an additional form of entreaty from Dr. Flint. However, much later in the narrative, Brent writes letters to Flint (from within the garret to which she "escapes") that are mailed and postmarked from New York. She convinces Flint of her successful "escape" to the North, ensuring "he had no suspicion of [her] being any where in the vicinity."[18] The scene of writing sketched here is more mediated; literacy and the construction of texts are taken up by diverse and conflicting hands and acquire their truth or potency by means of circulation and marks of that circulation. Here, one sees how language, literacy, and the construction and interpretation of texts operate "constitutionally"—that is, in a formative but always incomplete manner—to "confer explanatory power with regard to a wide range of evidence."[19] Scenes of writing are scenes in which occur struggles for and determinations of "explanatory power," as well as the disposition "of evidence." Certainly, the texts of both Douglass and Jacobs suggest this state of affairs; nevertheless, they have been traditionally understood to do so in a manner that privileges the more private interstitial and marginal aspects of their inscriptional scenes.

Conversely, the climactic scenes of Delaney's text place the dynamics of language, literacy, and interpretation as they bear on African American "subjectivity" at the most literal and open site of interpretive activity, the American courtroom. The courtroom is a site at which one is not prompted to understand the scene of writing in terms of inscriptions made between the lines or in intramural spaces. The courtroom neither resembles a garret nor confines its proceedings to the margins of used, discarded sheets of paper. Rather than an interstitial space, it is apparently one in which matters are brought into the open and settled. Moreover, the courtroom is a space in which presentations of "evidence" and conferring of "explanatory power" concerning African American identity have sweeping and enduring repercussions. At the site of the courtroom, statutory law is interpreted and upheld and and, all too plainly, the particulars of the presence of African Americans in the United States have been meaningfully determined by statutory law. Scenes of writing in African American autobiographies, in this sense, are the site of struggles for the right of individuals to control this "explanatory power" and to determine the disposition of the "evidence" of their own existence. The setting of Delaney's climactic scene of writing in a courtroom brilliantly allows her text to represent the problematic nature of this struggle. It allows her to stage, via the representation of an autobiographical self, the multiple fictions of selfhood that are the only resort of those for whom the "constitutional" issue of their identity already has been settled without their participation or consent. Just as the "fact" of her family is an elusive fiction, so is the ostensible subject of Delaney's narrative. In the end, what the courtroom scene allows her to represent is the enforced fictionality of any subject defined by the impersonality of the law's "constitutional" power, even when that power is employed on behalf of the freedom of the subject.

It is useful to consider briefly the nature of statutory law.

Statutory law is a distillation of some of the society's most cherished values, or at least of the class that wields the hegemonic power that produces laws. Statutes are one way, and a solemn and formal one, for the elite that imposes its values on a society to state what those values are and how behavior should conform to them. No other social act performs this function so conspicuously and directly. Statutory law is thus a valuable window on the hopes and fears of a society, of its images of itself, and of the ways it hoped to shape the time to come.[20]

Statutory law represents the convergence and "distillation" of a plurality of discourses, a formalizing of values, practices, and customs. The courtroom is the site at which this synthesis is understood and rehearsed. Historically, this site has provided the most far-reaching determinations of African American identity, an identity that cannot be understood as a "unified and autonomous" subjectivity in light of its determination at a site so open to the influences of diverse pressures, agencies, and convergences. Although "the idea of racial inferiority certainly did not appear in colonial law with the introduction of Negroes," and although "the legal determination of who might be slaves developed slowly," as American colonial law was refined, according to William E. Moore it allowed African Americans identity only as a collective, "not as individuals." Colonial law, in its attempt to confine slavery "to those who quite obviously were different in appearance," and in its attempt to justify itself "on the basis of [African Americans'] inferior background as a people, not as individuals . . . [took] the position that slavery is justified as a status properly attaching to a different and inferior people."[21] Thus, one finds in the colonial courtroom the binding interpretation (promoted by mechanisms of "explanatory power") that African Americans bear little estimable resemblance to any community other than that of African Americans and that African Americans bear little estimable difference from one another. The dilemma of the African American autobiographer—and of African Americans—is part of the story American law has written.

The construction of the African American self in this way has been contested as a fiction by African American rebellions, by expressive cultures (dance, song, oral performance) and, within the concerns of this discussion, by autobiographical texts. To grant that, in the words of Paul Finkelman, a leading scholar of early African American legal history, "slavery must be understood not only as a social, economic, or political institution but also as a legal institution"[22] is not simply to acknowledge the brutalizing determinations of African American identity in the legislature and then in the courtroom; it is to recognize, in addition, the persistent challenges to those determinations, as well as their troublesome ramifications. The fictiveness of the established legal "facts" concerning African Americans requires that interpretations separating fiction from fact be made again and again in the American courtroom. The courtroom remains a site of powerful interventions into these perpetual deliberations.

The establishment of the legal principle that slavery was a status properly belonging to the Negro, as inherently inferior, went far toward the legal determination of who might be slaves. But because slavery was *not* uniformly the status of Negroes from their first introduction, because not all Negroes were slaves even after slavery was established as being proper to them, and finally, because anti-miscegenation laws were not in force from the first and not uniformly obeyed thereafter, so that physiological criteria were variable and fallible, for all these reasons the legal criteria of the status of slavery required further elaboration.[23]

This is to say, the identity of African Americans "required further elaboration." Ultimately, however, this conflict between fiction and fact concerning African American identity proved unmanageable even for the "explanatory power" of the antebellum courtroom. Historian Eugene Genovese observes in his review of Paul Finkelman's *An Imperfect Union: Slavery, Federalism, and Comity* that "the 'judicial secession' that Finkelman describes paralleled a moral and ideological secession that struck the deepest sensibilities, and together they prepared the way for the political secession that formally declared the existence of contrasting views of civilization."[24] Equally, one might say the political secession dramatically declared the existence of contrasting views of African Americans in that civilization.

The courtroom, in its interpretation of statutory law, thus stands as a preeminent site for the construction of African American identity. It allows Delaney to dramatize the fictional nature of the forms that identity has been forced to take. Her courtroom scenes heighten the ideological drama of perceiving the fictive nature of the self; they heighten the ideological drama of "a total rejection of that notion of the subject." In the text, Delaney's appearance in court in a suit for her freedom is precipitated by an altercation with her mistress, Mrs. Mitchell. Several times Delaney is entrusted "to do the weekly washing and ironing . . . [even though she] had no more idea how it was to be done than Mrs. Mitchell herself" (p. 24).

Delaney is treated as if the particulars of menial servitude are innate, and her failures and protestations to the contrary prompt Mrs. Mitchell to sell her. Delaney flees and hides in the home of her legally free mother, who subsequently "on the morning of the 8th of September 1842 . . . sued Mr. D. D. Mitchell for the possession of her child" (p. 33). The issue brought before the court is who rightfully possesses the child Lucy Ann Berry, and it is precipitated by Delaney's headstrong self-determination—self-determination out of place in a situation in which that determination is a foregone conclusion.

In the courtroom the tale of the illegal abduction of Delaney's mother is rehearsed, and witnesses attest to the fact that Delaney "to the best of [their] knowledge and belief" (p. 40) is her biological child, and hence illegally enslaved. It is important to note that Delaney's defense is not premised on Delaney's personal identity, but on the very law that defines the status of African American slaves—taken as a collective entity—as perpetually the property of their masters. Delaney's defense depends on the condition of her mother, since "a master who owned a female slave owned also her increase."[25] It is the courtroom scene that occurs after the testimonies, however, that is most memorable to Delaney:

After the evidence from both sides was all in, Mr. Mitchell's lawyer, Thomas Hutchinson, commenced to plead. For one hour, he talked so bitterly against me and against my being in possession of my liberty that I was trembling, as if with ague, for I certainly thought everybody must believe him; indeed I almost believed the dreadful things he said, myself, and as I listened I closed my eyes with sickening dread, for I could just see myself floating down the river, and my heart-throbs seemed to be the throbs of the mighty engine which propelled me from my mother and freedom forever! (p. 40)

The power of the law here resides in the power of Thomas Hutchinson's rhetoric and his construction and interpretation of the "facts" before the court. This power is not negligible, for it challenges Delaney's sense of herself. The words "I could just see myself" introduce a vision of herself that strongly contradicts the identity she is struggling to maintain and to validate by means of legal sanction. Moreover, this vision may well be the one that will receive that sanction. Delaney recalls that "on the day the suit for [her] freedom began . . . the jailer's sister-in-law, Mrs. Lacy, spoke to [her] of submission and patience; but [she] could not feel anything but rebellion against [her] lot" (p. 39). This rebellion matches her earlier one against the "government" of Mrs. Mitchell for, in the dispute over the laundry, Delaney "would not permit [Mrs. Mitchell] to strike her; [Mrs. Mitchell] used shovel, tongs and broomstick in vain, as [Delaney] disarmed her as fast as she picked up each weapon" (p. 27). Nevertheless, that rebellious character dissipates as Hutchinson pleads, and the character in which Mrs. Mitchell would cast her seems confirmed—even in Delaney's own mind. In the arena of the courtroom, Delaney represents herself as having no say concerning who she is to be.

Only when Hutchinson concludes his pleading does Delaney find respite from the "constitutional" power of the law over her identity. "Oh! what a relief it was to me when he finally finished his harangue and resumed his seat! As I never heard anyone plead before, I was very much alarmed, although I knew in my heart that every word he uttered was a lie! Yet, how was I to make people believe? It seemed a puzzling question" (pp. 40–41). Yet that respite is brief. Delaney, in her apprehension, stumbles upon the disconcerting issue that "explanatory power alone does not guarantee the truth of interpretation. Nothing does and nothing could."[26] It is apparent that fictions may assert themselves in any circumstances, in any place, in any construct, even those that may appear most legitimate and convincing. It is also apparent that, as Delaney represents herself, her "self" is essentially a fiction constructed by others. It becomes clear that in the courtroom what are determined as facts are for Delaney fictions constructed through the determining technologies of legal discourse.

Confronting Delaney is the overwhelming trouble that "problems of multiple authorship," the competing textual activities of various agents, "have . . . separated the text from its original authors and given it a life of its own."[27] The terms "life" and "text" become interchangeable in this scene and at this point of the narrative. They achieve a strange equivalence, as they do in all autobiographical acts, but with recognizably greater force in African American autobiography. Delaney's autobiographical self-representation exposes the way in which the always preexisting construction of her life in the impersonal text of the law relies on "structures of discourse that so often contribute to the [African American] writers' oppression."[28] The life that is written in this scene is literally not her own. Even though the scene ostensibly produces her freedom, it dramatizes an enduring state of subjugation. Of course, such a predicament or analogous predicaments in the courtroom are not exclusive to African Americans. Nevertheless, it is imperative to see that for African Americans the issue does not involve any precipitating activity on their part. At issue in the case of African Americans are not the complications of precedent actions but an a priori state of being, the determination of an identity on which social existence and relations depend. One immediately understands, then, that African Americans and African American autobiographers must revise or recast in the terms of their lives a story that is already (unacceptably) written—and writ large—by American law and custom. They attempt to write a story already recorded and on which the book, for the most part, has been closed.

Among the issues in the balance is the issue of "authorship," and most particularly self-authorship. Hence, it proves more than incidental that the power to resist and abrogate Hutchinson's interpretations of the "facts"—or, equally, to elaborate an alternative fiction—rests not with Delaney, but with Edward Bates, who acts as her attorney. In this representation of her life, he "represents" her, not just as her advocate, but also as one more practitioner of the law who wields its power to construct and construe her life in accord with its letter.

Judge Bates arose, and his soulful eloquence and earnest pleading made such an impression on my sore heart, I listened with renewed hope. I felt the black storm clouds of doubt and despair were fading away, and that I was drifting into the safe harbor of the realms of truth. I felt as if everybody *must* believe *him*, for he clnng [*sic*] to the truth, and I wondered how Mr. Hutchinson could so lie about a poor defenseless girl like me. (p. 41; emphasis in original)

The eloquence and "explanatory power" of Judge Bates are beyond question, as is his role in securing the relief and victory of Delaney. The emphasis falls on his actions and influence, while Delaney appears as merely acted upon. The turning point in the crisis of her self-determination depends upon the force and efficacy of a self constructed by another. In her own rendition of the climax of her quest for and attainment of self-determination, Delaney has no authority, self-authority or any other kind. Indeed, in Delaney's self-representation in this scene she ironically dramatizes her inability to represent herself in any terms but those supplied by those whose law and customs have enslaved her and will also set her "free." The conventional bathos of "a poor defenseless girl like me" underlines her self-representation as a tactic undertaken within a world of always polite fictions that systematically determine the discourse of self-representation and identity for African Americans. Drawn in the courtroom and in anxiety as "a poor defenseless girl," she possesses less proximity to her "self" than Bates or, for that matter, Hutchinson. Delaney, in deference to the commanding power of the competing renditions of her self, is a negligible player at this point, and the irony is underscored rhetorically; "defenseless" is an interesting term to employ in reference to a life that turns precisely on a legal "defense" successfully upheld.

As with the narrative's privileging of the term "family" and its equivocal representation of Delaney's representativeness, the courtroom drama belies the notion of a "unified and autonomous" subject. Delaney represents her identity as decisively and variously constituted by the representations of others. The proceedings of the court as well as the autobiographical act that both renders them and is rendered possible by them expose the fictiveness of such a belief. This autobiographical act and its central terms—the privileging of the family, the claim of representativeness, and the climactic legal drama—also challenge the "ideological foundations" of that belief, the principles determining which fictions do and do not count. Because it alludes to the manifest fiction operating at the site of the courtroom itself, the peroration of Judge Bates forms a further element of this exposition. Bates commends the court as a site at which laws attain their most imposing, and thus inviolate, status, and Delaney transcribes his statement as follows:

"Gentlemen of the jury, I am a slave-holder myself, but, thanks to the Almighty God, I am above the base principle of holding anybody a slave that has as good right to her freedom as this girl has been proven to have; she was free before she was born; her mother was free, but kidnapped in her youth, and sacrificed to the greed of negro traders, and no free woman can give birth to a slave child, as it is in direct violation of the laws of God and man." (p. 42)

This ultimately successful argument turns on a larger set of ironies. What ultimately secures the court's determination of Delaney's identity is an act of self-definition by her legal representative ("I am a slave-holder myself") enabling a local, limited condemnation of slavery that remains clearly subordinate to an approbation of slavery in general. In his argument the laws of God and man rest surely on Delaney's side, yet the laws of God and man stand as surely behind slavery in general.[29] And to assert thus confidently the unequivocal meaning of divine and human law in this setting is to advance one further fiction. As Bates's activity as an advocate and Delaney's anxiety over whose definition of her identity will prevail attest, the courtroom is a site of equivocation. It is a site at which multiple determinations converge, conflict, and are deliberated. Delaney, furthermore, sets out explicitly a critique of the notion of unquestioned determinacy, a notion that assigns her an identity by a process that her narrative puts into question.

The courtroom would be transformed by Bates's appeal to the uncontestable will of God and to the mandates of man, not of men (not of individuals but of a species), into a site where there is no room for interpretation, since all determination has already been made. Because the courtroom is the site and mechanism of statutory interpretation—of the choosing of a particular meaning because a variety of possibilities presupposes and demands the deliberation—Bates's rhetorical gesture can only be understood as another fiction, "a supposition at variance with the facts." Rather than accepting appeals to unquestioned determinacy, courts make determinations "in the way that all knowledge is secure[d], by virtue of its acceptance within a community of interpretation whose existence is a prerequisite to the production of knowledge itself."[30] In other words, the courtroom gathers representatives of a community in order to determine what the community knows because conflicting interests have put into question what it knows. The knowledge that courts are charged to research, discover, and possess emanates from and returns to the civic and political communities from which the law is constructed.

This point is underscored by the lack of clear legislative origins for the law of American slavery. "Slavery was not established by law in any American colony, but its development by custom was later recognized by legislation."[31] Law and custom interact to the point at which their distinctions blur; upon scrutiny law is premised on custom, while custom manages to manifest itself as law. The two equally enlist one another, as colonial laws of American slavery continually remind us.

When Rhode Island legislators began the gradual statutory abolition of slavery in their state in 1784, they declared in a preamble that slavery "has gradually obtained [in Rhode Island] by unrestrained custom and the permission of the laws." This pithily restated the accepted explanations of the legal origins of slavery in the American states. To create slavery by law it was not necessary, as United States Supreme Court Justice John McLean later observed, to pass legislation providing "that slavery shall exist"; and no such statute was ever adopted in any American jurisdiction. Rather, as an anonymous Garrisonian abolitionist maintained in a retrospective survey of the statutory law of slavery in the British American mainland colonies, the legal origins of slavery are found in "the provincial legislative acts, which establish and sanction the custom [of slaveholding] and stamp it with the character of law."[32]

The situation Delaney narrated in her courtroom scene was related to the collective wills, conflicts, machinations, and imaginations of those segments of civic and political communities best able to command "the legal process . . . as an expression of social control."[33] The determined intermingling of custom and law composing the legal process demands that both be understood in relation to one another.

What law, custom, and the court, as it superintends them, struggle to define in Delaney's autobiography is her identity, her self as that self is complicated by being African American in communities in which African Americans are at worst enslaved and at best marginalized. If one understands the climactic courtroom scene of *From the Darkness Cometh the Light* as the autobiography's preeminent scene of writing, one understands—in addition to the manifest fictiveness of self-determining inscriptions—the manner in which some fictions are enforced and thus acquire greater sanction and power than others. Fictions transcend their provisional status always to someone's or some group's interest. In doing so, they acquire a further provisional status that is less discernible. Scenes of writing turn on issues of power, as is made clear by the conclusion Delaney assigns to the courtroom drama. The conclusion of the scene directly represents her continued confinement by a process of "constitutional" definition that always will determine her identity, even after it has defined her as "free." After Bates's peroration, "the case was then submitted to the jury, about 8 o'clock in the evening, and I was returned to the jail and locked in the cell which I had occupied for seventeen months, filled with the most intense anguish" (p. 43). The courtroom is a site at which fictions are fabricated and acquire legal and social sanction, one at which the peculiar situation of African American identity is made clear. The determination of her freedom and of the various forms of her continued subjugation rests with a community that takes it upon itself to measure, imagine, and (re)cast who she must be. Indeed, once American slavery was a fully formed legal institution, "statutory provisions directly or indirectly securing the rights of slaves were scanty. The only positively accorded right [in the mid-eighteenth century] appears in South Carolina's code of 1740 and Georgia's derivative code of 1755, where blacks could bring suit to test the legality of their enslavement."[34] Equally illustrative of the distinct association courts bear to African American subjectivity is the observation that "these suits, the only type of civil action a slave could take, did not begin until the nineteenth century."[35] Besides criminal prosecution, American courtrooms admitted African Americans primarily to determine their identity.

Hence, the individual scene of writing of the African American autobiographer is always matched by socially and legally prescriptive scenes of writing best imagined in terms of the courtroom, and for these reasons Delaney's autobiography effects an exposition of the concerns of the genre. Delaney seizes and begins to fill for African American autobiography "a prime fictive space"[36] that holds great priority for African Americans in determining the terms of their lives. It would seem that to write African American autobiography is not only to write "from behind the veil" but also to write in the public, yet confining "constitutional" space of American custom and law.

It is fair to say that Delaney's "story undercuts the authority of both points of view presented in the story: the personal and the legal."[37] In Delaney's text "the personal and the legal" converge at the peculiar nexus that is the courtroom, enabling the critical reader to see in the interrelated fictions of the personal and the legal how African American autobiography necessarily challenges the ideological foundations of the genre and the ideological foundations of American life. In undercutting both, Delaney exposes the dual fictions of unity and autonomy in the autobiographical subject and its claim to self-identity. Fictions may assert themselves in any circumstances, in any place, in any construct, even those that may appear most legitimate and convincing. The self is one such fiction, legality another, and the convergence of the two in terms of African American identity another still.

The Mexican Immigrant as *:
The (de)Formation of Mexican Immigrant Life Story

Genaro M. Padilla

The first thing the reader notices about *Between Two Cultures: The Life of an American-Mexican*[1] is the omission of the name of Ramón Gonzales* from the "autobiography's" front cover. We are advised that an American Mexican's "life" has been "told to John J. Poggie, Jr." but who that American Mexican is we do not know until we open the book, and even then we never really know whose life we are reading. Staring out from behind the ethnographic title of the front cover, however, is the photograph of a man's face—presumably the subject of the "life"—masked in dark glasses and veiled in greenish tinge. What is weird about the photo is that the man we are seeing appears to be at the center of an infrared telescopic sight, or, more unnerving, his forehead appears at the center of the scope, as though someone is drawing a bead right between his eyes. The visual representation of a man whom we assume to be Ramón Gonzales* appears in disguised, fugitive form, partially hidden by the title, but obviously the target of the text.

When the subject does make his appearance in the book, he has already been constituted as a representation of the split ethno-subject about whom the social scientist can "formulate scientific problems." The trope of marginality that characterizes the entire trajectory of the Mexican immigrant subject in prior social science discourse is present in the title's bold marking as well as in the photograph that appropriates and conceals the face it claims to represent. And because it is the formulation of the subject as a problematized sociological figuration rather than as an individual historical person, a man of *sangre y hueso*, the face in dark glasses recedes into an asterisk within the anthropological text that bodies forth his "life" for him.

At question in this essay is the formation of an ethnographic discourse on the Mexican immigrant that authorizes autobiographical narrative as the basis for constructing a sociological profile of immigrant behavior and personality within a discipline where autobiography has been derogated as overly subjective. What follows explores the problematic presence of autobiographical forms within a discipline where methodological objectification of the immigrant life story, manipulation of immigrant narrative performance, concealment of subjects' personal names, and structuring of fragmented subjectivity all conspire to construct such men and women as Ramón Gonzales* into a generalizable figure supposed to represent the in-the-flesh Mexican. I shall return to Ramón Gonzales* toward the end of this essay, but, since his is a persona already determined by a larger and older discursive matrix, I must reach back to other discourses by means of which his concealment in the asterisk has been doomed.

The first sustained Mexican immigrant autobiographical narratives were published only as recently as the 1970's, in 1973 and 1975 respectively, during the same period that national attention and sympathy were gathering on the farmworker organizing efforts of Cesar Chavez. The first of these is a narrative collected by the anthropologist John J. Poggie, Jr. titled *Between Two Cultures: The Life of an American-Mexican*. The subject of this "as-told-to" autobiography is a man pseudonymously referred to as Ramón Gonzales*, a man who, although born in Mexico, had immigrated to the United States with his parents when he was a child. Like many other such children, he had spent his culturally formative years in the United States without legally becoming an American citizen, and he was deported for the first of many times when he was twenty years old—hence, the logic of the subtitle, "The Life of an American-Mexican," a label that otherwise sounds backwards to most Mexican Americans.[2] The second "as-told-to" autobiography, *Pablo Cruz and the American Dream*, was collected by Eugene Nelson, a journalist active in Cesar Chavez's farmworker union. Unlike the life of Gonzales*, Cruz's story presents the more typical immigrant account of the Mexican who makes his way to the border, crosses only to be deported, recrosses again and again, and after some twenty years of pseudonymous self-disguising assumes his own name when he becomes an American citizen. Cruz relates his life story in Fresno, California, fully dignified as a new citizen, albeit one whose American dream comes in the form of odd jobs and seasonal farm labor. Gonzales*, on the other hand, having been thrown out of the United States, tells his story from "the central highlands of Mexico" where, Poggie explains, given his "fluent and idiomatic English" he is "selling arts and crafts in a tourist shop."

Both of these "bi-cultural, composite" autobiographies, as Arnold Krupat refers to such narratives,[3] were part of a wider discourse treating Mexican American farmworkers, illegal immigrants, and general Chicano political, socioeconomic, and cultural concerns. During the decade of the seventies scores of books, newspaper and magazine articles, and visual documentaries described the conditions under which both Mexican American and illegal Mexican farm laborers worked and lived, as well as the conditions under which these farmworkers struggled to organize their own labor union, with Cesar Chavez, the charismatic leader of the United Farmworkers Union, the focus of much of the literature.[4] Books by distinguished writers such as Peter Matthiessen, Stan Steiner, and John Gregory Dunne followed Nelson's own work on the United Farmworkers in *Huelga—The First 100 Days of the Delano Grape Strike* (1966).[5] Although Poggie's anthropological work was not directly connected to such topical political issues, his interest in the effects of modernization on third world people and its bearing upon Latin American immigration to the United States reflected broader political concerns motivating the production of ethnographic literature in the 1970's.

Although *Between Two Cultures* and *Pablo Cruz and the American Dream* were generated by the agricultural unionizing and general civil rights activism of the period, the construction of the immigrant subject represented in both texts emerged out of earlier social science discourse on the Mexican immigrant. Both Poggie, the anthropologist, and Nelson, the muckraking journalist, were served by the methodological development of informant life-history narrative that undergirded the findings of earlier scholars. The discursive formation underlying this construction of the immigrant subject appears most clearly in Julian Samora's contemporary *Los Mojados: The Wetback Story* (1971), a study of the undocumented Mexican workers based not only upon interviews with "Wetbacks" but upon a (re)construction of one immigrant's experience. This is not a Mexican's narrative of his own experience but a product of social science methodology. It is, Samora writes, the narrative of "one of our own researchers using one more sociologists' tool, participant observation" (p. 12).

The genealogy of this discursive formation, its practices, and its products, goes back to investigations of the Mexican cultural subject in the 1920's. John Poggie, in his acknowledgments, notes that Oscar Lewis, the author of such "multiple autobiographies" as *Five Families* (1959) and *The*

Children of Sanchez (1961), as well as single-subject autobiographies like *Pedro Martinez* (1964), was a direct influence on his own method for collecting and organizing the ethnographic material presented in *Between Two Cultures*. It is in prefatory acknowledgments that we often discover the traces of discursive genealogy, and it turns out that with Lewis's own tribute to Manuel Gamio, "who was Mexico's elder statesman among social scientists," we arrive at the proximate source of such constructions of the Mexican cultural subject.[6] With Manuel Gamio, recent immigrant autobiographical formations of the I-speaking voice, simultaneously privileged and dismissed by the social scientist, may be said to begin. I am not interested in tracking down origins here, however. Instead, what follows is devoted to thinking about the sociodiscursive production of the immigrant subject as the specimen-object of social science research. I am interested in identifying the specific discursive practices by which a voice is projected into a body in order to tell a story that serves sociology as a representation for a set of generalizations about immigration and immigrants. As a scholar of autobiography, I also wish to discover how this process is resisted—how and when the immigrant Mexican ceases being the object about whom the social scientist can "formulate scientific problems," the embodiment of the discipline's typical concerns, and becomes, rather, the autonomous subject of his or her own narrative fascination, an autobiographical agent rather than a de-named object of speculation. Thinking about this development can best begin by examining the work of Manuel Gamio.

Although Mexicans had freely crossed the border since 1848 and considerable migration to the United States was in process around the turn of the century, it wasn't until between 1910 and 1930 that great waves of Mexican people fled North from severe social, political, and economic conditions. The internal social trauma and socioeconomic destabilization that resulted from the Mexican Revolution of 1910–1920, coupled with the rise in agricultural business in the American West and the accelerated industrial economy that accompanied the United States's entry into World War I, created what Paul Taylor referred to as the "push" and "pull" that initiated a massive labor exodus to the United States. It has been estimated that over the ten-year period, the "number of border crossings was . . . nearer a total of 2,000,000 than the 330,000 counted by the United States immigration officials."[7]

The earliest extensive studies of this vast Mexican immigration to the United States were undertaken by the eminent Mexican anthropologist

Manuel Gamio and Paul Taylor, an American labor economist, between 1926 and 1932. The findings of Gamio's "preliminary survey" were published as *Mexican Immigration to the United States: A Study of Human Migration and Adjustment* (1930) and *The Mexican Immigrant: His Life-Story* (1931). Taylor's *Mexican Labor in the United States* appeared as a seven-volume monograph series between 1928 and 1932.[8] Although much of the data they collected was statistical (demographic employment figures, school enrollments, wage tables, money order receipts, and so on), the findings of both scholars relied heavily upon interviews conducted with hundreds of Mexican laborers over a wide terrain from California to Texas, from Chicago to Pennsylvania. As Taylor wrote in the foreword to the second volume, "literally hundreds of persons from coast to coast and from the Rio Grande to the Canadian border have been interviewed" (p. iv). Whereas Taylor spliced scores of voices into the texts of his findings, Gamio presented 76 self-contained "Autobiographic Documents" in *The Mexican Immigrant: His Life Story*. These autobiographical documents collected by Gamio and his assistants exemplify the problematics of ethnographic theorizing, collection tactics, and subject manipulation characteristic of the discursive practices that Gamio helped formulate.

In the introduction to *Mexican Immigration to the United States*, Gamio describes the strategies he established in order to gather personal narratives from a wide-ranging group of informants on a migratory phenomenon of extraordinary proportions. Given the fact that Mexicans by the scores of thousands had migrated to the United States since 1910, the potential scope of the project was so enormous that Gamio "had to be content with mere observation, objective and subjective" of a relatively small field of subjects (p. xi). The objective portion of the study required that Gamio and his assistants spend considerable time following their subjects into "their fields of work, factories, railroad camps, mines, schools," as well as "their homes . . . their prisons and hospitals" and even "their funerals" (p. xi). Such "objective observation" was to form the basis for an anthropology of the Mexican immigrant that relied upon—even as it dismissed—"subjective observation," which "consisted in finding out from the individual himself what had been the character of his material and mental life" (p. xii). Gamio interviewed Mexicans of varying ages, employments, regional and racial backgrounds, with different durations of residency in the United States, and recorded these "guided interviews" as background for his sociological project. The autobiographical statements taken from these subjects were not intended to privilege individual immigrant lives, but rather to undergird the objective data, and presumably to introduce a human touch to the study without contaminating the project by making it too human.

Even though getting inside the "mental life" of the immigrant was one of Gamio's objectives, scientific skepticism about individual social and personal memory was set not only against the credibility of those subjects whose "biographies were of doubtful veracity" but against the value of biographical and autobiographical information in general. Aligning himself with the depersonalizing methodological tactics developing in social science discourse during its formative period, Gamio qualifies, and as much as apologizes for, his use of personal statements: "Our first experiences . . . confirmed what modern sociological methods had already indicated, that the value of autobiographies is generally slight and relative" (p. xii). Personal narratives—the articulations of men and women with distinct names and personal histories—were regarded with suspicion, since to place too much emphasis on the individual subject might undermine the generalizing discourse. As Robert Redfield, Gamio's editor for *The Mexican Immigrant: His Life Story* and an eminent anthropologist himself,[9] wrote in his introductory remarks to the edition:

The value of concrete materials such as these lies in the fact that they enable us to get an intimate acquaintance with the field of interest. By means of such materials we may come to know just what is important for study. They . . . give us some degree of understanding of the Mexican immigrant; after reading them we know better what to expect of him, and we are in a better position to formulate scientific problems about him. (p. xii)

Redfield went on to point out that although the immigrant "is apt to tell the truth about where he was born, where he has worked, and how much he was paid . . . other more critical experiences and situations . . . are not likely to be reported objectively" (p. vii). Presumably tainted by personal subjectivity and social contingency, such "concrete materials" must be made to remain subordinate to "scientific study" because they are autobiographical and tend to report contingency. The problem, it appears, was that personal narratives are at once not concrete enough, that is, not empirical enough, and too concrete, too real in the flesh, too close to lived experience, too much inside the skin of their own language and personal concerns.

Once "the person's own view" attached itself to the relation of events, personal narrative was regarded as contaminated by self-aggrandizing "viewpoints and rationalizations." The nullification of immigrant personal statements as "rationalizations" oddly enough reopened the "field of study," since "rationalizations . . . are useful in explaining and anticipating conduct" (p. vii). When people engage in interpretative activity about their lives, the resulting personal narrative both exposes and permits the containment of suspicious behavioral tendencies. In Gamio's ethnographic practice, the Mexican subject no sooner engaged in autobiographic disclosure than he or she was recontained within a discourse operating to control aggravating intimate perceptions about self in the world. Autobiographical self-articulation had to be regulated in order to guarantee its function in creating a fit object for scientific study.

Although Gamio privileged "objective" observations, he was not content to dismantle entirely the subjective "Life-Story" portion of the project—the slight(ed) value of autobiographic statement notwithstanding. To his credit, Gamio reconsidered the difficult position of the immigrant during personal questioning, and conceded that his informants were perhaps misrepresenting themselves out of self-defense against "our abrupt and intrusive interrogation," which "created emotional reactions to our presence, such as fear, distrust, displeasure . . . or else satisfaction or vanity" (p. xxi). Following such self-criticism, Gamio "gradually corrected the method of observation" for eliciting personal statements. If ethnographically elicited personal narratives were suspect, it might be attributed to inappropriate contact between anthropologist and subject, with the anthropologist in a position of power that intimidated peasants and common laborers. "Fear, distrust, displeasure" might manifest themselves in evasion, hostility, or silence. "Satisfaction or vanity" might serve as strategic deceptions, exaggerations, or lies meant to sidetrack intrusions by pencil-and-paper wielding strangers. Gamio and his assistants, after all, were intent upon reducing people to the status of "informants," with all the term connotes.

The challenge for Gamio, therefore, was to bring the oral text of social experience into the "scientific" realm without alienating people into silence or deception. Awakening what he called a "true process of introspection" proved central to his method. Rather than abruptly intruding into the lives of selected subjects, Gamio and his assistants would ease their way into conversation with the immigrant only "when he was in the company of other persons." Even then the immigrant subject was to be "ignored," the observer exercising great "care not to question him or even refer to his person or life." This strangely bifurcated positioning by the field observers—affecting detachment and yet gesturing tacit interest—somehow succeeded in prompting narrative performance by people who began to tell their life stories alongside those they heard others tell. This necessarily surreptitious method, Gamio insisted, stimulated the subject's "memory," awakening the "true process of introspection" that gave greater warrant to personal narrative. Immigrant subjects would presumably express themselves truthfully and entirely only when they did not perceive themselves being perceived.

Gamio referred to this practice as producing "a state of voluntary eloquence." Gamio's revised strategy for obtaining subject information recalculated elicitation methods through a form of sociological *power of suggestion* aimed at awakening the deeper introspective desire in the subject that would yield a truth (some deeply profound sociological Truth?) Gamio had missed in his "first experiences." It is a technique by which the social scientist structures an environment in which unselfconscious articulations speak the *truth*, a truth the scientist is prepared to recognize precisely because it is a product, a response to a scientifically applied stimulus. It is a technique that produces a satisfactory, scientifically validated version of subjectivity. Gamio described this invasive technique as a necessary behavioral manipulation of the immigrant informant. I prefer to think of it as a form of anthropological hypnotism:

We chatted in simple language upon subjects suited to his interests and interposed remarks and comments upon other persons and their lives; after this we waited patiently for his response. . . . Our pretense of interest in the persons and lives of other individuals as well as in affairs entirely foreign to the persons interviewed and our own silence and indifference in regard to himself generally awoke in his mind a process of introspection: His memory was stimulated; reactions relating to the present arose and reactions of the past were recalled—all of which yielded a body of statements and confidences satisfactory because of their sincerity and spontaneity. When the confidence of the individual was thus once gained and he found himself in a state of voluntary eloquence, the observation was completed by direct questioning. (p. xiii)

The accommodation the social scientist makes to "simple language," a concession to working-class dialect that apparently swings away from official and formulaic sets of questions standard in the field questionnaire, is aimed at generating the subject's own concession. What the subject is made to concede, however, is the autonomy and contingency that so vexed Gamio's early attempts to produce reliable autobiographical information. In this remarkable account of ethnographic practice, the autobiographical voice that the subject brought to the encounter is extracted from the immigrant's too subjective existence and re-embodied in a more objective, more reliable form. It becomes "satisfactory" because its "sincerity" and "spontaneity" are not unregulated expressions but responses that the scientist himself has been able to produce via a limited and reproducible procedure. In this satisfactory form, the subjectivity of the subject can be seen as objective. It can be incorporated into a "body of statements and confidences" because it has been in-corporated into the form objective facts must display as part of the scientific body of knowledge.

But autobiographical consciousness proved troubling, even in this "satisfactory," regulated, objective form. Questions revealed psychological wounds in the body of statements and confidences the ethnographic procedure produced. More anguish and self-doubt than joy appeared in the results of ethnographic inquiry about intercultural experience. There can be no doubt that Mexican immigrants—whether those of the 1920's or those crossing the border today—have experienced difficulty, dislocation, disorientation. However, the immigrant subjects of Gamio's study—as well as those subjects of succeeding studies—in responding to the social scientist's systematic perturbation of memory have had their painful experiences of liminality and cultural difference structured in a particular way. The construction of the immigrant subject was not intended to open sustained, self-authorizing, autobiographically free terrain for immigrants to think about the fullness of experience in any sustained manner: memory, rather, was orchestrated to produce data in a form that could be contained, an account of cultural otherness, a narrative of the immigrant subject as marginal, suspended in a stasis between two cultures, not an active participant in the life of the United States.

The informal but nevertheless always formulaic structure of Gamio's questions not only elicited social and cultural information but placed the immigrants in the awkward and often anguished position of having to rationalize their decision to remain in the United States for any duration. Their motives for residing in the United States and their loyalty to Mexican cultural practices in the face of long residence here were at once called forth and implicitly derided by culturally comparative questions in which the immigrant subject was directed to comment—in his or her own words, of course—on the sense of displacement or liminality in which they discovered themselves. Inquiry into intercultural attitudes was structured to elicit affective comparisons between life in Mexico and that in the United States with "special attention to the social medium and the psychological environment in which [the immigrant] lives."[10]

In the appendix to *Mexican Immigration to the United States* called the "Guide For Field-Workers," Gamio warned that the questions "should not be formulated exactly like those suggested, but the wording and ideology should be adapted to the grade of mentality and culture of the individual under observation."[11] The questions may have been worded col-

loquially during interviews, but the personal statements they called forth
on the whole show that they produced a generalized kind of response. The
more substantive—or "eloquent"—responses were about intercultural relations, although the particular questions that produced them were about
religious affiliation ["Do you confess, partake of communion, go to
mass?"], reading habits ["Do you read Mexican or American newspapers
or both?"], and food customs ["Do you have Mexican cooking in your
house?"]. Some questions called for elementary comparisons of U.S.-
Mexican sociocultural experience: "What impressions do the big build-
ings, the trains, the many automobiles, the factories, the moving-picture
houses, and schools of this country make upon you?" "Do you know who
were Washington, Hidalgo, Lincoln, Juarez?" "Do you like American or
Mexican music or both?" Yet, inquiry ultimately seemed designed to establish disparities between the linguistic, cultural, and national characteristics of the two countries, and to situate the immigrant subject firmly in
the gap between them.

As the immigrant moved into a state of voluntary eloquence, the interview arrogated the subject's private experience and converted it into an
objective split in the subjectivity of the Mexican American, a split named
by the ethnic label itself. When asked why they left Mexico, often people
described personally painful family fragmentation—abuse or neglect by
parents, loss of loved ones during revolutionary crisis, joblessness and hunger. Notwithstanding the obvious motives created by such anguishing experiences, the interviewers put the subject on the defensive about choosing
to remain in the United States, where material and physical security were
possible, instead of returning to Mexico, where civil war raged and the
economy was in shambles. However much they might think of themselves
as Mexicans, despite their long stay away from their homeland, those
people who had been living in the United States for long periods officially
had been situated in the special category of "Mexican-Americans and Naturalized Mexicans." Many of the questions put to this group are edgy,
aimed not only at measuring cultural knowledge but at testing loyalty to
the homeland:

In case of war with the United States, would you side with the Americans and
fight the Mexicans?

Do you like American women on account of their white skin, because they are
more beautiful than the women you know, or because you think your social position would be improved?

Do you believe that those who constitute "The Race"[12] are destined to a happier future or to be absorbed by the Anglo-Saxon race on this continent?

Such questions seem unnecessarily provocative, sensationalizing the national loyalties and racial identities to which they appeal. After a history of conquest, intervention, and manipulation by the United States, Mexicans naturally regarded U.S. military and economic interests with suspicion, but when Gamio posed the hypothetical war question in the late 1920's it must have sounded extreme, since the two countries were hardly poised on the brink of war. Moreover, what Mexican in his right mind would say, or even be expected to say, that he would fight against his own people? And the question about beautiful white-skinned American women is both blatantly sexist and racist: in addition to objectifying American women, it simultaneously teases men of color with the image of the forbidden white goddess while, in the same breath, denigrating Mexican women, who the question presumes are uglier than their white sisters. The final question, which should measure assimilation/acculturation, feeds upon the Mexican's own historical disinclination to surrender culture; it also operates upon the assumption that given his low socioeconomic status the immigrant is unhappy, and can thus only vaguely imagine a condition of happiness in some uncertain future, or resign himself to the doom of being absorbed by the Anglo-Saxon race—the ultimate unhappiness.

Such questions provide an index to the beliefs and concerns of the investigators who employ them because they create a condition of discomfort in which the subjects are asked to speculate on experiences they perhaps never themselves have had or never have thought about. They betray a comprehensive anxiety about the otherness of the immigrant. Even seemingly innocuous culturally comparative questions ("Do you have Mexican cooking in your house?") seem aimed at testing cultural and national loyalties: under the section on "Assimilation," for example, one finds a Mexican whose taste for American cooking signals assimilative (traitorous?) tendencies: "The food seems to me to be better when American, more healthful. . . . I eat at home and I digest well but when I go to the homes of relatives and they give me Mexican dishes I am sick at night." And under "Conflict and Race-Consciousness," another immigrant's food loyalty is part of his overall distaste for American culture: "I eat according to Mexican style, for my wife makes my food. . . . In everything I am like the Mexicans, that is to say, like they live over there. I don't like anything about this country."[13] The Mexican American subject, when interrogated according to Gamio's procedures, consistently produced accounts of a self divided against itself.

The ends served by producing self-representations in these particular forms were not simply those of the emerging social sciences. The social scientist's production of an objectified, yet split immigrant subject, predictably, served as the basis for determining ways to contain and control the otherness that subject brought into Anglo-American culture. Despite the expressions of conflict, ambivalence, uncertainty, and anger revealed in nearly all of the personal narrative responses to "directed interviews," it is still surprising that Redfield would see fit to draw a comparison between the immigrant autobiographic documents and the findings of other sociologists who were studying criminal behavior. Redfield's principal examples of the use of "life-history materials" for "explaining and understanding [the] conduct of immigrants" were two books by sociologists that relied upon the value of "autobiographical accounts in understanding and in treating cases of delinquency" (p. vii). Resort to these, in place of any reference to immigrant autobiographies from the period of the great European migrations, doomed the Mexican immigrant to the status of outlaw, a status now fully extended into the contemporary degrading term "illegal alien." As one of the original editors of Gamio's autobiographic documents, Redfield's ideologically charged analogy between Mexican immigrant workers and juvenile delinquents instantly established an image of the Mexican as suspect, a person whose deceptive and duplicitous motives must be carefully scrutinized and rationally explained. Gamio's collection of brief personal narratives therefore functioned as the original handbook for Americans needing to be schooled in Mexican social and psychological behavior, in the hope, as Redfield says, that they will be "better able to understand and deal with Mexican immigrants." Establishing better understanding between Mexicans and Americans may indeed be a positive use for personal narratives, but any ideal of intercultural understanding projected in the opening phrase is subverted when the second part of the phrase darkens, almost nullifies such understanding.

That Americans continue to require handbooks for "dealing with" the Mexican and, more recently, the Central American immigrant "other" may be witnessed in Lewis's popular ethno-fictive autobiographies of the 1960's, Poggie's and Nelson's immigrant ethnographies of the 1970's, recent *testimonios* by Central American refugees, and John Donovan's *Coyotes: A Journey Through the Secret World of America's Illegal Aliens*, a participant narrator study of undocumented Mexican workers that appeared to wide acclaim in 1987.

Thanks to Gamio's wide influence, the modalities of intercultural liminality, or cultural split, structured into his ethnographic inquiry have been reproduced in the configurations of liminality reinscribed in the work of successive social scientists whose elicited autobiographical data form the basis for a social theory of marginalization. Redfield anticipated the influence that the discursive practices underlying Gamio's collection of autobiographic documents would exercise on another generation of ethnographers when in the introduction to *The Mexican Immigrant* he commended the extended "life-history technique" as a way to get "as complete a picture as possible of the successive events in the individual's life" (p. vii). Such sustained "life-history" would provide material for deep analysis of one subject while also opening space for generalization.

Perhaps the most notable example of detailed ethnographic reconstitution of the "successive events in the [Mexican] individual's life" is to be found in Oscar Lewis's *Five Families, The Children of Sanchez,* and *Pedro Martinez.*[14] These long, novelistic narratives focus ethnographic concentration on the individual subject in a manner consistent with Redfield's suggestion that "an immigrant life history would be an extensive autobiographic statement of the subject's career, the result of long study of the case by the investigator, and obtained from the subject only after suitable rapport had been established" (p. vii). Brief personal statements "made to hurried investigators in the course of casual contacts" eventually developed into Lewis's sustained multiple autobiographies, which privileged individual subjects as autonomous human beings. Or so it seemed. For Gamio's objectivist intention was both reproduced and refined in Lewis's ethnographic autobiographies; that is, there was a noticeable shift from Gamio's skepticism about the representational value of autobiography to the valorization of sustained autobiography. Yet Lewis's psychological pronouncements on his subjects were possessed of a smug Freudianism that seems both unnecessary and unwarranted. Of Pedro Martinez, whose father died when he was young and whose mother left him with his grandmother, he writes: "The lack of identification with a strong male figure and his close attachment to his mother may have created in Pedro some feelings of ambivalence about his masculinity and led to some passive, dependent feelings at a deep unconscious level" (p. xxxv). Similar psychologizing inserts itself into Poggie's reading the personality of Ramón Gonzales* as "emotionally flat," as evidenced by a "strategy for handling conflict situations [that] was to avoid or deny them" (p. x). As in Gamio's work, the protagonists of these immigrant autobiographies function as representatives for the marginalized, psychologically divided, culturally liminal Mexican immigrant. The immigrant as a subject split between two cultures— as the title of Poggie's text makes explicit—has, it turns out, long been determined by the discursive practices by which anthropology and sociology organize the Mexican immigrant experience. One need only scan the front covers of *Between Two Cultures* and *Pablo Cruz and the American Dream* and read their introductions to note the ponderously representative split subjectivity into which Ramón Gonzales* and Pablo Cruz are fashioned by their amanuensis-editors, John Poggie and Eugene Nelson. From Gamio through Lewis to Poggie and Nelson we witness the use of autobiographical statement in the construction of a prevailing image of the immigrant subject as the site of division, uncertainty, fragmentation—and a site of contention from which the name is removed.

The attachment of the personal name to an individual's life story is a cornerstone upon which autobiography rests, but, as we have already seen with Ramón Gonzales*, the Mexican immigrant proper name has typically been erased, only to be replaced with a generic Mexican name that represents a person talking, but talking through a mask. In his role of Gamio's editorial overseer, Redfield notes that in addition to eliminating "some passages and about twenty whole documents that seemed to me to throw no light on the behavior of the Mexican immigrants," he policed the law of subject confidentiality: "I have changed all the personal names and removed many of the place names, in recognition of the terms of confidence under which the statements were made to the original investigators" (p. ix).

So who were the people behind the 76 proper names listed in *The Mexican Immigrant: His Life Story*? Jesús Garza, Elisa Reciños, Angel Ruiz, Anastacio Torres, Doña Clarita, Elena Torres de Acosta, Elías Sepulveda, Epifanio Aguirre, Santiago Lerdo, Miguel Padilla—are they pseudonyms, disguises, partial names, echoes of the original personal names? We will never know, since the social scientist, in subordinating the individual to the field of study, long ago decided that it was in the best interest of the informant subject to keep him quiet under the guise of protective privacy and confidentiality. The Mexican immigrant was given voice in a text only to have the name that identifies the autobiographical utterance textually concealed, cancelled by a fabricated name. What would happen were we to trace Doña Clarita or Miguel Padilla? Because we begin with the proper name, a genealogical search for either person would evaporate into namelessness almost before beginning. Of course, hypothetically we might search through the field notes Gamio submitted to the Social Science Research Council, where true names are presumably attached to their life stories. I say hypothetically, because such archival rescue would do little to alter the textual presence of pseudonymous inscriptions in *The Mexican Immigrant: His Life Story*, which remains in print today.

I am not arguing that "terms of confidence" should be casually breached, or that subject confidentiality be abrogated altogether. I am pointing to something about the tone of Redfield's words, the quickness, the rhetorical authority casually voiced, the juridical finality with which policy is stated, that troubles me: "I have eliminated some passages . . . I have changed all the personal names." Subject confidentiality in the service of protecting people from political persecution, or deportation, may be warranted, but Redfield in 1930 never explained why changing "all the personal names" was necessary. I understand the division here: the social scientist will charge that as a literary scholar—"one of those mushy-headed humanists," as a sociologist friend recently called me—I am questioning a convention that is simply requisite for funding projects with human subjects and that protects the privacy of individuals from various intrusions. I understand this, but it also seems to me that the confidentiality rule has developed into a self-authorizing instrument for deciding what is in the best interest of the human subject, for dominating the human subject, for controlling discourse about the human subject. I am not convinced, therefore, that the policy of subject confidentiality is a practice always intended to protect the individual, without also always protecting the power the social scientist holds over his informants, who are, after all, merely the source of data. As Redfield says, documents failing to meet his criteria of intelligibility, failing to "throw light on the behavior of Mexican immigrants," must be edited out, banished from the field of study, nullified. What in the content of such personal statements was not illuminating information? Were the statements perhaps too personal, too occupied with concerns alien to the investigators, or too subjective to be of any use in a totalizing sociological project? Since the individual body, with its experience, is subordinate to the body of knowledge, the proper name can be dispensed with, subrogated, the subject dis-identified, severed from the sound that turns the head in attention to another's voice, lost to its own genealogical presence, turned into one of Maxine Hong Kingston's no-name ancestors.

The Mexican immigrant, therefore, has too often remained an anonymous entity, a cipher to be assigned meaning in a sociological play of statements. Such has been common practice from Gamio's work of the 1920's until the 1970's, when Ernesto Galarza wrote his name on the title page of *Barrio Boy*, and, perhaps more significantly, when in narrating his life story Pablo Cruz describes how he rescued his own proper name from the multiple pseudonyms he had hidden behind while an illegal immigrant in the United States. Yet, at the same time that Cruz's name came out of hiding, John Poggie's ethnographic narrative of a man born in Mexico but raised in the United States reaffirmed the convention—and the de-facing effects—of human subject confidentiality.

The methodological chain of influence extending from Gamio to Poggie through the widely acclaimed work of Oscar Lewis reveals the power of arrogation by which the deletion of the personal name has become a casually enforced convention. Poggie acknowledges the groundbreaking use of the "tape recorder, a method brought to attention by Oscar Lewis" (p. xi), just as in the introduction to *Pedro Martinez* (1964) Lewis acknowledges the influence of Manuel Gamio, who had sponsored his earliest work in a Mexican village in 1943. In their introductory comments, all three scholars maintain that the confidentiality of the proper name is necessary. Reiterating official policy, Lewis thanks the Martinez family "for their co-operation and friendship," and then de-faces them, saying their "true identity must remain anonymous." But why? What had they done that they should fear having their lives presented as theirs to the world? Notwithstanding his strong political views, Pedro Martinez* was no radical subversive whose identity had to be guarded, or an undocumented worker like Pablo Cruz who must disguise his name until legalizing it as an American citizen, or a repeatedly deported "American Mexican" like Ramón Gonzales*. On the contrary, Lewis says that Martinez's "name was given to me by local officials who suggested that he could tell me a great deal about his barrio and about the village." The social scientist's adherence to the convention of confidentiality in fact conceals a colonizing strategy by which he alone will control the articulation of the subject.

As a literary scholar questioning in my turn the social scientist, I can ask my friend the sociologist why names are necessary at all, if what we are interested in is generalizing discourse about Mexican immigrants as a sociological abstraction. Why not just use case numbers or letters? But notice the contradiction: a name, some name picked from the group's storehouse of names, is necessary. The social scientist, it turns out, believes that a personal name will confer immediacy and the warmth of human speech on the face and body of experience moving through narrative space. This desire for putting names to those whose stories we hear, shared by social scientist and literary scholar, announces a central contradiction in social science discourse: it appropriates the narrative practices common to the novel even as it privileges the scientific method. The social scientist's data—the meandering, elliptical, cacophonous voicings of human experience—must be arranged, ordered, given the kind of narrative coherence that the historian gives to scraps of evidence, or that the novelist imparts to characters in fiction. In the discourse of the social sciences, such novelistic practice is quickly framed as scientifically containable, a play toward the fictive that won't get out of hand. Literary scholars know better.

The hint of complicity between fictive and ethnographic narrative lies in the mark of the asterisk. The asterisk appears as the marker and reminder that ethnographic narrative is a serious, scientifically controlled project, not fictional art. And yet the asterisk novelizes ethnography. Oscar Lewis's commentary on the ethno-literary methods exercised in his work may be the most revealing example of how the narrative desires of the anthropologist and the novelist meet in the presentation of the Mexican subject. Lewis describes his intentions as purely anthropological: "In this tape-recorded story of a Mexican peasant family as told by three of its members*—Pedro Martinez, the father, Esperanza, his wife, and Felipe, his eldest son—I hope to convey to the reader what it means to be a peasant . . . how peasants feel, how they think, and how they express themselves." But the reader who follows the asterisk to the bottom of the page lands in the terrain of the novel, where the fine print reads: "Except for historical figures, the characters in this book have been given fictitious names, to protect their anonymity" (p. xxix). It is as if the Martinez* family has become characters in a novel about the peasantry after the fashion of Zola, Hardy, or Steinbeck. The asterisk protecting the anonymity of the subject functions as a sign of the anthropologist's self-licensing appropriation of a set of narrative procedures, beginning with renaming the subject and proceeding through an entire orchestration of narrative events that transforms disjointed statements, trailing monologues, whispers and mutters—the stuff of people speaking in the world—into the kind of reconstituted, planed speech found in a novel. In this instance an American anthropologist uses those procedures to instruct us in how peasants "express themselves."

My concerns here are fully warranted by Lewis's introductory notes to another ethnographic text, Five Families (1959), where he elaborates on, while apologizing for, the competing claims of social science and its appropriation of the novelist's structuring narrative:

The study of days presented here attempts to give some of the immediacy and wholeness of life which is portrayed by the novelist. Its major commitment, nevertheless, is to social science with all of its strengths and weaknesses. Any resemblance between these family portraits and fiction is purely accidental. Indeed, it is difficult to classify these portraits. They are neither fiction nor conventional anthropology. For want of a better term I would call them ethnographic realism, in contrast to literary realism. (p. 18)

When Lewis valorizes novelistic procedures because they confer "immediacy and wholeness" to data, but disclaims the organizing procedures common to the novel, he rightly implies that such techniques disrupt the empiricist imperative. Even if he is not writing "conventional anthropology," he nevertheless wants to claim for that writing the status of ethnographic truth, and to insist on the difference between the discourse of that truth and the "literary" techniques by which "fiction" is constructed. Sensing himself too close to the terrain of the fictive, Lewis draws back to legitimating empiricist ground—any resemblance to fiction, he says, is "purely accidental," which is just the opposite of the usual prefatory disclaimer found at the beginning of novels that "any resemblance between these characters and real people is purely accidental."[15] His "ethnographic realism" attempts to divest itself of the contaminations of the "literary" that threaten to depose the documentary claims of social science discourse.

It is just such claimed "ethnographic realism" that one discovers again and again in the ethnographically constructed autobiographies of third world people, native Americans, or Mexicans crossing the border into the United States. Through all of these externally imposed and controlled discursive mechanisms, the people who tell their lives are shaped and reshaped into sociological, ethnographic, and ethno-novelized representations of Mexican peasants. Like Ramón Gonzales*, Mexicans who live in the United States become the material of ethnographic narrative for whom the asterisk flashes its contradictory signal of protective concealment and disempowering disguise.

Between Two Cultures: The Life of an American-Mexican opens with John J. Poggie offering Ramón Gonzales* as an example of cultural marginality in the flesh: "Ramón Gonzales* is a man who is part of two very different cultures—American and Mexican. This is his autobiography." This American Mexican, found in a tourist shop close to the Mexican pyramids, one is led to imagine, has seized the moment to speak his autobiography to the world. But to what degree is the life represented in *Between Two Cultures* "his autobiography"? This is not a "life" in the conventional autobiographical sense but a social science case study. As Poggie says in the introduction, "Ramón is characteristic of a larger class of humans all over the world: people who feel that they do not belong solidly to one cultural group. These are the world's marginal men" (p. xiii). Why doesn't Poggie just say that the Gonzales* text is an ethnographic case study on marginality? Why insist this is an autobiography? And more importantly, why insist upon an autonomous autobiographical status for the subject of the text in the same breath that the name is hidden in the asterisk of subject confidentiality? "*Pseudonyms have been used in this volume when actual names of persons or places would intrude on the privacy of individuals" (p. ix).

So who is this man whose voice we hear calling: "My name is Ramón Gonzales. I was born in Pueblo Nuevo, Guanajanto, on August 31, 1922"? Given Poggie's startling and disorienting note on the necessary blurring/masking of personal and place names, is it unreasonable to wonder whether someone actually named Ramón Gonzales might have been born in a town called Pueblo Nuevo on August 31, 1922? Perhaps the subject of Poggie's book was actually born in a town called Pueblo Viejo on September 13, 1922, or 1925. And what are we to think when the pseudonymous speaker claims his immediate family: "My father's name is Nazario Gonzales and my mother's name is Candelaria Gonzales. I have three brothers [David, Jaime, Edward] and two sisters [Alicia, Guadalupe]." Are the characters in this pseudonymous genealogy partly or fully fabricated?

Poggie's concealment of his subject behind an asterisk puts the reader in a puzzling situation relative to a narrative that purports to be autobiography. For no matter how compelling I find the narrated life of Ramón Gonzales*, the asterisk looms before me, a reminder that Poggie's subject had little control over the narrative product in which he is represented. The asterisk—ever-present even though Poggie removes it from onerous duty by the conventional trick of showing it only once—reminds me that I am reading an ethnographically constructed autobiography, or an autobiographical case study: in this essay, I reactivate the * whenever Gonzales's "name" appears to remind myself and other readers that the proper name is always suspended in doubt. Given all the mechanics of ethnographic construction—directing the interview, transcribing and editing the tapes, eliminating material and organizing the narrative for publication—my first concern is that anything I say about the narrative as autobiography must at once be mediated by my doubts about the status of the autobiographical voice, notwithstanding Poggie's claim that the "narrative remains essentially in Ramón's own words." As usual, I find myself in the position of having to read through externally constructed narrative as a means of understanding and assessing the sociodiscursive operation out of which self-fashioned autobiography later emerges. While waiting for such a self-constituted and self-empowering formation, I must read through an * that deports the proper name. What is really at stake in considering *Between Two Cultures*, therefore, is the structure of power relations between the ethnic subject and the social scientist who gives voice to Ramón Gonzales*, empowered by the asterisk to omit where he will, rearrange where he must, and clarify where necessary to fashion a coherent narrative.[16]

Having argued at length that the subject of ethnographic autobiography is dominated by a matrix of manipulations over which he or she exercises little control, I wish to intervene in my own argument to ask where the subject assumes narrative authority over that story, however mediated, momentary, and subordinate to ethnographic intention that authority may be. Even though we recognize that the text is produced by someone else, part of our responsibility as readers of ethnographic autobiography is to find out the person speaking to us through the matrix of manipulations, the person who originally narrated the story of a life based on a body of felt experiences, a body of knowledge unmediated by the techniques and procedures of social science. This story contains its own logic, its own necessity. The original subject's need to tell this story, this basic narrative desire, as I call it, invests narrative performance with a claim to presence in the world that it is our responsibility to help validate in the act of reading. In other words, there are two narrative planes: the one I have detailed at length belongs to and is controlled by the social scientist; the other belongs to the person speaking into the ethnographer's microphone. Since we are implicated at every turn in the power relations between the "subject-informant" and the social scientist, unless we distinguish these narrative planes we are guilty of perpetuating the ethnographer's appropriation of the life we choose to read. We therefore read ethnographically constructed autobiography skeptically, but we nevertheless read it, hoping to make contact with someone's life, hoping to hear what another person says about that life, and finally, helping (rather than just hoping) to release personal narrative from its confinement in the ethnographic matrix.

A brief reading of *Between Two Cultures* will suggest a mode of analysis for distinguishing its surface articulation of its ethnographic agenda from the plane of the subject's life narrative, a way to read the life of a man whose name we can never know, whose narrative must remain in doubt, but who nevertheless is contending for narrative control as he speaks his life. *Between Two Cultures* has two distinct narrative openings that I think give evidence of the battle for narrative control between Poggie and the nameless subject whose life he appropriates. The first is an ethnographic opening in which Gonzales* appears as an adult, describing his work in a tourist shop while living "permanently" in the Mexican highlands; the second resembles the opening of a *Bildungsroman*, beginning with the subject's birth in Mexico and including a genealogy of family names, together with his earliest memories of his family's migration to California when he was six months old. What is immediately apparent about the anthropological opening is that Gonzales* is positioned to present himself as the perfect representative of Poggie's "marginal man" split between two cultures. The autobiographical opening, in contrast, focuses on the private anguish Gonzales* feels as the result of being abandoned by his mother when he was a small child. These two planes of narrative contend for authority throughout the book: Poggie structured his work into categories of behavioral and social development. There are chapters on "Early Experiences and Family Life," "Adolescence," "First Deportation," "Work Experiences on Both Sides of the Border." Gonzales*, responding to directed questioning by Poggie within these experiential categories but also waging a struggle for narrative autonomy, meanwhile emphatically staked out narrative territory of his own.

The two openings have a good deal to suggest about the interplay of narrative motives and the relation between ethnographic function and autobiographical desire. Each opening, it seems to me, operates from a distinct, if not always contradictory, set of motives. The manner in which ethnographic motive contravenes its subject's own autobiographical self-discovery is crucial to an understanding of the relations between the cultural subject and the anthropologist who in the introduction presumes to say: "We agreed that it would be worthwhile to present his life in the form of an autobiographical book" (p. xi). For whom, it should be asked, is this "life" presumed to be "worthwhile," and in what respect? Poggie's narrative motive arises from a desire to "present" the cultural subject as an anthropological specimen. I can hardly believe that his informant agreed to the objectifying public reading Poggie projected for him in the introduction: "I hope, as did Ramón in relating to me his life story, that this personal document will enable others to know what it is to be one kind of marginal man" (p. xiii). Who are these "others" to whom Poggie refers? Does he mean to suggest that other "marginal men," inhabitants of the third world, working-class people, Mexican migrants, will find Poggie's book under "Anthropology" on the shelves of their local library in Fresno or Teotihuacan? Will their own lives be alleviated by reading this "life"? Will they be "enabled" by the text? The answer, of course, is no. Poggie must be referring to students and scholars in the United States whose own anthropological interests are likely to find representational affirmation in the Gonzales* text.

My thinking is warranted by Poggie's use of a section of the Gonzales* narrative in another of his texts, *The Evolution of Human Adaptations:*

Readings in Anthropology.[17] This is an anthology of diverse readings on social, political, economic, and psychological adaptive behavior, mostly in the third world, intended for use in the anthropology classroom. Poggie includes the opening ["Introducing el Pocho"] and closing ["Mexico, Marriage and Future"] chapters of *Between Two Cultures* in a section called "Rethinking Modernization: The Present and the Future." In the preface to this section of the book, Poggie's single-subject ethnography is presented as a model study of the manner in which "transformations related to modernization not only affect whole regions and social structures, but also impinge on the lives of individuals" (p. 416). The chapter headnote refers to the "influx of peoples from Europe, Latin America and other parts of the world into the United States in search of the 'American dream'" (p. 417) and identifies the "considerable difficulty and hardship in their adjustment to the new social and environmental setting." Poggie's ethnography is therefore presented in this context as the "story of an individual whose life was complicated by the migration of his family from Mexico" (p. 417).

Yet, as Ramón Gonzales* represents his own life history, his dilemma seems less an example of the disorienting effects of migration and modernization than the result of a broken family. As far as marginality is concerned, he makes it perfectly clear that he felt at "home" in the United States. Given his own articulations of his cultural situation, one must question the imperious anthropological enforcement of Gonzales* as a specimen of the way "modernization creates the conditions whereby peoples become marginalized in a variety of ways." This isn't to argue that Mexican immigrants aren't typically caught in a push and pull between underdeveloped economies like those of Latin American countries and the strong, technologically developed economy of the United States. Manuel Gamio, Paul Taylor, Julian Samora, and more recently Amado Padilla and others have shown that immigrants experience acute intercultural stress and anxiety, a normal result of border crossing and cross-cultural trauma.

For the narrator whose story Poggie has appropriated, however, the most profound affective turmoil is rooted in the still-unreconciled disappearance of his mother when he was a young boy. She, rather than the border patrol, has disrupted his psychological equilibrium. It is the home she broke that he is always trying to reconstruct in his narrative of the past. He seems a good deal more traumatized by his mother's betrayal of the family than by his intercultural subjectivity, by the "marginality" that Poggie's narrative emphasizes. The familial crisis is a deep emotive tangle he has never figured out, while the cross-cultural dilemma, he understands, is a social fact of life. Although he misses "the States," is nostalgic for an earlier

American social life, and is understandably uncertain about his economic situation in Mexico, he appears reconciled to that situation. But he simply cannot forget the ghost of his mother's eternal presence-in-absence as the reminder of his own homeless life. He cannot forget her when, at the end of the narrative, he describes his married life and thinks aloud about how having a baby will transform his life of restless wandering: "That would change my whole life," he says, "because I think I would try to set up a home, you know, a decent home like I never had myself" (p. 92).

This need to remake the emotive home his mother disrupted is at the center of his narrative desire, while the sociocultural experiences that constitute his *pocho*[18] marginality are at the center of Poggie's efforts to fashion him into Gonzales*, an object of anthropological speculation. A close and sensitive reading of *Between Two Cultures* identifies behind Poggie's construction of Gonzales* a human and historical subject whose need to speak his life emerges from familial fragmentation, dispossession, loneliness, and his need for parental recognition and love. This narrator's preoccupations seem closer to what we think of as autobiographical narrative: the disclosure of formative personal experience, the crises and achievements that shape personality and the emotional life. Poggie's preoccupations situate the Mexican subject in a field of complex intercultural play, out of which a human representation of marginality may be bodied forth in a text that will "enable others to know what it is to be one kind of marginal man."

A stunning autobiographical moment closes the narrative, during which narrative control seems to elude Poggie and his agenda and return to the anonymous subject. His desire for a stable home to replace the one shattered by his mother's betrayal all at once appears more significant than Poggie's emphasis on the uncertain legal and economic position of Gonzales*. It is as though the scores of jobs he has had, the constant jumping of borders, the cultural discomfort he feels in Mexico and the legal dilemma he faces in the United States all along have been the result of this quest for the home he never had. This of course puts a different twist on the immigrant life story. His socioeconomic and juridical status is less an issue than the broken ecology of the family—for this particular person, at least. His mother's abandonment of him is responsible for the psychic fragmentation he feels. Her betrayal, rather than his successive deportations, appears to be the cause of his unending sense of dislocation. Although he never directly mentions his mother in the closing section of the narrative, it is obvious that he has her in mind when he promises his wife Augustina that he "would never leave her" because to do so would doom his children to "running around" as he did. The narrative closes autobiographically, with the narrator explaining how he met Augustina, the first person other than a phantom adolescent girlfriend with whom the narrator—and the reader—can finally imagine some idea of permanence, some possibility that he will end his driven wandering between different jobs and towns and finally find a home.

Of course, such narrative closure is crucial for Poggie's presentation of Gonzales*. It promises an end to his fugitive status as a marginal subject forever lost between two cultures, and gives coherence to a life history that otherwise seems doomed to a proliferation of jobs, women, and geographic locations. Ending as it does, with Gonzales* at least imagining a stable life for himself, gives some relief to the marginality Poggie condemns him to represent. But those moments at the end of the narrative in which he broods over his prospects for a stable job, for a place where he can settle with his wife and children, and for insuring that his new family will never suffer what he experienced as a child are also the sort of significant junctures of self-disclosure and self-gathering that we have come to expect of autobiography. Although we cannot pretend away the ethnographic manipulations operating in this or any other part of the narrative, or suspend skepticism about the external construction of the subject in such a text, I would argue that we can, and must, parse those competing registers of intent within the text in order to identify the immigrant subject's own narrative terrain. We must distinguish the junctures where ethnography gives way to autobiography, where the ethnographic subject becomes autobiographer. The asterisk will always loom before us as the symbol of the social scientist's ownership of the text, but within the asterisk's concealment of the face and name is a voice we hear calling its own presence. A narrative that ends by reiterating its subject's primal anxiety about the crisis of family fragmentation articulates an enduring hope, not for some vague "place in the world" as Poggie imagines (p. xiii), but for a home with children who will know what a home is. Its narrator's desire to articulate this may not displace the asterisk that enables the ethnologist's narrative agenda, but it does voice the existence of a man who is both more and less than a representation of one of "the world's marginal men."

What Happened in Mecca:
Mumtaz Mufti's 'Labbaik'

Barbara D. Metcalf

𝒯ravel often stimulates autobiographical reflection.[1] It offers marvelous potential for disjunction and irony as travelers move in a world different from their own and confront the gap between expectations and actuality.[2] Travelers not only move in space, but often in time, to places whose history they seek, and even in social hierarchy. In a new place they can abandon or question their customary identity, and, Paul Fussell writes, "among strangers a new sense of selfhood can be tried on, like a costume."[3] One well-known type of travel writing is that of the European escaping the modern, industrialized world in quest of an older simplicity or authenticity. The subject of this paper, however, is a non-European postcolonial "bicultural" who nevertheless also is absorbed in what is seen as the conflict between the old and the new—between East and West, faith and doubt, the spiritual and the material. He seeks what may be his roots, in no less a place than Mecca.[4] Travel writing like this allows, above all, a personal exploration of the perceived inconsistencies of modern life and gives occasion for the fundamental modernist experience—that cultural truths are inevitably contested.

In the mid-1960's Mumtaz Mufti, one of Pakistan's most celebrated novelists and intellectuals, a self-proclaimed "nominal Muslim," encountered—or so he tells us—a series of disconcerting events, not quite explicable, all of which worked together inexorably to bring him to the point of undertaking the pilgrimage to Mecca. Some time after he returned from Mecca, Mumtaz Mufti was prevailed on by friends to write out his experiences. They first appeared in sixteen installments in an Urdu journal; a revised account was published as a book in 1975 and has been in print ever since.[5] Mufti used a simple and evocative one-word title for the book ver-

sion—*Labbaik*, "I am here," the humble Arabic call of the pilgrim arrived
at Mecca. He identifies his account as an *ap biti*, an autobiography or,
literally "what happened to oneself" (p. 10). He also repeatedly and somewhat disingenuously calls it *reportage*, transliterating a word known from
English, perhaps to protest any suggestion that his account might be anything less than fact. The work is unconventional—at times phantasma-
gorical—vibrant and original.

The account opens with a storylike heading, "The Madman of Fawara
Square." One evening as Mumtaz Mufti was crossing the square, a dark-
skinned person with a frightening face, wild hair and burning eyes suddenly accosted him. "You will go on hajj, you will go on hajj," he cried.
Taking him to be a *faqir*, Mumtaz offered him some change. But then—in
a move that lifts the story from the predictable—the faqir turned the tables,
reached into his pocket, and pressed money on *him*: "Take this, take this,
you will need money on hajj" (p. 24).

Other episodes glide imperceptibly from observation to the author's
zany imagination. The middle of the night, finally on the PIA plane from
Karachi to Jiddah, Mumtaz Mufti is sitting among the pious pilgrims in
coach, dressed in their ritual garb, faces solemn, telling their beads. In first
class the Pakistan Hockey Team, off to a match, periodically explodes in
rollicking laughter. In Mumtaz Mufti's mind an alternate vision takes
place: the hockey players are hijackers; the pilgrims, the hijacked; the
laughter, the triumph of conspirators whose plans are working (pp. 50–
51).

On finding himself in Jiddah, lodged in an absurdly luxurious hotel
with every Western-style amenity—when, as he mocks himself, his vision
of being a pilgrim turns on deserts and camels—he entertains himself with
a fantasy of his room as a *honimun swit* where a tall, long-haired beauty
would glide into view saying "Hi . . . " (p. 57).

The continuum from strange episode to almost-real fantasy reaches its
culmination in the Ka'ba itself. Mumtaz, distressed at his lack of feeling
as he passes through the marble outer courtyard, suddenly looks up at the
roof of the plain stone building that is his goal and sees someone leaning
out, a face looking at him, showing forth "a storm of love, eyes moist with
boundless sympathy, the face radiant, an affectionate smile on his lips." As
he watched, he writes, the house swelled and swelled until it filled all creation. The face, described with all the lexicon of Hindi or Punjabi idolatry,
became the *but*, the idol of his devotion. He fled from the pilgrim guide
leading him in the ritual prayers. He read the prayers from his own book
until it too began to spread, covering everything—the mosque, the house,

the smiling face—so that he threw it too away. Allah was before him. "For my sake he had become a *but* so that my heart could delight in secret idolatry" (p. 82).

Days later, about to leave the sanctuary, Mumtaz knows the house now to be empty. He is riveted by the appearance of a procession of Africans, desperate at grief over departing, in humility exiting backwards from the shrine. It is, quite simply, the most moving spectacle he has ever seen in his life. He is not alone; every other pilgrim is fixed on the procession, too, "as if by sorcery turned into stone." Suddenly he thinks that perhaps Allah is leaving with the Africans. It is Allah, "flowing from their eyes, distilled into tears, glowing from their foreheads, changed into light." As they leave and the Ka'ba becomes, for him, nothing but a stone idol, he feels he must join them, find them so that he too can for a few minutes be "soaked in God," "become God." He runs to the door, only to find the procession gone—and sinks down in despair. When he lifts his eyes, there is God, sitting on the outer stairs, his clothes in tatters, his face wrinkled. As every pilgrim leaves, God holds out his finger, he tugs at their skirt, asking to be taken along. "Don't leave me, take me along, take my finger and take me along. . . . The house is empty. I am sitting here watching for you, waiting for you, wanting to go with you." No one pays attention. And Mumtaz, too, turns him down. "I am full of myself. . . . I have made a *but* of myself." (See Addenda, "The African Procession.")

Mufti has not given us a mainstream way of talking about God, or set himself in a heroic tale of triumph or conversion. Even these few episodes suggest the inconsistencies and ironies that make up the book. This is an account that defies both the religious skepticism of Mumtaz Mufti's coffeehouse intellectual circles and the conventions of those he calls the *ijaaradaars* (the leaseholders/monopolists) of Islam. The book is written by a cosmopolitan familiar with European literature—albeit with a time lag— and with an international world. Mumtaz Mufti can make an apt reference to Aristotle, William James, or H. Rider Haggard, as easily as he can to Shaikh Sa'di, the *Tazkiratu'l-ghausiyya*, or his son's letters from Prague. Here is a skeptic shaken by an encounter with a fortune-teller, a presumed pilgrim who fantasizes the pilgrimage as a hijacking, an irreligious person who more or less sees God. To write a travelogue whose goal is one's own presumably unscreened and discordant experiences is to participate in a cosmopolitan, Western-dominated genre of modern literature. At the same time, to go to Mecca is to say that one is a Muslim.

The authors of the other South Asian accounts of the pilgrimage to

Mecca that I have been able to identify are often, broadly speaking, people like this. Even the practice of writing accounts, and of course publishing them, is very much a product of the colonial period, and many of those who write are involved in colonial institutions.[6] Not all are as sophisticated as the author presented here: indeed part of the appeal of this genre is that it includes relatively modest authors as well, people for whom the account of the hajj may be the only substantial document they ever write. But by and large those who write about the central religious symbol of the hajj do so from a position that suggests, to varying degrees, familiarity with multiple cultural values. Far from being a site where essential shared cultural characteristics remain untouched, the hajj is precisely the kind of cultural symbol where contestations and cultural negotiations take place. In the process of writing about the hajj, new cultural truths are constituted and explored.[7] It is the "mongrels," as Salman Rushdie defiantly calls them, who have the most to contribute to these new cultural formations.[8]

If in this case the hajj account represents the experiences of someone familiar with Western institutions and literatures, it is at the same time a South Asian account. A modern mentality, engaged with cultural pluralism, finds expression in a distinctively non-European cultural milieu. The account has characteristics that differ from what seem to be widespread characteristics of life histories and autobiographies in European languages. These may help expand our sense of what the range of possibilities is in such writing and, indeed, in the way people think about themselves and their lives. Even in an account as unconventional as this, its three distinctive themes have long histories in biographical and autobiographical texts in the Urdu and, preceding it, the Persian traditions.

First, the definition of what is presented as part of life's experience is very inclusive. Put differently, magic is on the loose. There is a deep sense that reality is not limited to what is materially visible or subject to human control. An enduring model of dreams, for example, argues that any dream or vision involving God, prophets, or holy people is a visitation from beyond and not a product of one's own conscious or unconscious self.[9] (See Addenda, "A Conversation.") For example, one of the most celebrated books describing experiences in Mecca, the work of the great scholar of the eighteenth century, Shah Wali'ullah Dihlawi, is in no sense a travelogue but rather a compendium of visions and dreams.[10] What goes on in dreams is taken as fact and is intended to have continuity with waking life: thus a point in a dispute can be established by reference to an experience in a dream. In Shah Wali'ullah's case, his visions were taken as legitimation of his role as religious reformer. Here is an example of one of his visions:

I saw that the Two Imams, Hassan and Hussain, have come to my house. Imam Hassan is holding a pen which has a broken point. He held out his hand towards me as if he wanted to give me that pen, and said that the pen belonged to his grandparent, the Prophet of Allah (Peace be upon him). But he stopped for a moment, and asked Imam Hussain to mend the point of the pen for me, because it was no longer the same as it used to be. . . . I felt a great joy in my heart on this.

Another vision even more clearly confirms his calling; its image of expansion recalls Mufti's own vision in the same place: "I was circumambulating the Ka'ba when I saw my own light before me and it was all majestic and magnificent. Then, I saw that this light covered everything—almost the whole of the world; and people living in lands, far and near, came under its brightness."[11] Such visions in a great religious leader of the past do not surprise us as do, perhaps, the similar experiences of Western-educated bureaucrats and coffeehouse intellectuals in Pakistan today.

The dreams and visions of Mumtaz Mufti's account are distinctive in their power and inventiveness, but such surreal experiences are part of the everyday life of many people of Mufti's background in this culture, people who are educated, traveled, and typically employed in what could be called the modern sector. (Nazir Ahmad uses the English word "paranormal" to describe Mufti's experiences in his introduction.) Many, including Mufti, present these experiences as subject to interpretation. Unlike Shah Wali'-ullah, they do not simply accept them as fact. They may or may not be effective interventions of the divine. Thus from the very first Mufti distances himself from the traditional model of dreams. In describing his first dream he writes, "I had the habit of writing down my dreams, not because I thought they carried messages or gave indications of the future, but simply because of an interest in the unconscious [*nafs la sha'ur*, a neologism]" (p. 2). Over and over he tells us that doubt, not faith, is the religious style (*maslak*, p. 33) or occupation (*pesha*, p. 140) of intellectuals. In the central vision of the *but* of the Ka'ba, however, no such caution or question is asked. And Mufti alludes to the extra-ordinary experiences of people he knows even in the course of retelling his own.[12]

Fatwas were pronounced against the book and some attempts were made to have it banned. One might think that the condemnation of Mumtaz Mufti stems from the same mentality that opposes Salman Rushdie. Both authors distance themselves from religious leaders and their teachings, and both play rather exuberantly with "reality." Rushdie, unlike Mufti, however, writes in the form that most alarms the absolutist, a form that denies that any one voice is the author's own.[13] Moreover, he sets out to explore the colonial Orientalist vision of Islam, and in so doing he has been read as having sold out to it. Mumtaz Mufti, by contrast, however much he creates an irony between his authorial omniscience and the foibles of his protagonist, the Mumtaz Mufti of the account, nonetheless claims to speak for himself.

Indeed, those who objected to his book did so not so much because of its content per se, which in basic ways has a long tradition, but because Mufti chose to tell what the pious often believe should be kept secret, not least because it could be misunderstood.[14] To tell any inner experience is problematic. Not only can such experiences be misunderstood, but they should be regarded as marks of divine favor likely to be withdrawn because what is told publicly can be seen as boasting. Once, for example, a university teacher told me extraordinary tales of his ability, over a period of several years, to "visit" the Ka'ba through meditation, seeing in these visions details he had no other way of knowing. He could tell me these experiences now, he explained, simply because the experiences were behind him: he never would have told them while they were in process.[15] (See Addenda, "An Interview.")

Mufti's play with multiple realities and his euphoric appropriation of a Hindu language for relationships to God, coupled with a skepticism of mainstream, ritually oriented religion, puts him squarely in the Sufi emphasis on interior religion. He flamboyantly identifies himself with what is local and mixed—the Sufism of pre-Partition Punjab—against those so prominent in Pakistan in recent years who have asserted an Islam meant to be universal and unalloyed. He is ambivalent throughout, yet mocks the skepticism he cannot escape. In one vignette he places God on church steps in Europe, just as he has put him on steps in Mecca. One day, he writes, the Europeans will discover God and take him East, and then we will adopt faith as the latest fashion just as now we've taken up miniskirts and irreligion (pp. 193–94). For all that, the thrust of the book, however ironically circumscribed, is to assert that Mumtaz Mufti is someone who confronts and is shaped by a dramatic series of what are taken as divine interventions into everyday life over a period of many years.

Besides this expanded sense of reality, a second striking feature of this account also has long roots in local tradition, namely a particularly pervasive way of thinking about the person and, above all, an assumption of the givenness of personal qualities. In this model, which resonates with old Eurasian humoral theories, a person is endowed with certain qualities that persist throughout life. A biography then becomes an occasion for showing contexts in which those qualities are manifest. As one scholar has written, "the telling of lives in much Islamic biographical material does not present events or cumulative reflections as constituting character. Rather, biographical notices serve to establish origins and display a person's type through his or her discrete actions and sayings." The self is evident at any well-chosen moment.[16]

Since character does not develop over time, there is no need for chronology or for dwelling particularly on childhood as autobiographers informed by Romantic individualism and subjectivism unfailingly do.[17] A biography may well be organized by categories of activities, for example, not by periods, so that a biography of a pious person might be divided into two parts, *shari'at* (describing activities demonstrating obedience to divine injunctions) and *tariqat* (describing manifestations of spiritual realization), with no concern for a single chronology.[18] Early episodes will be adduced only to illustrate what later become characteristic attitudes or activities. In this intensely personal account Mumtaz Mufti tells us virtually nothing about his childhood, his past, or even his present life except what is specifically relevant to the Mecca trip.

A recent study of Muslim conversion narratives, focusing on people who become part of reform organizations or movements that call for far-reaching change in behavior and community, finds that even there Muslim accounts do not posit the radical break in self-perception that Christian narratives do. Muslims are not "born again."[19] What might be viewed as a cataclysmic spiritual experience, namely the hajj, can mark a deepening of faith, a change in everyday patterns, or the adoption of a new name, but it cannot be seen as a change in fundamental identity. At best one returns to one's real self in a religion that posits to human character not original sin but an essential Muslim nature (*fitrah*) and that focuses on assiduity in obedience, not on vicarious redemption, for salvation. Life stories are thus marked by continuity, not by breaks. Malcolm X, in telling his life, draws on a model that is quintessentially American, not on this mainstream Muslim tradition.[20]

One of the favorite South Asian genres for showing personality, especially the personality of holy men, is that of *hikaayaat*, tales, or *malfuzaat*, "table talk," where strings of little anecdotes are given that illuminate a personality from different angles. A personality is like a prism, held up to the light of multiple contexts so that its constant characteristics are revealed. In "A Story," in the Addenda, I have included a typical anecdote, in this case meant to show not only the givenness but the social acceptance of a type of personality. A person is taken for what he is. Thus, presumably without wounding either, Mumtaz Mufti can refer to the authors of the two introductory essays in his account as Nazir Ahmad "who is nothing but brains" and Zu'lfiqar Ahmad Tabish "who is nothing but heart" (p. 10).

We can see, I believe, the author Mumtaz Mufti treating his protagonist Mumtaz Mufti as do the recounters of *hikaayaat*, placing himself in contexts where the characteristics of his nature are revealed, turning himself around to refract dimensions of an essential self. What kind of person is he? He is the unconventional idiosyncratic, a revealer of ironies, always finding ways to distance himself and surprise the conventional, even if they are his fellow intellectuals baffled by his journey. He explicitly employs the alternate European model of personal development, only to insist that it does not apply to him. He does not change in essence, and does not, he claims, change even in detail. He mocks his expectation that he will be venerated as an ideal hajji would be. He deserves nothing—he is the same. The headings of the final sections of his book make his point plain: *jaissee ga'ee waisee lautee,* "back as I left," *wahiin mumtaz mufti,* "the same Mumtaz Mufti."

Mufti articulates one model of personal change, but in his claims exemplifies the old humoral model of personality. Is he not using this convention with some sense of irony? He is to be sure the same person who boasts a lively and critical eye on human behavior and emotion, including his own. He is the same distanced critic of formal religion that he always was, but by the very act of choosing to go on hajj and writing about it, he has realized himself as part of the crowd. In a characteristically modern move, he has sought authenticity by showing himself part of popular culture expressed in a popular tongue. He is now a man of some kind of faith, even if it is idiosyncratic, unconventional, and embedded in ironic layers. He saves himself from commitments or expectations by claiming nothing at all—except the implicit claim to now be more than a "nominal Muslim" made by the very fact of the pilgrimage and its record in this book.

Finally, a third characteristic of the account again draws on a long-standing Muslim model of human behavior, namely that the subject does not shape events but responds to events that happen to him. This is a common emphasis in the representation of human behavior in life histories. Again, the particularities of Mumtaz Mufti's case make this conventional structuring significant. One has to be called to go on hajj—ultimately the choice to go is beyond individual will. Moreover, the actual achievement of the hajj is often attributed to the grace or the prayers of someone else. Here, however, we have someone who, far from waiting for God's invitation or for the mediation of the pious, claims he never even thought of going on hajj and yet finds himself propelled into it. The convention of passivity gives this skeptic his excuse.

Mufti presents himself as someone upon whom religious experience is thrust. He places himself, or sees himself placed, in a succession of events and observes his reactions, measuring his feelings. His account is cinematic, as scene after scene is presented: at one key moment, in the Prophet's mosque in Medina, when (perhaps) the Prophet himself emerges (*utarna*, incarnates, as the Hindi verb has it), Mufti resorts to the metaphor of a zoom lens to convey the power with which he sees him approach from afar (pp. 236, 247).

The book jolts open: "No desire to go on hajj ever appeared in my heart. But strange things happened." We are then bombarded with some half-dozen vignettes, partaking, or not partaking, of something more than normal, though no explicit claim is ever made. This is, after all, reportage. The first vignette, the encounter with the faqir, is told above. The next episode is a dream. This time an uncle, as much a superficial believer as he (*allah t'aala ko sirf munh zabaanii maantee thee*) appears with suitcases and a ticket for the hajj (p. 27). The dream is remarkable, apparently, for its lucidity and coherence as much as for the implausibility of linking an irreligious uncle and the hajj. Mufti tells the story and lets it hang; he never systematically resolves the tension between his skepticism and the tradition that says dreams are communications from God. There is a surprising encounter with a pious man, yet another dream, even another madman. But the critical element in his decision to go, and in the trip itself, is the presence of the second major character of the book, Qudratu'llah Shahab, a distinguished civil servant who, for Mumtaz Mufti, emerges as a veritable Shams Tabriz, a realized self to act as spiritual guide.[21]

In creating Shahab in this role, Mumtaz Mufti evokes a long and rich tradition, both Indic and Islamic, of transformative personal relationships. A recent study has argued that the relationship of teacher and disciple holds for South Asians the kind of centrality that romantic love holds in Europe from the twelfth century on.[22] Mufti is explicit that without Shahab as guide he would never have gone on hajj. The trip depends on him; Shahab is his *lathi*, his stave and support (pp. 139–40). Shahab is an unlikely guide. An advisor to President Ayyub, he fills no conventional religious role. He is shown moreover to have his own vulnerabilities, particularly an oppressive immobility at moments of religious intensity (pp. 76–78). He is, Mufti writes, a person who knows simultaneously both doubt and faith. But like a classic spiritual guide he intuits Mufti's own conditions (p. 90);

he sends him on quests whose meaning is obscure (pp. 27–28); he offers only oblique answers to significant questions (pp. 29, 31–32); and he sets a model of humility (p. 32) and self-abnegation (pp. 216–17). He is at once in the world but detached from it, and is able to focus his attention (what Mufti calls *ganga jamni tawajjuh*, p. 90)[23] in any setting. He finds good in everyone. In the portrait of Shahab, as much as anything, the account resonates with central traditions of life accounts and life experiences in this culture, with the twist that Shahab is, again, such an unlikely guide.

It is possible, moreover, that Mumtaz Mufti is acted on by yet another spiritual leader, alluded to when he declines to take initiation at the hand of his mother's guide, who foretells that he will find another (pp. 196–97), a person possibly witnessed in one key episode when his skepticism about God is challenged in Lahore by an unknown passerby (pp. 70–71). Shahab himself suggests that the unknown person may have been the *bazorg* or elder through whose grace Mumtaz Mufti's journey takes place (p. 196). Mufti himself speculates on this, troubled at the thought that one's personality, one's attitude or shape (*rukh*) as he calls it, is not of one's own making but can be reoriented through the intervention of someone else. He now explicitly adduces a model of personal development in which personality is the sum of one's own efforts and striving. If an elder or even God can change you, what is your "contribution"? he asks (p. 199). He clings to the Western notion of self-generated personal development, but plays with the possibility of external intervention. And, when it comes to everyday life, he entrusts himself wholly to Shahab.

A series of inexplicable events leads Mumtaz Mufti to the point of imploring Shahab to take him on hajj when he goes (p. 350). Then, once he has taken such an initiative, all his actions prove futile. Shahab takes up a European post as ambassador and is not free to leave. Mumtaz puts in his name for the hajj lottery—certain, he says, mocking himself, that Allah Miyan would personally pull it out—only to fail (p. 39). The mysterious advocate, whose intercession has or has not secured offspring for Shahab (pp. 42–43), who has seen "the list" (not the lottery results but the heavenly list, pp. 41–42), tells him that his name is not there. Agency does not rest with the individual.

In the very telling of his story he makes clear the extent to which he conceives of his life as subject to outside influences. Indeed, even the act of writing is seen as outside his own initiative. Mumtaz Mufti, like virtually every writer of these accounts, insists that he had no intention of writing until pressed. This recalls the conventional modesty of Urdu orators who begin haltingly and apologetically only to warm up to their powerful style.[24] Mumtaz Mufti specifically insists that he lacked the courage to write, since he had neither the emotion nor the knowledge to justify writing. Mufti, recalling the conventional attributes of humility that authors use, calls himself ignorant (*jaahil, anjaan*) but insists, as a nineteenth-century Urdu author would not feel constrained to do, that he is also sincere (*mukhlis*) (p. 10). He wrote, he explains, first, to keep a promise to an editor and friend, and second, because, having begun, God "grabbed him" and he, "not knowing what happened," kept on writing. God becomes yet one more person who impinges on his life.

The burden of his account is distance and ambivalence. He mocks himself for even being on the hajj. He holds up the pretensions of his fellow pilgrims, freighted with "ritual" and mundane concerns. He celebrates feelings and inner experience—only to recognize their fragility and immaturity. He does not know how to evaluate supernatural happenings and refers to his initial imbroglio as fairy tales, *tuta mina kahaaniyaan* (tales of a parrot), or, alternatively, *alis aur wandarland*. The advocate's spiritual power, nurtured through ceaseless prayer, for example, is expended in securing a child for Shahab against all medical opinion. "Yet," he concludes, "[the birth] was just a coincidence" (p. 43), knowing we cannot accept it as such, given its presentation.

His insistence on his own limitations makes his presentation of intense moments of spiritual encounter more powerful. He sees himself in ritual dress and calls himself a *bahrup*, a mimic: "the person dressed in *ihram* looking at me from the mirror made me want to laugh" (p. 48). At every stage he fails to react as he thinks he should, finding each town no different from home, maybe even less lively: Jiddah airport looks like the one he had just left (p. 52); the inn en route to Mecca feels like the frontier (p. 69); Mecca reminds him of Siyalkot (p. 73) and Medina, again, seems like an ordinary qasba in Punjab (p. 212). Entering the sanctuary in Mecca, he writes, he found he had as little religious feeling as would a tourist surveying the Taj (p. 78).

At both Mecca and Medina he is unable to pray in areas of particular sanctity. In Mecca he is driven out by an overwhelming sense that a buzzing noise attacks him and that he is radiating an overwhelmingly offensive smell (pp. 106–10). In Medina he sees the special cell of revelation as a kind of sports arena where people are being knocked over, and he is unable to stand (pp. 220–23). He mocks other people for their distractions and falls victim to them himself. After describing each moment of illumination, moreover, he retreats in his prose to flat description as a way of deflating his euphoria, adducing such conventional tropes as the racial unity of the hajj, or reminding the pilgrim to bring along a good pair of scissors (pp. 83, 112, 176).

Mumtaz Mufti shows by the very act of writing that he is part of a plural intellectual world. Here the characteristics of Urdu come into play. Mumtaz is regarded today as one of the best living novelists in Urdu, a language known to linguists as Hindi-Urdu since it is written in two scripts, one based on Sanskrit (Hindi) and one on Perso-Arabic (Urdu).[25] Urdu lends itself to a wide variety of registers, drawing as it does on vocabulary and expressions from the local languages (in this case Punjabi), from Persian and Arabic, and from English. The capacity to utter a well-turned phrase is valued in this culture; to open your mouth is to convey who you are. Great value is placed on eloquence, and those whose Urdu is free from rustic vocabulary or accent hope to be known as *ahl-i zaban*, masters of language. Mumtaz Mufti flouts that standard and makes his virtuosity in exploiting the options available to Urdu part of his success.

His use of English loan words is telling. He turns to English for a vocabulary that describes much that is summed up by "the West": science (*micrometers, test tube, transmitter, receiver, neutrons*); materialism; obsessive cleanliness (he mocks a pilgrim complaining of an unfulfilled promise of a *nit and klen bath*, p. 126); sex. When he complains of the writers of travelogues who focus only on externals, he has one, "Shibli, B. Comm.," come into the sanctuary with his tape measure, saying *ai baig yur pardun* (p. 183).[26] At the same time, it is to an English vocabulary that he turns to explicate Shahab's psychology and religion. He speaks of his psychological *resistance*, of the problem of *reversion* (p. 165), of the goal of *divine unconcern* (p. 91), of *identification* as a key to worship (p. 71). What comes from the "West" is not easily dismissed.

Yet simultaneously he seeks an identity with the ordinary pilgrim, an identity that the very act of coming on hajj permits. Again, his lexicon makes the point. At the sanctuary he persists in referring to God's house not with the conventional words: *bait* in Arabic, *khana* in Persian and in Urdu, or even *ghar* in ordinary Hindustani. Instead he uses the Punjabi word for hut, *kotha*. When a companion finally protests that this is disrespectful (*be-adabi*), he answers that the word does not convey contempt. He is Punjabi, not *ahl-i zaban*, and for him the word is dear (*piyara*) and conveys a sense of belonging (*apnaaiyat*). To treat the whole creation of God as a *but* and to use a local vocabulary is self-consciously to make a claim to what is indigenous and not part of a cosmopolitan or high tradition.

Mumtaz Mufti thus pictures himself as torn between the styles of faith and skepticism. In Mecca, placed in his luxurious hotel, which he has peopled with relics of the *raj*, he says he feels like a man with two mistresses: one is the secluded, modest housewife of the Ka'ba, the other is the old "mem" of the hotel who sits on his lap and says, "*darling dont be so superstishus.*" At the time of stoning the pillars (meant to represent the devils who tempted Abraham), he discovers that they are throwing stones at him. Are they telling him that he is the tempter to disobedience, that the enticer is within? he asks. He tries to shout out to everyone to make him the target of their stones: "I am the one who led people astray, sowed doubts, planted seeds of infidelity and skepticism. I am an intellectual who makes doubt the foundation of knowledge. . . . I am an educated person who set infidelity as the foundation of culture and defined faith as the mark of ignorance" (pp. 175–76). He consoles himself that he does not come like a trader storing up merit, and he says he watches his fellow pilgrims treating the hajj like a booking office for paradise, a dry-cleaning factory for removing sins (p. 115). Now he uses a Hindu vocabulary to mock them: *jap, mala, puja*, their frolicking under the *mezab-i rahmat*, a veritable *holi* bacchanalia of reversals (pp. 116–18).

Is Mumtaz Mufti culturally marginal? He would be part of the masses but shrinks back in dismay. He finds anomalies, incongruities, and mixed motives everywhere, especially in himself. He travels intellectually to Europe, physically to Arabia. But if this is marginality, it is of a sort that is increasingly the mainstream in *our* ever more integrated world. Bharati Mukherjee, as an immigrant American, asks who speaks for "us," but, addressing her *New York Times* reader, explains that "who speaks for us" means "who speaks for you."[27]

Mumtaz Mufti may, at one point, say he has not even completed the hajj, caught up as he is in his vision at the Ka'ba. But if he does not, his book does. He lays claim, by the very act of writing a pilgrimage narrative, to a place within the religious tradition and at the heart of his society. Mumtaz Mufti has, in a sense, now made possible the pilgrimage for people like himself. He has found some sort of God in Mecca and something like the Prophet incarnate in Medina, even though he decides he must leave them behind. He comes back knowing that somewhere—back there, out there—there is a benign force that every now and then, in ways that are unexpected, even bizarre, comes home. His account is a tutor to the emotions and intellectual ambivalences of people—ever more numerous—like himself. This is not a conceptual resolution, but a resolution achieved by narrative art.

Conventionally, pilgrimage accounts have little to do with the personality of the pilgrim. They are not written as occasions for self discovery; if anything, the particularities of the writer are suppressed.[28] The text itself is seen as a kind of ritual continuation of the duty of pilgrimage. An aid to later pilgrims and a stimulus to their piety, it is nothing less than a further act deserving reward, *sawab*. As the reader, typically invited to do so in the text, prays blessings on the author, that *sawab* continuously grows. If the goal of authors of the classic accounts was humbly to seek *sawab*, in the end Mumtaz Mufti does too. For the second edition of *Labbaik*, as mutterings were still to be heard about its heresies, Mumtaz Mufti turned to the then Minister of Religious Affairs, Maulana Kausar Niyazi, a distinguished writer himself and a member of the "fundamentalist" Jamaʿat-i Islami, to provide a kind of *nihil obstat* in the form of a jacket blurb. This book, the Maulana wrote, far from being heresy, would secure for the author nothing less than paradise itself.[29] *Sawab* indeed. And again, Mufti, in the freedom that comes from travel and art, takes a cultural chord that resonates deep and claims it for his own.

Addenda: Three Everyday Visions and a Teaching About Character

The African Procession, from *Labbaik*

Everyone's gaze had shifted from the House of God to the courtyard of the sanctuary (*harm sharif*). It was the first of the farewell processions.

An African procession. The procession was made up of 40 or 50 Africans, men as well as women, children too. They were all standing on the road that leads directly to the outer gate.

The faces of these Africans, engaged in making their farewells, were distorted with disproportionate love and the pain of impending separation. Their eyes, flowing with tears, were fixed on the House of God; their foreheads virtually quivered to make prostrations. Every member of their body emanated humility, respect, and grief.

They were all going toward the outer door from the House of God backwards. With every step their emotions grew more intense and their longing increased. Depth in their grief and ever more tears. Their faces were oozing like sores from their anguish and the chants of separation. The procession, still going backwards, crept on and on.

All the pilgrims sitting in the sanctuary watched them struck dumb. In my life I have seen many profoundly moving sights but never such intensity as I saw that day in the sanctuary in this scene of farewell.

The pilgrims could not lift their gaze from this sight, as if by sorcery they were turned to stone.

Soaked. It seemed as if Allah had left his house to be absorbed in that procession.

Those fifty Africans at this point were soaked in Allah. Their faces had absorbed God's love as jalebis do sugar syrup. Allah was flowing from their eyes, distilled into tears, glowing from their foreheads, changed into light. At such humility Allah stood astonished, his finger in his mouth.

The procession kept creeping backwards. Centuries passed.

When the last person left from the outer gate, I started. I felt that they had taken Allah with them.

The whole sanctuary was empty and the house of the Ka'ba stood in the midst like an idol. An idol of stone.

I ran to the outer door.

Outside I found no trace of the African procession. Lost, I thought, lost. I had to join that African procession. I too would be soaked in God even for a few minutes; I would become God. Lost. Despairing, I sat down on a platform outside. I don't know how long I sat there, my head bowed.

The house and its master (makaan aur makiin). Then when I lifted my eyes I saw him sitting on the stairs of the outer gate with his chin on his knee. His clothes were patched, his face wrinkled, his eyelids covering his eyes.

When anyone leaving came out of the door, he looked up with love-filled eyes, held out his finger and said, "Don't leave me, take me along, take my finger and take me along. Don't sorrow over leaving the house (*kotha*). The house is empty. I am sitting here watching for you, waiting for you, wanting to go with you. Take my finger, take me along." He tugged at the skirt of everyone leaving.

But no one looked at him. No one heard him. No one paid attention to him. All were fixed on the house of stone. They were motionless in sorrow at leaving it.

They were so lost in the house that they forgot the master.

And the master just gazed at them, astonished and helpless.

Then he looked at me with suppliant eyes and extended his finger.

"No, no, I cannot take you," I said. "I am full of myself. I have grasped the finger of myself with both hands. I have made a *but* of myself. How can I take you along." (pp. 189–92)

A Conversation About Dreams at the Daru'l-'Ulum, 1970

In 1970 I was conducting research on a leading Muslim theological seminary, the Daru'l-'Ulum at Deoband, whose rector and other officials welcomed me generously. One day, seated at my table in the guest house, I was chatting with a few of the people connected with the school about political life immediately preceding independence. At that time most of the school's scholars supported the Indian nationalist movement and opposed the movement for a separate Muslim state. One young man spoke of the fact that people's confidence in the veracity of these religious leaders was shaken when both the leader of the nationalist scholars, Maulana Husain Ahmad Madani, and the leader of the smaller group supporting Pakistan, Maulana Shabir Ahmad Usmani, both claimed to have had dreams of the Prophet sanctioning their respective positions.

Caught up in the conversation, and influenced by the fact that this young man regarded himself as a bit of a skeptic, I interjected that it was perfectly possible that each should have had such a dream, that anyone could have such a dream, that after all I myself had once even had a dramatic dream in which the Prophet appeared. The stunned silence that greeted my remarks made clear to me that an epistemological chasm divided us. But the respect for dreams was so great that a sincere appreciation for my dream seemed to erase my "logical" gaffe—and earn me a status I felt undeserved.

Paraphrase of an Interview with a Poet and Scholar, Lahore, 1985

Although I had no particular connection to religious practices, my family, Pathans from Miyanwali, were religious, offering *namaz*, etc. My paternal grandfather was close to the English but inclined to Sufism. My father was a policeman but kept a beard and would repeat *namaz* even if he had to do it while wearing his regulation boots! As for me, I felt distant from God but not from Muhammad. It is Muhammad who is the way to know God, for there is no other man like him.

We were ten or eleven children in our family, but my father especially loved me. My father particularly wanted to go on hajj but was never able to do it. He was a "misfit" in the police. He died. Once he was dead I needed to know if he was finished, how I could continue to feel his love. I knew that Sufism (*tasawwuf*) was the only way for me to find out. . . . It could promote a meeting, a *real* meeting and not just thought, a meeting as real as all of us sitting here around this table. I began Sufi practices. . . . My father had had a spiritual guide (*pir*) who was very unattractive. Nonetheless, he had felt an immediate rapport with him.

A professor I knew, Naqwi Sahib, came to discuss socialism, etc., with me and I felt he was doing something to me. After a week I felt it even more. He was establishing some connection (*rabita*). He asked me if I wanted to meet Data Sahib [Data Ganj Bakhsh, a twelfth-century Sufi buried in Lahore]. I gave no answer but after he left I wept for no reason. When he came the next day we sat in a dark room, he on my right and I on his left, and he had me repeat the name of God (*zikr Allah*) with a pattern of breathing while paying attention to my heart. The breathing was fast and lasted about an hour. At the end I was very tired (though later when I got used to it I would not be). At the end I closed my eyes and lost all connection with the world. The room was filled with light although my eyes were closed; when I opened them, the room was dark. In this meditation (*muraqaba*) the light was ten times brighter than the sun. The light narrowed to a dot and came from Naqwi's heart directly to mine. I would awaken for the night prayer and meditate, often with him, until dawn. I wanted to meet my father more than I wanted to meet Data Sahib.

Although it was not necessary we went to my father's grave to secure this meeting. I was always on Naqwi Sahib's left, on the side of his heart. He told me to exert attention (*tawajjuh*) on my heart and told me to enter the grave. I sat with my father as I am sitting with you. There was no need for language. My heart felt the conversation which came directly from his heart to me. After that I could meet him anywhere. I consulted him, for example, on my sister's wedding. . . . Without *tasawwuf* no one is complete.

I met Naqwi Sahib's *pir* in Chakrala. He is a Naqshbandi, but very informal and does not require initiation. He keeps goats. He was in Allah Yar Khan. He was a *malik*, a *Jat*, and an ʿalim. He never heard radio or tv, nor did he read a newspaper, but he was very informed about the world. I met him often. He was very informal, we all sat on the ground. He is dead now.

The stages of meditation begin, first with *uluhiyat*, the divine essence, whose color is white. (I am not a Sufi.)

Then he would say, "Go to *ahdiyat*, oneness." I felt myself leave myself and go up, and everyone present could feel the others doing it.

The next stage was *maiʿyat*, companionship, whose color is green. No one taught me these colors.

The next stage is *aqrabiyat*, nearness, whose color is red.

The next stage is *fana*, extinction, whose motion is continually upward; one feels that all are finished.

There could be more than 300 of us meditating at one time. It would be completely dark, all of us with our eyes closed.

The next stage is *baqa*, abiding, whose color is white again.

When we reached it he would say *sair-i Kaʿba*, the trip or experience of the Kaʿba, and it was there, not just as a thought. Everything was before me, the water of Zamzam, Mina, everything, as if I were there. I had not even seen pictures of all this before. I would do this two times a day, at sunset and at the time of the supererogatory night prayer. It would take about two hours. I could do it myself or with a group.

I thus went on hajj thousands of times.

The *pir* himself had gone on hajj four times. He died at over 80 and in his whole life had never missed the prayer in community.

People say there is more pleasure (*maza*) in the hajj done during meditation than there is in the real hajj.

The final stage is *sair-i rasul*, experience of the Prophet, when I would feel myself in the Prophet's mosque in Medina. I cannot describe the feelings I would have afterward. The *pir* presented me to the Prophet. I put my knees toward him and could feel them touching him. I extended my hands and he took them. At the time of initiation, the Prophet gives a gift. I had not told the *pir* that I was a poet and for three years I had not even read a book. Yet he gave me a pen! The others sitting with me had the same experience and afterward when I asked them the color of the pen they all knew that it had been blue!

A Story Concerning the Eighteenth-Century Scholar and Sufi Maulana Muhammad Mazhar Jan-i Janan

One day one of the great notables of Delhi decided to test three of the most distinguished scholars of *hadith*, Shah Wali'ullah, Maulana Fakhru'd-din Chishti, and Hazrat Mirza Jan-i Janan, to see whose rank (*martaba*) was highest. He invited each to take the morning meal at his house, inviting them to come at half hour intervals. All accepted. The next day, as each arrived, he graciously escorted him to a separate room, assuring him that a meal would soon follow. The entire day passed. Finally, the host went to each and apologized profusely that problems in the household had made it impossible to prepare food; instead he offered each a gift of money. Shah Wali'ullah graciously accepted the gift, assured him that there was no need to be embarrassed, and departed. Similarly, Maulana Fakhru'd-din arose, insisted that he not worry, and ceremonially held out a handkerchief to receive the proffered gift. Mirza Mazhar Jan-i Janan, however, took the money, stuffed it in his pocket and told him, with a frown, "No problem, but don't bother me again." Then he left.

When this story was told to a group of scholars in the late nineteenth century, they are recorded as having pondered the three responses with a view to seeing who of the three emerged as the greatest. The narrator himself ranked Maulana Fakhru'd-din highest because he acted ceremonially, followed by Shah Wali'ullah who was also gracious, followed in turn by Maulana Mazhar Jan-i Janan who showed his displeasure. But the most revered of the scholars demurred. For him the greatest was none other than Jan-i Janan, a man endowed with such a brittle temperament (*nazuk mizaji*) that for him to have acted as he did required the greatest forbearance and self-control. (Paraphrased from Zuhuru'l-Hasan Kasoli, *Arwah-i salasa*, Saharanpur, 1950–51.)

So you are what you are. You can and should hone your personality—above all by acts of obedience to divine teachings—but you cannot change essentials. The goal is to direct what you are given in ways ordained by God.

"In *me* the solitary sublimity": Posturing and the Collapse of Romantic Will in Benjamin Robert Haydon

Roger J. Porter

On June 22, 1846, moments before he committed a kind of double suicide by shooting himself and slashing his throat, Benjamin Robert Haydon, historical painter, would-be savior of British art, and friend to both generations of romantic writers, wrote the final words in the diary he had kept for 38 of his 60 years: "'Stretch me no longer on this tough World'—Lear."[1] With a symmetrical gesture he could hardly have been conscious of making, Haydon was closing a parenthesis of allusion around his life. In 1808, at the beginning of what he envisioned—no less than did his companion Keats—as a grand and illustrious calling, Haydon noted in the first entry of his journal that he stood upon the cliffs of Dover where "Lear defied the storm" (1: 3) and when a storm actually broke over the coast Haydon fancied himself as the great white-haired king blasted by nature and fiendish daughters; he was moved to reread the play, and thus began a series of identifications with Lear that were to linger through thousands of pages of journal and hundreds of autobiography. At Dover Haydon envisioned a colossal statue of Britannia looming over the sea and facing France, as if in challenge to that country's art. We can take that defiance and heroic posturing at the start of his career, and its self-dramatizing end, as coordinates in his life and the signs and motives for his writing, which in both its magnitude and its obsessive self-aggrandizements became the rival of, if not the substitute for, his painting. With the exception of Van Gogh, there may be no other visual artist whose need to write—out of self-justification and compensation—was as great as Haydon's, and who created as extended a literary self-portrait as an alternate life to the one that brought him such grief.[2]

Virginia Woolf said of Haydon, "we catch ourselves thinking, as some felicity of phrase flashes out or some pose or arrangement makes its effect, that his genius is a writer's. He should have held a pen."[3] There is an amplitude to his journals that corresponds to the grandiose scale of his historical paintings, their sheer size and the heroism of their subjects, those he actually painted and those he only desired to paint: Achilles, Christ, Samson, Adam, Solomon, Antigone, Orpheus, Lear, Andromache, Macbeth, Caesar, Hercules. His writing similarly refuses to be narrowly focused; a partial list of topics might include meditations on the Bible; literary criticism of Homer, Dante, and Milton; discussions of human and animal anatomy; treatises on the Elgin marbles; character analyses of Wordsworth, Keats, and Napoleon; technical discussions of oil painting; attacks on debtors' laws (Haydon was imprisoned three times for debt); stories of betrayal by those whose patronage he had expected; gossip about other artists, M.P.'s, and critics; detailed descriptions of his progress on a given painting; critiques of English and continental politics; meditations on fleeting fame; endless self-analysis; attacks on the art establishment and its institutions; and long prayers to carry a painting to completion. But Haydon's *Diary* and his *Autobiography*, despite their sprawl and catch-all nature, have what we might call an autobiographical plot; I mean this not merely in the sense of a theme or cluster of related themes that we can trace through the life, whether they were composed with hindsight by the autobiographer or with relative spontaneity in the dailiness of the diary. I mean rather "plot" in the sense of its author's motive for writing, as De Quincey in *Confessions of an English Opium-Eater* urges us to understand a motif as a motive "in the sense attached by artists and connoisseurs to the technical word *motivo*, applied to pictures."[4] The themes reveal Haydon's motive for writing, and indeed he makes the impelling need to write the dominant theme of autobiography. Writing stands beside painting, if it does not virtually displace it, in Haydon's own order of importance.

Haydon was born at Plymouth on January 26, 1786. He began serious sketching at 6, and although an inflammation of his eyes permanently and early dimmed his sight he pursued his profession as if possessed. From an early age he assiduously read biographies of ambitious men and prophesied his own fame, drawing up a list of painterly subjects that would bring about this result. He was the first English artist to see the importance of the Elgin Marbles, and they greatly influenced him all his life. He soon entered into embattled relations with the Royal Academy, which he had attended as a boy, especially chagrined at not being elected to membership. His continuously disputatious life led to numerous fights with patrons over financial matters, alienated friendships, and a belief that the entire art es-

tablishment was bent in opposition to him. His life was a constant oscil-
lation between an obsessive devotion to the cause of British historical
painting and a history of debt. In between his stays in debtors' prison, he
set up a school to rival the Academy, fought rancorous battles with everyone, and continued to rail against portrait painting as insufficiently heroic.
He finally received substantial requests for work, but five of his children
died, and the loss of commissions to decorate the Houses of Parliament
rendered him particularly bitter. When he committed suicide, the coroner's
report included a verdict of insanity.

At 22 Haydon started the journal that was to last throughout his life,
and he made almost daily entries in 24 volumes. When he was 53 he began
writing his *Autobiography*, and labored several years on the work, carrying his life only to 1820, 26 years before his death at 60. It is likely that
writing about the succeeding years would have caused too much pain; to
describe and analyze the difference between his early glory and the later
neglect, or at least what he had come to perceive as a lifetime of failed
promise and constant oppression from an unappreciative public and a system of reluctant patronage, would doubtless have frayed an already deli-
cate psyche. It was difficult enough for Haydon to record on a daily basis
his defeats and embattled status; to place the events in a structure of impending disaster would have been too anguishing. But the large questions
remain: why did he write at all, and why was he so committed to some
form of autobiography? What function did it serve, and what is its relation
to his art?

Walter Jackson Bate, in his biography of Keats, has described Haydon's
"vivid, simple-hearted energy" and his "endless, booming confidence."[5]
These traits do emerge from Haydon's writing, especially in his heroic
claims to outdo the greats of the past. One of the dominant voices is that
of the young man staking his place in history:

People say to me: "You can't be expected in your second picture to paint like Titian
and draw like Michel Angelo"; but I will try; and if I take liberties with nature and
make her bend to my purposes, what then? "Oh yes, but you ought not to do what
Michel Angelo alone might try." Yes, but I will venture—I will dare anything to
accomplish my purpose. If it is only impudent presumption without ability I shall
find my level in the opinion of the world; but if it be the just confidence of genius
I shall soon find my reward.[6]

Even his endless prayers to God for blessings have the self-assured tone of
a man who, if he cannot cajole the deity to shower talent upon him, at least
is on intimate and easy terms with that authority. Much of the autobiographical writing is a trying out of such attitudes, and even towards the

end Haydon persists in his confident address to the world: "My position still is solitary and glorious. In *me* the solitary sublimity of High Art is not gone" (5: 407).

The *Autobiography* and the *Diary* are filled with assertions of his own greatness and immortality, the devotion to a high calling almost as if it were a divine mission. When the serious eye disease he suffered as an adolescent left him temporarily blind, Haydon defiantly proclaimed he would be the first great sightless painter. Later he described the cure as if it were the work of destiny, and his own spirit as if it were sanctified: "It would have been quite natural for an ordinary mind to think blindness a sufficient obstacle to the practice of an art, the essence of which seems to consist in perfect sight, but 'when the divinity doth stir within us,' the most ordinary mind is ordinary no longer" (*Autobiography*, p. 15). Much of the *Autobiography* takes the form of a *Bildungsroman*, with Haydon the hero who overcomes the obstacles of disease, official resistance to his youthful bravado, the Academy's timidity toward historical painting, and its insistence that artists conform to the vogue of portraiture that Haydon detests. There is a description of a ritual moment of stocktaking as he begins his first painting, an allusion to the close of *Paradise Lost* as the world of promise opens before him, a prophecy that he will bring honor to England with his art, and a characteristic belief that difficulties are stimulants that discourage only the indolent. Again and again we hear of his monumental labors, the anticipation of glory, greatness and fame, and his posturing in the style of Julien Sorel.

I was so elevated at . . . the visit of crowds of beauties putting up their pretty glasses and lisping admiration of my efforts, that I rose into the heaven of heavens, and believed my fortune made. I walked about my room, looked into the glass, anticipated what the foreign ambassadors would say, studied my French for a good accent, believed that all the sovereigns of Europe would hail an English youth with delight who could paint a heroic picture. (*Autobiography*, p. 104)

Every encounter is a test, every creative act a competition with past greatness, and Haydon uses the *Autobiography* to convince himself that he is correct in his defiance, or if he misjudges things, that he is nonetheless heroic in his convictions. There is an ebullience and daring in his self-congratulation: "I had proved the power of inherent talent, and I . . . had shown one characteristic of my dear country—bottom. I had been tried and not found wanting. I held out when feeble, and faint, and blind, and now I reaped the reward" (*Autobiography*, p. 199).

When Haydon wrote this passage, describing the reception of his work "The Judgement of Solomon," it was 1844 and the painting was gathering dust in a warehouse. Haydon sees its ignominy as a metaphor for his own decline in popular and official esteem, but prophesies "shame on those who have the power without the taste to avert such a fall; who let a work which was hailed as a national victory rot into decay and dirt and oblivion! But it will rise again; it will shine forth hereafter, and reanimate the energy of a new generation" (*Autobiography*, p. 236). This challenge corresponds to Haydon's motives for autobiography: vindication in the Rousseauean mode; and a nostalgic reliving of past greatness from a perspective in which, as he moves towards the close of the autobiography, his powers and fame are waning. Autobiography sanctions Haydon's struggles not by merely recording them but by elevating them to a heroic status in spite of, or rather because of, the difficulties they brought upon himself. Haydon deeply overestimated the greatness and originality of his own work, and this misjudgment makes his condemnation of his critics suspect, unlike the way Van Gogh's self-justification gains our credence. Nevertheless, despite the fact that, as Haydon's biographer has argued, the "myth of ill-usage was one he cultivated assiduously throughout his life,"[7] the autobiography reveals how Haydon refused to "bear affliction and disappointment" and often acted in a self-destructive way against all his better judgment. He claims his work can serve as a guide to the young, who will exercise more caution and avoid the fatal consequences arising from reckless behavior, but Haydon's tone suggests he also relishes those actions, and relived them as much for his own morbid pleasure as to convince the world of his integrity.

As he writes the *Autobiography* his own life is gradually crumbling about him—several children have died, he has spent months in debtors' prison, he fears his creative juices may be drying up, his work has been attacked in the press, and even former supporters have deserted him. To compose autobiography is to risk further pain, perhaps even to cultivate this pain as a sign of stoical resignation and ultimately of heroic courage. The most common psychological move that Haydon makes throughout both the *Autobiography* and the *Diary* is to embrace struggle and difficulty as a sign of superiority. He encounters "ceaseless opposition" from the first, and there is a kind of energizing joy in confrontation with his enemies, a power that only contentiousness confers. Indeed controversy and conflict are the very animators of his writing. In an argument with Leigh Hunt, Haydon determines to get the better in print; Hunt is a dangerous opponent because he is editor of the *Examiner*, in whose pages they will do battle. In the *Autobiography* Haydon's punning metaphor draws the fight with Hunt into Haydon's own domain: "Though this is not the first time

Leigh Hunt is mentioned it is the first opportunity I have had of bringing him fairly on the canvas. . . . This controversy consolidated my power of verbal expression and did me great good. . . . I resolved to show I could use the pen against the very man who might be supposed to be my literary instructor" (*Autobiography*, pp. 142, 144). Failure is a great stimulus for Haydon, a kind of tempering mechanism to test his invincibility. There is a determination not to be defeated in any competition. To complete a painting under trying circumstances is analogous to composing autobiography itself: ruthless honesty through the analysis of emotional complexity or foolish action testifies to a willingness to face difficult home truths and to avoid easy evasions. Too luxurious a climate would encourage indolence; too uncomplicated a romance would undermine the value of the love; too charmed a life would dull its vigor. "Some faculties only act in situations which appall and deaden others. Mine get clearer in proportion to the danger that stimulates them. I get vigour from despair, clearness of perception from confusion, and elasticity of spirit from despotic usage. . . . want and necessity, which destroy others, have been perhaps the secret inspirer of my exertions" (2: 397–98).

How does conflict produce this feeling of well-being? In Haydon's case it creates the illusion that he has, in the very act of facing difficulty, justified his life and reached down into deeper resources of being. It is true that Haydon avoids excessive difficulty, arguing, for example, that his painting keeps him from madness and pain, and dulls his sensitivity to really disastrous experience; he even inserts into his journal a bit of doggerel claiming a purgative function for painting, writing, and love. The last line anticipates inadvertently the twin weapons of his suicide, as if he were invoking them as a talisman to ward off what later happens.

> Oh hail, my three blessings of Life,
> My pencil, my Book, and my Wife,
> Never mind the alloy,
> While these I enjoy,
> I defy both the bullet & knife. (4: 321)

Yet he constantly writes about difficulty as a catalyst for creativity, and links this strategy with the trope of heroic identification. Napoleon and Nelson are only two of many figures Haydon views as different from the run of ordinary men (as presumably Haydon himself is) exactly because to men of genius insurmountable difficulties are stimulants to action.

Nelson is an illustrious example of what persevering, undivided attention to one Art will do; of how far a restless habit of enterprise will carry a man; to what a length never resting in indolent enjoyment after exertion will go. He began the war unknown . . . and concluded it famous throughout the World. . . . The same eagerness, the same enthusiasm, the same powers, the same restlessness, the same determination to go on while in existence, in any art, will carry a man the same length, because such conduct begets a confidence in others, as well as yourself. (1: 284)

Throughout his work Haydon wavers between the egotistical sublime of heroic self-assertion and the negative capability of self-effacement or identification with other men, primarily Napoleon (see Fig. 1), Wellington, and Michelangelo. It would seem that the latter impulse is no less self-projecting, since Haydon takes on the identities of triumphant figures. Nevertheless, I would suggest this strategy is an ironic form of self-denigration, in that the identification implicitly asserts the failure of originality and the need to subsume other selves. Unlike such autobiographical writers as the Keats of the *Letters*, writers who playfully try out a series of roles, inventing spiderlike from within themselves, Haydon often defines himself by taking on the personae of historical or artistic figures. Haydon's autobiographical writing meets the problem of unavailable originality by allowing him to assert a range of identifications, as though mimicry could substitute for genius, if not validate it.

Bate has elsewhere described the burden such demands for originality placed on writers and painters by the end of the eighteenth century:

The eighteenth-century "Enlightenment" had created, and had foisted upon itself and its immediate child . . . an ideal of "originality": sanctioned both officially (theoretically, intellectually) and, *in potentia*, popularly. As a result the vulnerability of the [artist], already great enough, was accentuated by having his uneasiness now given a "local habitation and a name." For the first time in history, the ideal of "originality"—aside from the personal pressures the artist might feel to achieve it anyway—was now becoming defined as necessary, indeed taken for granted.[8]

That pressure on Haydon comes not from external sources but from within himself. Again and again he declares he will be the salvation of British art by raising it to a level formerly attained only in ancient Greece and Renaissance Italy. He aspires to the achievements of Raphael and Michelangelo (Haydon literally dreams that the latter comes to him; in a Wordsworthian echo he muses: "I certainly think something grand in my destiny is coming on, for all the spirits of the illustrious dead are hovering about me," 3: 510), and he will not bow to any contemporary or obey any obsolete rule if it will inhibit the value of his work. "Genius is sent into the world not to obey laws but to give them" (*Autobiography*, p. 95). A decade

Fig. 1. *Napoleon Musing at St. Helena.* Formerly owned by the Metropolitan Museum of Art, New York. Current owner unknown.

later, in 1815, he expresses the feeling of power and buoyant self-assertion in an entry suggesting not merely confidence but something like a self-apotheosis:

Never have I had such irresistible, perpetual and continued urgings of future greatness. I have been like a man with air balloons under his arm pits and ether in his soul. While I was painting, or walking, or thinking, these beaming flashes of energy followed and impressed me! . . . Grant that they may be the fiery anticipations of a great Soul born to realize them. They came over me, & shot across me and shook me. (1: 430)

And in a letter to Keats, Haydon sounds like both Prospero and a Hotspur of the creative spirit, the elements of water and earth substituting for the fire and air of the previous passage: "I have no doubt you will be remunerated by my ultimate triumph. . . . By Heaven I'll plunge into the bottom of the sea, where plummets have now never sounded, & never will be able to sound, with such impetus that the antipodes shall see my head drive through on their side of the Earth to their dismay and terror."[9] What disturbs about the autobiographical writing, however, is Haydon's continual need to identify himself with other beings or with forces of nature. To be sure, it is hard not to admire the Tamburlaine-like desire to seize upon elements outside the self and to absorb and incorporate them as a way of vitalizing his longed-for power. And yet, on another view of the case, each identification undermines the very claims Haydon makes for originality and implies the need to compensate for disappointment or uncertainty with an endless series of self-dramatizations. As part of the autobiographical motive this process answers the twin needs to be original and to be like others, especially like persecuted men. The irony is that while Haydon desired to join himself to greatness, whether in the role of Wellington, Michelangelo, Achilles, or Christ, he never could make his influence felt. When the news of Haydon's death reached Hunt he remarked, "I looked upon [Haydon] as one who turned disappointment itself into a kind of self-glory,—but see how we may be mistaken" (5: 561).

Throughout the *Diary* and the *Autobiography* Haydon's view of himself veers between those of a misunderstood, martyred man (the oppressors include patrons, critics, rival painters, the general public, and the Royal Academy), and of a successful, dominating will. Haydon's identification with satanic energy ("Give me the sublimity of chaos, give me the terror of Hell, give 'Hail, horrors, hail . . . and thou profoundest hell receive thy new possessor,'" 1: 309) appears as a Romantic strategy to achieve power while it recoils against orthodox Christian beliefs. The impulse here is to equate greatness with suffering wherever it can be found, but the seminal figure behind both the *Autobiography* and the *Diary* is not Satan but Rousseau.

Often Haydon asserts the absolute sincerity of his efforts as autobiographer; he will not be outranked on this score: "There I will defy any man, let him be Raffaele himself, to beat me" (*Autobiography*, p. 90). He is talking not about painting but about honesty and confessional integrity. The

"Author's Introduction" to the *Autobiography* bears a striking resemblance to the famous opening paragraphs of Rousseau's *Confessions*; Haydon claims that his writing originates from a sense of unjust persecution, and that although he has made occasional mistakes, and has even been sinful, his sincerity, decent intentions, and perseverance will serve to exonerate him in the eyes of his readers. But sincerity is not the real issue. Haydon's deeper instinct is for a Rousseau-like cultivation of suffering, which he hopes will testify to a misunderstood genius; indeed he is self-congratulatory about his willingness to acknowledge anguish: "I am one of those beings born to bring about a great object through the medium of suffering. . . . Adversity to me, individually, is nothing" (3: 334). Haydon's aspiration to be raised above the world gradually gives way to an awareness of futility and a corresponding nurturing of defeat, almost as if it were an alternate proof of greatness.

In a crucial diary entry Haydon distinguishes between sublimity and the pathetic. Sublimity is unconnected with the earth, freed from mundane emotions; it speaks to the imagination and genius, unavailable to the mass of mankind; pathos speaks to the heart and is common. The sublime corresponds to what he calls "the grand conception," ambition and glory. Pathos contains the realization of heart-aching failure, the impossibility of achievement, and the recognition that he might be "born the sport and amusement of Fortune" (2: 362).

Both aspects of personality—heroic genius and ill-usage—receive their due in the writing; it is difficult to say which myth gives Haydon more pleasure in the recording. There is a curious luxuriating in the numerous long passages documenting and expanding upon the instances of persecution and official neglect, almost as if oppression itself were a valid sign of genius. Each mode produces its characteristic rhetoric of hyperbole, whether in the high Romantic sublime or in the Rousseauean complaint.

In 1824, after losing commissions, being rejected for membership in the Academy, getting arrested for debt with no help from patrons, and failing to persuade influential M.P.'s to appropriate government funds for the support of painting, Haydon laments: "Of what use is my Genius—to myself or to others? . . . All this was bearable when I was unknown because the hope of fame animated me to exertions in order to dissipate my wants; but now, what have I to hope? My youth is gone! every day and year will render me more incapable of bearing trouble; at an age when I ought to have been in ease, I am ruined!" (2: 474). It would be absurd to claim that Haydon simply takes pleasure in his losses or enjoys the sensation of defeat; nevertheless the self-dramatizing easily adheres to whatever the situation, and "the glories of a great scheme" are no more ecstatically described than "the troubles, the pangs, the broken afflictions, the oppressions, the wants, the diseases of life" (*Autobiography*, p. 165). Haydon stands simultaneously inside and outside his life, not only a public man concerned with the impact of art on the social body, or a private man tracing each particular nervous agitation in the self, but one who dramatizes a self for the public even as he speaks to himself within the privacy of his journals.

Haydon seems drawn to the most dramatic gyrations of fortune, the sinusoidal curve of his life providing evidence of both sensitivity and recovery. Even here the exemplary figure is Napoleon, advancing on Moscow, retreating, escaping from Elba, defeated once again. The pleasure of triumph, says Haydon, is that we no longer look up (we are there) but down (Haydon longs to excite envy); and yet looking down already anticipates an inevitable decline to the grave. Haydon was of two minds regarding Napoleon: he revered his titanic power and aloofness from ordinary men, yet was comforted by Napoleon's ordinariness and vulnerability. This fascination with the swings of fortune appears throughout Haydon's writings: he receives a commendatory sonnet from Wordsworth that cheers him; immediately after he relapses into melancholy. He walks the streets in grief, and within moments enters a drawing room "like a comic hero in a farce." Following an arrest for debt he goes from the bailiff's house into a room full of beautiful women and elegant pictures. "What a destiny is mine! One year in the Bench, the companion of Demireps & Debtors—sleeping in wretchedness & dirt, on a flock bed, low and filthy, with black worms crawling over my hands, another, reposing on down & velvet, in a splendid apartment, in a splendid House, the guest of Rank & fashion & beauty!" (3: 167).

The inconsistencies of his own personality intrigue "that mysterious, incomprehensible, singular bit of blood, bottom, bone, & genius, B. R. Haydon" (2: 273). The same perplexity of human character not surprisingly attracts him to Shakespeare's mixed style and juxtaposition of character types (this of course is a common Romantic attitude). The *Diary* is filled with instances of incongruity, such as the laughter in his infant son's sleep at the moment Haydon's wife is lying in agony in the next room. Haydon appears drawn to rather than dismayed by these turns and violent contrasts; his autobiographical writing stands in opposition to the classical certitude and careful planning of a life such as Gibbon's, who perceives his existence as a work of art given compositional grace and symmetrical order corresponding to schemata ordained by prudence. For Haydon there are no models to follow with confidence, for even the ostensible exemplars are patterns of inconsistency.

Haydon holds a mirror to himself, but each event witnessed, every book read, seems to reflect a different self. In 1844 he had painted some 25 portraits of Napoleon, and while there was an economic motive for this obsession, it also reflects his penchant for finding infinite variations in an emulated figure, and thus a desire to be many different persons—an indirect version of Rembrandt's life-long series of self-portraits. Haydon's journals fight against the tendency of autobiography to freeze the self into a fixed image; they express not merely the implicit fragmentation we expect from journal writing, but a subtle pleasure in the act of creating multiple perspectives.

This book is a picture of human life, now full of arguments for religion, now advocating virtue, then drawn from chaste piety, & then melting from a bed of pleasure, idle & active, dissipated & temperate, voluptuous & holy! burning to be a martyr when I read the Gospel! ready to blaze in a battalion when I read Homer! weeping at Rimini and at Othello. Laughing & without sixpence, in boisterous spirits when I ought to be sad & melancholy when I have every reason to be happy! (2: 273)

The irony of this dissipation of self is that once again the powerful impulse toward ego does not hold. Whether we call him a manic-depressive or a doubt-ridden genius, there is continual self-qualification that undermines the foundations of his own confidence and makes the autobiographical writing less Cellini-like than might otherwise be the case.

Perhaps the roots of this fragmentation are to be found in Haydon's dwelling on fleeting fame, passing time and loss. In a world that presents to him so many images of frustrated ambition, unexpected suffering and diminished power, it is not surprising that the self appears unstable. Frequently at the end of a calendar year Haydon identifies the year's passing with death in terms imaged as either an eternal waterfall churning into a gulf below or an irresistible tide sweeping everything away in its wake. We are vulnerable children, and neither our hopes, raptures, calculations nor our art can prevent us from sinking into sorrow. In other passages time is a reptile devouring men, who are born to putrefaction, or a Conqueror who exceeds Napoleon for power. At such moments Haydon's voice is that of an evangelical preacher, or of Leonardo da Vinci in the *Notebooks*, foreseeing universal ruin in the deluge, the swirling and anarchic water of our helpless condition. This is a sublime, visionary moment: "The sun shines, winds blow, ships are wrecked, men are drowned, children are born,

women are in labour, youths in love, in one ceaseless round!. . . Matter &
events seem to be in one eternal reaction & destruction" (2: 347). Haydon
struggles to affirm existence, for he cannot bear this ceaseless round: de-
spondency takes over, and he sees himself as a desperate chaser of an unattainable happiness that diminishes as he approaches it, and an overrater
of joy that lies just ahead but is darkened by folly and wickedness. What
appears sweet and beautiful on the outside is revealed as "bitter & corky
& putrid & full of ashes."

Like an Old Testament prophet, Haydon dramatizes his vulnerability
and isolation, and then turns and acts out an imaginary retribution, as if
retaliating against all the authorities who have humiliated him. His fragile
sense of self, controlled by a susceptibility to natural process and social
attack, finds a reprieve in fantasy. In one of the most melodramatic passages, he imagines himself a self-exiled Romantic wanderer.

If I were alone again I would leave my Country for ever—buried in Italy or Greece,
I would pass my days in the lowest avocations, could I get by it peace! ay, peace! I
would lie out in the Acropolis and hail the ruins about me, as congenial to my own
destroyed hopes. I would wander in the Alps, sleep in ravines, and be lulled by the
invisible roar of foaming floods, and be waked by echoing screech of soaring eagles!
I would willingly have footed, scrambled over rugged barks, fallen pines, and climb
sharp cutting flinty rocks, & plunge with the flood, & rise from its depths, & lie
panting & breathless on its banks, till Nature recovered sensation, & my desola-
tion returned to me! Or I would . . . vent my rage on the trees, the stones, the birds,
the animals, & glory with ecstatic rapture, to meet a *solitary human* being *without
defence* on whom I might vent my hatred of human nature! and gratify my tiger
feelings by tearing out his heart & drinking his blood! and then strip my body, my
half clothed & ragged body, & paint it with grinning faces in the blood yet warm
and unclotted by the air! Ah, ah, Revenge, thou dear, dear, dear passion! (2: 475)

This passage, with its powerfully suggestive echo of Milton's Satan, implies
that within the confines and shelter of the *Diary* he can enact his fantasies
of retribution without having to confront his adversaries. He can play out
with impunity a range of roles, allowing him to justify himself and to appear as oppressed scapegoat. These strategies find a place in the privacy of
the book, but even as we witness the Romantic will sublimely asserting
itself against all opposition, we also see the luxury of self-effacement. For
Haydon, autobiography simultaneously permits a therapeutic assertion
and an unembarrassed diminution of self.

In designating the *Diary* and *Autobiography* as shelters I am claiming
that his writing (especially in the *Autobiography*, where the events have
occurred at least two decades earlier) is part of an elaborate process of im-

age formation. He is pleased to be thought a fighter, and the autobiographical writings are filled with verbatim letters and essays in which his career and public self is launched against others. Haydon revels in his status as pariah because within the writing he is free to vindicate his actions without public consequence. Haydon may relive his experiences but he need not account to others for his actions. There is no evidence that he intended publication of either the journals or the autobiography during his lifetime. He took great pleasure in the force of his attacks upon painters, critics, and patrons, the very strength of the offended opposition confirming him to himself as a man of convictions.

But if aggrieved outrage regarding a painting hung in a dimly lit exhibition space, or a patron who reneged on a commission, marks one pole of Haydon's sensibility, reckless self-destruction marks another. There are numerous litanies of self-accusation:

I had always a tendency to fight it out, a tendency most prejudicial to artists, because it calls off his mind from the main point of his being—perfection in his art. . . . My will had not been curbed, or my will was too stubborn to submit to curbing; Heaven knows. Perhaps mine is a character in which all parts would have harmonised if my will had been broken early. The same power might have been put forth with more discretion, and I should have been less harassed by the world. (*Autobiography*, p. 116)

These sentiments contrast with the more vituperative ones directed outward against the world. Harold Bloom has remarked how, according to Freud, part of the ego's own self-hatred is projected onto an outward object but part remains in the ego. Such a description precisely fits Haydon's situation.[10] "The heart . . . sinks inwardly in itself & longs for a pleasure calm & eternal, majestic, unchangeable. I am not yet 40 and can tell of a Destiny melancholy and rapturous, severe, trying, & afflicting, bitter beyond all bitterness, afflicting beyond all affliction, cursed, heart burning! heart breaking! maddening, not to be dwelt on lest its thought scathe my blasted heart and blighted brain." (2: 499). There is as much self-hatred as loathing of the world in this entry. Puritanical disgust and guilt for not working harder or achieving greater stature dominate his writing in the middle years. But Haydon's fundamental strategy is to escape the implications of his particular, idiosyncratic behavior by lamenting both a crippled self and the disappointments of living. Chastened by his growing awareness that he is simply not as great a painter as he had thought, he cannot bear to acknowledge that truth, even to himself within the confines of writing. Instead, he turns on the world and on the general state of human misery without facing the possibility of self-delusion regarding his own skill. Autobiographical writing defers the problem by allowing endless options for the perpetuation of ambivalence towards himself. All Haydon could hope for was that his sufferings alone would vindicate him, but the more he stresses them the more it appears he has brought them on himself.

Haydon's biographer Eric George claims that Haydon's ultimate tragedy would have been not to be noticed, and that all his efforts were bent on avoiding that final humiliation. But one can also argue that Haydon knew, as all the Romantics did, the impossibility of fulfillment, and that the autobiographical writing testified to what could not be avoided. This awareness seems to have come early to Haydon, whose endless prayers for the energy to conquer obstacles soon turned into prayers to bear up under stress and defeat. Loss of power and the crises brought by its realization were Haydon's subject from the start, as if in his desperate need to find models in history for his desire, he envisioned a radical emptiness even as he projected a powerful libido.

When he is most critical of a life without design, when most ashamed of his drift, the prose becomes fragmented, as Haydon dramatizes the disconnected moments in the life.

My mind fatuous, impotent—drewling over Petrarch—dawdling over Pausanias— dipping into Plutarch. Voyages and Travels no longer exciting—all dull, dreary, flat, weary, & disgusting. I seem as if I should never paint again. I look at my own Xenophon, & wonder how I did it—read the Bible—gloat over Job—doubt Religion to rouse my faculties, and wonder if the wind be East or S.S. West—look out of the window and gape at the streets—shut up the shutters, & lean my hand on my cheek—get irritable for dinner, two hours before it can be ready—eat too much, drink too much—and go to bed at nine to forget existence! I dream horrors, start up, & lie down, & toss & tumble, listen to caterwauling of cats, & just doze away as light is dawning. Delightful life!—fit attendents on Idleness. With my Ambition! my talents! my energy! Shameful. (3: 549)

The *Diary* can be read as the gradual recognition that hope is less salvation than nemesis, in the sense that it not only holds out impossible illusions but, if miraculously gratified, is followed by inevitable disappointment. For Haydon all dreams are enchantments; the nearer we get to their fulfillment the less desirable they become. We live in a world of time and imperfection, but deceive ourselves that we can remedy our plight. There are moments of relief, when Haydon endows his Muse-like precursor painters, his friends, a beloved, and of course his creative work with the potential to redeem his despair. He even declares that similarly wretched men "shoot themselves—but not me" (5: 412). Nevertheless he seems to know that nothing will come of his hopes, that all "grand conceptions" and "elevated sensations of an ambitious and glorious soul" (*Autobiography*, p. 165) are flimsy constructions, much like love objects who can never make good the expectations with which we have freighted them.

Haydon's reluctance to submit to the reality of events and to the diminution of his life in its contingencies has its analogy in his attack on realism and portrait painting, and on the need for a heroic scale. There is something almost visceral in his passionate commitment to painting that is heroic in both size and subject matter, as if his very being could not tolerate limitation. He constantly seeks a form of transcendence, and the sheer scale of his work becomes the measure of escape from the trivial and mundane aspects of existence. In his public life Haydon craved largeness of scale as if to proclaim his greatness; smallness (or portrait painting) was equated in his mind with obscurity. When he painted large canvases he felt important and significantly controversial. His *Autobiography* in fact concludes with a description of his beginning to work on a painting of Lazarus, "determined to make it my grandest and largest work" (*Autobiography*, p. 345), and the *Autobiography* breaks off not after a description of the work or its execution, but after a meditation on size per se: "I always filled my painting-room to its full extent; and had I possessed a room 400 feet long, and 200 feet high, and 400 feet wide, I would have ordered a canvas 399-6 long by 199-6 high, and so have been encumbered for want of room, as if it had been my pleasure to be so" (*Autobiography*, p. 346). The painter, hemmed in and striving to create a gigantic world, is a Titanic figure wrestling with resistant material. The desire to transcend limits is a projection of heroic striving into both the principal figures of the painting: the Christ who performs a miracle, and the Lazarus who achieves his rebirth. (From the vantage point of the composition of the *Autobiography*, two decades after this scene from 1820, Haydon no doubt saw Lazarus as a symbol of his own hoped-for rebirth after twenty years of public defeats and private unhappiness.) Painting is a form of combat "because [in the eyes of a misguided public] Reynolds beat West in force, depth & color, Portrait Painters beat Historical Painters" (3: 118). Losing the game is inevitable, because "the Historical Painter, whatever be his talent . . . is considered half cracked or completely mad" (3: 311). In the face of public disdain, Haydon turns to the autobiographical writings, where the intensification of these struggles magnifies his sense of being both victim and scourge.

Paul de Man's acute observation about autobiography applies to Haydon's need to live within the writing: "We assume the life *produces* the autobiography as an act produces its consequences, but can we not suggest, with equal justice, that the autobiographical project may itself produce and determine the life and that whatever the writer *does* is in fact governed by the technical demands of self-portraiture and thus determined in all its aspects, by the resources of its medium?"[11] Haydon's life was partly shaped by the achievement of the writing, in that autobiography granted him a certain freedom to experiment in his life by trying out and anticipating within the security of the writing all possible consequences of his action. Then, as he confronted lost commissions and official neglect, he turned to the autobiographical project for solace, the very privacy of the writing compensating for and justifying his unacknowledged work. A myth of self-defeat emerges as the dominating one, as in a remark appended to an earlier entry where an inner voice urges him not to miss out in proposing designs for the Nelson Monument: "And yet it ended in nothing, & here my old voice deceived me" (4: 525). Triumph or even desire inevitably turns to loss, and the writing unfolds this design as if Haydon—against his will—were both compelled actor and composing author of his tragedy.

Haydon, both sinned against and sinning, finds the causes for disappointment wherever he can—in the public world, in his own misapprehensions, in the way life is. He bows to a course of ineluctability, even as he asserts that he will not submit to suicide; time is inexorable and surrender is half-sweet in the contemplation. He alleges he would plunge over the falls of Niagara if he could, those sublime torrents that always stand for the deadly rush of time. Reading through great stretches of the *Diary*, we see that passages of calm and ordinary experience inevitably give way to passages of hysteria and nightmare: whether Haydon meditates on his own self-destructive impulses, his dreams of revenge, his marriage as the ruination of his art and of those whom he drags down with him, or the overestimation of his chances for greatness, he is aware of a tragic arc to his life, yet unable to accept it. The autobiographical writing, veering as it does between hope and despair, expresses the instability of its author as he attempts both to write himself into tranquility and to lash out against the failures he can no longer deny.

In a moment that looks like melodrama but really suggests a fascination with the course of his own psyche, we see why Haydon could never let any emotional problem rest without examination: "I do not think any man on Earth ever suffered more agony of mind than I have done, & so would the World think if it knew why, and yet I always had an abstracting power, & that saved my mind and made me look down & meditate, as it were, on my own sufferings. They became a curious speculation" (3: 38). Haydon reveals both a therapeutic benefit from self-exploration and also a morbid excitement from his own pain. Writing brings peace—it helps dispel the uncertainty of things—but it also intensifies the anguish as he relives it and explores every detail. He is unable to escape from the circle of curiosity he has drawn.

Haydon claims he writes to show the reader how to "bear affliction and disappointment" (*Autobiography*, p. 164); it is an autobiographical commonplace for a writer ostensibly to address his work to an audience who will benefit from his wisdom, but Haydon, like so many autobiographers, writes largely to console himself and to assert an irrepressible claim for his own genius. We have noted that early in the *Diary* he imagines himself as a figure of fiery greatness: "I have been like a man with air balloons under his arm pits and ether in his soul. While I was painting, or walking, or thinking, these beaming flashes of energy followed and impressed me! . . . Grant that they may be the fiery anticipations of a great Soul born to realize them" (1: 430). Twenty-six years later he is still unquenchable, his imagery equally Promethean. "Had a most glorious idea of Genius at 4 this morning. I awoke saying what is Genius? It is a spark from the Deity's Essence which shoots up into the Heavens fiery & blazing over an astonished World, & when it has reached its elevation, drops back into his Being like lava from a Volcanic Mountain" (5: 82). The Romantic ego expressed here is in the high mode of natural supernaturalism and self-renovation. But the defeated dross of nature, unresponsive society, and an unwilling self combine to check those enthusiasms. Nevertheless, Haydon celebrates the self even in and through its defeats; autobiography replaces the painted self-portrait (he did only one; see Fig. 2), and expresses a belief that in his solipsism he can gather strength against his detractors and assert a radical "I am" even as he slowly kills himself with recrimination.

But, ironically, Haydon's problem is that he can never fully turn inward, at least without extreme self-consciousness; too often he has his eyes on others, on their judgments and their determination of his fortune. Haydon enacts what Bloom calls the first stage or Promethean mode of the "internalized quest-romance," defined as an "involvement in political [and] social . . . revolution, and a direct, even satirical attack on the institutional orthodoxies of . . . English society."[12] Haydon's condemnation of the Royal Academy and of misplaced patronage figures here. But he is ultimately fixated on these issues—he can never shake free of a preoccupation with the accusing voices, even when he internalizes them. He needs others' condemnation in order to assert himself; trapped in the process, he becomes fully absorbed with defense of his worth. His obsession with avatars

Fig. 2. Self-portrait. Courtesy of the National Portrait Gallery, London.

suggests that he cannot separate himself from the past and from judgment. (Does Michelangelo in the dream come to inspire or to judge?) It is not surprising that he was unable to paint in an original style.

Just as he can never turn from his elders, so he exhibits an adolescent petulance in his life-long insistence that he is better than anyone else. The *Diary* and the *Autobiography* express his attempt to re-beget himself and to assert an identity without the defining imperatives of others, but Haydon cannot sustain this posture. Defiance is as crucial as achievement; indeed one is impossible without the other. Frustrated or defeated creativity is mandatory for self-assertion. "In reading over my journals of 1818, I gloried to see how I suffered . . . how I vanquished," and "It is my destiny to perform great things, not in consequence of encouragement, but in spite of opposition, & so let it be. . . . 'Impossibility is the Element in which he glories.'—Hazlitt" (5: 447, 430).

He is plagued not only by the expectations of others, but also by his own heroic demands, the images he must live up to. Here is Haydon's essentially oxymoronic position: it is in a purgatorial mode, expressing hopeful labor and fear of entrapment. Autobiographical writing is both an escape from sorrow and the net that enmeshes him more tightly in his grief; that writing is not merely reflective, composed at the end of a long life, but an almost daily tracing of the torment of his failure to meet his own expectations. Self-absorption becomes a tragic game in Haydon's hands, his writing both the vantage point from which to perceive his life's slow dying, and the virtual instrument of that death.

Hogarth's Self-Representations

Ronald Paulson

William Hogarth wrote an autobiography (or at least notes and drafts toward one) and he produced in his graphic works self-representations, including self-portraits. He wrote the autobiography in the early 1760's as an old man; he included self-representations in his paintings and prints from the 1720's onward.

The autobiographical notes were both public and private: they gave an official public account but they were never finished or published in Hogarth's lifetime. The notes fall into three stages of a narrative: youth, overcoming obstacles and exploiters; success, creating a new graphic form, the "modern moral subject," and launching into sublime history painting; and in the 1750's–60's, jealousy, misunderstanding, and persecution, a return to the paranoid first stage of the narrative. The passages most rewritten—perhaps only because they came first—were those of his childhood, apprenticeship, and early manhood, running up to the success of his conversation pictures (1728–30) and of *A Harlot's Progress* (1732), his "modern moral subject," something "not struck out before in any kingdom."

In these notes there are three highlights: the first is the emphasis on his father, his shabby treatment at the hands of the booksellers, and his subsequent death (Hogarth implies it was the result of their treatment). Parallel with the fate of his father, Hogarth presents his own early experience with the printsellers who pirated his prints and stole his livelihood (until he succeeded in getting an engravers' copyright act passed in 1735); and his later experience in the 1750's–60's with patrons, politicians, and other artists that prompted him to write the autobiographical notes. The second emphasis falls on his problems as a young engraver: his late-coming to the art, his hatred of the "drudgery" of reproducing "the monsters of heraldry" on silverplate, and his escape from this profession into independent engraving and then painting—but also his steep and remarkable ascent from engraving to painting and the priority of the mode he invented. The third emphasis, a correlative of the second, is the stress he put on the need for both his "pleasures" and his "studies," words he repeats over and over. "Pleasures" takes on quite a burden of meaning for Hogarth, all the way from *dulce* (as opposed to *utile*) to play (the "love of pursuit" he advocated as the basis of a reading of his prints and an important aspect of the Beautiful) and "idleness," but in the polarities with "studies" it sums up the private aspect of his life in tension with the public, moral, didactic, and professional.

All three of these situations were embodied indirectly in his art. For example, the "monsters of heraldry" is only another term for the decorative high art that he constantly played off against forms of low or empirical reality. The dichotomy of "pleasures" and "studies" appears in his obsessive use of the Choice of Hercules (which is between Virtue and Pleasure) and comes to a focus in his series of 1748 called *Industry and Idleness*.

What we notice when we turn from Hogarth's written autobiography to his graphic self-representations is that while the first presents a self, William Hogarth, the second begins by presenting this self as other, and specifically as marginalized other—a figure that may recall the story of his father and of his own early years. As soon as he started to paint, in his conversation pictures of 1729–32, Hogarth introduced a dog—the pug who stands with his paws up on a chair, mimicking the dignified pose of the host, while creating a wrinkle in the carpet (Fig. 1). The innocent questioning of a dog confronts a world of imposed human order: society, or (in conversation picture terms) the family. The dog's continued presence in Hogarth's conversations strongly suggests that this was intended as his signature—permitted, even perhaps encouraged by his sitters, who commissioned him expecting some touch of puggish liveliness. But one also wonders why, so early in his career, Hogarth includes himself, or an aspect of himself, however conventionalized, insistent though self-deprecating, in almost every picture.

In some conversations the pug is contrasted with the dog of the family Hogarth is painting. In one the pug worries a small wicker hamper, while the well-behaved spaniel of the household by contrast sits upright to join his master in admiring a work of art instead of nature. In another the pug growls opposite the family dog who has a bone on his prosperous plate. Finally, precisely this same pug appears in Hogarth's self-portrait of 1740 alongside his own face, which the dog's face clearly resembles (Fig. 2).

There is of course a conventional aspect to this dog: I refer to the Dutch

Fig. 1. *The Wollaston Family* (detail); painting; 1730; 39×49 in. Courtesy of the executors of the late H. C. Wollaston.

"Dissolute Family" scenes on the one hand and—closer to Hogarth's intention—Watteau's *fêtes galantes* on the other, for example, *The Shepherds* (Berlin), where the dog's "natural" pose clarifies the artist's attitude toward the idealized love of the human couple. The dog also, especially in the self-portrait, relates mockingly to the tradition of the art treatises that connected animals with the old masters: Michelangelo with a dragon, Leonardo with a lion, Titian with an ox—in Hogarth's case with connotations of down-to-earth common sense and an awareness of the resemblance to his own profile.

After a series of self-representations as other, at the peak of his career in the 1740's, Hogarth joins the dog with his own face in a "self-portrait": and he accompanies the two doggish faces with an artist's palette inscribed

Fig. 2. *Gulielmus Hogarth*; engraving; fourth state; Mar. 1748/9; 13½ × 10⁵⁄₁₆ in. Collection of the author.

with his contribution to aesthetic theory, the "Line of Beauty," and with volumes labeled Shakespeare, Milton, and Swift. Like his ancestors the Puritan spiritual autobiographers, he defines himself in terms of others—not Christ or St. Paul, but Shakespeare and the pug. He is defining himself as he had Tom Rakewell define himself in *Rake's Progress 3* where, in a brothel, Tom breaks the mirror, destroying his present self, and replaces it by cutting out the faces of all the Roman emperors hanging on the brothel wall except Nero. The juxtaposition of the English writers and the pug draws attention to Hogarth's need in these images to make himself both singular and exemplary; to emphasize both the spiritual and the animal in him and—what he regards as the same thing—in his art.

In other works, in particular *Boys Peeping at Nature*, the subscription ticket for his first "modern moral subject," *A Harlot's Progress*, the dog's function is taken by a young satyr with the same connotations of satiric disrespect and animal hunger, or sexuality, and the same association with the artist, although these are here complemented—domesticated—into a kind of *concordia discors* by a more respectable putto who restrains his attempt to lift Nature's veil. This plate reminds us that in his conversation pictures Hogarth had also employed children to comment on the over-ordered society of their parents. Like the dog, they are the commentary of nature on culture.

In the huge history paintings Hogarth made for St. Bartholomew's Hospital in the late 1730's, the *Christ at the Pool of Bethesda* and the *Good Samaritan* are accompanied—down below, as the Samaritan's wounded man is accompanied by his wounded alter-ego, his dog—by three small reddish monochrome panels telling the story of the jongleur Rahere, the founder of St. Bartholomew's Hospital, in this way connecting divine charity with an even more human and outcast Samaritan. Rahere was a public entertainer who recounted tales of comic heroes, sang, tumbled, and led dancing bears, but he rose by way of his comic gift from humble origins and little education to be the favorite entertainer of King Henry II, and with his wealth he endowed the church and hospital.

Hogarth, whose childhood had been spent in the shadow of St. Bartholomew's, and who by this time was a successful artist and a governor of the hospital, suggests the parallel to his own career of painting comic histories, which had now ascended to this large gift of charity in the form of the most exalted painterly genre. And while he painted the public message of Charity, his own and his age's primary virtue, depicted larger than life above, he adds his personal message, in monochrome, self-deprecating but at the same time self-assertive, below: the human version of the divine Charity in *The Pool of Bethesda*. And the two stories are connected by the figure of a dog leaning over from the upper to peer down at the lower.

But there is a further subtext in these sublime histories. The positive subject of Charity (human and divine, the Good Samaritan and Christ) evokes the negative subject of the Pharisees' pursuance of the letter rather than the spirit of the Old Testament law. Characteristically, Hogarth connects the subject of religion with another, for him cognate, subject of the English artist ("William Hogarth Anglus pinxit," as he signed one painting), in which the biblical law equals the rules imposed on him by academic and usually foreign art critics. The references to Pharisaic law in both of the stories he illustrates make a comment on the rules of high art as well as on those of religion and society, emphasized by the commentary

Fig. 3. *Characters and
Caricaturas* (detail);
engraving; April 1743.
Collection of the author.

of the Rahere panels. The paintings say something in favor of the artist-
Samaritan, the painter as well as his subject, who refuses to follow blindly
the rules of the art treatises or of patrons—and is an outcast, always an
outcast. One such rule is that a painter of drolls, the Rahere of painters,
does not attempt the highest genre, history painting, as Hogarth is doing
in these paintings. The singular and the exemplary are conjoined: this is
only Hogarth, while at the same time Hogarth wants the figure to be exemplary for other English artists. These paintings are supposed to show
them how to paint in England in the 1730's; the story of the Samaritan and
the priests is to show them how to avoid the rules-bound theorists of academic art.

The exemplary self-image continues from the self-portrait with Shakespeare, Milton, and Swift: Hogarth also links himself with contemporaries
with whom he wishes to associate himself—primarily Fielding, but also
Garrick, Sterne, and others. For example, near the bottom (or source?) of
the cloud of character-heads in *Characters and Caricaturas* he places his
own face grinning at Fielding's—and below this, in words, a reference to
Fielding's preface to *Joseph Andrews*, where the novelist associated his
"comic epic in prose" with Hogarth's "comic history-painting" (Fig. 3).

But there is also a paranoid fiction, the equivalent of his father's story,
that runs through Hogarth's works. It becomes specifically autobiographical in *The Gate of Calais*, a nevertheless humorous scene based on an experience during a trip Hogarth made to the continent in 1748 (Fig. 4). The
animus is against the French, who had arrested him for sketching (as they
suspected) the fortifications of Calais: But the scenario and the composition establish the form of his less humorous paranoia in the 1750's–60's.
There is the misunderstanding of his intentions; there is the tiny, almost
obliterated, figure of the artist in the background at the left, marginal to
the scene of folly but about to be unjustly imprisoned, however momentarily, for this misunderstanding (Fig. 5). This was, of course, again the
story of his father, the unjustly imprisoned.

Fig. 4. *The Gate of Calais, or The Roast Beef of Old England*; engraving; second
state; Mar. 1748/9; 13⅝ × 17⁵/₁₆ in. Collection of the author.

Fig. 5. *The Gate of Calais* (detail).

The cause of his paranoid fictions was the attacks on him by his fellow artists that began when he opposed the plan for a national academy of art. It was important for them to discredit him, the most famous living English artist, if the plan was to succeed. And some of the attacks were grossly personal as well as professional. The basis of the latter—intensified after he wrote his aesthetic treatise—was the folly of the Rahere figure who aspires to history painting, the engraver who tries to paint becoming the painter who thinks he can write.

In his last years, when Hogarth had taken an equally unpopular position in politics, the paranoid fiction took the form of actually erasing his face from the self-portrait with his pug, replacing it with Charles Churchill's bearish physiognomy to indicate that in this world of the 1760's Hogarth and all he stood for had been replaced by *this*. Only the pug remains, showing the same puggish disrespect we saw in the conversation pictures (Fig. 6). In his final print, *The Tailpiece* of 1764, his anticipated death (and the closing of the volume of his prints) coincided with the breaking of all serpentine continuities, all Lines of Beauty, all signs of his art, by the new fashion for the Sublime in theory (Burke), painting (Reynolds), and politics (Pitt).

But the paranoid fiction, masked or inverted, concealed or displaced, had begun to appear in Hogarth's first series, his first great success, *A Harlot's Progress* of 1732. Here is the ostensible pattern of an innocent girl from the country drawn into the ambience of the "great," the fashionable, the respectable, in London; turning against her own nature she imitates this "greatness," and comes to grief while the "great" themselves go their merry way. Her initials in Plate 3 are fleshed into "Moll [or Mary] Hackabout." The *Dictionary of Cant* defines "*Hacks* or Hackneys" as "hirelings." "*Hackney-whores*, Common Prostitutes. *Hackney-Horses*, to be let to any body," but also "Hackney-*Scriblers*, Poor Hirelings, Mercenary Writers." "Hack" links prostitute and bookseller and thus may contain a submerged memory of Richard Hogarth, or an inscription of Hogarth's own case with the printsellers.

The personal pattern is unmistakable. Besides the public facts found in newspapers about Col. Charteris, his rape of Anne Bond, and the rest, there was also Hogarth's father, who had come down to London and tried to live by London standards as a scholar and man of letters. The lad from the north country, attempting to be a Latin scholar and schoolmaster, ends as a literary hack, an inmate of debtors' prison, and dies, driven to his death by the exploitive London booksellers, as Hogarth recalled bitterly half a century later.

Fig. 6. *The Bruiser*; engraving; seventh state; Oct. 1763; 13½ × 10⅚₆ in. Collection of the author.

Equally relevant are Hogarth's own refusal to accept his status as a silver engraver's apprentice, his rejection of his indentures, his struggle to survive against the printsellers who pirated his early plates. Subscription, the method of distribution he inaugurated with the *Harlot*, was aimed against the mediation of the printseller (the equivalent of the harlot's bawd), a constant threat to his livelihood.

One wonders whether Hogarth read (though one can hardly doubt that he did) Defoe's preface to *Serious Reflections During the Life and Sur-*

prising Adventures of Robinson Crusoe (1720), where Defoe/Crusoe affirms of *Robinson Crusoe* "that the story, though allegorical, is also historical," that is a "real history": "All these reflections are just history of a state of forced confinement, which in my real history is represented by a confined retreat on an island; and it is as reasonable to represent one kind of imprisonment by another, as it is to represent anything that really exists by that which exists not." One wonders if this aim—essentially the goal of self-discovery as the finding of the self by losing the self—explains the way Hogarth felt about the *Harlot's Progress*, the extent to which he rationalized the "allegory" of that history as his own. The story of the closed rooms he represented in these early "progresses" that are regresses suggests the representation of "one kind of imprisonment by another."

No English artist painted more prison interiors than Hogarth. His first major painting was of Newgate and his second of the Fleet Prison. The first was *The Beggar's Opera*, where the prison was not a real one but a painted set on the stage of a theater; the second was of a real prison and the House of Commons committee that was investigating its cruelty and corruption. But with his first series of invented pictures, *A Harlot's Progress*, he abandons all sense of play. These show a room, which appears to be a drawing room or a boudoir, that is in reality a prison. The Harlot is literally imprisoned in Bridewell, but from the second to the final plate she is in spaces that are ever more closed and confining, and these are metaphorical equivalents for the confining choice she made in Plate 1.

In 1747, Hogarth published *Industry and Idleness*. Contemporaries who knew Hogarth or even his London-wide reputation would have perceived an obvious parallel between the industrious apprentice and Hogarth himself, who married his own "master's" daughter—Jane Thornhill, daughter of Sir James Thornhill, Serjeant Painter to the King—and succeeded to his business, carrying on history painting, reestablishing Thornhill's academy, and defending Thornhill's reputation as a painter (Fig. 7). The question was the degree of the Hogarthian irony. Goodchild's face, with its handsome, bland, almost sheeplike features, is idealized almost to the point of caricature (Fig. 8). One recalls the look of self-satisfaction on his face, the heartlessly academic poses he assumes, the affected manner in which he holds his teacup (perhaps trying to emulate the manners of the West End) in Plate 6. It may be significant that Hogarth originally called him William Goodchild but, thinking better of it, changed his name to Francis.

It is, however, Tom Idle's face that resembles Hogarth's own puggish,

Fig. 7. *Industry and Idleness*, pl. 6; engraving; second state; 1747; 10 × 13¼ in. Collection of the author.

Fig. 8. *Industry and Idleness*, pl. 6 (detail).

plebeian profile (Figs. 9 and 10), which can be seen in *The Gate of Calais*, in his self-portrait of a few years later, or in *Hogarth Painting the Comic Muse* (Fig. 11). If only to inject enough self-irony to make the portrayal palatable in his own mind, Hogarth must have introduced some sense of himself into his opposite: he was so unlike Idle, so like the industrious one. Yet one side of him clearly sought, as he put it, his "pleasure" as well as his "studies." "Idleness" is one of the key words of his autobiographical notes. Looking back on his time as an apprentice, both in silver engraving and in painting at Vanderbank's academy, he emphasized his idleness, saying that he required a mnemonic technique "most suitable to my situation and idle disposition"; the system he developed and wrote about (a few lines on his thumbnail expanded, back in his studio, into full figures) allowed him "to make use of whatever my Idleness would suffer me to become possest of."

It sounds very much as if there is a humorous self-portrait included in the portrait of the other, Tom Idle, hinting at that aspect of Hogarth that kept him from finishing his apprenticeship, liked to go wenching, was deluded by illusions of ease and grandeur, and, perhaps, unconsciously associated the creative act (as opposed to the successful businessman's practice) with guilt and public execution. Perhaps it was the Harlot (and also the Rake) in him that needed to be exorcised or at least accommodated.

The ballad "Jesse or the Happy Pair" being sung by a beggar at the lower left in Plate 6 leads the spectator, in a characteristically Hogarthian reading, to the memory of earlier apprentice-master relationships that also involved the master's daughter. The "Happy Pair" refers to Goodchild and his master ("West and Goodchild" on the shop sign) as well as to Goodchild and his bride, the master's daughter. There appears to have been no such ballad, but what one remembers of the biblical Jesse is his genealogy (given twice in the Old Testament) and his son David, who married Michal, his master's daughter. Out of this marriage a distinguished tree was to grow—the Tree of Jesse, the outcome of which was Jesus himself (Isaiah 11.1–4).

But Goodchild and David were both "apprentices": David, originally engaged in a lowly capacity as harper to King Saul, becomes his master's close companion, best friend to his son Jonathan, and lover of his daughter (in each case a "happy pair"), and finally "takes over the business" as king of Israel. Saul's anxiety over the fact that David is destined to replace him as king led to attempts on David's life and to his own eventual ruin. To secure Michal's hand David was required to slaughter a hundred Philistines for Saul, to impress whom he doubled the number. Shortly thereafter,

Fig. 9. *Industry and Idleness*, pl. 3; engraving; first state; 1747; 10⅛ × 13⁶⁄₁₆ in. Collection of the author.

Fig. 10. *Industry and Idleness*, pl. 3 (detail).

Fig. 11. *Hogarth Painting the Comic Muse*; engraving; seventh state; 1764.
Collection of the author.

Michal saved him from the assassins her father had sent to kill him (1 Samuel 19.11–27). Saul in fact forced her to marry another, and David only reclaimed her after Saul's death (1 Samuel 25.44; 2 Samuel 3.13–16).

If the story of his childhood in debtors' prison was one plot or myth Hogarth could not help retelling, another was the story of the boy who is adopted by a second father, presented with his dazzling daughter, and then denied her because he has not lived up to expectations (or, in *Industry and Idleness* not denied her—but then he has split himself into the apprentice who gets her and the other who does not). He does not write in his autobiographical notes about his marriage to the daughter of Sir James Thornhill, but this private life is precisely what he takes up in his paintings: his relationship to his wife Jane and to his father-in-law, and perhaps (by implication) to other women as well. This becomes the self-representation of his "modern moral subject" following the *Harlot's Progress*.

George Vertue, the contemporary engraver whose diary records much of Hogarth's career, remarked that Hogarth had married Sir James Thornhill's daughter (this was in the spring of 1729) "without his consent," and John Nichols, fifty years later, possibly from an independent account, envisaged an elopement. Thornhill may have been disturbed by the difference in their stations, but the age difference—he was 32, she at most 20—and Hogarth's probably too convivial years on the town may also have given Thornhill pause.

There is a reconciliation story (recounted by John Nichols) in which Lady Thornhill is supposed to have restored good feeling between the generations by advising Hogarth to place some of his *Harlot's Progress* paintings in his father-in-law's way. In this story it is the enterprising Jane, rather than Hogarth himself, who conveys his canvases to the Thornhill dining room, acting as a sort of mediator, and persuading her father to be reconciled.

Thornhill's disapproval of the marriage had to be reconciled with his obvious fondness for his young protégé. As to Jane Hogarth, we know little about her except that she was accustomed in later years to sail into the local parish church, very much the grande dame, and that she fiercely defended Hogarth's reputation long after his death. And there is one surviving letter from Hogarth to "Jenny," from 1749, that demonstrates both his fondness (in writing at least) and the fact that she spent much time in their country house in Chiswick while he worked in the Leicester Square house in London. The fact is that whenever Hogarth turned to history painting based on a literary text he chose a story that dealt with a trio resembling Thornhill, Jane, and himself.

A decade after his wedding, and shortly after Thornhill's death, Hogarth painted *A Scene from Shakespeare's "The Tempest"*: He chose Act I, scene ii, the first meeting of Ferdinand and Miranda, which also includes Prospero, who serves to introduce the two parties and to hover over the scene as playwright-magician (Fig. 12). Ferdinand, saved from shipwreck, recalls "Sitting on a bank, / Weeping again the king my father's wreck," and he repeats more than once the paramount fact that his father has drowned ("my drown'd father," "the king my father wreck'd"). Prospero has befriended him and now, in the scene Hogarth illustrates, introduces him to his daughter, with whom he immediately falls in love. The parallel is ob-

Fig. 12. *A Scene from Shakespeare's 'The Tempest'*; painting; ca. 1735?; 31½ × 40 in. Courtesy of Lord St. Oswald; Nostell Priory Collection.

vious. Hogarth's father had spent some years in prison and emerged a ruined man to die a few years later. Then Hogarth had met Thornhill and fallen under his spell—a spell we can recognize in the influence the older painter had on his assumptions about history painting of the sort being attempted in *A Scene from "The Tempest."*

But having introduced the young couple, Prospero says, aside,

> They are both in either's powers; but this swift business
> I must uneasy make, lest too light winning
> Make the prize light.

He therefore tests Ferdinand, accusing him of treason and attempting to turn him into another wood-toting Caliban. Ferdinand, outraged, draws his sword, which Prospero's magic prevents him from raising.

> *Miranda*   O dear father,
> Make not too rash a trial of him, for
> He's gentle and not fearful.

. . .

> *Prospero*   Silence! one word more
> Shall make me chide thee, if not hate thee. What!
> An advocate for an imposter! hush!
> Thou think'st there is no more such shapes as he,
> Having seen but him and Caliban: foolish wench!
> To the most of men this is a Caliban
> And they to him are angels.
> *Miranda*   My affections
> Are then most humble; I have no ambition
> To see a goodlier man.

"Come on," says Prospero; "Obey," and of course Ferdinand does carry out such menial tasks for Prospero as gathering wood.

Miranda is the woman who has never seen a man, shown by Hogarth with her aged father Prospero behind her and a lamb nearby; and Hogarth gives her the colors of the Virgin Mary and a pose roughly like that of Mary at the Annunciation—crossed with Mary in a Nativity scene, thus relating Prospero to Joseph: a scene very like the parodic Annunciation used in the *Harlot's Progress* 3, a few years earlier, applied to the Harlot as a failed Miranda.

This sounds like a witty private joke between Hogarth and his wife—though the fact that Thornhill had recently died might give one pause. Some of it sounds like a joke only Hogarth himself would have enjoyed. But the story was already present in his earliest finished painting, *The Beggar's Opera* (and a few years later in *A Scene from "The Indian Emperor"*). The plot convention parodied by Gay in *The Beggar's Opera* has the father-king imprisoning the hero because he is in love with the king's daughter. Captain Macheath's relationship to old Peachum is essentially the same, on a low level, as Montezuma's with the Inca or any of Dryden's rebellious tragic heroes with his king. Aspects of this fiction must have appealed to Hogarth in the years following 1728, when he had his own Polly and Mr. Peachum to contend with and was constructing his own "modern moral subject." And he returned to it from time to time in the years to come. The question of course is: Did his interest in the story lead him to Jane or Jane (whom he would have known before January 1728 when *The Beggar's Opera* premiered) to the story?

The plot reappears in its most sinister form in the painting *Satan, Sin, and Death*, made around the same time as *The Tempest*, though it's safe to assume a bit later. As in the *Tempest* painting, Hogarth chooses the aspect of the *Beggar's Opera* painting that makes Polly a mediator (rather than the other aspect, or gestalt, of Macheath as Hercules at the Cross-

Fig. 13. *Satan, Sin, and Death*; painting; date unknown; 24×29 in. Courtesy of the Tate Gallery, London.

roads choosing between his two wives, Polly and Lucy), but in *Satan, Sin, and Death* Sin's face is turned toward her father-lover and away from her son-lover, and—subsidiary figures eliminated—the woman is now unambiguously the central figure (Fig. 13). The context makes it clear that the father and the lover/son are fighting for the daughter. They are not only held apart by her but are contending for her favors. By emphasizing the triangular psychological relationship Hogarth has not only lifted the trapdoor on the conflicting instincts at work in Milton's scene, hitherto unnoticed by illustrators, but he has also exposed the deepest level of conflict in his *Beggar's Opera* and *Tempest* paintings, and in many of his other compositions.

The painting *Sigismunda* of 1759, the immediate cause of Hogarth's self-justification in his autobiographical notes, was an embarrassment from the start. There were stories about the posing of Jane Hogarth for Sigismunda and the bloodiness of Guiscardo's heart in the goblet, the object of her mourning or meditation (Fig. 14). John Wilkes noted unkindly

Fig. 14. *Sigismunda*; painting; 1759; 39 × 49½ in. Courtesy of the Tate Gallery, London.

(after he and Hogarth had broken off their friendship) that it was Jane "in an agony of passion, but of what passion no connoisseur could guess," and a housemaid of the Hogarths at Chiswick recalled that it was Jane grieving for her dead mother.

Hogarth cites Dryden's version of the story in his *Fables*. In this version, though not in any earlier one, Sigismunda and Guiscardo have not merely become lovers despite her father's disapproval, but have gotten married. That is, her crime is only marrying without her father's consent—marrying beneath her. It is a very hasty and perfunctory marriage ceremony followed immediately by their falling into bed. Secondly, Sigismunda stands up to Tancred; she is not frail, as she is in Boccaccio's version, but active. The parallel to Hogarth's own experience with Jane and Sir James Thornhill is all too precise.

Sigismunda's father Tancred selfishly sequesters her, but she falls in love with a young man

> Of gentle blood, but one whose niggard fate
> Had set him far below her high estate:
> Guiscard his name was called, of blooming age,
> Now squire to Tancred, and before his page.

Guiscardo is a young plebeian, raised up by Tancred to be his protégé, but when he discovers the youth has fallen in love with his daughter he forbids the match. Dryden recounts the story of their secret courtship under Tancred's eyes, how they steal away and are married, and how, after their marriage, they are discovered by the angry father, who kills Guiscardo and sends his heart in a goblet to Sigismunda; she fills the goblet with poison and drinks. Hogarth's persistent efforts to have the painting engraved, to show it to the public, and to sell it for an exorbitant price all suggest something of the deep personal feeling that accompanied it—exacerbated, of course, by Sir Richard Grosvenor's rejection of it (perhaps a memory of Sir James Thornhill's rejection of 1729) and by the adverse criticisms overheard at the Society of Artists exhibition of 1761, which caused him to withdraw the painting.

It may be significant that by this time Hogarth paints only the face and upper body of the woman, focusing on her face—her expression—and her hands. As he explained the painting in his autobiographical notes, he was responding to a head-and-shoulders painting attributed to Correggio, but in fact (as Hogarth sensed) by a minor follower. And here we have to ask once again: Did the "Correggio" lead him to choose the opportunity to challenge the old master, or was it the story of Sigismunda that caught his attention? The simple composition, dictated by the challenging of "Correggio," is augmented, however, by a few symbolic objects. The heart of the lover in the goblet is balanced against Sigismunda's bracelet that bears the head of a king, apparently her father. (In his portrait of Jane he shows her holding an oval portrait of Sir James.)

There is a kind of transformational grammar in effect in Hogarth's imaginative works. Richard Hogarth is reconceived as a naive young woman trying to succeed in London. She in turn is transformed, in the *Rake's Progress* (1735), into a male figure, one who destroys his loved one as well as himself. But in the *Rake* a new figure appears, a good woman named Sarah Young, who attempts (albeit unsuccessfully) to redeem the Rake. She derives from the Polly Peachum in *The Beggar's Opera* paintings who tries (unsuccessfully, it should be noted) to mediate between her father and lover/husband. Sarah Young tries to mediate between Tom Rakewell and the outside world, paying his debts at one point and accompanying him to debtors' prison and Bedlam, in the last posing as a Mary-the-Mother of a *Pietà* in the Rake's final agonies.

This figure, we have to conclude, is either Jane Hogarth or simply "the wife," as opposed to the Harlot, Hogarth himself, and all the rest. This version of the other is good, though undeniably oppressive, the Samaritan as opposed to the wounded man or his wounded dog, and she moves to the center of the picture. In his St. Bartholomew's Hospital paintings (which immediately followed the *Rake* in 1736) she is carried directly over into the figure of Christ (Christian Charity-Love mediating between God the Father and his fallen creation), ministering to a figure who distinctly resembles the unclothed Rakewell in Bedlam. Love as Charity is contrasted with the Eros of the nude courtesan who (presumably suffering from a venereal disease) is being thrust by her wealthy keeper ahead of the poor so she will be first into the pool.

I must pause to mention the fact that in Jonathan Richardson's book on Milton, published in 1734 and read to Hogarth's club of artists at Slaughter's Coffeehouse, Christ is presented as the "Mediator" between God and man. Also I must recall that Hogarth affixes the name of Athanasius to the wall of a madman's cell in Bedlam in *Rake's Progress* 8. William Whiston, also inscribed on the Bedlam wall, was notorious for his anti-Athanasian pamphlets. Given the presence of Rakewell and Sarah in the pose of Christ and Mary, Hogarth may be making an ironic reference back to Rakewell Senior (a heavy presence, though recently deceased, in Plate 1), suggesting a parodic Trinity of these three.

The argument concerning the Trinity was the most vexed of the religious controversies surrounding deism. The heretical views filled a complicated spectrum labeled Arian, Socianian, anti-Trinitarian, semi-Arian, Tritheist, and so on. Pantheism formulated three distinct gods; deism one God, with Christ a much lesser and relatively unimportant figure (though still a god), and so on. Arianism was attributed even to high-ranking churchmen like Archbishop Tillotson and John Sherlock. Milton, believing in the son as Mediator, was regarded by many as an Arian: In his own writings on the subject he pointed out that Christ himself had said there is only one God; and that if he were a mediator, "it cannot be explained how anyone can be a mediator to himself on his own behalf."

In general all these unorthodox views held that the Holy Spirit and the Son were to be distinguished from the Supreme God and could not therefore be regarded as part of him and his omnipotence—three distinct spirits or independent minds, three different essences. Thus it is possible to see Hogarth, with his own private concerns, as he moved from the *Rake's Progress* into sublime history, developing a story of an omnipotent father, a son who maintains his separateness, and a spirit (female) that tries to join them; or, to take Richardson's thesis of Christ as mediator, a father, his mediating daughter, and a fallen, "low" (Rahere, pug, apprentice) son: in other words, a story about both separateness and undifferentiation; about the power and threat of the father; or about a second father who replaces, obliterates in some guilty sense, the first and real father; or about a "trinity" of separate elements, two opposed and the third attempting to mediate between them, all variants of the tension between division and union.

The figure of the woman, as mediator as well as sexual object, continues to appear in the prints about art that Hogarth published between 1736 and 1741 in which a pretty young woman (again in the pose of Polly, Miranda, or Sin) mediates between an artist and the threat of external disorder directly aimed at him by the chaotic external world. On the surface the pictures are about the beautiful woman as one form of nature (*la belle nature*). In *The Distressed Poet* and *The Enraged Musician* she is bridging the gap between the artist and intractable things-as-they-are: between an over-formalized artist, a poet or musician, and the subculture, underclass world of street noises, bill collectors, and hungry dogs (Fig. 15). In the former she still carries New Testament associations, especially in the painting, in which she is in the color as well as pose of a Virgin Mary in a Nativity.

Parenthetically, we might note how the Christ child is projected in the story of "Jesse or the Happy Pair" as well as in the Nativity Scenes (*Harlot 3*, the *Scene from "The Tempest*," as well as the *Distressed Poet*), and then recall the Hogarths' childlessness. In fact, the children who bore the name William and Jane Hogarth were in a sense miraculous children: they were foundlings. The orphans who were placed in London's Foundling Hospital were named after the governors, of which Hogarth was one, and there was always a William and Jane Hogarth in residence—and also, when the governors' and their wives' names were used up, a Tom Jones and Sophia Western, and so on into current fiction.

In any case, Hogarth presents a story—at least in his experiments in high art (his history paintings) and his prints about art and the artist—in which his wife Jane is the center of his world, the mediator between a poor foolish artist trying to find and impose order (trying to equal the old masters, and so on) and the threats of intractable experience, or perhaps between the father or the superego who imposes the ideal and the idle apprentice who violates it, or some such dichotomy. Either Jane has become the center of his imaginative world, or he has found a substitute for her (what he would have wanted her to be) in this figure: a Jane or a Jane-substitute.

There is another detail that has not been explained in *Characters and Caricaturas*: Fielding and Hogarth are grinning at each other, as if sharing a good joke. But Hogarth's head is attached to another, growing out of the back of his head, clearly indicated by the shading of his neck that joins the

Fig. 15. *The Enraged Musician*; engraving; second state; Nov. 1741;
13¹/₁₆ × 15¹¹/₁₆ in. Collection of the author.

two faces into a Janus (see Fig. 3). No other face in the print is attached to
another. This gently smiling face, the only female face shown, I take to be
Jane's, and I do not doubt that Hogarth was playing on the words Jane-
Janus. He is showing the other, gentler aspect of himself. For corroboration
I have only the two surviving portraits of Jane, one certainly by Hogarth,
the other—with the mouth of the face in *Characters and Caricaturas*—possibly by Sir James Thornhill.

The Janus-reference—seeing himself divided—returns us to the question of his self-representation: What does Hogarth, as a person of his time,
see as the shape of a life? To judge by his "biographies" of a Harlot, Rake,
and so on, he sees a life in terms of the Puritan model of conversion. But
these "conversions" are parodies, not the replacement of our face by
Christ's but its replacement by some fashionable model. And Hogarth did

not see his own life in terms of a conversion. Rather, both his father's and his own life adapt the form, in the recounting, of a satire (or a sentimental satire), something between Juvenal's Third Satire and Mackenzie's *Man of Feeling*. The man of sensibility and originality is misunderstood, persecuted, and destroyed.

But then there is the other story of his split identities and the woman who tries to heal them. He seems to see himself, insofar as he allegorizes himself as the artist, with a profound ambivalence—as both Harlot-victim and Rake-destroyer/self-destroyer, as well as both industrious and idle apprentice. This is where the young woman fits in, trying to bridge in some way this antinomy. But when, as in *Industry and Idleness*, Hogarth has the courage to follow through, from the single plate showing mediation to the narrative account, his self-representation, beginning as bifurcation (into pleasures versus studies, industry versus idleness, order versus chaos) is then leveled out, undifferentiated until either pleasures join studies or industry is no longer distinguishable from idleness in terms of intentions, actions, or consequences.

A final example, from 1745, just after *Characters and Caricaturas*: The small etching called *The Battle of the Pictures*, which Hogarth used as a ticket for his sale of the paintings for his engravings, was an attempt to prove that his paintings were not merely *modelli* for his enormously popular engravings but art objects in themselves, fit to stand up against the old masters (Fig. 16). For his ticket he adapts to art history Swift's *Battle of the Books* in which the moderns, materialized as their books, attack and are repulsed by the old folios of the ancients.

The question I want to ask about this print is why Hogarth chose to show two almost identical paintings, one above the other, in the lower center of the design. One is a Penitent Magdalen slashing into *Harlot 3*, and the other is a saint cutting into the pious old woman of *Morning* (the first of the *Four Times of the Day*). The saint is in a very similar pose, with similar altar, skull, and crucifix, perhaps merely at his devotions but parallel to the Magdalen, seemingly penitential. The first refers to the Harlot, a Magdalen who does not repent, and the second to the cold exclusive piety of the old woman, a contemporary version of a holy hermit.

The horizontal relationship between the contending ancient and modern paintings is clear enough, but the relationship is less clear between the vertical series of subjects and compositions. Hogarth never made such juxtapositions without a reason. These two canvases are placed below two scenes of revelry: a Feast of the Gods versus a brothel scene, and a bacchanal versus a drinking scene. They are scenes of revelry and penance, two

Fig. 16. *The Battle of the Pictures*; engraving; 1744/5; 7 × 7⅞ in. Collection of the author.

and two, with the exception of the one pair of paintings that appear within the cutaway of Hogarth's house, where the painting of *Marriage A-la-mode* 2 is shown still on his easel (this series was not included in the sale). The opponent in this case is the *Aldobrandini Marriage*, sharing the subject of matrimony—the one not only antique but ideal; the other modern and a degeneration of that ideal. I suppose the other paintings could be said to represent a decline, as well as candid realism, in the modern as opposed to the ancient—if, that is, we take the classical gods and the Christian, in fact, Roman Catholic, saints to be ideals. There is the sense that these old paintings are no longer appropriate to be copied, though they remain—as they do in *The Battle of the Pictures*—models in terms of which the world of eighteenth-century London can be understood.

Off to the left, out of the contest between ancient and modern, are series of copies of other old master paintings: a Flaying of Marsyas (with, behind it, a row of St. Andrews and crosses) and a Rape of Europa. These must be regarded, in the context of other Hogarth prints, as emblems that inform the central action, the scene of combat. One *Marsyas* and one *Rape of Europa* are shown flying toward the fray. First there is the story of Marsyas, the underclass modern Hogarth, who challenges Apollo and is flayed for his impertinence (the opposite, by the way, of the emphasis in Pope's allusion to the story in his "Epistle to Arbuthnot" of 1735). The crucified St. Andrew offers a Christian version of the classical martyrdom. But why the Rape of Europa? Does Europa represent the continental tradition of art, the old masters, being carried away by Hogarth the bull, who is "raping" the ancients? That is the way he was seen by unsympathetic connoisseurs. Is the bull a larger version of the aggressive pug? Or is Hogarth perhaps also pairing himself and Jane in this print of 1745 as in the *Characters and Caricaturas* of 1743? If Europa is Jane, then the bull is once again the impatient William carrying her away from her father King Agenor—in this case by force and pursued by Agenor's son. There has been a strange sense in which Hogarth has seen his story in terms of—against the antique model of—the New Testament story of Christ, so why not set it against the story of the classical gods?

About all we can conclude is that something is being said, on some level, about Hogarth's painting and his marriage, both art and Jane, as well as about revelry and guilt accompanied by penance. And it is being said in a representation that is ostensibly only about art. The movement of Hogarth's imagination from this point on into the 1750's is relentlessly toward aesthetic theory, and the personal ("pleasures") serves as the basis of his metaphor for his theory. But it is notable that the S-curve does not stand for self; Hogarth places his aesthetic theory, and its figure, in the other, in "Jane"; he projects his thoughts onto a woman. The ultimate end of his *Beggar's Opera* triangle of Macheath-Polly-Peachum is the diagram of the triangle on which is inscribed the serpentine line, Hogarth's "Line of Beauty," on the title page of *The Analysis of Beauty* (1753). This figure schematizes the curves of the female body, has the head of a serpent, and is accompanied by an epitaph from Eve's fall in *Paradise Lost*. It "mediates" the three points of the triangle as it connects the opposing elements of architecture, decoration, pieces of furniture, and the successive positions of a dance. Within the illustrations accompanying *The Analysis* it is embodied in the figure of Venus or a beautiful contemporary woman, both involved in an adulterous triangle with a husband and lover.

I am not contending that Hogarth's subconscious drove him to produce these distinctive fictions, images, and finally this theory; or that they are predicated on the limitations of the discourses provided him by his society; but rather that Hogarth mythologized himself, his story, and in particular his marriage. First the story of his childhood, his father's failure and imprisonment, and then the story of his substitute father, that father's daughter, and their marriage, allowed him to chart the successful slide from the father down to the son through the mother-daughter, with his ambivalences expressed in the story of paternal opposition, rivalry, denial, and threat. It is quite possible to imagine him seeking out and selecting stories that in some sense validated or made public and respectable these elements of his personal life. He found public, accessible, ennobling (and enabling) equivalents in literature and history, and his paintings of them both drew upon and authorized his own experience.

The Self as Other

Robert Folkenflik

*M*y title may seem to be an abstract version of Rimbaud's "Je est un autre," and this is certainly a line to which I will return, but what I have in mind, at least initially, is the moment in autobiography in which the subject perceives himself, or less frequently herself, as another self, a frequent though not inevitable feature of the genre.[1] I will start with Augustine, not simply because he stands at the beginning of the most influential tradition in autobiography, but because he presents the process in a clear-cut and characteristic form. In book 8, chapter 7 of the *Confessions* he says:

This was what Ponticianus told us. But while he was speaking, O Lord, you were turning me around to look at myself. For I had placed myself behind my own back, refusing to see myself. You were setting me before my own eyes so that I could see how sordid I was, how deformed and squalid, how tainted with ulcers and sores. I saw it all and stood aghast, but there was no place where I could escape from myself. If I tried to turn my eyes away they fell on Ponticianus, still telling his tale, and in this way you brought me face to face with myself once more, forcing me upon my own sight so that I should see my wickedness and loathe it. I had known it all along, but I had always pretended that it was something different. I had turned a blind eye and forgotten it.[2]

Augustine's translators typically have some trouble with this passage because of the physical impossibility—it is literally preposterous—of Augustine's original locution "behind my own back." This placement of the self makes of the true self an other, for though we are not normally present to our selves, yet we can in some sense see ourselves by means of a mirror. What we get is an image of our exterior self (it is not quite accurate, for right and left are reversed) that enables self-contemplation. Some of the images of bodily displacement that follow in this passage suggest a vision in a mirror—"you brought me face to face with myself once more." And in a few paragraphs he says "the time had now come when I stood naked before my own eyes, while my consciousness upbraided me." Jacques Lacan has claimed that in the infant there is a "mirror stage" in which the infant gains a sense of self by seeing itself in a mirror. Perhaps there is a similar state in those autobiographers who undergo a conversion experience that is registered in their autobiographies and provides the point of departure from which the autobiography is written.

In any case, there are a number of things of importance to be noted here. First, concern with the self comes about through self-hatred rather than self-love. This will be typical of the religious conversion autobiography. In the English and American traditions it is especially characteristic of Puritan autobiographies of the seventeenth century. The form that the opposition between the two selves takes is accompanied by imagery of sickness versus health (here the "ulcers and sores"), darkness (often blindness) versus light, bondage versus freedom, sleeping versus waking, birth versus death. This imagery runs throughout the book, and it is easy to see how Manichaeism, with its emphasis on good and evil as equally powerful oppositions, appealed to Augustine in his earlier days. Just after the quoted passage he registers in a famous sentence the pulls he felt in adolescence: "I had prayed to you for chastity and said 'Give me chastity and continence, but not yet.'" This is, to use in another context the term that Sacvan Bercovitch has revived from Puritan usage, an "automachia," a battle of the self against the self.[3]

But we have not yet considered the nature of the "mirror" in which Augustine sees himself. It is a narrative told by Ponticianus. On a chance visit to Augustine, Ponticianus notices a book on his game table. It turns out to be Paul's epistles, and this leads him to relate the biography of St. Anthony of Egypt and then collective biographies of monks in the desert, followed by an account of the monastery at Milan led by Ambrose. All this is new and astonishing to Augustine, but it leads to the story of how Ponticianus strolled with a friend while another pair of friends went off to a house and found a book containing a biography of Anthony. It converted the one who read it on the spot. He, "labouring under the pain of the new life that was taking birth in him," conveyed to his friend his decision "to serve God," and his friend decided to follow his example. When they returned to the other pair, "Ponticianus said that he and the other man did not change their old ways, but they were moved to tears for their own state of life" (p. 168).

The shifts here are complex, more complex than I wish to work out in detail in this essay, but some aspects should be noted. The finding of a book bearing Christian witness leads to biographies of saintly men and then to a story of how a saintly biography converted one man who conveyed his conversion experience to another who was in turn converted by his argument. And though the other pair (the balance is neat) is not converted by the story, they are moved by the disparity between it and their own lives.

This is the narrative that serves Augustine as a mirror of his own life. And yet it is both mirror and anti-mirror. It shows him, in the converts, a model that he admires but has not followed, and it shows him a parallel to his own action in that of Ponticianus and his friend. The image is a self that he has not seen, but it is a hateful self, not what he has characterized a little earlier as his "true self" (p. 164), a self that his faulty will has kept from coming into being. His emphasis, however, is on the difference between himself and the converts: "I hated myself in comparison with them." We should be reminded, then, that although this book is a confession directed to God, both in the sense of a confession of sins and a praise of God (*confessio laudis*) conveyed in the first paragraph of the book, it is also intended for a less exalted audience: "I need not tell all this to you, my God, but in your presence I tell it to my own kind, to those other men, however few, who may perhaps pick up this book" (p. 45). Hence, the chance reading of this private confession made public may itself act like the life of Anthony upon the friends of Ponticianus, like the story told by Ponticianus upon Augustine himself. And Augustine's *Confessions* will be that other that will show the true self to the unconverted Christian. (This is his primary audience, though his career, which moves through the errors of Pagan philosophy and Manichaeism, provides a wide net in which other sorts of believers may be caught, only to find their way.) Augustine shows us how the narrative of another about narratives of others yet becomes his narrative, his testament, as the praise of God found in the Old and New Testaments becomes the very words he speaks. So his book provides a model that may become part of our narratives if it converts us in turn; he is that other in whom we may recognize our selves.

The retrospective consciousness converts the early events of his life to a series of continuously ironic activities, as for example in his reading of Virgil: "I was obliged to memorize the wanderings of a hero named Aeneas, while in the meantime I failed to remember my own erratic ways. I learned to lament the death of Dido, who killed herself for love, while all the time, in the midst of these things, I was dying of love for you, my God and my Life, and I shed no tears for my own plight" (p. 33). Here the chiasmus and antitheses oppose two ways of being that were not present at the time and can only be seen together through the narrative that makes of the early self a false self and of the later a true.

At the beginning of book 8 Augustine says that although he was sure of God's eternal life, "I had only seen it like a confused reflection in a mirror," an allusion to the passage from St. Paul that we know better as "through a glass darkly" (1 Cor. 13: 12). Of course the whole of the book is composed of Biblical quotation and allusion—it is almost a cento—with the greatest number coming from the Psalms, which provide a model of a continuous, intimate song of praise to God and a proto-autobiography of sorts, and, though far fewer, from St. Paul's epistles, which themselves provide a model of conversion in an autobiographical context. And we should remember that the conversion only comes about when Augustine hears a child's singsong voice saying *"Tolle, lege; Tolle, lege"* (Take up and read; take up and read). Though he had been contemptuous of the use of random Virgilian passages as guides, he finds that the words of Romans 13: 13–14 with its injunction to "put ye on the Lord Jesus Christ" are meant for him.

The very language Augustine uses, then, is the language of the true self, the convert to God's ways, whose every word is intended to fall within his mode, just as Augustine pays tribute to God's continuous presence in his life from the first, even though he was unaware of it. Augustine's work is in the tradition of the *imitatio Christi*, but it in turn provides an exemplary life for contemplation, and the mirror is central image both within the book and for the book itself. The "mirror" as a literary form would last until the Renaissance and provide images of both exemplary and negatively exemplary behavior. *The Mirror for Magistrates*, to take a well-known example, provides a series of tragic falls of princes and great men.

A later churchman uses the image of the mirror directly to account for a stage in his shift from Anglicanism to Catholicism. John Henry Newman in the embattled *Apologia Pro Vita Sua* (1864) speaks of his reading the *History of the Monophysites*: "My stronghold was antiquity; now here, in the middle of the fifth century, I found as it seemed to me, Christiandom of sixteenth and nineteenth centuries reflected. I saw my face in that mirror, and I was a Monophysite."[4] Here we have again not a literal mirror, but a book, and one that reflects not just individuals but whole epochs. What is characteristic of the metaphor is that Newman's perception of self is in advance of his rational recognition. He does not go to the mirror to see what he looks like; he sees in the mirror of the book a face that is his, but it is a fifth-century Christian of a forgotten sect peering out at him. In this strange and moving defense of Newman's religious change, he must see that the other is himself before he can apprehend his true self.

It is not surprising to find that a few pages after this account of a mirror that is a book Newman speaks of the power of words by reference not only to Augustine's words in his attack on the Donatists but also to a key passage in the *Confessions*: "For a mere sentence, the words of St. Augustine, struck me with a power which I never had felt from any words before. To take a familiar instance, they were like the 'Turn again Whittington' of the chime, or, to take a more serious one, they were like the 'Tolle, lege—Tolle, lege' of the child, which converted St. Augustine himself" (pp. 98–99). Newman shifts from the story of Dick Whittington's decisive reversal, which leads to his becoming Lord Mayor of London, to the more meaningful instance of Augustine's hearing the child's command to "Take up and read, Take up and read," which leads him to turn to a Biblical passage that seems providentially guided. The whole of Augustine's *Confessions* would seem to provide just such a reading experience for Newman.

There is an extraordinary—I am tempted to call it unique—autobiographical document written by Newman that is sometimes given the title (not his) "An Autobiography in Miniature":

John Newman wrote this just before he was going up to Greek on Tuesday, June 10th, 1812, when it only wanted 3 days to his going home, thinking of the time (at home) when looking at this he shall recollect when he did it.

At school now back again.

And now at Alton where he never expected to be, being lately come for the Vacation from Oxford where he dared not hope to be—how quick time passes and how ignorant are we of futurity. April 8th 1819 Thursday.

And now at Oxford but with far different feelings—let the date speak—Friday February 16th 1821—

And now in my rooms at Oriel College, a Tutor, a Parish Priest and Fellow, having suffered much, slowly advancing to what is good and holy, and led on by God's hand blindly, not knowing whither He is taking me. Even so, O Lord. September 7, 1829. Monday morning ¼ past 10.

And now a Catholic at Maryvale and expecting soon to set out for Rome. May 29, 1846.

And now a Priest and Father of the Oratory. having just received the degree of Doctor from the Holy Father. September 23, 1850.

And now a Cardinal. March 2, 1884.[5]

We might be inclined to call this the work of a lazy diarist, but it is different and more. What makes it remarkable is the spread in the writing, conducted at intervals over a period of nearly 72 years, and only conveyed to us as what it is through the suppressed present tense and the anaphoric "and now." If the locution were "and then," and the tense, like that of the first entry, past, we would have a typically autobiographical form (pro-

vided also that it adhered to first-person narration). But as either autobiography or biography it would be unexceptional: after childhood a mere
dating of high points or stages. Even less exceptional: the dates, as Jonathan Loesberg notes, may be exhorted to speak, but they do not, for they
are frequently at some remove from the event to which they may point
when the event is significant.

The use of "and now" insists upon the identity of the changing being
whose voice comes to us in different registers at each point and whose
shifts must be composed of "far different feelings" even when he does not
say so. The locution begins in earnest when he picks up the single word
from the second entry ("And at school now back again") and uses it with
a sense of the irony of the situation ("And now at Alton where he never
expected to be"). The generalization established here operates as a figured
bass for the entries of the next 65 years: "how quick time passes and how
ignorant we are of futurity." With each succeeding entry he knows the difference between what he was and what he is (the "far different feelings" he
has), but he does not know what the future holds. Throughout the whole
document there is a sense of expectation, whether that of going home or
being "where he never expected to be," which gives way to "slowly advancing . . . led on by God's hand blindly, not knowing whither He is taking me." This in turn is succeeded by his "expecting soon to set out for
Rome" and the final reticence and mystery of "And now a Cardinal."
Home turns out to be Rome in a way he never could have guessed. In this
serial autobiography, the suggestion is that the self may be "other" at every
given moment. What looks like a conundrum for the philosophers of personal identity is presented as the mystery of God's leading the blind self
into an unknowable future.

Newman uses third person at times in this passage, and such usage is
characteristic of a small but significant portion of writers of autobiography
in the Western tradition, with a greater percentage before the early modern
period. In the Chinese tradition third-person autobiography has been the
norm, a fact that leads a recent investigator of this neglected field to call
them "self-written biographies."[6] In a sense this convention reminds us of
how unusual a genre autobiography is, for it is dependent not on the subject but on the identity of subject and writer. It would be easy for the writer
of a third-person autobiography to pass off his work as a biography,
though in most cases there are internal signs that the work could not have
been written by a biographer (or perhaps only by a bad biographer, one
given to mind reading or unwilling to make available the basis for his in-
ferences about the feelings and thoughts of his subject). Third-person au-

tobiographies have been written by such important autobiographers as Vico (see John Sturrock above), Mme d'Aubigné, and Henry Adams, and this convention, which has different meanings at different times, is worth closer examination, for it would seem to insist upon the self as an other.[7]

Before doing so, however, I would like to glance at a still rarer convention, the use of the second person to refer to the self. Julia Watson (above) finds it occasionally in the work of Christa Wolf, but perhaps the strangest of formal breaks representing the self as other appears as the dedication, "The Author to Herself," of the *Narrative of the Life of Mrs. Charlotte Charke* (1755), an autobiography discussed above by Linda Peterson. Charke's second-person address is preceded, as far as I know, only by Smollett's dedication to himself of the novel *Ferdinand Count Fathom* and Fielding's mock dedication of *Shamela*, "The Editor to Himself," an attack on Charke's father Colley Cibber among others. I know of no earlier autobiographies so dedicated. Charke plays against the form by criticizing rather than flattering her dedicatee through a mock encomium: "That thoughtless Ease (so peculiar to yourself) with which you have run thro' so many strange and unaccountable Vicissitudes of Fortune, is an undeniable Proof of the native indolent Sweetness of your Temper." She wants to call herself "FRIEND; a Name, I own, I never as yet have known you by." In what seems a characteristic move by this cross-dressing actress of the eighteenth century, the dedication dramatizes the difference between her former behavior and what she hopes to become, her self-division and her awareness of her "Oddity," something she represents while reprehending it.[8]

Early third-person autobiographers, like Vico, could be said to attempt impersonality, if not entirely objectivity, but the appearance of the convention in more modern writers is apt to be complex. In perhaps the greatest of them, Henry Adams, this seeing of the self as other is part of a strategy operating at various levels and highly thematized in his work. He did not want *The Education of Henry Adams* to be taken as an autobiography at all. It was to be seen rather as a plotted point to be lined up with *Mont-Saint-Michel and Chartres*, a geometric basis for his "scientific" history. The book was originally privately published and sent to a number of friends, who were to regard it "in the nature of proof-sheets" and to return it (which most, of course, did not).[9] He characterized it as an "experiment" (p. 513), a "last Will and Testament" (p. 508). It is also "a mere shield of protection in the grave," and he advises the recipient of the letter in which he says this, Henry James, "to take your own life in the same way, in order to prevent biographers from taking it in theirs" (pp. 512–13). Adams metaphorically recommends autobiography as suicide, a way to avoid being murdered by biographers. Despite his claim at times that it is not an autobiography, he asks William James in a letter if he has ever read "the Confessions of St. Augustine, or of Cardinal de Retz, or of Rousseau, or of Benvenuto Cellini, or even of my dear Gibbon?" in order to insist upon Augustine as the only one with "an idea of literary form" (p. 511), and to establish that his own book is "rotten"—though in another letter naming Augustine as his "literary model" he indicates that like himself, Augustine was a failure as an artist.

All of this has its bearing on the third-person form. If the impetus for his third-person form comes from his quest for historic detachment from the self to give it historic meaning, this is neither the sole function nor the significance of his strategy. It is as though, unlike those egotists of autobiography, Adams cannot say "I." He seems to suffer from low self-esteem, as a popular psychologist might put it. And certainly the self-characterizations of Adams throughout the book denigrate and diminish him. He is "The American insect" (p. 143), "a little dog" (p. 146). In comparison to others he has no importance. When he accompanies his father, the ambassador to England, as private secretary, he is a "cabin-boy" (p. 112). He summarizes his activity at the embassy by claiming that "he never gave his father the smallest help, unless it were as a footman, a clerk, or a companion for the younger children" (p. 117). To the poet Swinburne, "he could be no more than a worm." In the social world of England he is a shapeless "cub" (p. 122), for in society he was "a young man without any position at all" (p. 145). He remains "a mere student" (p. 153), and "a clerk at five dollars a week would have done the work [at the embassy] as well or better" (p. 171). He even loses what identity he has (typically, at the hands of a servant):

No one knew him—not even the lackeys. The last Saturday evening he ever attended [one of Palmerston's parties], he gave his name as usual at the foot of the staircase, and was rather disturbed to hear it shouted up as "Mr. Handrew Hadams!" He tried to correct it, and the footman shouted more loudly: "Mr. Hanthony Hadams!" With some temper he repeated the correction, and was finally announced as "Mr. Halaxander Hadams," and under this name he made his bow for the last time to Lord Palmerston who certainly knew no better. (p. 134)

He has a powerful awareness of his own small stature that takes on metaphoric force. In the text he says that "Adams had tried his own little hands" on the problem of Grant's administration (and failed), but in the preface he presents himself in an image adapted (along with much else) from Carlyle's *Sartor Resartus* as a "mannikin," obviously a dummy upon which clothing is draped, but a "little man" as well (pp. 280, xxx). And later in the book he devises an epitaph for himself that begins "Hic jacet / Homunculus Scriptor," portraying himself as a virtual embryo (with perhaps a glance at Sterne's *Tristram Shandy*).

Painfully shy and self-conscious, Adams is further reduced by the tireless narrative voice that describes him and refuses to comfort him or make compact with him. Its mordant irony does not allow Adams to find a place in the present or a retrospective purchase on his being through telling his own tale. He even breaks with autobiographical decorum by insisting that "to the end of his life he labored over the lessons then taught." This is what no autobiographer can say, and what no honest biographer can say of a living man. This sentence is the work of a disembodied voice from beyond the grave, one who has successfully "taken" his own life in writing his autobiography. He knows that the book will only be "published" after his death, despite the printed copies he has sent out while alive.

This is the self as other with a vengeance. It is as though Adams, through the strategy of historical detachment, is able to disown his self, to make believe he is not he. In a strange and usually unremarked scene, the only one that may remind us that Adams and Lewis Carroll were contemporaries, he comments on the barrenness of his "diplomatic education": "Still another nightmare he suffered at a dance given by the old Duchess Dowager of Somerset, a terrible vision in castanets, who seized him and forced him to perform a Highland fling before the assembled nobility and gentry, with the daughter of the Turkish Ambassador for a partner. This might seem humorous to some, but to him the world turned to ashes" (p. 118). Here nations are united in a dance, but everything is out of synchronization in this grotesque wonderland version. The English Duchess holds Spanish castanets and the young American is forced into a Scottish dance (a highland fling no less) with a Turk. He calls it a "nightmare" and certainly the idea of being not just commanded but "forced" to dance a dance one does not know before a society filled with authority figures, nobility, gentry, and ambassadors must be that for the shy young man. Even the ironic and generally detached narrator seems momentarily to sympathize with him.

Joyce's description of his own fictional James Duffy in "A Painful Case" could be designed for Adams: "He had an odd autobiographical habit which led him to compose in his mind from time to time a short sentence about himself containing a subject in the third person and a predicate in the past tense." And the sentence before this one seems to also make its comment on Adams: "He lived at a little distance from his own body, regarding his own acts with doubtful side-glances." I cannot say that Adams did this in fact, but his style in the *Education* certainly does. Something more than an inferiority complex is at stake, though Adams was painfully aware of being a very short man. He was also aware of coming short of expectations, for his grandfather and great-grandfather had been presidents of the United States. The very first paragraphs of the book dramatize that heritage, typically as a disabling fact. He is born "under the shadow of Boston State House" and christened "by his uncle, the minister of the First Church in the tenets of Boston Unitarianism, as Henry Brooks Adams." This provides the basis for a characteristically strange analogy: "Had he been born in Jerusalem under the shadow of the Temple and circumcised in the Synagogue by his uncle the high priest under the name of Israel Cohen, he would scarcely have been more distinctly branded, and not much more heavily handicapped in the races of the coming century" (p. 3). This is the initial self-denigration, for Adams was a visceral anti-Semite, and the bitter humor here comes at the expense both of himself and Jews. Much later in a chapter called "The Press" he again energetically compares himself negatively to a Jew in the ugliest passage in the book: "Not a Polish Jew from Warsaw or Cracow—not a furtive Yacoob or Ysaac still reeking of the ghetto, snarling a weird Yiddish to the officers of the customs—but had a keener instinct, an intenser energy, and a freer hand than he—American of Americans, with Heaven knew how many Puritans and Patriots behind him and an education that had cost a civil war" (p. 238). He achieves something of the intensity he claims he lacks in the envious contempt he displays toward this anti-self (what Erik Erikson would call a "negative identity fragment") with whom he has in some ways metaphorically identified himself at the outset of the book. This is not just a matter of "period" anti-Semitism. One can see here the scapegoating that comes from a genuine feeling of inferiority that is there despite all the irony.

Autobiography as the story of failure or tragedy is relatively unusual. Most autobiographies are success stories, even if not crassly so, despite the fact that the older autobiographers are of necessity nearing death (and as W. B. Carnochan indicates speaking of Hume, we can even read the autobiography of a man who knows that he will be dead shortly after he finishes writing).[10] But Adams is possibly unique in his continued insistence upon his own failure. One of the later chapters in the book is called "Failure," and the title might have been used for the whole. This insistence, of course, cuts two ways, and the irony operates both for and against him. Another sort of autobiographer might take the facts of Henry Adams's life, his ancestry, education, and achievements as the material for a fulsomely self-congratulatory and complacent book. As R. P. Blackmur puts it, he should be regarded "as a representative example of education: but education pushed to the point of failure as contrasted with ordinary education which stops at the formula of success."[11] Hence we also see what the self-denigration and diminishment tend to underplay, the heroic standard by which all of Adams's thoughts and actions are judged, and one could put the emphasis, as Adams's best biographer, Ernest Samuels does, on the egoism of the man, though it would have to be far different from the egoism of Rousseau.

One very special form of the self as other is dependent on the lie. The telling of a lie as a way of presenting the self to others as different from what one consciously knows oneself to be differentiates one from others and at the same time makes of one's self a private thing (one's "own" self) that cannot be known by another. The lie seems particularly important in autobiographies devoted in whole or in part to childhood. Edmund Gosse's *Father and Son* provides a good sense of the process involved, even though an actual lie as such is not told at this point in the narrative. His father, an authoritative figure and member of an obscure fundamentalist Christian sect, the Plymouth Brethren, one day says something factual that is mistaken. Since the six-year-old boy has "confused him in some sense with God; at all events I believed that my Father knew everything and saw everything," this otherwise insignificant event changes reality for him entirely:

The shock to me was as that of a thunderbolt, for what my Father had said 'was not true.' . . . Nothing could possibly have been more trifling to my parents, but to me it meant an epoch. Here was the appalling discovery, never suspected before, that my Father was not as God, and did not know everything. The shock was not caused by any suspicion that he was not telling the truth, as it appeared to him, but by the awful proof that he was not, as I supposed, omniscient.[12]

This is, of course, not a lie but an error, yet it is the first step toward conscious lying on the part of the boy. The next comes soon after and involves the boy's keeping quiet as his Father speculates that some plumbers have put a hole in a waterpipe that the boy himself had pierced: "No suspicion fell on me; no question was asked of me. I sat there, turned to stone within, but outwardly sympathetic and with unchecked appetite" (p. 34). In essence here there are two selves, an inner real self and the outer one playing a role. But this in turn leads to a corresponding sense of another inner self that seems more important even than the discovery of his Father's fallibility:

But of all the thoughts which rushed upon my savage and undeveloped little brain at this crisis, the most curious was that I had found a companion and a confidant in myself. There was a secret in this world and it belonged to me and to somebody who lived in the same body with me. There were two of us, and we could talk with one another. (p. 35, and compare p. 158)

And he will lie, will keep his inner realities known only to himself as he becomes a hypocritical "infant Samuel," the cynosure of a sect that he leaves long after losing his faith.

The lie plays a special role in differentiating the self from others. Here the need to lie is part of the need to be oneself, despite the powerful personal and ideological demands made upon the self by the authoritative Father. To see that the Father is not congruent with the self and does not have the omniscience of God is crucial. The failure of the self to obtain such knowledge may lead to a very different kind of perception of the self as other, that obtained not through lies but through sickness. Schizophrenia has come to be perceived by some analysts as a means for the protection of the real self from others through the projection of a false self that keeps the other from penetrating to the self.[13] Returning to Gosse, we would not have a hard time proving that this narrative, which he insists upon calling a "document," is a fiction itself.

The network of themes surrounding the lie found in Gosse also appears in somewhat different form in Rousseau's *Confessions*. He has experienced that key event of early life, the "first injustice":

There ended the serenity of my childish life. From that moment I never again enjoyed pure happiness, and even to-day I am conscious that memory of childhood's delights stops short at that point. We stayed some months longer at Bossey. We lived as we are told the first man lived in the earthly paradise, but we no longer enjoyed it; in appearance our situation was unchanged, but in reality it was an entirely different kind of existence. No longer were we young people bound by ties of respect, intimacy, and confidence to our guardians; we no longer looked on them as gods who read our hearts; we were less ashamed of wrongdoing, and more afraid of being caught; we began to be secretive, to rebel, and to lie.[14]

In Rousseau the distinction is between an external world that remains paradisiacal and the paradise lost within. Thus the false accusation of a stolen comb (which has a later counterpart in the ribbon he does steal) leads to the parent figures becoming gods no longer because the nature of their godhood was their ability to read the hearts of Rousseau and his cousin. If in Gosse a lie leads to this state, in Rousseau the state leads to a guilty selfhood, one that expresses itself through secrets and lies. And the theme of the damaging relation of self to others is writ large in his work, to which we will now turn.

Rousseau is, as he himself insisted, a special case. Although we could follow our theme in that splitting of the self that is *Rousseau, juge de Jean-Jacques*, the *Confessions* supplies some very interesting variations. One of the more obvious causes of the self's being perceived as other is a split between what a man appears to be and what he knows himself to be. Rousseau's whole autobiographical project can be seen as an attempt to present the real Rousseau to an audience that knows him only as writer and rebel and at the same time to define and apprehend the self that is conscious of worth even when its actions are not worthy. Rousseau presents himself as a man of the *esprit d'escalier*, and perhaps we should look on his autobiography as the articulation of the tongue-tied man's real life. Is the self the body, the mind, a continuum of the two, or something else? Obviously Rousseau thinks himself something other than what his awkward body does or what he says to others.

Frequently Rousseau's position in life is at variance with his real worth. Even others recognize from time to time that, as he says, "I was not in my true place" (p. 85). At times he even gets some help: "In my succession of desires and fancies I had always struck too high or too low, always played either Achilles or Thersites; now hero, now scoundrel. M. Gaime took pains to put me in my place, to make me see myself as I was, neither sparing me nor discouraging me" (p. 92). This man, upon whom Rousseau drew for the Vicaire Savoyard, taught Rousseau an unforgettable lesson, "that if every man could read the hearts of others there would be more men anxious to descend than to rise in life" (p. 93). And Rousseau elsewhere in the book claims as much for his own case. Soon after this the Count de la Roque tries to find Rousseau a suitable place. Though Rousseau initially seems to be a lackey, there is a difference: he is welcomed ceremoniously, eats at the steward's table, and wears no livery (p. 94). And when the Abbé de Gouvon comes on the scene, Rousseau quickly finds that "by one of those strange tricks that were to recur so often in the course of my life, I was at the same time above and below my station. I was a pupil and a valet in the same house, and, although a servant, had a tutor so highly born that he should have taught none but the children of princes" (p. 98).

These are rightly *Confessions*, for if his secular version of what Augustine had called his work is basically self-justifying (in the eyes of man and God), it is at the same time shot through with a pervasive sense of guilt, a guilt that takes its point of departure from the death of his mother in giving him birth and can only have been enhanced by his Calvinist heritage, a religious tradition that by yoking guilt and autobiography has given us some of the strongest autobiographical writings, those of Pepys, Boswell, and Bunyan, as well as Rousseau (and perhaps even Adams):

So much am I a slave to fears and shames that I long to vanish from mortal sight. If action is necessary I do not know what to do; if I must speak I do not know what to say; if anyone looks at me I drop my eyes. When roused by passion, I can sometimes find the right words to say, but in ordinary conversation I can find none, none at all. I find conversation unbearable owing to the very fact that I am obliged to speak. (p. 44)

This is the man whose voice we hear speaking to us, usually without shame. In part it is his very distance from us, the fact that he does not have to see us or know that we are apprehending his story that allows him to tell us what he obviously could not say in his own person. But we should also be aware that what he regards as his real self can only be known through such writings, and the *Confessions* is filled with accounts of his being taken for an idiot because he is unable to express himself in the way that he wants. His most shameful incident, the story of his accusing a young servant girl of stealing a ribbon that he had stolen himself, is given as an example of an unpremeditated action that comes about through his inability to express himself: "I grew confused, stammered, and finally said with a blush that it was Marion who had given it to me" (p. 86). Rousseau had never been able to tell anyone, even Mme de Warens, of this shameful incident, which continues to haunt him, and indeed "I can affirm that the desire to some extent to rid myself of it has greatly contributed to my resolution of writing these *Confessions*" (p. 88). Ridding himself of guilt and saying the things he could not say thus become two sides of the same coin.

We might also remember Rousseau's activities as an exhibitionist in this connection (pp. 90–91), for he is surely trying to make contact socially in a direct way and to present himself (at least one version of himself) as he really is. And when he says "Since I have undertaken to reveal myself absolutely to the public, nothing about me must remain hidden or obscure" (p. 65), we may see in retrospect his *Confessions* as the literary equivalent of his exhibitionism. This is also apparent in his claim at the beginning of the book: "I have bared my secret soul" (p. 17). The key term in the original is *dévoilé*, unveiled. I do not, of course, intend to belittle him by this observation.

Conversion autobiographies usually contain, as in the case of Augustine, turning points in the life, those moments of conversion that divide the true and the false self. In Rousseau's case there were many, but they ironically function as moments that seal him off from the life he should have led. At the end of book one he recounts the incident of the gates closing the city of Geneva before he could get back inside as the decisive moment that causes him to leave his apprenticeship. But instead of celebrating this decision as the foundation of his freedom and fame, he bewails it as the start of his "fatal destiny" and depicts the happy obscure life he would have led as an engraver with busy daily activity and his imagination left free. Better a mute inglorious Rousseau than the persecuted Jean-Jacques he becomes (p. 51). This may be posturing of the sort that Roger Porter discusses above in the work of that inheritor of Rousseau's tradition, Benjamin Robert Haydon.

Another such incident, and certainly the most important, is Rousseau's reading, while walking along the road, of the essay prize proposed by the Dijon Academy on the subject, "Has the progress of the sciences and arts done more to improve morals or to corrupt them." "The moment I read this," says Rousseau, "I beheld another universe and became another man" (p. 327). But if we are apt to take this as a secular version of Paul's conversion on the road to Damascus, we ought to recognize that the winning of that prize, which leads to Rousseau's fame, is another false turning point. Diderot encouraged him to try for the prize, "and from that moment I was lost. All the rest of my life and of my misfortunes followed inevitably as a result of that moment's madness" (p. 328). But, as we have already seen, Rousseau's actions on the moment-to-moment level are usually both mistaken and untrue to his real self. He is condemned to an unhappy actual life because the life he wants seems to exist only as afterthought. Although he does not take it as symbolic, even his vision seems to work this way: "My short sight is constantly deceiving me" (p. 45). And, as he says in recounting his original exile from Geneva, "Never mind how great the distance between my position and the nearest castle in Spain, I had no difficulty in taking up residence there" (p. 50). Perhaps in the long run the major theme of his life is the reality of his imagination and the unreality and pain of the life he leads.

A very different relation to the self is found in Jean-Paul Sartre's *Les Mots*, which I think better translates as *Words* than as *The Words*. In this text Sartre's continual attempt to arrive at an authentic self is presented in two parts, "Reading" and "Writing." It begins with Sartre's great-grandfather, not because Sartre wants to give an account of his ancestry, but because it enables him to show how the "family play-acting" forces roles upon others and ultimately upon him: he has a role in effect before he is even born. His mother is a good example of someone who has been educated to accept distortions of reality:

Anne Marie, the younger daughter [of Charles Schweitzer, Sartre's maternal grandfather], spent her childhood on a chair. She was taught to be bored, to sit up straight, to sew. She was gifted: the family thought it distinguished to leave her gifts undeveloped; she was radiant: they hid the fact from her. . . . Fifty years later, when turning the pages of a family album, Anne Marie realized that she had been beautiful.[15]

Just as Anne Marie, his own term for the woman who seems more his elder sister than his mother, suffered unknowingly from miseducation and the imposition of roles, Sartre himself has ideas imposed upon him by her and by others. Seemingly acting of his own accord, he actually is trapped by the form of her words: "She does not give me orders; she outlines in light words a future which she praises me for being so kind as to bring into being: 'my little darling will be very nice, very reasonable. He'll sit still so I can put drops into his nose.' I let myself be caught in the trap of these coddling prophecies" (p. 22). Rather than being ordered to do something, he is cooperating in bringing a preformed future into being. In doing so he is encouraged not to be responsible for his own acts but to perform an action that has already been given shape and presupposes what he will do.

His grandfather's form of the family play-acting takes other delusive and self-delusive shapes:

He was a man of the nineteenth century who took himself for Victor Hugo, as did so many others, including Victor Hugo himself. This handsome man with the flowing beard who was always waiting for the next opportunity to show off, as the alcoholic is always waiting for the next drink, was the victim of two recently discovered techniques: the art of photography and the art of being a grandfather. He had the good and bad fortune to be photogenic. The house was filled with photos of him. Since snapshots were not practiced, he had acquired a taste for poses and *tableaux vivants*. Everything was a pretext for him to suspend his gestures, to strike an attitude, to turn to stone. He doted upon those brief moments of eternity in which he became his own statue. (p. 24)

The grandfather attempts to monumentalize his poses. He seems to live only to be caught eternally in a role that he dramatizes. Sartre's observation that the role he plays is that of Victor Hugo is given an added twist by the aside that Victor Hugo himself plays that role too. Hugo is also implicated in playing the role of the grandfather, an art ironically paralleled to the art of photography through an allusion to the title of Hugo's book, *The Art of Being a Grandfather*. In a sense he lives for others, for their gaze upon him in his chosen poses. In Sartre's narrative, culture becomes the mirror in which man looks at himself.

Sartre's dissatisfaction with biography stems in part from his recognition of the way an already known future operates in the form to let us at any given point take the main character in terms of what we know will come. In Sartre's terms, we cannot help seeing Robespierre at each point in the story of his life with his head under his arm. The main problem, as Sartre's Roquentin puts it in *La Nausée*, is that "a man . . . seeks to live his life as if he were telling its story." Yet one contemporary line of thought would argue that the narrative encoding of "reality" is inescapable.

Sartre's atheism begins as a debate with "another me, my grim brother" (p. 100). Like Gosse, he keeps up the outer form while the inner self shifts: "I said my prayers every day, but I thought of God less and less often." Here one might notice what is frequently apparent in autobiography: the self as other may come about through an opposition between exterior and interior, between outer expression or appearance and consciousness, between body and mind.

Sartre recognizes his position in relation to *La Nausée* as a superior sort of conjuring trick:

At the age of thirty, I executed the masterstroke of writing in *Nausea*—quite sincerely believe me—about the bitter unjustified existence of my fellowmen and exonerating my own. I *was* Roquentin; I used him to show, without complacency, the texture of my life. At the same time, I was *I*, the elect, the chronicler of Hell, a glass and steel photomicroscope peering at my own protoplasmic juices. Later, I gaily demonstrated that man is impossible; I was impossible myself and differed from others only by the mandate to give expression to that impossibility, which was thereby transfigured and became my most personal possibility, the object of my mission, the springboard of my glory. I was a prisoner of that obvious contradiction, but I did not see it, I saw the world through it. Fake to the marrow of my bones and hoodwinked, I joyfully wrote about our unhappy state. Dogmatic though I was, I doubted everything except that I was the elect of doubt. I built with one hand what I destroyed with the other, and I regarded anxiety as the guarantee of my security; I was happy. (pp. 251–52)

Without hypocrisy (he is demonstrating, among other things, the inadequacy of sincerity when one speaks of authenticity) Sartre is the happy registrar of man's unhappiness. As Roquentin and as himself he can have it both ways. He can be, in the scientific metaphor that merges with the religious metaphor running throughout the book, the objective observer of his own self-consciousness, the dogmatist whose right answers proclaim him of the elect while he damns the human race.

Sartre defines authenticity in his essay on Nathalie Sarraute as "the real connection with others, with oneself and with death."[16] His description there of her "protoplasmic vision of our interior universe" may remind us of his description here of viewing himself under the microscope. Sartre's irony at his own expense, conveyed by a series of nearly oxymoronic oppositions between his own state as writer and our human situation, certainly is his last word on self-deception in this book and he presents himself as "cured": "I've lost my illusions" (p. 253). Yet the wisdom of the text suggests that the man who says this must be suffering from illusions, and we may well wonder what "Sartre" is thinking and feeling while the "I" of the narrative tells us what he has learned. Could it be that the second volume he never lived to write would have demystified the first? Sartre recognizes that "that old, crumbling structure, my imposture, is also my character: one gets rid of a neurosis, one doesn't get cured of one's self" (p. 254). The price of authenticity, Sartre seems to say, is eternal vigilance. Yet Sartre's autobiography suggests, as he himself does not, that the quest for authenticity is like the peeling of an onion, or perhaps that it can only be a quest, for each attempt to come into contact with the real self is only the shedding of another layer of falsehood. The value of Sartre's autobiography resides in the satirical demystifications of the self performed by the narrative "I" on all those earlier selves, but surely the logic of this work is that we must be led to a conclusion in which nothing is concluded. This is not Sartre's conclusion, which ends unsatisfactorily: "If I relegate impossible Salvation to the proproom what remains? A whole man, composed of all men and as good as all of them and no better than any" (p. 255). Yet this position too is ripe for demystification, and some of Sartre's comments in interviews suggest that he recognized its inadequacy to sound the firm note of closure and finality of the text.[17]

Where can we go from here? *Roland Barthes par Roland Barthes* breaks the self into an alphabetical series of topics as likely to be in the present tense as the past and in the third person as the first. Despite the paradigmatic quality of the title, an autobiographical mirror image, Barthes claims to have written a text, not an autobiography: "Once I produce, once I write, it is the Text itself which (fortunately) dispossesses me of my narrative continuity" (p. [4]).[18] This strategy—though Barthes abjures strategy because it implies structure—effects a radical break between subject and writing. His comment under "Lucidity" can be taken as a critique of autobiography from Augustine to Sartre: "This book is not a book of 'confessions'; not that it is insincere, but because we have a different knowledge today than yesterday; such knowledge can be summarized as follows: What I write about myself is never *the last word*: the more 'sincere' I am, the more interpretable I am, under the eye of other examples than the old authors, who believed they were required to submit themselves to one law: *authenticity*" (p. 120). What we have in this case is the anatomy of autobiography and an unwillingness to let the self turn into a story, though as with those modern French novels scissored into separate pages and read in an arbitrary order, a story will assert itself even in the absence of plot through the interpretative acts of the reader. We have been too well prepared by fiction for Barthes' non-narrative. Indeed, he is aware that "All this must be considered as if spoken by a character in a novel—or rather by several characters" (p. 119), an admonition, I would add, that need not preface a novel.

Sartre's anxieties about the correspondence of the represented self to the actual self cannot obtain here, for the "I" of the writing is textual and not to be judged in relation to a biographical Barthes whose characteristics nonetheless appear. Yet the anxieties remain in a thoroughly textualized form. The "risks" and "dangers" of which Barthes frequently speaks (compare these with Sartre's "traps") are risks of going beyond the text or making a structure of the text. If "the subject speaks about himself" there is a risk of "psychologism." Because the book is written in fragments, he risks "aphorism" (p. 152). This last is a particular danger for the editor of Rochefoucauld—as he notes later, "An aphoristic tone hangs about this book" (p. 179).

With ironic appropriateness this book appeared in the series "Par lui-même." Each volume consists of autobiographical statements by someone who has not necessarily written an autobiography, and the editor chooses and orders them. Barthes edited *Michelet par lui-même* for this series and could have stuck to the general form of the title, but he wished to overcome its reflexivity. He denies that *Roland Barthes* can be *par lui-même*. He includes photographs and an outline biography as in the *Michelet*, however, and he could as easily have billed this discourse as "images et textes présentés par Roland Barthes." It is worth noticing that once a book *par lui-même* is actually composed by an editor it takes on the appearance of a collection of fragments. Barthes is aware that fragments can be organized (as they were in his unmentioned *Michelet*; or, I would argue, as they frequently are in *Roland Barthes*), but he is even more aware that "the fragment (haiku, maxim, *pensée*, journal entry) is *finally* a rhetorical genre" (p. 95), and hence cannot fully deconstruct the self. He might have added that the fragment as genre has an important Romantic history from the late eighteenth century (Sterne in prose and Macpherson in poetry). In the escape from the inadequacies of autobiography through alphabetized fragments and the shifting usage of first and third person, Barthes takes contemporary autobiography as anti-autobiography to its endpoint.

This brings us back to our starting point. Rimbaud's observation, "I is another," registers through its fractured syntax the incompatibility of saying "I" and by that means asserting an identity of self and statement. Modern linguistics, which serves as the explicit or implicit model for so much of the most recent critical theory, has produced formulas that highlight such distinctions. Emile Benveniste, following Saussure, has made the analysis that enables a series of important observations. The "I" comes into existence only in relation to some "you." That is, it is defined by its difference from some other. Furthermore, "I" according to Benveniste, is a shifter. As opposed to other pronouns, it is unable to refer of itself: "'Ego' is he who says 'ego.'"[19] Therefore, "it is in and through language that man constitutes himself as a subject," and "the condition of man in language is unique." The suggestion is strong that the self can only exist in language, that the self in autobiography is the only thing that we can call a self.

The idea of the self as other is a condition of the autobiographical narrative, for there is generally some distinction between the "I" who is talking and the figure in the past who is described (call them "narrator" and "protagonist," for both comprise the "character"). An autobiography will often take shape as a way of dealing with the otherness of the figure in the past. This *dédoublement* in autobiography may or may not have its counterpart in the frequent occurrence of two selves within the lives of the subjects, though the pastness of a false self versus the presentness of a true self frequently provides the point of departure for the writing of autobiography. The sense that there are two selves, which may be negative or positive (Augustine as opposed to Gosse or Wordsworth), is both an assertion of difference and an assertion of identity. Gosse, we note, however, finds that his other self, a hidden consciousness, is that other with whom he communes, a friend of the friendless boy.

Perhaps instead of talking of those crucial moments I have been discussing as a "mirror stage" in the autobiographies, one can think of autobiography itself as a mirror stage in life, an extended moment that enables one to reflect on oneself by presenting an image of the self for contemplation. This does not happen in early childhood, but, if at all, in adulthood or old age. And the self is not that of the mirror or photograph. In Lacan's terms it is part of the symbolic, not the imaginary.[20] I say this because if the "I" relates to a "you," it is not simply narcissistic, as in the infantile "mirror stage." Autobiography promises intersubjectivity, not just intrasubjectivity. Because autobiography manipulates the prestige of the self in relation to the other, it enters the play of desire that constitutes the symbolic order. Here the self as a point of reference outside the text and the self as represented, constructed within the text, are in rightful tension.

Notes

Notes

Folkenflik: Introduction

1. For earlier accounts, see Georg Misch, *A History of Autobiography in Antiquity* (Cambridge, Mass.: Harvard University Press, 1951; orig. ed., 1907), vol. 1, pp. 5–7; Jacques Voisine, "Naissance et évolution du terme littéraire 'autobiographie,'" in *La Littérature comparée en Europe orientale*, conference proceedings, Budapest, Oct. 26–29, 1962 (Budapest: Akademiai Kiado, 1973), pp. 278–86; James Olney, "Autobiography and the Cultural Moment: A Thematic, Historical, and Bibliographical Introduction," in James Olney, ed., *Autobiography: Essays Theoretical and Critical* (Princeton, N.J.: Princeton University Press, 1980), pp. 1–48; Jerome Hamilton Buckley, *The Turning Key: Autobiography and the Subjective Impulse Since 1800* (Cambridge, Mass.: Harvard University Press, 1984), pp. 18–19, 38–39; and Felicity Nussbaum, *The Autobiographical Subject: Gender and Ideology in Eighteenth-Century England* (Baltimore: The Johns Hopkins University Press, 1989), pp. 1–4. The consequences of inaccuracies and ignorance for even the most recent books are readily apparent. Compare, for example, the brief account of the term in Valerie Sanders, *The Private Lives of Victorian Women: Autobiography in Nineteenth-Century England* (New York: Harvester Wheatsheaf, 1989), p. 25 n. 13. Sanders also seems unaware that some women called their books autobiographies in the 1830's and 1840's. At the same time I recognize that my own findings, like those of others before me, must be labeled tentative.

2. Robert Southey, "Portugueze Literature," *Quarterly Review*, 1 (1809): 283. The *OED* omits the hyphen. Southey speaks of a poem by Francisco Vieira.

3. See James Ogden, "A Note on 'Autobiography,'" *Notes and Queries*, 206 (1961): 461–62. This was also noticed (independently?) by Arnaldo Momigliano in *The Development of Greek Biography* (Cambridge, Mass.: Harvard University Press, 1971), p. 14.

4. William Taylor, *Monthly Review*, 24 (1797): 375. Taylor of Norwich's identity as author can be established from Benjamin Christie Nangle's indexes, *The Monthly Review, Second Series, 1790–1815* (Oxford: Clarendon Press, 1955).

5. The preface is now easily available in Moira Ferguson, ed., *First Feminists: British Women Writers, 1578–1799* (Bloomington: University of Indiana Press, 1985), pp. 382–86.

6. Robert Southey, introductory essay to John Jones, *Attempts in Verse* (London, 1831); C. C. Southey, ed., *The Life and Correspondence of the Late Robert Southey*, 6 vols. (London, 1849–50). James Ogden, in *Isaac D'Israeli* (Oxford: Clarendon Press, 1969), p. 96, mentions a letter D'Israeli naively wrote to the *Monthly* recounting how much pleasure one of Taylor's reviews of a book of his had given him.

7. Ogden notes the use in 1809; see "Autobiography," p. 462. His claim, however, that "D'Israeli did not substitute 'autobiography' for 'self-biography' in later editions of *Miscellanies*" misses the ways in which D'Israeli takes up the new term. See Isaac D'Israeli, "Memoirs of Percival Stockdale," *Quarterly Review*, 1 (1809): 386.

8. Isaac D'Israeli, *Curiosities of Literature*, 7th ed., second series, 3 vols. (London: John Murray, 1823), vol. 2, p. 161; vol. 3, p. 285; ibid., 6th ed., 3 vols. (London: John Murray, 1817), vol. 3, p. 172.

9. Christian Friederich Daniel Schubart, *Leben und Gesinnungen von ihm selbst, im Kerker aufgesezt* (Stuttgart, 1791), vol. 1, pp. 120–21. Unless otherwise noted, all translations are mine.

10. Hippel is quoted from *Biographie . . . Th. G. von Hippel* (Gotha, 1801), p. 343, and the anonymous writer from "Ueber Selbstbiographien. Aus dem Nachlass des verstorbenen Herrn Hofraths Fritze," p. 157, by Günter Niggl, *Geschichte der deutschen Autobiographie im 18. Jahrhundert: Theoretische Grundlegung und literarische Entfaltung* (Stuttgart: J. B. Metzler, 1977), p. 103n.

11. The notion of publishing collections of autobiographies, which would wait in England until 1826 (see text below), was undertaken in Germany by Johann Georg Müller led by Herder in 1791, and by David Christoph Seybold from 1796 to 1799. My account of the relation of Seybold to Herder differs a little from those of Niggl and Misch. Niggl cites as examples of the uncertain use of the terminology at this time the foreword to Bogatzky's *Lebenslauf* (1801), Laukhard's *Leben und Schicksale* (1802), and Schlozer's *Offentliches und privat-Leben* (1802).

12. It is worth noticing here that there is more of what might properly be called theory of autobiography and biography in the eighteenth century than has been recognized and that a number of scholars of autobiography in English wrongly credit Herder with the first use of "Selbstbiographie." Jenisch uses both *Selbst-Biographien* and *Autobiographie*. See Daniel Jenisch, *Theorie der Lebens-Beschreibung Nebst einer Lebens-Beschreibung Karl des Grossen: Einer Preisschrift* (Berlin: bei Heinrich Frölich, 1802), pp. 39, 42, 170.

13. Karl Philipp Moritz, *Grammatisches Wörterbuch der deutschen Sprache* (Berlin, 1793), p. 168.

14. Friedrich Schlegel, *Athenaeum* (Darmstadt: Wissenschaftliche Buchgesellschaft, 1960; orig. ed. 1798), pp. 227–28; trans. Ernst Behler and Roman Struc, in Friedrich Schlegel, *Dialogue on Poetry and Literary Aphorisms* (University Park: Pennsylvania State University Press, 1968), p. 143.

15. Georges Gusdorf, "De l'autobiographie initiatique à l'autobiographie genre littéraire," *Revue d'histoire littéraire de la France*, 75 (1975). Gusdorf connects it to "the formation of a technical vocabulary of criticism at the beginning of the nineteenth century" (p. 963).

16. Schlegel, *Athenaeum*, p. 183; trans. Behler and Struc, p. 134.

17. I found the English quoted by Behler and Struc, pp. 42–43, before I stumbled upon the original quoted by Hans Eichner in his introduction to Friedrich Schlegel, *Literary Notebooks: 1797–1801* (Toronto: University of Toronto Press, 1957), p. 3, from a letter of A. W. Schlegel to Schleiermacher on Jan. 22, 1798.

18. See Momigliano, *Greek Biography*, p. 14, where he instances the autobiography of Nicolaus of Damascus for the Greek title.

19. Quoted by Georges May, *L'autobiographie* (Paris: Presses Universitaires de France, 1979), p. 29. This account draws on May, pp. 118–20.

20. Buckley, *The Turning Key*, p. 18.

21. T. F. Dibdin, *The Library Companion* (London: Harding, Triphook and Lepard, 1824), p. 543.

22. Henry Mackenzie, *The Anecdotes and Egotisms of Henry Mackenzie*, ed. Harold William Thompson (London: Oxford University Press, 1927), p. 184. Carlyle also used *autobiography* in the 1820's.

23. Leigh Hunt, *The Reflector*, 2 vols. (London: J. Hunt, 1812), vol. 2, p. 244. James Field Stanfield, *An Essay on the Study and Composition of Biography* (Sunderland: George Garbutt, 1813), pp. 28, 34, 35, 315.

24. *Autobiography*, 34 vols. (London: Hunt and Clarke, 1826–33); John Galt, *The Member: An Autobiography* (London: James Fraser, 1831); idem, *The Radical: An Autobiography* (London: James Fraser, 1831); idem, *The Autobiography of John Galt* (London: Cochrane and McCrone, 1833). William Brown, *The Autobiography, or Narrative of a Soldier* (J. Patterson, 1829); Matthew Carey, *Autobiographical Sketches. In a Series of Letters Addressed to a Friend* (J. Clark, 1829); Asa Greene, *A Yankee Among the Nullifiers: An Auto-biography* (New York: Stodart, 1823); James Browne, *The "Life" of the Ettrick Shepherd . . .* (Edinburgh: William Hunter, 1832). I omit other short and manuscript examples. The use of *autobiography* in titles of essays came earlier: "Observations on the Autobiography of Bishop Watson," *Blackwood's Magazine*, 2 (Feb. 1818): 479–85, and the first part of the fictional "Autobiography of Timothy Tell, Schoolmaster of Birchendale," *Blackwood's Magazine*, 12 (Oct. 1822): 395–409, are the first known to me.

25. Sir Egerton Brydges, *The Autobiography, Times, Opinions, and Contemporaries of Sir Egerton Brydges* (London: Cochrane and McCrone, 1834); Elizabeth Wright McCauley, *Autobiographical Memoirs* (London: printed for the author, 1834); Caroline Fry, *Christ Our Example, to Which Is Prefixed an Autobiography* (New York: American Tract Society, 1839).

26. Sir Egerton Brydges, ed., *A True Relation of the Birth, Breeding, and Life of Margaret Cavendish, Duchess of Newcastle* (Kent: Johnson and Warwick, 1814), p. 1; Samuel Weller Singer, in Joseph Spence, *Anecdotes . . . of Mr. Pope* (London: W. H. Carpenter, 1820), p. xiv; Charles Armitage Brown, *Shakespeare's Autobiographical Poems . . .* (London: James Bohn, 1838).

27. Nussbaum, *The Autobiographical Subject*, p. xiv; H. Porter Abbott, "Autobiography, Autography, Fiction: Groundwork for a Taxonymy of Textual Categories," *New Literary History*, 19 (1987–88): 597–615; Domna C. Stanton, "Autogynography: Is the Subject Different?" in Domna C. Stanton, ed., *The Female Autograph* (Chicago: University of Chicago Press, 1987), pp. 3–20; Jacques Derrida, *The Ear of the Other* (New York: Schocken Books, 1985), originally published as *L'Oreille de l'autre* (1982).

28. Samuel Johnson, *The Idler and The Adventurer*, ed. W. J. Bate, John Bullitt, and L. F. Powell (New Haven, Conn.: Yale University Press, 1963), p. 262.

29. Mme de Staël, *De la littérature*, ed. Paul van Tieghem (Geneva: Librairie Droz, 1959), p. 238.

30. Karl Joachim Weintraub, *The Value of the Individual: Self and Circumstance in Autobiography* (Chicago: University of Chicago Press, 1978), p. xiv.

31. May, *L'autobiographie*, p. 9.

32. Ibid.

33. William C. Spengemann, *The Forms of Autobiography: Episodes in the History of a Literary Genre* (New Haven, Conn.: Yale University Press, 1980), p. xi.

34. Estelle C. Jelinek, ed., *Women's Autobiographies: Essays in Criticism* (Bloomington: University of Indiana Press, 1980), pp. ix, 1. Some recent collections are Stanton, ed., *The Female Autograph*; Shari Benstock, ed., *The Private Self: Theory and Practice of Women's Autobiographical Writings* (Chapel Hill: University of North Carolina Press, 1988); Bella Brodzki and Celeste Schenck, eds., *Life/Lines: Theorizing Women's Autobiography* (Ithaca, N.Y.: Cornell University Press, 1988).

35. Georges Gusdorf, "Conditions et limites de l'autobiographie," in Günter Reichenkron and Erich Haase, eds., *Formen der Selbstdarstellung: Analekten zu einer Geschichte des literarischen Selbstporträts* (Berlin: Duncker & Humblot, 1956), pp. 105–23, also available as "Conditions and Limits of Autobiography" in Olney, ed., *Autobiography*, pp. 28–48, and "De l'autobiographie initiatique," pp. 957–94; Paul de Man, "Autobiography as De-Facement," in *The Rhetoric of Romanticism* (New York: Columbia University Press, 1984), pp. 67–81, also published in *Modern Language Notes* 94 (1979): 919–30; Derrida, *The Ear of the Other*.

36. Spengemann, *The Forms of Autobiography*, p. 188; Northrop Frye, *An Anatomy of Criticism* (Princeton, N.J.: Princeton University Press, 1957), pp. 307–8.

37. Charles Ryecroft, "Viewpoint: Analysis and the Autobiographer," *TLS*, May 27, 1983, p. 541.

38. Jeffrey Mehlman, *A Structural Study of Autobiography: Proust, Leiris, Sartre, Lévi-Strauss* (Ithaca, N.Y.: Cornell University Press, 1974); James Olney, *Metaphors of Self: The Meaning of Autobiography* (Princeton, N.J.: Princeton University Press, 1972); Paul Jay, *Being in the Text* (Ithaca, N.Y.: Cornell University Press, 1984).

39. Paul John Eakin, *Fictions in Autobiography: Studies in the Art of Self-*

Invention (Princeton, N.J.: Princeton University Press, 1985), p. ix; Sidonie Smith, *A Poetics of Women's Autobiography: Marginality and the Fictions of Self-Representation* (Bloomington: Indiana University Press, 1987), p. 3; Herbert Leibowitz, *Fabricating Lives: Explorations in American Autobiography* (New York: Alfred A. Knopf, 1989), p. xi.

40. I have in mind here such characteristic essays as Louis A. Renza, "The Veto of the Imagination: A Theory of Autobiography," *New Literary History*, 9 (1977): 1–26; Michael Sprinker, "Fictions of the Self: The End of Autobiography" in Olney, ed., *Autobiography*, pp. 321–42; and Marc Eli Blanchard, "The Critique of Autobiography," *Comparative Literature*, 34 (1982): 97–115. The most powerful of such critiques is that of de Man, mentioned above.

41. Quoted by Alan Bowness, "The Painter's Studio," in Petra Ten Doesschate Chu, ed., *Courbet in Perspective* (Englewood Cliffs, N.J.: Prentice-Hall, 1977), p. 127. Pierre Borel, *Le Roman de Courbet* (Paris: Editions E. Sansot, 1922), p. 37, prints the original.

42. Philippe Lejeune, *L'autobiographie en France* (Paris: Colin, 1971), p. 14.

43. See Spengemann, *The Forms of Autobiography*, and de Man, "De-Facement."

44. See John Sturrock, "The New Model Autobiographer," *New Literary History*, 9 (1977): 51–63.

45. Paul Fussell, "Private Lives," *Partisan Review*, 37 (1970): 288.

46. Robert Graves, *Goodbye to All That* (Garden City, N.Y.: Doubleday, 1957), p. 1.

47. E. L. Woodward, *Short Journey* (New York: Oxford University Press, 1946), p. 3.

48. John Locke, *An Essay Concerning Human Understanding*, ed. Alexander Campbell Fraser (New York: Dover, 1959), vol. 1, p. 449 (II, 27, 9).

49. Sigmund Freud, "A Childhood Recollection from *Dichtung und Wahrheit*" (1917), in *Character and Culture*, ed. Philip Rieff (New York: Collier Books, 1963), p. 192.

Sturrock: Theory Versus Autobiography

1. Richard N. Coe, *When the Grass Was Taller: Autobiography and the Experience of Childhood* (New Haven, Conn.: Yale University Press, 1984), p. xiv.

2. Paul de Man, "Autobiography as De-Facement," in *The Rhetoric of Romanticism* (New York: Columbia University Press, 1984), pp. 67–68.

3. Friedrich Nietzsche, *Ecce Homo*, trans. Anthony M. Ludovici (London: Foulis, 1924), p. 1.

4. Jean-Jacques Rousseau, *Confessions*, trans. J. M. Cohen (Harmondsworth: Penguin Books, 1953), p. 5.

5. René Descartes, "Discourse on Method," in *Descartes' Philosophical Writings*, trans. Norman Kemp Smith (London: Macmillan, 1953), p. 163.

6. Ibid., p. 122.

7. Ibid., p. 118.

8. Gottfried Wilhelm Leibniz, letter to Louis Bourguet, cited in Giambattista Vico, *The Autobiography of Giambattista Vico*, trans. Max Harold Fisch and Thomas Goddard Bergin (Ithaca, N.Y.: Cornell University Press, 1944), p. 5.

9. Vico, *Autobiography*, p. 113.

10. Ibid., p. 111.

11. Nelson Goodman, *Of Mind and Other Matters* (Cambridge, Mass: Harvard University Press, 1984), p. 1.

12. Vico, *Autobiography*, pp. 121–22.

13. Sigmund Freud, *An Autobiographical Study*, trans. James Strachey (London: Hogarth Press, 1935), p. 87.

14. Ibid., p. 110.

15. Jean-Paul Sartre, *The Words*, trans. Bernard Frechtman (New York: Vintage Books, 1964), p. 204.

16. Ibid., p. 255.

Bruner: The Autobiographical Process

1. *Autobiography and the Construction of Self* (Cambridge, Mass.: Harvard University Press, forthcoming).

2. Donald Spence, *Narrative Truth and Historical Truth: Meaning and Interpretation in Psychoanalysis* (New York: Norton, 1982); Roy Schafer, "Narration in the Psychoanalytic Dialogue," in W. J .T. Mitchell, ed., *On Narrative* (Chicago: University of Chicago Press, 1981).

3. Sir Frederic Bartlett, *Remembering* (Cambridge: Cambridge University Press, 1932), p. 206. See especially chapter 10.

4. Sidonie Smith, *A Poetics of Women's Autobiography: Marginality and the Fictions of Self-Representation* (Bloomington: Indiana University Press, 1988). But see also Karl Joachim Weintraub, *The Value of the Individual: Self and Circumstance in Autobiography* (Chicago: University of Chicago Press, 1978).

5. Philippe Lejeune, *On Autobiography*, ed. Paul John Eakin, trans. Katherine Leary (Minneapolis: University of Minnesota Press, 1989).

6. Ibid., pp. 4–5.

7. One can conceive of self-revelation as a class of self-reflexive commissive speech act in which one promises to be true to one's own memories. Or perhaps it might better be conceived simply as a particularly stringent instance of applying the Gricean maxims of brevity, sincerity, relevance, and perspicuousness to communications about a private domain. In any case, see John Searle, *Speech Acts* (Cambridge: Cambridge University Press, 1969), and Dan Sperber and Deirdre Wilson, *Relevance: Communication and Cognition* (Oxford: Blackwell, 1986).

8. Charles Taylor, *Sources of the Self* (Cambridge, Mass.: Harvard University Press, 1989), chapter 1.

9. Michelle Rosaldo, *Knowledge and Passion: Ilongot Notions of Self and Social Life* (Cambridge: Cambridge University Press, 1980); Bertrand Russell, *Autobiography of Bertrand Russell* (London: Allen and Unwin, 1967–69), vols. 1–3.

10. James Boyd White, *Heracles' Bow: Essays on the Rhetoric and Poetics of the Law* (Madison: University of Wisconsin Press, 1985).

11. Wilhelm Dilthey, *Descriptive Psychology and Human Understanding* (The Hague: Nijhoff, 1977; orig. ed., 1911).

12. For a particularly thoughtful discussion of these issues, see Alexander Nehamas, *Nietzsche: Life as Literature* (Cambridge, Mass.: Harvard University Press, 1985).

13. Algirdas Greimas, *On Meaning: Selected Writings in Semiotic Theory* (Minneapolis: University of Minnesota Press, 1987). See particularly chapter 6, "Elements of a narrative grammar," pp. 63–83.

14. While the English translation of Greimas's book of essays, *On Meaning*, is highly sensitive, it is impossible to render the French modal verb system into English "word by word." I have inevitably taken some liberties in my own rendering. The reader is referred to the original papers in French cited in the English edition.

15. I mean "localness" in the sense that Geertz speaks of "local knowledge" in the adjudication of disputes in different cultures: the accepted form in which the genuineness of testimony is weighed. His discussion provides the locus classicus for what I mean by "constitutive rhetoric" in the sense that the three forms of jurisprudence he analyzes—Arabic *haqq*, Malaysian-Indonesian *adat*, and Indian *dharma*—each provide a way of defining and determining guilt and innocence, admissible and inadmissible evidence, appropriate and inappropriate punishment and penance. One cannot understand a legal proceeding without appreciating the system of distinctions it rests upon. And by the same token, one cannot understand an autobiography unless it is composed in the system of folk psychology that creates the distinctions to which people customarily respond or see others responding. See Clifford Geertz, "Local Knowledge: Fact and Law in Comparative Perspective," chapter 8 in *Local Knowledge* (New York: Basic Books, 1983), pp. 167–234.

16. Carol Laderman, *Taming the Wind of Desire: Psychology, Medicine, and Aesthetics in Malay Shamanistic Performance* (Berkeley: University of California Press, 1991).

17. Bruner, *Autobiography and the Construction of Self.*

18. For a discussion of the "diatactical," see Hayden White, *Tropics of Discourse: Essays in Cultural Criticism* (Baltimore: The Johns Hopkins University Press, 1978), p. 4.

19. Patrick White, *Flaws in the Glass: A Self Portrait* (New York: Penguin, 1981); Tennessee Williams, *Memoirs* (New York: Bantam, 1976); Richard Feynman, *Surely You're Joking, Mr. Feynman: Adventures of a Curious Character* (New York: Norton, 1985).

20. For a fuller discussion of verisimilitude in narrative generally, see Jerome Bruner, *Actual Minds, Possible Worlds* (Cambridge, Mass.: Harvard University Press, 1986).

21. See, particularly, Erving Goffman, *The Presentation of Self in Everyday Life* (Garden City, N.Y.: Doubleday, 1959).

22. For an especially revealing review of this literature, see Roger Brown, *Social Psychology: The Second Edition* (New York: Free Press, 1986).

23. See, particularly, the chapter I coauthored with Joan Lucariello in Katherine Nelson, ed., *Narratives from the Crib* (Cambridge, Mass.: Harvard University Press, 1989), pp. 73–97.

24. See S. Baron-Cohen, A. Leslie, and U. Frith, "Does the Autistic Child Have a Theory of Mind?" *Cognition*, 211 (1985): 37–46; and Francesca Happe, "The Autobiographical Writings of Three Asperger Syndrome Adults: Problems of Interpretation and Implications for Theory," in U. Frith, ed., *Autistic Theories of Mind* (forthcoming).

25. Erik Erikson, *Childhood and Society* (New York: Norton, 1950). See my *Acts of Meaning* (Cambridge, Mass.: Harvard University Press, 1991), chapter 4, for a discussion of the "private-to-public" dimension in contemporary American "spontaneous" autobiography.

26. Vincent Crapanzano, "On Self Characterization," *Working Papers and Proceedings of the Center for Psychosocial Studies*, 24 (1988).

27. Smith, *A Poetics of Women's Autobiography*.

28. Perhaps the "generation of 1968" has not yet reached the "age of autobiography." When leading figures in the protests of the generation have put pen to paper, little new has emerged. Todd Gitlin's *The Sixties: Years of Hope, Days of Rage* (New York: Bantam, 1987), interesting though it may be as a political memoir, travels along well-worn realist tracks.

29. James Young, *Writing and Rewriting the Holocaust: Narrative and the Consequences of Interpretation* (Bloomington: Indiana University Press, 1988).

30. Primo Levi, *The Periodic Table* (New York: Schocken, 1984), p. 140.

31. Idem, *The Drowned and the Saved* (New York: Summit Books, 1986).

32. J. Kirk T. Varnedoe, Introduction, in J. K. T. Varnedoe, ed., *Modern Portraits: The Self and Others.* A catalog for an exhibition organized by the Department of Art History and Archeology of Columbia University at the Wildenstein Gallery in New York, October 20–November 28, 1976. (New York: Trustees of Columbia University, 1976), pp. xii–xxv.

33. Nelson Goodman, *Of Mind and Other Matters* (Cambridge, Mass.: Harvard University Press, 1984); *Ways of Worldmaking* (Indianapolis, Ind.: Hackett, 1978); *Languages of Art* (Indianapolis, Ind.: Hackett, 1976).

34. Roberto Unger, "The Critical Legal Studies Movement," *Harvard Law Review*, 96 (1983); White, *Heracles' Bow*; Robert Cover, "Nomos and Narrative: The Supreme Court 1982 Term," *Harvard Law Review*, 97 (1983).

35. Roland Penrose, *Picasso: His Life and Work*, rev. ed. (New York: Harper and Row, 1973), pp. 121–22.

36. *The National Law Journal*, Dec. 10, 1990, p. 27. The report is written by Rosalind Resnick.

37. Don DeLillo, *Libra* (New York: Viking, 1988); *White Noise* (New York: Viking, 1986).

38. Philip Roth, *The Facts: A Novelist's Autobiography* (New York: Farrar, Straus, and Giroux, 1988); *Deception* (New York: Simon and Schuster, 1990).

39. Hazel Markus and Paula Nurius, "Possible Selves," *American Psychologist*, 41 (1986): 954.

40. *The National Law Journal*, p. 27. Brackets in the original.

41. Nicholas Humphrey and Daniel Dennett, "Speaking for Ourselves," *Raritan: A Quarterly Review* (Spring 1989): 68–98.

Watson: Toward an Anti-Metaphysics of Autobiography

An early version of this essay was first presented as a paper, "Destabilizing the Theory of Autobiography: Challenges from the Margin," at the conference "Autobiography and Biography: Gender Text and ConText" organized by the Center for Research on Women, Stanford University, April 11–13, 1986. The responses of Sidonie Smith, Caren Kaplan, and Mary Louise Pratt were particularly helpful, as were those of the faculty and graduate students at the University of California, Irvine, notably Alexander Gelley, Robert Folkenflik, and Renée Riese Hubert, who also heard the paper. My work was facilitated by a National Endowment for the Humanities Summer Seminar at Barnard College in 1987 led by Nancy K. Miller, who offered insightful advice and support, as did Rebecca Hogan and Nancy Paxton. I presented a related essay, "Women's Autobiography—A Separable Genre?", at the Nonfictional Prose Section meeting of the 1988 Modern Language Association conference, where Bella Brodzki's comments were illuminating.

1. Cited by Stephen Spender, "Confessions and Autobiography," in James Olney, ed., *Autobiography: Essays Theoretical and Critical* (Princeton, N.J.: Princeton University Press, 1980), p. 115. Spender takes issue with this definition because he rightly sees self-reference as unlike other modes of reference. But he excludes most modern autobiography from consideration because it does not fulfill what he sees as the fundamental requirement of the genre, namely to engage simultaneously the doubled selves of historical objectivity and subjective self-revelation that constitute for him the order of autobiographical "truth" occasionally attained by such autobiographers as Rousseau, Restif de la Bretonne, or Augustine. "It is understandable that most people who write their autobiographies write the life of someone by himself and not the life of someone by his two selves" (p. 122).

2. William Spengemann, *The Forms of Autobiography: Episodes in the History of a Literary Genre* (New Haven, Conn.: Yale University Press, 1980), p. xi. Spengemann argues that autobiography moves between biographical and fictive modes and should not be limited to "self-written biography," although what he calls its historical and philosophical models are in this mode. Modernist poems, plays, and novels that are self-reflexive "make the very idea of literary modernism seem synonymous with that of autobiography" (p. xiii). Despite this concession, Spengemann seems to equate *bios* unproblematically with self and concludes that autobiography's forms were fixed by the nineteenth century: "However various critics have defined autobiography, their ability to recognize one has always depended on some evidence that the writer's self is either the primary subject or the principal object of the verbal action. . . . Historical self-explanation, philosophical self-scrutiny, poetic self-expression, and poetic self-invention—these are, so far as I

know, the only procedures available to autobiography, and the list was exhausted by the time Hawthorne finished *The Scarlet Letter*" (pp. xvi–xvii). The intervening decade in autobiography studies argues for decidedly different emphases.

3. Georges Gusdorf, "Conditions and Limits of Autobiography," in Olney, ed., *Autobiography*, pp. 29, 47.

4. Roy Pascal, *Design and Truth in Autobiography* (Cambridge, Mass.: Harvard University Press, 1960).

5. *New Literary History*, 9, 1 (Autumn 1977). "Self-Confrontation and Social Vision" was a special issue with several important essays on rethinking autobiography, among them Louis Renza's "The Veto of the Imagination: A Theory of Autobiography" (pp. 1–26), John Sturrock's "The New Model Autobiographer" (pp. 51–63), and Philippe Lejeune's "Autobiography in the Third Person" (pp. 27–50). *NLH*'s remapping of positions was extended in James Olney's important 1980 collection, *Autobiography*, cited above. But for all the revisionism of these essays, canonical texts remain prominent in their discussions of autobiography.

6. Philippe Lejeune, "The Autobiographical Pact," in Paul John Eakin, ed., *On Autobiography*, trans. Katherine Leary (Minneapolis: University of Minnesota Press, 1989), p. 20. Lejeune's discussion of the proper name as "the deep subject of autobiography" and his validation of the proper name as verification of the subject exclude women and those of slave ancestry, whose names signify at best their linkage to a patriarchal chain, as both Nancy K. Miller and Domna Stanton have pointed out elsewhere.

7. Louis Renza discusses Teresa extensively in "The Veto of the Imagination" and in his dissertation. Mary G. Mason, in "The Other Voice: Autobiographies of Women Writers," discusses Julian of Norwich, Margery Kempe, Margaret Cavendish, and Anne Bradstreet, in Olney, ed., *Autobiography*, pp. 207–35. Her anthology of women's autobiographical writings includes selections, mostly excerpted, from a range of British and American women autobiographers. See Mary G. Mason and Carol Hurd Green, eds., *Journeys* (Boston: G. K. Hall, 1979).

8. In, for example, Paul John Eakin's *Fictions in Autobiography: Studies in the Art of Self-Invention* (Princeton, N.J.: Princeton University Press, 1985), the autobiographers discussed extensively are Mary McCarthy, Henry James, Jean-Paul Sartre, Frank Conroy, Saul Friedländer, and Maxine Hong Kingston. While both the book's thesis and its attention to neglected writers are important acts of critical revision, the readings postulate a kind of universalized subject that is, in its attention to linguistic innovation, informed by an assumption of mainstream/male modernism.

9. Here I have in mind especially John Sturrock and Jerome Bruner, above.

10. Paul de Man, "Autobiography as De-Facement," in *The Rhetoric of Romanticism* (New York: Columbia University Press, 1984), pp. 67–81.

11. Michel de Montaigne, "Of Giving the Lie," in *The Complete Essays of Montaigne*, trans. Donald Frame (Stanford, Calif.: Stanford University Press, 1965), book 2, essay 18, pp. 503–6. All references will be to this edition and will appear in the text.

12. Plutarch, "On Inoffensive Self-Praise," in *Moralia* (Cambridge, Mass.:

Harvard University Press, 1969), pp. 115–67. Plutarch recommends including one's shortcomings, one of several strategies for avoiding the audience's displeasure, which would prevent them from believing in the self-portrait.

13. James Olney's conception of "the doubled self," for example, is deeply informed by Montaigne's notion of consubstantiality as a metaphor of intersubjective dialogue in the *Essais* that refuses a representational split into subject and object. See his chapter on Montaigne in *Metaphors of Self: The Meaning of Autobiography* (Princeton, N.J.: Princeton University Press, 1972).

14. The Cretan liar paradox is a famous logical conundrum attributed to Zeno: "All Cretans are liars, says Epidaurus of Crete." If his statement is true, he is lying; if it is false, he is telling the truth. The statement engages the audience because it is verifiable only by reference to their assessment of the ethos of its speaker. Rosalie Colie extensively discusses the retrieval of this and other paradoxes of antiquity in several Renaissance writers, including Montaigne, whom she describes as exploring epistemological paradox. See *Paradoxia Epidemica* (Princeton, N.J.: Princeton University Press, 1966), especially pp. 374–95.

15. Michel Beaujour, *Miroirs d'encre: Rhétorique de l'autoportrait* (Paris: Seuil, 1980). See especially pp. 7–26 and pp. 113–26.

16. Philippe Lejeune, in essays such as "The Order of Narrative in Sartre's *Les Mots*," has described the critic's work as using biographical information to complete the project of self-representation in most autobiographies. But he has acknowledged that Montaigne and Stendhal create circles of self-presentation that do not allow this act of critical explanation. In that sense he views their writings as "complete" autobiographies and inimical to his sense of what autobiography is (discussion on Sept. 30, 1989, after Lejeune's presentation of a paper at the University of Southern Maine on the autobiographical critic's work). For the Sartre essay, see Eakin, ed., *On Autobiography*, pp. 70–107.

17. Thomas De Quincey, *Confessions of an English Opium Eater*, ed. Alethea Hayter (London: Penguin Books, 1971), based on the 1821 version. *Confessions* was first published in 1821, then expanded by De Quincey through numerous appendices, commentaries, and revisions in the edition of 1856, which Hayter considers an inferior version.

18. "Not the opium-eater, but the opium, is the true hero of the tale; and the legitimate centre on which the interest revolves" (De Quincey, *Confessions*, p. 114).

19. See Hayter's Introduction to *Confessions*, p. 18. De Quincey comments on how sensory experience, under the agency of opium, makes memory present: "[The music] displayed before me . . . the whole of my past life—not as if recalled by an act of memory, but as if present and incarnated in the music" (*Confessions*, p. 79). As memory is activated, the boundaries of past and present experience are blended. Like Montaigne, De Quincey has recourse to a sacramental metaphor (incarnation) to describe this experience of self-revision.

20. "There is no such thing as forgetting possible to the mind; a thousand accidents may, and will, interpose a veil between our present consciousness and the secret inscriptions on the mind . . . whether veiled or unveiled, the inscription remains for ever" (De Quincey, *Confessions*, p. 104).

21. Rainer Maria Rilke, *The Notebooks of Malte Laurids Brigge*, trans. M. D. Herter Norton (New York: W. W. Norton, 1949). Published in German as *Die Aufzeichnungen des Malte Laurids Brigge*, in *Werke in drei Bänden*, vol. 3 (Frankfurt am Main: Insel Verlag, 1966), pp. 109–346. *Aufzeichnungen* are quick sketches; the word is derived from the verb *zeichnen*, to draw. The *Aufzeichnungen*, then, is a repository of visual, momentary images, rather than a verbal diary, as the English translation implies.

22. Ralph Freedman discussed *Notebooks* as lyrical fiction, but dismissed it as too fully lyrical to be considered in his boundary genre. See *The Lyrical Novel* (Princeton, N.J.: Princeton University Press, 1963), pp. 8–10.

23. Rilke explicitly rejected reading *Notebooks* as a literary biography of himself: "One would be wrong in working *Malte Laurids Brigge* . . . as a mine of biographical material" (letter to Robert Heinz Heygrodt, Dec. 24, 1921, #102, *Wartime Letters*, trans. M. D. Herter Norton [New York: W. W. Norton, 1940], p. 226). But Rilke's statement, which rejects the *bios* character of life writing, does not apply to the redefinition of autobiographical writing that I am pursuing here; indeed it supports the distinction of self-reflexive writing from "self-written biography."

24. For a Lacanian reading, see Eleanor Honig Skoller, "Threads in Three Sections: A Reading of *The Notebooks of Malte Laurids Brigge*," *SubStance* 32 (1981), pp. 15–25.

25. "Ich lerne sehen." Malte writes this repeatedly throughout the initial sections of *The Notebooks*: "I am learning to see" (p. 14); "Have I said it before? I am learning to see" (p. 15); "I think I ought to begin to do some work, now that I am learning to see" (p. 26).

26. Bella Brodzki and Celeste Schenck, eds., *Life/Lines: Theorizing Women's Autobiography* (Ithaca, N.Y.: Cornell University Press, 1988), p. 11. Brodzki and Schenck take to task the representations of experimental autobiography by Michael Sprinker and Paul Jay and argue for Stein as a more radical experimenter than dominant theorists have acknowledged. See Michael Sprinker, "Fictions of the Self: The End of Autobiography," in Olney, ed., *Autobiography*; and Paul Jay, *Being in the Text* (Ithaca, N.Y.: Cornell University Press, 1984). Brodzki and Schenck's project is summed up in the call for "the imperative situating of the female subject in spite of the postmodernist campaign against the sovereign self" (p. 14).

27. Mason, "The Other Voice," p. 210.

28. "The egoistic secular archetype that Rousseau handed down to his Romantic brethren in his *Confessions*, shifting the dramatic presentation to an unfolding self-discovery where characters and events are little more than aspects of the author's evolving consciousness, finds no echo in women's writing about their lives" (Mason, "The Other Voice," p. 210).

29. Susan Stanford Friedman, "Women's Autobiographical Selves: Theory and Practice," in Shari Benstock, ed., *The Private Self: Theory and Practice of Women's Autobiographical Writings* (Chapel Hill: University of North Carolina Press, 1988), pp. 41, 42.

30. Domna C. Stanton, "Autogynography: Is the Subject Different?" in Domna C. Stanton, ed., *The Female Autograph* (Chicago: University of Chicago Press, 1987), pp. 14, 15, 17.

31. Sidonie Smith, *A Poetics of Women's Autobiography: Marginality and the Fictions of Self-Representation* (Bloomington: Indiana University Press, 1987). See especially the discussion in chapter 3, "Woman's Story and the Engendering of Self-Representation."

32. Carolyn G. Heilbrun, *Writing a Woman's Life* (New York: Norton, 1988), pp. 47, 60.

33. Cherríe Moraga and Gloria Anzaldúa, eds., *This Bridge Called My Back: Writings by Radical Women of Color* (New York: Kitchen Table, Women of Color Press, 1981, 1983).

34. For a more extensive discussion of the relevance of *Bridge* to autobiography, see my review in the special Women's Autobiography issue of *a/b: Auto/Biography Studies*, 4, 1 (Fall 1988): 77–79.

35. Biddy Martin, "Lesbian Identity and Autobiographical Difference," in Brodzki and Schenck, eds., *Life/Lines*, pp. 77, 103, 90.

36. Trinh T. Minh-ha, "Grandma's Story," *Woman, Native, Other* (Bloomington: Indiana University Press, 1989), pp. 119–51.

37. Trinh, *Woman, Native, Other*, p. 132.

38. Ibid., p. 148.

39. Françoise Lionnet, *Autobiographical Voices: Race, Gender, Self-Portraiture* (Ithaca, N.Y.: Cornell University Press, 1989).

40. Since the reunification of Germany, Wolf has been under attack by the German Left for the privilege and fame she enjoyed in the German Democratic Republic and her unwillingness either to denounce the state unqualifiedly or to flee it. In *Was bleibt?* Wolf responded to her critics by publishing a revised story written in 1979 that depicts a day in the life of a woman observed by the security police (Berlin: Aufbau Verlag, 1990). No final judgment on her reputation can be ventured at this time.

41. Christa Wolf, *Patterns of Childhood*, originally titled (inaccurately) *A Model Childhood*, trans. Ursule Molinaro and Hedwig Rappolt (New York: Farrar, Straus, and Giroux, 1980). Originally published as *Kindheitsmuster* (Aufbau Verlag, 1976). I am generally indebted to Bella Brodzki's insightful analysis of the interwoven texts of memory and mothering in this book. See "Mothers, Displacement, and Language in the Autobiographies of Nathalie Sarraute and Christa Wolf," in Brodzki and Schenck, eds., *Life/Lines*, pp. 243–59.

42. Christa Wolf, "Conditions of a Narrative: *Cassandra*," in *Cassandra: A Novel and Four Essays* (New York: Farrar, Straus, and Giroux, 1984), p. 142. Originally published as two volumes, *Voraussetzungen einer Erzählung: Kassandra* and *Kassandra, Erzählung* (Luchterhand, 1983). All subsequent references to this work are in parentheses in the text. This passage is discussed in Linda Schelbitzki Pickle, "'Scratching Away the Male Tradition': Christa Wolf's *Kassandra*," *Contemporary Literature*, 27, 1 (1986): 33. I prefer Pickle's translation: "There is and there can be no poetics which prevents the living experience of countless perceiving subjects from being killed and buried in art objects."

43. The parallels are extensive. Jack Zipes sums them up and reads the text biographically: "*Kindheitsmuster* makes it quite clear how Christa Wolf must have been bewildered by and suffered from the initiation into the fascist system which

is associated with bestial and irrational behavior. . . . she felt herself to be a victim of Nazi propaganda. She especially keeps returning to the traumatic break in her life, 1945–46, when she was forced to flee her home and to rethink her situation in light of the allied occupation" ("Christa Wolf: Moralist as Marxist," in *Divided Heaven*, trans. Joan Becker [Berlin, GDR; Seven Seas Books, 1965]).

44. The notion of "present-ifying"—reanimating of memory as present—was extensively developed in Louis Renza's important essay on autobiography, "The Veto of the Imagination." Renza's conceptual framework would prove useful for reading the subtle and complex mingling of pasts and present in Wolf's writing.

45. Anna Kuhn rightly points out that, unlike *Patterns of Childhood*, which is constructed of multiple commentaries that gloss one another, "*Cassandra* makes it the reader's responsibility . . . to establish connections between the self-reflective essays and narrative," a task that would require a longer exploration than I can provide here. See Anna Kuhn, *Christa Wolf's Utopian Vision: From Marxism to Feminism* (Cambridge: Cambridge University Press, 1988), p. 184. Kuhn focuses on "the exclusion and objectification of women" in the novel as a consequence of patriarchal values in both prehistoric Troy and the twentieth-century West.

Peterson: Institutionalizing Women's Autobiography

1. Mary G. Mason, "The Other Voice: Autobiographies of Women Writers," in James Olney, ed., *Autobiography: Essays Theoretical and Critical* (Princeton, N.J.: Princeton University Press, 1980); Estelle C. Jelinek, *The Tradition of Women's Autobiography: From Antiquity to the Present* (Boston: Twayne, 1986); Sidonie Smith, *A Poetics of Women's Autobiography: Marginality and the Fictions of Self-Representation* (Bloomington: Indiana University Press, 1987); and Carolyn G. Heilbrun, *Writing a Woman's Life* (New York: Norton, 1988). Heilbrun's book is not, strictly speaking, a historical study, but it assumes the historical development of a women's tradition in its discussion of certain modern texts as "revolutionary" (Adrienne Rich's autobiographical works), as a "turning point" (May Sarton's *Journal of a Solitude*), or as otherwise exemplifying progress in the genre. Collections that include attempts to define a women's tradition are Estelle C. Jelinek, ed., *Women's Autobiography: Essays in Criticism* (Bloomington: Indiana University Press, 1980); Domna C. Stanton, ed., *The Female Autograph: Theory and Practice of Autobiography from the Tenth to the Twentieth Century* (Chicago: University of Chicago Press, 1987); and Shari Benstock, ed., *The Private Self: Theory and Practice of Women's Autobiographical Writings* (Chapel Hill: University of North Carolina Press, 1988).

2. Jelinek, *The Tradition of Women's Autobiography*, p. 8. Cf. Susan Stanford Friedman's conclusion to "Women's Autobiographical Selves: Theory and Practice," in Benstock, ed., *The Private Self*, pp. 55–56: "Women's autobiography comes alive as a literary tradition of self-creation when we approach its texts from a psycho-political perspective based in the lives of women. . . . Individualistic [male] paradigms do not take into account the central role collective consciousness of self plays in the lives of women and minorities."

3. The exclusion of women's autobiographies from major theoretical studies is

documented in Jelinek, *The Tradition of Women's Autobiography*, pp. 1–8; Smith, *A Poetics of Women's Autobiography*, pp. 3–19; and Friedman, "Women's Autobiographical Selves," pp. 34–44. About this exclusion, Smith writes: "The poetics of autobiography, as the history of autobiography, thus remains by and large an androcentric enterprise. Despite the critical ferment brought about by feminist critiques of the academy, of disciplinary methodologies, of the canon, the majority of autobiography critics still persist in either erasing woman's story, relegating it to the margins of critical discourse, or, when they treat women's autobiographies seriously, uncritically conflating the dynamics of male and female selfhood and textuality" (p. 15).

4. See the Introduction to this volume for an account of the term.

5. Mason, "The Other Voice," p. 210.

6. Paul de Man, "Autobiography as De-Facement," *Modern Language Notes*, 94 (1979): 920.

7. I use the term *auto/biography* throughout this essay to designate texts that combine both autobiographical and biographical modes, or collections that include both biographies and autobiographies.

8. William Evans and Thomas Evans, eds., *The Friends' Library* (Philadelphia: Joseph Rakestraw, 1837–50), 1: 1–2. Besides the rationale provided by the prospectus, it is probably the case that the Evans brothers shared the concern of many Victorian Friends that Quakerism was losing its spiritual center and thus needed models to restore its members to a purer form of faith.

9. Because Augustine's influence on the tradition of English spiritual autobiography was negligible (or at least indirect) until the nineteenth century, it is more accurate to speak of a "Bunyanesque" tradition. Even this label, meant to acknowledge the crucial influence of *The Pilgrim's Progress* as well as of *Grace Abounding to the Chief of Sinners*, neglects the early contributions of women writers to the formation of the English tradition.

10. *The Life and Testimony of that Faithful Servant of the Lord, Elizabeth Stirredge*, in Evans and Evans, eds., *The Friends' Library*, 2: 187–212. Stirredge's account was written in the 1690's, first published in 1711, and reissued throughout the eighteenth century.

11. *A Brief Account of the Life and Travels of Thomas Wilson*, in Evans and Evans, eds., *The Friends' Library*, 2: 319–33.

12. Richard T. Vann, "The Theory and Practice of Conversion," in *The Social Development of English Quakerism, 1655–1755* (Cambridge, Mass.: Harvard University Press, 1969), pp. 1–46. Howard T. Brinton summarizes the major episodes of the Quaker formula in *Quaker Journals: Varieties of Religious Experience Among Friends* (Wallingford, Pa.: Pendle Hill Publications, 1972).

13. For the episodes summarized in this paragraph, see in Evans and Evans, eds., *The Friends' Library: The Life of Elizabeth Ashbridge*, 4: 11; *Some Account of the Life of Joseph Pike*, 2: 358; *A Short Account of Alice Hayes, Minister of the Gospel*, 2: 73–74; *Memoirs of the Life and Convincement of Benjamin Bangs*, 4: 224–25; and Wilson, 2: 330.

14. Hayes, in Evans and Evans, eds., *The Friends' Library*, 2: 71; compare Malachi 3:2–3 and Ezekiel 22:17–22.

15. Prospectus, Evans and Evans, eds., *The Friends' Library*, 1: 1–2.

16. See, for example, Cynthia S. Pomerleau's statement that "for seventeenth-century women, much more than men, love acted as a defining force" ("The Emergence of Women's Autobiography in England," in Jelinek, ed., *Women's Autobiography*, p. 25). Pomerleau's judgment results from an emphasis on secular texts and, perhaps, from a neglect of accounts written by male autobiographers.

17. See Nancy Chodorow, *The Reproduction of Mothering: Psychoanalysis and the Sociology of Gender* (Berkeley: University of California Press, 1978); and Carol Gilligan, *In a Different Voice: Psychological Theory and Women's Development* (Cambridge, Mass.: Harvard University Press, 1982). The models proposed by these two fine studies, highly influential on recent feminist criticism, are problematic when applied to seventeenth-century accounts. Criticism needs to maintain the historical and cultural limits that Chodorow and Gilligan themselves recognize.

18. Stirredge, in Evans and Evans, eds., *The Friends' Library*, 2: 193. The practice of including "testimonies" (character references) holds for all autobiographers, male and female alike.

19. Hoskens, *The Life of that Faithful Servant of Christ, Jane Hoskens, A Minister of the Gospel*, in Evans and Evans, eds., *The Friends' Library*, 1: 471.

20. *Some Account of Circumstances in the Life of Mary Pennington* (London: Harvey and Darton, 1821), pp. 10–13, 68–70. The first half of Pennington's account is a spiritual record left to her daughter, Gulielma Maria Springett, which focuses on the mother's history before marriage and with her first husband; the second half, a family memoir intended for her grandson, focuses on the paternal heritage. One knows only after reading both halves that Mary Pennington had two children—one daughter, one son.

21. Benjamin Bangs, *Memoirs of the Life and Convincement of that Worthy Friend Benjamin Bangs* (London: Luke Hinde, 1757), p. 48.

22. The revision in Evans and Evans, eds., *The Friends' Library*, 4: 227, reads: "Although we had often met together before in our journeys, I never so much as mentioned to her; though my spirit was united in a Divine fellowship with her." The original "Word of Courtship" disappears.

23. See Arnold Lloyd's discussion of Quaker marriage in *Quaker Social History, 1669–1738* (London: Longmans, Green, 1950), pp. 48–65.

24. In Evans and Evans, eds., *The Friends' Library*: Hayes, 2: 68; Pike, 2: 351; Oxley, *Journal of Joseph Oxley's Life and Travels*, 2: 415. The rationale for autobiography as a spiritual legacy is formulaic, though not universal in the Quaker tradition.

25. Hayes, in Evans and Evans, eds., *The Friends' Library*, 2: 75, 78. When Hayes first attended Quaker meetings, Smith was quite a cruel husband, locking up her clothes to prevent her attendance and threatening to desert her and the children unless she renounced the Friends.

26. Stirredge, in Evans and Evans, eds., *The Friends' Library*, 2: 190, 192. The editorial materials surrounding Stirredge's account seem to clarify the question of her motherhood. The "testimonies" mention her late husband but no children; the

biographical notice attached by the Hemel Hempstead Friends, however, is signed by a James Stirredge, presumably her son.

27. Nancy Armstrong, *Desire and Domestic Fiction: A Political History of the Novel* (New York: Oxford University Press, 1987).

28. *Memoirs of Lady Fanshawe*, ed. E. Harris Nicolas (London: Henry Colburn, 1829).

29. Some modern historians like Natalie Zemon Davis do, indeed, treat them as a form of history. See her "Gender and Genre: Women as Historical Writers, 1400–1820," in Patricia H. Labalme, ed., *Beyond Their Sex: Learned Women of the European Past* (New York: New York University Press, 1980), pp. 153–82. For my argument, fixing their genre is less important than noticing the autobiographical designation that Victorians chose.

30. *The Autobiography of Mrs. Alice Thornton of East Newton, Co. York*, ed. Charles Jackson (London: Surtees Society, 1875), p. v.

31. *The Autobiography of Anne Lady Halkett*, ed. John Gough Nichols (Westminster: Camden Society, 1875), p. i; *Memoirs of Lady Fanshawe*, p. viii; *Autobiography of Mary Countess of Warwick*, ed. T. Crofton Croker (London: Percy Society, 1848), p. xi; *Memoirs of the Life of Colonel Hutchinson . . . to which is prefixed The Life of Mrs. Hutchinson, Written by Herself*, ed. Rev. Julius Hutchinson, 3d ed. (London: Longman, Hurst, Rees, and Orme, 1810), p. xxiv. See also the prefaces to *A Pairt of the Life of Lady Margaret Cunninghame* (Edinburgh: James Ballantyne, 1827) and *A True Relation of the Birth, Breeding, and Life of Margaret Cavendish*, ed. Sir Egerton Brydges (Kent: Johnson and Warwick, 1814).

32. Mary Beth Rose, "Gender, Genre, and History: Seventeenth-Century English Women and the Art of Autobiography," in Mary Beth Rose, ed., *Women in the Middle Ages and the Renaissance* (Syracuse, N.Y.: Syracuse University Press, 1986), pp. 245, 273. Although Rose initially states that she is "not attempting to establish the extent to which women may be credited with influencing the development of secular autobiography" (p. 247), throughout her essay and especially at its close she refers to women's "contributions" to the genre.

33. See my "Gender and Autobiographical Form: The Case of the Spiritual Autobiography," in James Olney, ed., *Studies in Autobiography* (New York: Oxford University Press, 1988), pp. 211–22.

34. See the index to William Matthews, *British Autobiographies: An Annotated Bibliography of British Autobiographies Published or Written Before 1951* (1955; reprint, Hamden, Conn.: Archon Books, 1968), s.v. "religion." Most of the nineteenth-century women's accounts that Matthews lists as spiritual autobiographies are in fact private diaries to which biographical accounts have been added by an editor.

35. See Matthews, *British Autobiographies*, s.v. "diplomats' and consuls' wives" and "politicians' wives." As in the seventeenth century, such accounts are written primarily by women from the upper classes.

36. Matthews, *British Autobiographies*, s.v. "domestic and family life" and "housewives." Women wrote two-thirds of the memoirs listed.

37. The quest for tradition underlies Elaine Showalter's account of nineteenth-

century women's fiction, *A Literature of Their Own: British Women Novelists from Brontë to Lessing* (Princeton, N.J.: Princeton University Press, 1977).

38. Thornton refers to "the first book of my life" (p. 174), to a "first booke of my widowed condition" (p. 154), to a "2nd booke" (p. 184), and to "my booke of meditations" (p. 142). Her editor simply arranged the entries in chronological order, omitting repetitious material and deleting many of her meditations or thanksgivings for God's mercy.

39. Presumably, Lady Cunningham thought it appropriate to appeal to her errant spouse in the language of Scripture, although the consequence is a vagueness about her plight and her specific demands. The religious discourse seems to have had little effect on his behavior.

40. Chodorow, *The Reproduction of Mothering*, pp. 166–69, 173–77. See also Gilligan, *In a Different Voice*.

41. From the spiritual autobiographies of Francis Power Cobbe and Annie Besant, to the *Bildungsromane* of Charlotte Brontë and Margaret Oliphant, to the artists' autobiographies of Oliphant, Fanny Kemble, Charlotte Riddell, and Mary Cholmondeley, women writers felt the pressure of the domestic memoir. Sometimes, as in Cholmondeley's *Under One Roof*, they turned this pressure into productive literary channels. More often than not, the pressure was counterproductive, as their artistic goals were to circumvent the domestic tradition and reclaim another.

42. These categories and names appear in the Advertisement that prefaces *Autobiography: A Collection of the Most Instructive and Amusing Lives Ever Published, Written by the Parties Themselves* (London: Hunt and Clarke, 1826), unpaginated. In 1829 the series was taken over by Whittaker, Treacher, and Arnot, who were more interested in translating and publishing contemporary accounts, as vols. 27–34 show. The series ceased publication in 1833.

43. Hunt and Clarke applied a fairly rigorous definition of "autobiography," including retrospective accounts like the memoir but not spontaneous forms like the diary or personal correspondence; this choice categorically excluded some of the most common forms of women's self-writing.

44. For an extended discussion of the relations of these plots, see my "Female Autobiographer, Narrative Duplicity," in *Studies in the Literary Imagination*, 23 (1990): 165–76.

45. For examples, see *Memoirs of the Late Mrs. Robinson, Written by Herself: From the Edition Edited by Her Daughter* (London: Hunt and Clarke, 1826), 7: 34, 59–60, 64, 86–87.

46. *A Narrative of the Life of Mrs. Charlotte Charke* (London: Hunt and Clarke, 1827), pp. 34, 48. This edition is based on the 1755 book version of Charke's autobiography. Page numbers in the text are to the 1827 edition.

47. See Patricia Meyer Spacks, "Female Identities," in *Imagining a Self: Autobiography and Novel in Eighteenth-Century England* (Cambridge, Mass.: Harvard University Press, 1976), pp. 57–91.

48. The title page to the series states that the accounts will include "brief introductions, and compendious sequels carrying on the narrative to the death of each writer."

49. A *Narrative of the Life of Mrs. Charlotte Charke* (London, 1755), pp. 276–77. The autobiography was first issued in eight installments during March and April 1755, and then in a bound volume for two shillings and sixpence.

50. Dedication, ibid., pp. viii–ix. For another view, see Robert Folkenflik, "The Self as Other," in this volume, p. 221.

51. Twentieth-century editions have continued the distortions of the Hunt and Clarke version. In 1929 Constable and Company reissued *A Narrative of the Life of Mrs. Charlotte Charke* in their "Miscellany of Original and Selected Publications of Literature," again with a preface that focused on the author's pathetic demise; the next year an identical American edition appeared (New York: Richard R. Smith, 1930). A recent facsimile edition, ed. Leonard R. N. Ashley (Gainesville, Fla.: Scholars' Facsimiles and Reprints, 1969), avoids prejudging Charke and gives a reliable, appreciative introduction to her work. Fidelis Morgan's *The Well-Known Troublemaker: A Life of Charlotte Charke* (London: Faber and Faber, 1989), a reproduction of Charke's autobiography with biographical supplements, seems both fascinated by and judgmental of its subject.

52. "Vagabondism" may signal transvestism or, more generally, sexual deviance. In *The Female Husband* Fielding's Mary Hamilton was arrested and tried for "vagrancy"; in the nineteenth century the antiquarian John Ashton retold stories of male impersonators in a collection called *Eighteenth Century Waifs* (London: Hurst and Blackett, 1887).

53. Mason, "The Other Voice," p. 210.

54. Smith, *A Poetics of Women's Autobiography*, p. 104.

Barrett: Self-Knowledge, Law, and African American Autobiography

1. Lucy A. Delaney, *From the Darkness Cometh the Light, or Struggles for Freedom* (c. 1891), in *Six Women's Slave Narratives*, intro. William L. Andrews (New York: Oxford University Press, 1988).

2. Marion Wilson Starling, *The Slave Narrative* (Washington, D.C.: Howard University Press, 1988), p. 106.

3. Michel Foucault, *The History of Sexuality: An Introduction* (New York: Vintage, 1978), p. 127. I am prompted to use this phrase by Teresa de Laurentis's understanding and explanation of it in her essay "The Technology of Gender." De Laurentis suggests that cultural formations and identities such as gender, race, class are produced by cultural technologies "in the sense in which industrial machinery produces goods or commodities, and in so doing also produces social relations" (*The Technologies of Gender: Essays on Theory, Film, and Fiction* [Bloomington: Indiana University Press, 1987], p. 12).

4. Mark Tushnet, *The American Law of Slavery, 1810–1860: Considerations of Humanity and Interest* (Princeton, N.J.: Princeton University Press, 1981), p. 229.

5. Stephen Butterfield, *Black Autobiography in America* (Amherst: University of Massachusetts Press, 1974), pp. 2–3.

6. Roger Rosenblatt, "Black Autobiography: Life as the Death Weapon," in James Olney, ed., *Autobiography: Essays Theoretical and Critical* (Princeton, N.J.:

Princeton University Press, 1980), p. 174. Rosenblatt also makes the observation that "no black American author has ever felt the need to invent a nightmare to make his [or her] point" (p. 172).

7. Georges Gusdorf, "Conditions and Limits of Autobiography," in Olney, ed., *Autobiography*, p. 43. The terms supplied in brackets, however awkward they may seem, open the possibilities of the genre in ways that the original's gendered nouns and pronouns prohibit.

8. Candace Lang, "Autobiography in the Aftermath of Romanticism," *Diacritics*, 12 (Winter 1982), p. 5.

9. Abraham Lincoln, "First Joint Debate, Ottawa, August 21: Mr. Lincoln's Reply," in Robert W. Johannsen, ed., *The Lincoln-Douglas Debates* (New York: Oxford University Press, 1965), p. 52.

10. Valerie Smith, *Self-Discovery and Authority in Afro-American Narrative* (Cambridge, Mass.: Harvard University Press, 1987), p. 21.

11. Lucy A. Delaney, *From the Darkness*, p. 10.

12. Constitution of the United States, Thirteenth Amendment (1865).

13. Frances Smith Foster, *Witnessing Slavery* (Westport, Conn.: Greenwood Press, 1979), pp. 5–6.

14. Lang, "Autobiography," pp. 5, 10.

15. Hazel Carby, *Reconstructing Womanhood: The Emergence of the Afro-American Woman Novelist* (New York: Oxford University Press, 1987), p. 164. At this point in her argument, Carby is considering the vexed dynamics of representation both "in relation to art and creative practices, and as it applies to intellectuals who understand themselves to be responsible for the representation of 'the race,' defining and constructing in their art its representative members and situating themselves as representative members of an oppressed social group" (p. 164).

16. Lang, "Autobiography," p. 5.

17. Frederick Douglass, *Narrative of the Life of Frederick Douglass, An American Slave Written by Himself*, ed. Benjamin Quarles (Cambridge, Mass.: Harvard University Press, 1960), pp. 58, 59.

18. Harriet A. Jacobs, *Incidents in the Life of a Slave Girl, Written by Herself*, ed. Jean Fagan Yellin (Cambridge, Mass.: Harvard University Press, 1987), p. 132.

19. Walter Benn Michaels, "The Fate of the Constitution," in Sanford Levinson and Steven Mailloux, eds., *Interpreting Law and Literature* (Evanston, Ill.: Northwestern University Press, 1988), p. 391.

20. William W. Wiecek, "The Statutory Law of Slavery and Race in the Thirteen Mainland Colonies of British North America," in Kermit L. Hall, ed., *The Law of American Slavery* (New York: Garland, 1987), p. 683.

21. William E. Moore, "Slave Law and the Social Structure," in *The Law of American Slavery*, p. 332.

22. Paul Finkelman, *Slavery in the Courtroom* (Washington, D.C.: Library of Congress, 1985), p. 14.

23. Moore, "Slave Law," pp. 338–39.

24. Eugene D. Genovese, "Slavery in the Legal History of the South and the Nation," in Paul Finkelman, ed., *Law, the Constitution, and Slavery* (New York: Garland, 1989), p. 162.

25. Moore, "Slave Law," p. 340.

26. Michaels, "The Fate of the Constitution," p. 391.

27. Ibid., p. 390. It is important to note that in this and all my uses of quotations from Michaels's "The Fate of the Constitution" I am using the author's prose in the service of a position that he particularly argues against. In its entirety the sentence I am now quoting reads: "Instead, they [theorists who think that texts can be separated from intention] imagine that the passage of time and the problems of multiple authorship have eventually separated the text from its original authors and given it a life of its own." Michaels states that at present "it may seem perverse not only to defend intention but to claim that every interpreter is always and only looking for authorial intention" (p. 390); he writes further that, despite this climate, it is precisely his intention to do so. I repudiate Michaels's stance in regard to autobiography generally and African American autobiography in particular. Indeed, the issue, or problem, is exactly who the author is. The problem is especially exasperating for the African American autobiographer for whom the terms of life to be written appear (unacceptably) already written.

28. Smith, *Self-Discovery and Authority*, p. 6.

29. Perhaps one might even go so far as to say that in this discourse Delaney emerges as an ironic figure in a pro-slavery argument. Certainly, these passages strike a very different chord from, say, the somewhat analogous concluding moment in Harriet Jacobs's *Incidents in the Life of a Slave Girl*, when Jacobs's freedom is purchased.

30. Kenneth S. Abraham, "Statutory Interpretation and Literary Theory: Some Common Concerns of an Unlikely Pair," in Levinson and Mailloux, eds., *Interpreting Law and Literature*, p. 129.

31. Moore, "Slave Law," p. 325.

32. Wiecek, "Statutory Law of Slavery," p. 661.

33. A. Leon Higginbotham, Jr., *In the Matter of Color: Race and the American Legal Process—The Colonial Period* (New York: Oxford University Press, 1978), p. 13.

34. Wiecek, "Statutory Law of Slavery," p. 668.

35. Moore, "Slave Law," p. 342.

36. Robert B. Stepto, telephone conversations, June 22 and 23, 1991. One might imagine the courtroom as "a prime fictive space" because, in the words of Stepto, "barred from a certain context, especially as it involves voice and telling one's own story," it is inevitable that you finally arrive there.

37. Brook Thomas, *Cross-examinations of Law and Literature: Cooper, Hawthorne, Stowe, and Melville* (New York: Cambridge University Press, 1987), p. 110.

Padilla: The Mexican Immigrant as *

1. John J. Poggie, *Between Two Cultures: The Life of an American-Mexican* (Tucson: University of Arizona Press, 1973).

2. Although there are different labels—Chicano, Hispanic, Latino—the term "American-Mexican" is one that I had never seen or heard prior to reading the

Poggie text. Poggie clarifies the term when in the introduction he points out that although Gonzales was living in Mexico—"permanently"—when the narrative was recorded, he had spent most of his life in the United States until being deported repeatedly after he was twenty. Gonzales is presented as a man whose experience represents further complication of the confounding situation in which many Mexican Americans discover themselves.

3. Arnold Krupat, *For Those Who Come After* (Berkeley: University of California Press, 1986), pp. 31–35.

4. Jean M. Pitone, *Cesar Chavez: Man of the Migrants* (Staten Island, N.Y.: Alba House, 1971); James Terzian and Kathryn Cramer, *Mighty Hard Road: The Story of Cesar Chavez* (Garden City, N.Y.: Doubleday, 1970); Jacques E. Levy, *Cesar Chavez: The Autobiography of La Causa* (New York: Norton, 1975); Winthrop Yinger, *Cesar Chavez: The Rhetoric of Non-Violence* (Hicksville, N.Y.: Exposition Press, 1975); Ronald Taylor, *Chavez and the Farmworkers* (Boston: Beacon Press, 1975).

5. Peter Matthiessen, *Sal Si Puedes: Cesar Chavez and the New American Revolution* (New York: Random House, 1969); Stan Steiner, *La Raza: The Mexican Americans* (New York: Harper & Row, 1970); John Gregory Dunne, *Delano* (New York: Farrar, Straus & Giroux, 1971); Eugene Nelson, *Huelga—The First 100 Days of the Delano Grape Strike* (Delano, Ca.: Farm Worker Press, 1966).

6. Oscar Lewis, *Pedro Martinez: A Mexican Peasant and His Family* (New York: Random House, 1964), acknowledgments.

7. Lawrence Cardoso, *Mexican Emigration to the United States, 1897–1931* (Tucson: University of Arizona Press, 1980), p. 53.

8. Paul Taylor, *Mexican Labor in the United States*, 7 vols., University of California Publications in Economics (Berkeley: University of California Press, 1928–32); Manuel Gamio, *Mexican Immigration to the United States: A Study of Human Migration and Adjustment* (Chicago: University of Chicago Press, 1930); idem, *The Mexican Immigrant: His Life Story* (Chicago: University of Chicago Press, 1931). Initiated and funded by the Social Science Research Council, both Gamio studies had the objective of tracing migration patterns and observing immigrants' general "conditions of life" in order to "determine the character of their contacts with the people of the United States and with the American civilization." The SSRC's rationale for funding the study, it appears, was to gather information on immigration that "had reached astonishing proportions" by about 1925 and to consider "how best to deal with the situation" (*Mexican Immigration*, p. xi).

9. Among Robert Redfield's numerous publications on Mexican culture and social practice are *Tepoztlan, A Mexican Village: A Study of Folklife* (Chicago: University of Chicago Press, 1930); *Chan Kom, A Maya Village* (Washington, D.C.: Carnegie Institution, 1934); *The Folk Culture of Yucatan* (Chicago: University of Chicago Press, 1941); *A Village That Chose Progress: Chan Kom Revisited* (Chicago: University of Chicago Press, 1950).

10. Gamio, *Mexican Immigration*, p. 200.

11. Ibid., Appendix I, "Guide for Field-Workers Used in Connection with This

Preliminary Study," p. 199. Gamio suggested that attention should be directed "principally toward those individuals who are typical representatives of the Mexican immigrant—that is to say, the mestizos and full-blooded Indians who make up the greater part of both unskilled and skilled labor and the tenant and share farmers" (p. 197).

12. "The Race" is translated from the more expansive and commonly applied group designation of *La Raza*, or "our people," "our culture," and so on.

13. Gamio, *Mexican Immigration*, pp. 228, 158.

14. Oscar Lewis, *Five Families: Mexican Case Studies in the Culture of Poverty* (New York: Basic Books, 1975); *The Children of Sanchez: Autobiography of a Mexican Family* (New York: Random House, 1961); and *Pedro Martinez*. In *The Children of Sanchez*, Lewis describes the function of the "multiple autobiography": "This approach gives us a cumulative, multifaceted, panoramic view of each individual, of the family as a whole, and of many aspects of lower-class Mexican life. The independent versions of the same incidents given by the various family members provide a built-in check upon the reliability and validity of much of the data and thereby partially offset the subjectivity inherent in a single autobiography. This method of multiple autobiographies also tends to reduce the investigator bias because accounts are not put through the sieve of a middle-class North American mind but are given in the words of the subjects themselves" (p. xi).

15. As Lewis writes in *The Children of Sanchez*: "In preparing the interviews for publication, I have eliminated my questions and have selected, arranged, and organized their materials in coherent life stories. If one agrees with Henry James that life is all inclusion and confusion while art is all discrimination and selection, then these life histories have something of both art and life. I believe this in no way reduces the authenticity of the data or their usefulness for science" (p. xxi).

16. As Poggie writes: "This book represents about eighty percent of the unedited tapes. Only redundant or repetitious materials have been deleted. The major part of the editing task was arranging the material in roughly chronological order and pulling together pieces that fit together. . . . Except for elimination of some of the 'you knows,' with which Ramon often began and ended sentences, and occasional clarification of phrasing, the narrative remains essentially in Ramon's own words" (*Between Two Cultures*, p. xii).

17. John J. Poggie, Gretel H. Pelto, and Pertti J. Pelto, *The Evolution of Human Adaptations: Readings in Anthropology* (New York: Macmillan, 1976).

18. The term *pocho* is usually used pejoratively by Mexicans for those American-born or acculturated Mexicans who have lost their language, native culture, or sense of loyalty to the Mexican homeland.

Metcalf: What Happened in Mecca

I have been interested in hajj accounts for several years and have accumulated innumerable debts to institutions and individuals. I would particularly like to thank Robert Folkenflik, for inviting me to participate in the conference that led to this volume, as well as the National Humanities Center, for providing a tranquil setting to write. My thanks also to John Sturrock, a participant in the conference, at whose suggestion a shortened version of the conference paper was published in the *Times Literary Supplement* (June 1–7, 1990). I am particularly grateful to two fellow inhabitants of the Center, Morris Dickstein and Thomas Metcalf, and to three North Carolina neighbors, Katherine Ewing, David Gilmartin, and James Peacock, for many lively conversations during 1989–90.

1. See William C. Spengemann, "Eternal Maps and Temporal Voyages," *Exploration*, 2 (1974): 1–7.

2. On the subject of irony in travel writing, see Donald B. Howard, *Writers and Pilgrims: Medieval Pilgrimage Narratives and Their Posterity* (Berkeley: University of California Press, 1980).

3. Paul Fussell, Introduction, *The Norton Book of Travel* (New York: Norton, 1987), p. 13.

4. For a stimulating treatment of non-Western travel writing to Europe, see Timothy Mitchell, *Colonizing Egypt* (Cambridge: Cambridge University Press, 1987), chapter 1.

5. The journal, published in Lahore, was *Siyara Da'ijast*. The edition of the book used here is Mumtaz Mufti, *Labbaik* (Lahore: Al Tahrir, 1975), with introductions by Nazir Ahmad (pp. 11–16) and Zu'l-fiqar "Tabash" (pp. 17–24).

6. There is no continuing genre of travel accounts, despite the well-known works of the Arab geographers up to the fourteenth century. Travel accounts became common from the late eighteenth century on, and seem to have been products of the same intellectual impulse that stimulated other new genres, like autobiography and, later, the novel. See my "The Pilgrimage Remembered: South Asian Accounts of the Hajj," in Dale Eickelman and James Piscatori, eds., *Muslim Travellers: Pilgrimage, Migration and the Religious Imagination* (Berkeley: University of California Press, 1990), pp. 85–107.

7. See Renato Rosaldo, *Culture and Truth: The Remaking of Social Analysis* (Boston: Beacon Press, 1989).

8. Salman Rushdie, "In Good Faith: A Pen Against the Sword," *Newsweek*, Feb. 12, 1990, pp. 52–54.

9. See Gustav von Grunebaum and Roger Callois, eds., *The Dream and Human Societies* (Berkeley: University of California Press, 1966). For a study specifically related to this milieu see Katherine P. Ewing, "The Dream of Spiritual Initiation and the Organization of Self Representations Among Pakistani Sufis," *American Ethnologist*, 17 (Feb. 1990): 56–74.

10. Shah Wali'ullah, *Mushahadat wa ma'arif tarjama Fayuzu'l-haramain* [Visions and inspirations: A translation of "The excellences of the two holy places"], trans. from Arabic into Urdu by Muhammad Sarwar (Lahore: Sindh Sagar Akademi, 3d ed., n.d.).

11. The translations are from Gilani Kamran, *South Asian Muslim Creative Mind* (Lahore: National Book House, 1980), pp. 41–43.

12. For example, the Ko'ila Center's baba, pp. 59–60; Khawar's vision and transformation, pp. 68–69; and the return of the martyrs of Badr, pp. 209–10.

13. For a brief but powerful argument about why magic realism is "offensive,"

see Vinay Dharwadker, "'Offensive Books' and the Rhetoric of Outrage," *Public Culture*, 1 (Spring 1987): 76–79.

14. "Tabash," introduction to *Labbaik*, p. 22.

15. Interview with an academic and poet, Lahore, 1985.

16. Marcia Hermansen, "Interdisciplinary Approaches to Islamic Biographical Materials" (typescript, 1987), p. 4. See also Dale F. Eickelman, "Traditional Islamic Learning and Ideas of the Person in the Twentieth Century," in Martin Kramer, ed., *Extraordinary Lives: Methods and Sources in Middle East Biography* (forthcoming). This of course does not mean that there is no notion of coming to maturity in these writings. Quite the contrary, and other accounts, if not this one, stress the hajj as an occasion for ethical reflection and moral growth. In English, for example, see S. M. Zafar, *Haj: A Journey in Obedience* (Lahore: Ripon Printing Press, 1978). Ira M. Lapidus suggests that Muslim (auto)biographies tend not to map life stages and transitions but see positive change as a deepening of or return to faith. See his "Adulthood in Islam: Religious Maturity in the Islamic Tradition," *Daedalus*, 105 (1976): 93–107.

17. See Robert Folkenflik's introduction to this book; it is important to note that the generalization about a post-Romantic emphasis on childhood may not be true everywhere.

18. See for example Muhammad Ashiq Ilahi Mirathi, *Tazkiratu'r-rashid*, 2 vols. (Meerut: n.p., n.d.), which is divided into two sections, *shari'at* and *tariqat*, so that events are categorized as to whether they are primarily related to fulfillment of religious obligations or spiritual experience. See also Muhammad Ikramullah Khan, *Viqar-i hayat* (Aligarh, 1925) where events are categorized in relation to fulfillment of the so-called pillars of Islam.

19. James L. Peacock, "Religion and Life History: An Exploration in Cultural Psychology" in Edward M. Bruner, ed., *Text, Play, and Story: The Construction and Reconstruction of Self and Society* (Washington, D.C.: American Ethnological Society, 1984), pp. 94–116; and idem, "Dahlan and Rasul: Indonesian Muslim Reformers," in A. L. Becker and Aram A. Yengoyan, eds., *The Imagination of Reality: Essays in Southeast Asian Coherence Systems* (Norwood, N.J.: Ablex, 1979), pp. 245–68.

20. For a study linking the structure of Malcolm's autobiography to such American classics as the autobiography of Benjamin Franklin, see Carol Ohmann, "*The Autobiography of Malcolm X*: A Revolutionary Use of the Franklin Tradition," *American Quarterly*, 22 (Summer 1970): 131–49.

21. For Qudratu'llah's own account of a hajj (not the same one) see his *Shahabnama* (Lahore: Sangmel Publications, 1987), pp. 557–612. Shams-i Tabriz was the spiritual guide of the great thirteenth-century mystic poet of Konya, Maulana Jalalu'd-din Rumi.

22. T. G. Vaidyanathan, "Authority and Identity in India," *Daedalus*, "Another India," 118 (Fall 1989): 147–70.

23. Again, a pre-Partition allusion, here to the confluence of the Ganges and Jumna, a symbol of dualism in unity, sacred to Hindus.

24. David S. Lelyveld, "Eloquence and Authority in Urdu: Poetry, Oratory and

Film," in Katherine T. Ewing, ed., *Shariʿat and Ambiguity in South Asian Islam* (Berkeley: University of California Press, 1988), p. 108. This device, as Lelyveld points out, prevents the listener from questioning authority.

25. C. M. Naim calls him one of today's two most distinguished Urdu novelists. See Francis Robinson, ed., *The Cambridge Encyclopedia of India, Pakistan, Bangladesh, and Sri Lanka* (Cambridge: Cambridge University Press, 1989), p. 426.

26. The account is a real one. See ʿAbduʾr-rahim Shibli, *Rabb-i kaʿba ke huzur* [The noble presence of the Lord of the Kaʿba] (Lahore: Qamr Taskin, 1972). His presumed B. Comm. degree is not noted in the text.

27. Bharati Mukherjee, "Immigrant Writing: Give Us Your Maximalists!" *New York Times Book Review*, Aug. 28, 1988, p. 1.

28. Compare the treatment of Egeria's late-fourth-century *Pergegrinatio ad terram sanctam* in Mary B. Campbell, *The Witness and the Other World: Exotic European Travel Writing, 400–1600* (Ithaca, N.Y.: Cornell University Press, 1988). Campbell argues that Egeria deflects interest in her personality in favor of showing each place as a stimulus to the memory of a historic event; her presence, her response, is essentially irrelevant to what is primarily a didactic goal of enhancing the meditation of the reader who, in a sense, becomes a second pilgrim.

29. Interview with Maulana Kausar Niyazi, Delhi, Feb. 14, 1990.

Porter: "In *me* the solitary sublimity"

1. *The Diary of Benjamin Robert Haydon*, ed. Willard Bissell Pope, 5 vols. (Cambridge, Mass.: Harvard University Press, 1963), 5: 553. Further references to this edition by volume and page number will be in parentheses following the passage.

2. Midway between these entries Haydon described the birth of his first son like Lear pronouncing on the inevitable doom in store for the child: "I had been sitting on the stairs, listening to the moaning of my love, when, all of a sudden, a dreadful, dreary outcry, a tortured, passionate, dull, & throttled agony, gasping, breathless, & outrageous, announced intense suffering, and then there was a dead silence, as if from exhaustion, and then a puling, peaked cry, as of a little helpless living being, who felt the air, & anticipated the anxieties, & bewailed the destiny of his irrevocable humanity" (2: 392). Heroic defiance, prophetic doom, and exhaustion are all characteristics Haydon assigned to his own Lear-like being.

3. Virginia Woolf, "Genius," in *The Moment and Other Essays* (New York: Harcourt, Brace, 1948), p. 191.

4. *The Collected Writings of Thomas De Quincey*, ed. David Masson, 14 vols. (London: A. and C. Black, 1897), 3: 233.

5. W. Jackson Bate, *John Keats* (New York: Oxford University Press, 1963), pp. 98, 101.

6. *The Autobiography and Journals of Benjamin Robert Haydon*, ed. Malcolm Elwin (London: Macdonald, 1950), p. 94. Further references to the *Autobiography* will be in parentheses following the passage.

7. Eric George, *The Life and Death of Benjamin Robert Haydon* (Oxford: Oxford University Press, 1967), p. 92.

8. W. Jackson Bate, *The Burden of the Past and the English Poet* (New York: Norton, 1970), pp. 106–7.

9. *The Letters of John Keats*, ed. Maurice Buxton Forman (London: Oxford University Press, 1952), p. 278, letter from Haydon to Keats, Jan. 23, 1819.

10. Harold Bloom, "The Internalization of Quest-Romance," in Harold Bloom, ed., *Romanticism and Consciousness* (New York: Norton, 1970), p. 12.

11. Paul de Man, "Autobiography as De-Facement," *Modern Language Notes*, 94 (1979): 920.

12. Bloom, "The Internalization of Quest-Romance," p. 11.

Folkenflik: The Self as Other

1. An important line of feminist thought argues, as Mary G. Mason puts it, that "the self-discovery of female identity seems to acknowledge the real presence and recognition of another consciousness, and the disclosure of female self is linked to the identification of some 'other,' that is, of an 'other' who is not the self." See "Autobiographies of Women Writers," in James Olney, ed., *Autobiography: Essays Theoretical and Critical* (Princeton, N.J.: Princeton University Press, 1980), p. 210. See also the theoretical work of Carol Gilligan, *In a Different Voice: Psychological Theory and Women's Development* (Cambridge, Mass.: Harvard University Press, 1982). For the mirror image in particular, see Luce Irigary, *Speculum of the Other Woman*, trans. Gillian C. Gill (Ithaca, N.Y.: Cornell University Press, 1985), and Jenijoy La Belle, *Herself Beheld* (Ithaca, N.Y.: Cornell University Press, 1988). I discuss the equivocal case of Charlotte Charke in this essay.

2. Augustine, *Confessions*, trans. R. S. Pine-Coffin (Harmondsworth: Penguin Books, 1978), p. 169. All subsequent references will appear in the text. The literature on Augustine is vast, but any list of citations probably should begin with Pierre Courcelle's *Recherches sur les "Confessions" de S. Augustin* (Paris: Boccard, 1950). I have found especially helpful Peter Brown, *Augustine of Hippo* (Berkeley: University of California Press, 1969), and Kenneth Burke, *The Rhetoric of Religion: Studies in Logology* (Berkeley: University of California Press, 1970).

3. Sacvan Bercovitch, *The Puritan Origins of the American Self* (New Haven, Conn.: Yale University Press, 1975), p. 19.

4. John Henry Newman, *Apologia Pro Vita Sua*, ed. David J. DeLaura (New York: Norton, 1968), p. 96.

5. Idem, *Autobiographical Writings*, ed. Henry Tristram (New York: Sheed and Ward, 1955), p. 5. This text has, not surprisingly, received little attention. James Olney discusses it in another context in *Metaphors of Self: The Meaning of Autobiography* (Princeton, N.J.: Princeton University Press, 1972), pp. 28–29. For Jonathan Loesberg's account, see *Fictions of Consciousness: Mill, Newman, and the Reading of Victorian Prose* (New Brunswick, N.J.: Rutgers University Press, 1986), pp. 89–91.

6. See Pei-Yu Wu, *The Confucian's Progress: Autobiographical Writings in Tra-*

ditional China (Princeton, N.J.: Princeton University Press, 1990), especially pp. x–xi, 15–41. Avrom Fleishman warns that "autobiography's reputation as a peculiarly Western phenomenon" is overstated and subject to "refutation by example." See *Figures of Autobiography: The Language of Self-writing in Victorian and Modern England* (Berkeley: University of California Press, 1983), p. 13n.

7. For an account of "Autobiography in the Third Person," see Philippe Lejeune, *New Literary History*, 9 (1977): 27–50, now available in his collection *On Autobiography*, ed. Paul John Eakin, trans. Katherine Leary (Minneapolis: University of Minnesota Press, 1989), pp. 31–51.

8. I discussed this work in my paper "Generic Androgyny in the Autobiography of Charlotte Charke," Western Society for Eighteenth-Century Studies, University of San Diego, Feb. 1991.

9. *The Education of Henry Adams*, ed. Ernest Samuels (Boston: Houghton Mifflin, 1973), p. 507. All subsequent references will appear in the text. Samuels's three-volume biography of Adams has been helpful: *The Young Henry Adams*; *Henry Adams: The Middle Years*; *Henry Adams: The Major Phase* (Cambridge, Mass.: Harvard University Press, 1948, 1958, 1964). For a good critical account see John Carlos Rowe, *Henry Adams and Henry James: The Emergence of a Modern Consciousness* (Ithaca, N.Y.: Cornell University Press, 1976), chapter 4.

10. For Carnochan's account of Hume's very short autobiography, "My Own Life," see *Gibbon's Solitude: The Inward World of the Historian* (Stanford, Calif.: Stanford University Press, 1987), pp. 129–30, 138–41.

11. R. P. Blackmur, "The Expense of Greatness: Three Emphases on Henry Adams," in *The Lion and the Honeycomb: Essays in Solicitude and Critique* (New York: Harcourt, Brace & World, 1955), p. 80.

12. Edmund Gosse, *Father and Son: A Study of Two Temperaments* (New York: Norton, 1963), p. 33. All subsequent references will appear in the text. Gosse is discussed in slightly different terms in Vivian and Robert Folkenflik, "Words and Language in *Father and Son*," *Biography*, 2 (1979): 157–74.

13. R. D. Laing, *The Divided Self* (Harmondsworth: Penguin Books, 1969), especially chapter 6.

14. Jean-Jacques Rousseau, *The Confessions*, trans. J. M. Cohen (Harmondsworth: Penguin Books, 1978), pp. 30–31. All subsequent references to this book will appear in the text. Paul de Man's deconstructive reading of the purloined ribbon passage in the *Confessions* speaks to a range of the topics under consideration here. See chapter 12 of *Allegories of Reading: Figural Language in Rousseau, Nietzsche, Rilke, and Proust* (New Haven, Conn.: Yale University Press, 1979).

15. Sartre, *The Words*, trans. Bernard Frechtman (New York: Vintage, 1981), p. 14. All subsequent references to this book will appear in the text. Jeffrey Mehlman gives a somewhat Lacanian account in *A Structural Study of Autobiography: Proust, Leiris, Sartre, Lévi-Strauss* (Ithaca, N.Y.: Cornell University Press, 1974), chapter 3 ("Sartre and His Other"), which also treats *Saint Genet* as autobiography. Paul John Eakin's account in *Fictions in Autobiography: Studies in the Art of Self-Invention* (Princeton, N.J.: Princeton University Press, 1985), chapter 3

("Jean-Paul Sartre: The Boy Who Wanted to Be a Book"), takes as its point of departure the parable of the missing train ticket, a highly self-conscious fiction.

16. Jean-Paul Sartre, *Situations*, trans. Benita Eisler (New York: George Braziller, 1965), p. 199.

17. Philippe Lejeune prints the interview in *L'autobiographie en France* (Paris: Armand Colin, 1971), pp. 205–7.

18. Roland Barthes, *Roland Barthes*, trans. Richard Howard (New York: Hill and Wang, 1977). All subsequent references will appear in the text. A good short account appears in Paul Jay, *Being in the Text: Self-Representation from Wordsworth to Roland Barthes* (Ithaca, N.Y.: Cornell University Press, 1984).

19. Emile Benveniste, *Problems in General Linguistics*, trans. Mary Elizabeth Meek (Coral Gables, Fla.: University of Miami Press, 1971), p. 225.

20. Some of the key works here are Jacques Lacan, "The Mirror Stage as Formative of the Function of the I," in *Ecrits*, trans. Alan Sheridan (New York: Norton, 1977), pp. 1–7, and the essays now known in America as *Speech and Language in Psychoanalysis*, ed. Anthony Wilden (Baltimore: The Johns Hopkins University Press, 1968). Although Lacan provides models, they must be used warily, for both the mirror and language, the specular and symbolic, remain other, though the identification with the other is crucial to the self. Lacan denies the ability of the self to speak itself in the first person, but it would seem that it can be read.

Index

In this index an "f" after a number indicates a separate reference on the next page, and an "ff" indicates separate references on the next two pages. A continuous discussion over two or more pages is indicated by a span of page numbers, e.g., "pp. 57–58." *Passim* is used for a cluster of references in close but not continuous sequence.

Abbot, H. Porter, 7
Adams, Henry, 9, 13f, 19, 42; *The Education of Henry Adams*, 13, 42, 221–25
African American autobiography, 12, 18, 50, 68, 104–24, 257
Aristotle, 32, 151
Armstrong, Nancy, 87
Ashridge, Elizabeth, 84
Ashton, John, 255
Aubigné, Madame d', 221
Augustine, 19, 42, 61, 73, 82f, 227, 232f, 245, 251; *Confessions*, 15, 24f, 42, 215–19, 222
Autobiography: as English term, 1–6, 81, 89, 238f; as German term, 2ff, 238; vs. "self-biography," 3–7, 238; eighteenth-century, 4, 7, 91, 98, 166, 174, 260; as French term, 5, 7; nineteenth-century, 8, 81ff, 89–103 *passim*, 167, 239, 245, 251, 253; as narrative, 10, 15, 23, 29, 39–48 *passim*, 72, 101, 107, 140f, 145, 161, 231; as genre, 11, 13, 15, 22–26, 34, 36, 40–42, 47f, 58f, 62f, 67, 75, 80–83, 88f, 90, 92, 103–8 *passim*, 114, 123f, 152, 220, 245, 253, 260; and theory (deconstruction), 11, 13, 21–24, 27, 34f, 37f, 45, 48, 57, 59, 61ff, 71ff, 87, 238; and subjectivity

(fragmented), 12, 57, 59–79 *passim*, 90f, 94, 97, 106, 111–38 *passim*, 146ff, 158, 179, 220, 227, 232, 234, 246, 250; and (self-)portraiture, 12f, 23, 63f, 168, 185, 188–214; definitions of, 13, 15, 38, 41, 105, 184, 254; and fact/fiction debate, 13–15, 30, 59f, 75–77, 105–24 *passim*, 136, 141f, 144, 197, 209, 245; vs. biography (*bios*), 15, 57f, 61–79 *passim*, 245, 248; seventeenth-century, 18, 80, 83, 88–91, 93f, 216, 252f; spiritual (conversion), 19, 25, 82–91 *passim*, 155, 161, 191, 216, 218, 228, 251, 253f; as speech act, 41, 45, 108, 119, 121, 242; Western-centered, 44, 58–61, 66ff, 71–79 *passim*, 151, 158, 160, 220, 264; "new model" theory of, 57, 59f, 69f; and editorial shaping, 60, 86, 90–103 *passim*, 233, 253f; and ethnographic practice, 126–48; non-European, 149–67, 220, 264. *See also* African American autobiography; Domestic memoir; Feminism and autobiography; Freudian psychology and autobiography; Lacanian psychology and autobiography; Law and autobiography; Mexican American autobiography; Novel and

autobiography; Romanticism and autobiography; Women's autobiography
Autogynography, 7, 70

Bachmann, Ingeborg, 78
Backhouse, Edmund, 14
Baillet, Adrien, 29
Baldwin, James, 60
Bangs, Benjamin, 84, 86
Barrett, Lindon, 18
Barthes, Roland, 15, 19, 232f; *Roland Barthes by Roland Barthes*, 15, 232f
Bartlett, Sir Frederic, 40
Bate, Walter Jackson, 170, 174
Beaujour, Michel, 65
Benveniste, Emile, 234
Bercovitch, Sacvan, 216
Berry, Polly, 104
Besant, Annie, 254
Blackmur, R. P., 9, 224
Bloom, Harold, 181, 185
Boswell, James, 14, 227; *Life of Johnson*, 14
Bowdler, Thomas, 101
Breuer, Joseph, 33
Brodski, Bella, 69, 248
Brontë, Charlotte, 6, 254
Brooks, Cleanth, 10
Brown, Charles Armitage, 7
Brown, William, 6
Browne, James, 6
Bruner, Jerome, 18
Brydges, Sir Egerton, 6, 89, 93
Buber, Martin, 47
Buckley, Jerome Hamilton, 5
Bunyan, John, 83, 227, 251
Burke, Edmund, 195
Burke, Kenneth, 9
Butterfield, Stephen, 105

Carey, Matthew, 6
Carlyle, Thomas, 222
Carnochan, W. B., 224
Carroll, Lewis, 223
Cavendish, Margaret, Duchess of Newcastle, 6, 81, 88f, 93
Cellini, Benvenuto, 3, 5, 95, 179, 222
Charke, Charlotte, 18f, 98f; *A Narrative of the Life*, 100–103, 221
Chavez, Cesar, 126f

Chodorow, Nancy, 69, 92
Churchill, Charles, 195
Cibber, Colley, 19, 95, 98, 221
Clarke, Cowden, 82, 94f, 98–102, 254f
Cobbe, Frances Power, 254
Coleridge, Samuel Taylor, 4, 7; *Biographia Literaria*, 7
Colie, Rosalie, 247
Conroy, Frank, 14
Consubstantiality, 63ff
Courbet, Gustav, 12f
Cover, Robert, 53
Crapanzano, Vincent, 49
Cruz, Pablo, 126, 138f
Cumberland, Richard, 5
Cunninghame, Lady, 92

Dante, 14, 169
d'Aubigné, Madame, 221
Defoe, Daniel, 13, 196
Delaney, Lucy A., 12, 18f, 104f, 107–24, 257
de Laurentis, Teresa, 255
DeLillo, Don, 54f
de Man, Paul, 10, 13, 23, 62, 83, 183, 264
De Quincey, Thomas, 58, 61f, 65, 166–69, 247
de Retz, Cardinal, 222
Derrida, Jacques, 7, 10, 62
Descartes, René, 28–33, 35, 37, 60
de Staël, Germaine, 8
Diatactics, 45, 52
Dibdin, T. F., 5
Diderot, Denis, 229
Dihlawi, Shah Wali'ullah, 152f, 166f
Dilthey, William, 43
D'Israeli, Isaac, 1f, 4
Domestic memoir, 88–91, 94f, 254
Donovan, John, 136
Douglass, Frederick, 12, 50, 106f, 114
Dryden, John, 206f
Dunne, John Gregory, 127

Eakin, Paul John, 11
Einstein, Albert, 47
Eliot, T. S., 10
Elmwood, Elnathan, 6
Empson, William, 10
Equiano, Olaudah, 12
Erikson, Erik, 49, 224

Evans, Thomas, 83ff, 251
Evans, William, 83ff, 251

Fanshawe, Ann Lady, 88, 90–94
Feminism and autobiography, 41, 57, 73,
    251, 263
Feynman, Richard, 46
Fielding, Henry, 193, 221
Finkelman, Paul, 116f
Fleishman, Avrom, 264
Folkenflik, Robert, 259
Foster, Frances Smith, 111
Fox, George, 83, 86
Franklin, Benjamin, 261
Freedman, Ralph, 248
Freud, Sigmund, 33ff, 53
Freudian psychology and autobiography,
    10f, 17, 19, 33f, 39, 55, 137, 152,
    181f, 185, 214, 224, 226, 243
Friedman, Susan Stanford, 69f
Fry, Caroline, 6
Frye, Northrop, 10, 15
Fuller, Margaret, 50
Fussell, Paul, 14, 149

Galarza, Ernesto, 139
Galt, John, 6
Gamio, Manuel, 128–33, 135–39, 146,
    258f
Ganj Bakhsh, Data, 165
Garrick, David, 193
Geertz, Clifford, 243
Genovese, Eugene, 117
George, Eric, 182
Gibbon, Edward, 3, 5, 95, 178; *Memoirs*,
    5, 222
Gilligan, Carol, 92
Gilman, Charlotte Perkins, 70
Goethe, Johann Wolfgang, 17, 60
Goffman, Erving, 47, 56
Goldman, Emma, 50
Gonzales*, Ramón, 19, 125f, 137f, 140,
    142–48, 258f
Goodman, Nelson, 32, 52
Gosse, Edmund, 225–26, 231, 234
Graves, Robert, 16
Greene, Asa, 6
Greimas, Algirdas, 44, 243
Grosvenor, Sir Richard, 207
Gusdorf, Georges, 4, 10, 58f, 70, 106

Haggard, H. Rider, 151
Haley, Alex, 15, 60
Halkett, Ann Lady, 90–93
Harris, Mark, 14
Hawthorne, Nathaniel, 13, 246
Haydon, Benjamin Robert, 19, 168–82,
    184–87, 229, 262
Hayes, Alice, 84, 87
H.D., 70
Heilbrun, Carolyn, 71, 80
Hellman, Lillian, 60
Herbert, Edward, Baron of Cherbury, 5
Herder, Johann Gottfried, 3, 238
Hernadi, Paul, 61
Hippel, Theodor Gottlieb von, 2
Hobbes, Thomas, 35
Hogarth, Jane, 197, 202, 206f, 210, 213
Hogarth, Richard, 195, 203, 207, 211
Hogarth, William, 12, 19, 188–214
Homer, 169
Hoskens, Jane, 84f
Hugo, Victor, 230
Hume, David, 95, 224
Hunt, John, 82, 94f, 98–102, 254f
Hunt, Leigh, 5, 172f, 176
Husain Ahmad Madani, Maulana, 164
Hutchinson, Lucy, 90f, 93
Hutchinson, Thomas, 118f

Jackson, Charles, 90
Jacobs, Harriet, 12, 106f, 114, 257
James, Henry, 221, 259
James, William, 151, 222
Jay, Paul, 10, 248
Jelinek, Estelle C., 9, 80
Jenisch, David, 3
Johnson, Samuel, 7f, 13
Joyce, James, 223
Juvenal, 211

Kausar Niyazi, Maulana, 162
Keats, John, 168ff, 174, 176
Kingston, Maxine Hong, 14, 50, 60, 70,
    72, 139; *The Woman Warrior*, 14, 50
Krupat, Arnold, 127
Kuhn, Anna, 250

Lacanian psychology and autobiography,
    10, 19, 92, 216, 234, 265
Lactilla, the Milkmaid Poet, 2

Lang, Candace, 106
Larousse, Pierre-Athanase, 5
Law and autobiography, 43ff, 104f, 111–24
    passim
Leibniz, Gottfried Wilhelm, 30
Leibowitz, Herbert, 11
Leiris, Michel, 42
Leitner, Isabella, 70
Lejeune, Philippe, 13, 41f, 46, 48, 59f, 246f
Lentricchia, Frank, 61
Leonardo da Vinci, 179, 190
Levi, Primo, 19, 50f
Lewis, Oscar, 127, 137, 140f
Lilly, William, 95
Lincoln, Abraham, 107
Lionnet, Françoise, 73
Locke, John, 16f
Loesberg, Jonathan, 220
Lorde, Audre, 70
Lorrington, Meribah, 97f
Lowe, Mary, 86

Macauley, Elizabeth Wright, 6
McCarthy, Mary, 42, 60
Mackenzie, Henry, 5, 211
Macpherson, James, 233
Malcolm X, 155, 261
Marin, Louis, 15
Markus, Hazel, 54
Marshall, Paule, 70
Martin, Biddy, 72
Martinez, Pedro, 137
Mason, Mary, 60, 69, 80, 102, 263
Matthews, William, 91
Matthiessen, Peter, 127
May, Georges, 5, 7ff
Mehlman, Jeffrey, 10
Metcalf, Barbara, 19
Mexican American autobiography, 18,
    125–48
Michelangelo, 170, 174, 176, 186, 190
Miller, Nancy K., 246
Milton, John, 169, 180, 191, 193, 205, 208
Misch, Georg, 7, 59, 238
Molière, 37
Montaigne, 58, 61–65, 68, 247
Moore, William E., 116
More, Hannah, 1
Moritz, Karl Philipp, 3

Muhammad, 164
Müller, Johann Georg, 238
Mumtaz Mufti, 19, 149ff, 153–62
Munch, Edvard, 13

Napoleon, 169, 173f, 178f
Nazir Ahmad, 153, 155
Neihardt, Charles, 60
Nelson, Eugene, 126f, 136, 138
Nelson, Horatio, 173
Newman, John Henry, 19, 218–20
Nichols, Beverly, 14
Nichols, John, 202
Nietzsche, Friedrich, 26f, 34, 43, 73; *Ecce*
    Homo, 26
Niggl, Günter, 2f, 238
Nin, Anaïs, 70
Novel and autobiography, 13, 40, 46, 56,
    75, 87, 142, 144, 171, 209, 250, 254
Nurius, Paula, 54
Nussbaum, Felicity, 1, 7

Oglethorpe, James Edward, 8
Ohmann, Carol, 261
Oldenburg, Claes, 52ff
Olney, James, 10, 106, 247
Oxley, Joseph, 86

Padilla, Amado, 146
Padilla, Genaro, 18
Pascal, Roy, 59
Paulson, Ronald, 19
Pennington, Mary, 85
Pepys, Samuel, 227
Peterson, Linda, 18, 221
Picasso, Pablo, 53
Pike, Joseph, 84ff
Pitt, William, 195
Plato, 32, 55
Plutarch, 58, 63f, 247
Poggi, John J., 125ff, 136–48 *passim*, 258f
Pope, Alexander, 213
Porter, Roger, 19

Qudratu'llah Shahab, 157–60

Ranke, Leopold von, 43
Ransom, John Crowe, 10
Raphael, 174, 176

Redfield, Robert, 130, 136f, 139
Rembrandt, 13, 179
Renza, Louis, 59, 60, 250
Retz, Cardinal de, 222
Reynolds, Sir Joshua, 13, 183, 195
Richards, I. A., 10
Richardson, Jonathan, 208
Rilke, Rainer Maria, 58, 61f, 68, 248
Rimbaud, Arthur, 215, 233
Robinson, Mary, 18f, 95–98, 100
Rodriguez, Richard, 14
Romanticism and autobiography, 4, 7f, 19, 102, 155, 168, 178–85 *passim*, 233, 261
Roth, Philip: *The Facts*, 54f
Rousseau, Jean-Jacques: *Confessions*, 3, 5, 19, 26f, 61, 69, 82f, 102, 172, 176f, 222, 225–29, 245, 248
Rowbotham, Sheila, 70
Royal Academy of Arts, 169f, 176f, 185, 195
Rushdie, Salman, 152f
Russell, Bertrand, 42
Ryecroft, Charles, 10

Sa'di, Shaikh, 151
Samora, Julian, 127, 146
Samuels, Ernest, 225
Santayana, 42
Sarraute, Nathalie, 231
Sartre, Jean-Paul, 36f; *The Words*, 36f, 60, 229–33
Saussure, Ferdinand de, 234
Scargill, W. P., 6
"Scene of writing," in African American autobiography, 104, 114f, 123
Schenck, Celeste, 69, 248
Schlegel, August Wilhelm, 4
Schlegel, Friedrich, 3f
Schopenhauer, Arthur, 34
Schubart, Friederich Daniel, 2
Schweitzer, Albert, 47
Searle, John, 242
Seybold, David Christoph, 3, 238
Shabir Ahmad Usmani, Maulana, 164
Shakespeare, William, 178, 191, 193
Shange, Ntozake, 70
Sheridan, Richard, 97
Sherlock, John, 208

Singer, Samuel Weller, 6
Smith, Daniel, 87
Smith, Sidonie, 11, 49, 71, 80, 102, 251
Smollett, Tobias, 221
Sophocles, 43
Southey, Robert, 1f, 4f
Spacks, Patricia Meyer, 98, 102
Spence, Joseph, 6
Spender, Stephen, 245
Spengemann, William C., 9f, 13, 58, 245
Sprinker, Michael, 248
Staël, Germaine de, 8
Stanfield, James Field, 4f
Stanton, Domna C., 7, 70, 246
Stein, Gertrude, 15, 53, 60, 248
Steiner, Stan, 127
Stendhal, 247
Sterne, Lawrence, 193, 223, 233
Stirredge, Elizabeth, 83ff, 87
Stowe, Harriet Beecher, 109
Strauss, Richard, 13
Sturrock, John, 14, 17, 59, 221
Sufism, 154, 164f
Swift, Jonathan, 191, 193, 211
Swinburne, Algernon Charles, 222

Tate, Allen, 10
Taylor, Charles, 42
Taylor, Paul, 128f, 146
Taylor, Thomas, 2
Taylor, William, 1f, 4
Theresa of Avila, 60
Thornhill, Sir James, 197, 201–10 *passim*
Thornhill, Jane, *see* Hogarth, Jane
Thornton, Alice, 90ff
Titian, 190
Toklas, Alice B., 15
Trapnel, Anna, 88
Trevor-Roper, Hugh, 14
Trinh Minh-ha, 72

Unger, Roberto, 53

Van Gogh, Vincent, 172
Vann, Richard T., 84
Varnedoe, Kirk, 52–55
Vaux, James Hardy, 95
Vertue, George, 202

Vico, Giambattista, 19, 30–33, 35, 221
Virgil, 217f
Voisine, Jacques, 6
von Hippel, Theodor Gottlieb, 2
von Ranke, Leopold, 43

Wakefield, Gilbert, 5
Warwick, Lady, 90, 92
Washington, Booker T., 50
Watson, Julia, 18, 221
Watteau, Antoine, 190
Weintraub, Karl, 8
Wellington, Duke of, 174, 176
Wesley, John, 95
West, Benjamin, 183
Whiston, William, 208
White, James Boyd, 42f, 53
White, Patrick, 46
Whitfield, George, 95

Wilkes, John, 205f
Williams, Tennessee, 46
Wolf, Christa, 18f, 58, 73–79, 221, 249
Women's autobiography, 7, 18f, 49f, 58–
    61, 68–71, 79–95 *passim*, 100–107
    passim, 250–54 *passim*
Woodward, E. L., 16
Woolf, Virginia, 70, 169
Wordsworth, William, 7, 42, 61, 169, 174,
    178, 234; *The Prelude*, 7, 13
Wright, Richard, 50, 60

Yearsley, Ann, 1–2
Yeats, William Butler, 50
Young, James, 49

Zipes, Jack, 249
Zu'lfiqar Ahmed Tabish, 156